THIS BOOK BELONGS TO:

_____

OUR ANNIVERSARY:

_____

GOOD
HOUSEKEEPING

The Newlywed Cookbook

GOOD HOUSEKEEPING

The Newlywed Cookbook

125 Recipes to Celebrate Your New Life Together

Illustrations by **NIKKI ACKERMAN**
Photographs by **MIKE GARTEN**

HEARST HOME

7	Foreword by Kate Merker

Settling In

10	Gearing Up
18	Shop Smarter
28	DIY It

Weeknight Winners

36	Chicken Dinners
56	Meaty Mains
76	Noodle Night
96	Seafood Suppers
116	Plant-Powered Plates

Easy Entertaining

140	Date Night In
162	Game Day
174	VIP Dinner Party
184	Brunch for a Bunch
194	Fire Up the Grill

Holiday Cooking

208	The Main Event
218	Showstopping Sides
234	Delicious Desserts

252	*Index and credits*

FOREWORD

It's been a minute since I walked down the aisle, and though I no longer consider myself a newlywed, getting to that point was an incredible adventure. I still remember the nervous excitement that comes with building a home with the person you love. So whether you are headed toward getting married or the best day ever has already happened, congratulations!

As Chief Food Director, I cook and taste all the time in the Good Housekeeping Test Kitchen, and what we create runs the gamut, from quick to complicated and from healthyish to indulgent. No matter how many things we make (and we churn out thousands of recipes each year), the thing I like to cook most is, honestly, anything for the people I love. I am honored that I get to help you do so too.

Whether you are cooking for your boo on a Tuesday night (I love the Aleppo Grilled Steak with Farro Salad on page 57) or a Sunday supper for in-laws (I'd start building a menu with the Chicken à l'Orange on page 181 or the Everything Bagel Crusted Salmon with Herby Fennel Salad on page 211), we've got you covered. I hope these pages become worn and stained, full of the love you enjoy as the two of you grow together.

From our kitchen to yours, happy cooking!

Kate

KATE MERKER
Chief Food Director

PS: We've included a Love Notes section on each recipe so you can jot down thoughts about it, tweaks you might make to it for next time or details and memories regarding when (and for whom) you cooked it.

PART 1

Settling In

Combining kitchens with your partner can be exciting (and maybe a little stressful). Set yourself up for success with our registry must-haves along with strategies for optimal organization and tips on grocery shopping, meal planning and stocking your pantry, fridge and freezer so you can make memorable meals together.

Gearing Up

A well-equipped kitchen makes cooking a breeze, not to mention more fun. Start building your registry with the basics, then consider adding a few extras based on your cooking personality.

Sort Your Stuff

Before you start adding items to your registry, take a look at what you already have. When you combine kitchens, it's likely that you and your partner will have some similar items, so to create the most efficient space, you'll want to purge before you merge. Here, Home Care & Cleaning Lab Executive Director Carolyn Forté and Kitchen Appliances & Innovation Lab Director Nicole Papantoniou offer ideas to make that process a little smoother.

TAKE INVENTORY. Working with one category at a time (e.g., appliances, flatware, pots and pans), pull out your kitchen stuff so you can see it all at once. Before you can streamline, you have to know what you're working with.

DEAL WITH DUPLICATES. When you encounter two similar items, you'll need to make some decisions. "I would lean into keeping items that are better quality or that you think will last longer," says Papantoniou. "Also consider things that have sentimental value to you or your partner and try to compromise where it's helpful. You can share duplicates that are in good condition with family and friends or consider donating the items."

DECIDE WHERE OVERLAP IS OK. Having too many of the same items can lead to clutter, but there are a few reasons you might want to double up (or triple up, or even go beyond that). "Some things, like knives and cutting boards, make sense to keep multiples of so you can both cook at the same time," says Papantoniou. "It's always nice to have a little backup if something goes on the fritz," adds Forté, "but only if you have room to store extras."

DO A DOUBLE-CHECK. As you're sorting through your stuff, it's a great moment to get rid of dishware that is chipped as well as storage containers without lids (who among us hasn't ended up with those?) and other mismatched items. As you pare down your cookware, make sure you have the lid to any pot that came with one. Also, consider upgrading any kitchen item you feel "meh" about. "You're building this space together—it's a perfect time for a fresh start," says Forté.

BE HONEST WITH YOURSELF. If you want your kitchen drawers and cabinets to close, you will likely have to get rid of some things. Gadgets are often a good category to take a close look at. "You might say, 'I thought I was going to use this melon baller, but I never did,'" says Forté. "Now is a good time to get rid of it. You don't need everything."

CONSIDER HOW YOU COOK. When you're sorting, think about how you use the gear you have. Forté says there's really no set rule for when you should rehome something based on how long it has been since you last used it. The key is to think about how you cook. For example, if you're the kind of person who likes to bake a fresh cherry pie every summer, it might be worth keeping your cherry pitter around if you have the room, even if you don't use it more often. "But if you're never going to use it, if it's not useful for the kind of cooking you do and it's getting in the way, it's definitely time to let it go," she says.

Your Essential Kitchen Gear List

Now that you've reviewed what you have (and probably made some difficult choices about what to keep and what to get rid of—good job, you!), it will be easier to figure out what else you need. These are Papantoniou's and Test Kitchen Director Kate Merker's must-haves when equipping a kitchen.

KNIVES

Start with the essential trio below, then add to your collection based on your cooking routine.

Chef's knife A good, sharp chef's knife is key for quick and safe prep work in the kitchen. The long blade makes it the best choice for chopping, dicing and mincing as well as breaking down a roast chicken or slicing a steak for serving. See our best advice on buying a chef's knife at right.

Bread knife This long serrated knife is the optimal tool for slicing breads and so much more. Cutting through rugged, crusty bread can damage a chef's knife, but the teeth on a bread knife will saw right through it without smashing the loaf. A bread knife is also clutch for smoothly slicing tomatoes, peeling pineapple and leveling cake layers.

Paring knife This is the go-to knife for small jobs like peeling potatoes and apples (if you don't have a vegetable peeler), slicing strawberries and segmenting citrus.

POTS & PANS

It's worth investing in a high-quality set or individual pieces, as these will be used frequently. Buying good pans to begin with will save you a fortune in the future.

Dutch oven This is a kitchen workhorse. You can use an enameled Dutch oven to boil pasta; simmer soups, stews and chilis; make slow-simmered sauces and meats; bake bread; deep-fry chicken; and much more. A 5- to 7-quart version is a good size for most home cooks.

Saucepans Choose two or three saucepans with lids, ranging from 1.5 quarts to 4 quarts. Look for ones that are 4 to 5 inches deep so you can stir food without spilling.

Knife Know-How
Buying a new chef's knife? Tips to keep in mind:

Test it out. Try a knife in person so you can see whether it feels comfortable and balanced in your hand.

Consider your options. You're likely to find two versions: German-style knives typically are heavy and have thick blades. Japanese ones can be fragile but allow for more precise cutting.

Get a grip. Wide nonslip handles encourage a good hold, while thinner ones allow for more control.

Think about size. Chef's knives commonly have 8-inch blades; opt for a 6- or 7-inch one if you have smaller hands.

Make sure they will last. Look for knives with a full tang (a blade made of a single piece of metal that runs from the blade tip to the end of the handle).

GEARING UP | **SETTLING IN**

Skillets You'll need at least one large (12-inch) and one small (7- to 8-inch) skillet. The latter is great for eggs, so look for a high-quality nonstick one. Stainless steel skillets are ideal for searing meats and cooking at higher temps. Cast-iron skillets require a little TLC, but conduct heat well and can be used for baking, braising and frying. Plus, if you take care of them you can pass them down to the next generation.

BAKEWARE
Get ready for cookie making, cake creating and putting together a pan of lasagna for a crowd.

Baking sheets For baking cookies, roasting vegetables and making sheet-pan suppers, you need at least two 18-by-13-inch rimmed baking sheets (often called half sheet pans). You may also want a few smaller sheet pans. A quarter sheet pan measures 9 by 13 inches and is great for small batches and toaster oven cooking.

Baking pans A small square baking pan (8-by-8-inch) works for cakes, cobblers and brownies, and a large rectangular baking pan (13-by-9-inch) is better for bigger bakes like lasagna.

Cake pans Get a few 8- or 9-inch round pans—recipes like layer cakes tend to call for two or three.

Cooling racks Buy a couple of these (because, cookies!) and look for a stainless steel option with a grid pattern, which means a sturdier rack. You can also set cooling racks on a baking sheet to make crispy bacon or create a ad hoc roasting pan for a whole chicken. Check the dimensions to make sure the rack will fit in your pan.

Loaf pan Standard sizes are 9 by 5 inches (8 cups) and 8½ by 4½ inches (6 cups). Always read a recipe before beginning to make sure you have the right pan size.

Muffin pans These also come in handy for making other dishes like mini frittatas. A 12-well pan with 2½-by-1¼-inch cups is the standard, but toaster oven fans might consider buying two 6-well pans.

Cookware Costs
Buying a complete set of pots and pans can allow you to get individual pieces at a better price, but you might not need everything the set comes with. If you find one that works with your budget and the way you cook, consider it. Buying single pieces gives you the greatest control and flexibility, but can require spending more overall. (This applies to bakeware sets as well.)

HOW TO Measure a Pan
Not exactly sure what size your pan is? Get out the ruler (or the measuring cups). To know the dimensions, measure across the top of the dish from inside edge to inside edge and measure the depth on the inside of the dish from the bottom to the rim. To find out the volume, pour water by cupfuls (4 cups equals 1 quart) into the pan, right up to the top.

THE NEWLYWED COOKBOOK **13**

Pie plate While we found pros and cons in our Lab tests for glass, metal and ceramic pie plates, metal was the best overall.

SMALL GADGETS & TOOLS

With this gear, you'll be prepared for any recipe that comes your way.

Tongs The more, the merrier! It's great to have a mix of nylon-tipped (for use on nonstick surfaces) and stainless-steel ones in a variety of sizes. A 9-inch pair is good for serving; a 12-inch version will be your go-to for tossing; and 16-inch ones are great for the grill, where you want a little more distance from the heat.

Spatulas Flipping anything from fried eggs to pancakes requires something that can slide under each type of food. (Another use: removing cookies from baking sheets.) You'll want a plastic option to avoid scratching nonstick pans as well as a metal one to use when grilling burgers. A fish spatula with a long, thin, angled head is fantastic for turning delicate fillets, getting under veggies and more.

Silicone or rubber spatulas These are a go-to for stirring batter and scraping bowls. You'll use them a lot, so buy a few sizes (a large one for stirring risotto and rotating roasted veggies; a medium one for scrambled eggs; and a small one for scraping out jars). Look for a silicone spatula that's all one piece (versus one with a wooden handle) because it can go right in the dishwasher.

Whisk A balloon-style metal whisk is a good all-purpose tool for whipping cream and egg whites and bringing batters together.

Ladle You often don't think about it until you need one. A silicone ladle is both sturdy and flexible, which means it'll get into all the corners of that soup pot.

Kitchen scissors These come in handy for cutting a chicken into pieces, snipping kitchen twine and cutting parchment paper. Look for a pair with long, skinny blades and wide handles.

Vegetable peeler In general we find that a straight peeler (one that has a blade that's in line with its handle) is great for potatoes and carrots, and a Y peeler (one with a horizontal blade across the top) is best for larger produce like squash.

Handheld grater A box grater can take up a lot of room and can be a pain to clean. If you're grating a large amount (such as a block of cheese, or many carrots for carrot cake), use a food processor. For smaller jobs, a handheld grater works fine and is easier to store.

Microplane With smaller blades, a rasp-style grater is perfect for zesting citrus and grating hard cheeses like Parmesan.

Handheld juicer or reamer A hinge-style metal juicer is handy for juicing citrus for cocktails and dressings, but not every fruit will fit inside (we're looking at you, grapefruit!). Because of that, some cooks prefer a reamer, which requires a little more elbow grease.

Cutting boards For versatility and ease, it's hard to beat sturdy plastic cutting boards. They're easy on knives and can go right into the

14 THE NEWLYWED COOKBOOK

dishwasher. For a more aesthetic choice, consider a wooden cutting board, which can double as a cheese or charcuterie board.

Mixing bowls A nesting set can handle most of your mixing and prep needs and save room in the cabinet. We like glass ones with lids, which can be used for storage.

Measuring cups Get metal cups for dry ingredients and a 2-cup glass liquid measuring cup.

Measuring spoons A nesting metal set is the gold standard. If you can find one with a ½-tablespoon measure, grab it. (If not, just remember that half a tablespoon equals 1½ teaspoons.)

Salad spinner This tool, which dries foods via centrifugal force, is more than a single-use gadget. Sure its intended for lettuces, but it's also great for washing and, of course, drying other vegetables, fruits such as berries and fresh herbs.

Colander Choose a large colander with a stable footed base; the more holes it has, the more quickly liquid can drain out.

Thermometer Take the guesswork out of knowing when a protein is properly cooked with an instant-read thermometer, which will help you gauge meats' internal temps.

Ice cream/cookie scoop It's great for portioning everything from cookies to muffin batter to burgers and ice cream. We like the trigger-handled ones.

Ruler Have you rolled that dough out to the right size? How big is that pan? If you have a ruler in the kitchen, you can easily answer those questions. For easy cleanup, go for a metal or plastic ruler with no cork backing.

Corkscrew A winged design can set you up for success. You place the guide on the bottle and twist in the screw: As the corkscrew goes in, the wings on the side go up; push them down, and out pops the cork! (PS: The top also serves as a bottle opener.) If you drink wine often, an electric opener is nice to have.

SMALL APPLIANCES

Air fryer This powerful countertop cooker will easily revive leftovers or crisp up prepackaged frozen foods like french fries. It is also handy for cooking quick dinners (such as Air-Fried Steak Fajitas, page 61). When shopping, you can choose from a number of sizes and types: ones with a basket, air fryer ovens (with shelves) and air fryer toaster ovens (multifunctional appliances that also bake, roast and broil).

Blender Powerful models like the Vitamix can blend, grind, puree and chop with ease; personal blenders can be used for daily smoothies and single-serve cocktails and are easy to clean. An immersion blender is great for silky-smooth soups.

Electric mixer A stand mixer is essential for any baker, as it ensures fluffy whipped cream and meringues, light and airy cake layers and icing that's velvety smooth. A more affordable pick, an electric hand mixer, can also help with these tasks (though it requires some physical effort) and takes up a lot less space.

Food processor Cut down on prep time with this appliance that will dice, mince, grind, knead, puree, slice and shred in a fraction of the time it would take to do those tasks by hand. A mini processor is great for small-batch cooking, whereas a full-size one is more versatile, especially if the model includes shredding and slicing discs and a pulse setting.

Multicooker or slow cooker The former appliance operates in multiple modes — it can pressure cook, slow cook, brown, sauté, steam and sometimes air-fry — and the latter does just what its name suggests: It cooks food slowly at a low and steady temperature. If quick, versatile cooking is what you prefer, you probably want a multicooker. If you like to cook large batches of meat or simple soups and prefer your cooking to be hands-off, you likely want a slow cooker.

Toaster oven Opt for this over a regular toaster, as a toaster oven can do so much more than heat up slices of bread. It can be a good replacement for several kitchen appliances (some models toast, bake, roast and air fry) and can let you cook smaller portions of food without heating up your whole kitchen (a small batch of cookies, anyone?). It doesn't require much time to heat and may use as little as half the energy that a conventional oven does.

REGISTRY CHECKLIST
Discover the specific products the pros at the Good Housekeeping Institute recommend adding.

Register Right
Make the most of your wedding registry with these five tips.

1 Dream big. This is the time to ask for what you really want. Got your eye on an ice cream machine? Add it to the list! That fancy toaster oven that does everything? On the list it goes. Just don't go too overboard. It's important to register for things you believe you'll use as opposed to things that'll collect dust or sit in the back of a cabinet.

2 Shop around. Before choosing a domain, do some research. Certain sites let you pull in items from many stores instead of registering at just a few; this will allow friends and family members to do one-stop shopping. Some registries offer couples discounts on any unpurchased items left on the registry after the wedding.

3 Consider costs. Everyone is working with a different budget, so you want to be sure your registry includes options at a variety of price points. Also great: Unlocking "group gift" functions for larger items so people can pitch in whatever they're comfortable with but still get you something you really want.

4 Don't delay. Start building a registry soon after getting engaged so you'll have a link ready when people ask (which happens earlier than you'd think!). News travels fast and showers can happen quickly, so the sooner your registry is up and running, the better prepared you will be. Plus, who doesn't love browsing?

5 Be true to yourself. Don't add items out of obligation or peer pressure. If you don't care about fine china and would rather not deal with the care and maintenance of actual silverware, don't register for either. This list should be tailor-made for you and your partner rather than a reflection of whatever you think the "rules" might be.

16 THE NEWLYWED COOKBOOK

GEARING UP | **SETTLING IN**

Getting Personal

Now that you've got the basics covered, it's time to have some fun. Find your customized equipment list for how you like to cook.

The Baker
- Bundt pan
- Decorating bags and tips
- Extra baking sheets
- Extra cooling racks
- Kitchen scale
- Offset spatula(s)
- Pastry brush
- Precut parchment sheets
- Rolling pin
- Springform pan(s)
- Stand mixer
- Tart pan(s)

The Barista
- Burr grinder
- Coffee scoop
- Espresso machine or specialty coffee machine
- Espresso cups or specialty mugs
- Knock box
- Milk frother
- Pour-over gooseneck kettle
- Sugar bowl and creamer set

The Entertainer
- Bar tools and shaker
- Cloth napkins
- Dishes and drinkware
- Serving platters and bowls
- Servingware
- Tablecloths
- Fun drinkware
- Wine fridge

The Home Chef
- Carbon steel pan and/or wok
- Carving knife and cleaver
- Cast-iron skillets
- High-powered blender
- Ice cream maker
- Sous vide machine
- Mandoline
- Potato ricer

The Meal Prepper
- Chopper
- Containers (all sizes)
- Painter's tape (for easy labeling)
- Reusable silicone bags
- Silicone molds for preportioning food for freezing
- Vacuum sealer

The Mixologist
- Bar cart
- Bar tools and shaker
- Cocktail and wine glasses
- Ice buckets and/or wine chillers
- Mixing glass(es)
- Pitcher(s)
- Silicone ice cube trays

The Outdoor Enthusiast
- Grill and/or flat-top grill
- Grilling tools
- Grilling thermometer
- Outdoor pizza oven
- Skewers
- Smoker

The Pasta Lover
- Pasta machine (hand-cranked countertop model or stand mixer attachment)
- Pasta wheel
- Pot with pasta insert
- Ravioli molds

THE NEWLYWED COOKBOOK

Shop Smarter

These grocery shopping and food storage strategies will make your life so much easier. With a plan in place, you'll save money and time, and you'll also waste less food.

SHOP SMARTER | SETTLING IN

Check In Before You Check Out

In advance of going to the grocery store, be sure you're both on the same page about what you want to eat this week (or tonight!).

LOOK AT THE CALENDAR. Set up a shared digital calendar and devote time each week to planning out your meal schedule together so you can properly gauge how many nights you'll both be eating dinner at home and understand who will have time to cook and when. Then plot out how many meals you need to figure out and note if you're anticipating any nights when you'll both be home but will probably want takeout, leftovers or something pre-prepped.

SEE WHAT'S ON THE WAY OUT. Hang a dry-erase board near the fridge to keep a running list of everything that's about to go bad (say, that wilting bunch of kale in the crisper) and leftovers you need to use up (like last week's extra takeout container of rice). Use that information to start your recipe search and begin to build your meal plan. Cooking this way will help reduce food waste and can be fun because you might find a creative way to cook with half a can of coconut milk or discover a new method of reimagining leftovers (see page 21 for some ideas!).

BRAINSTORM TOGETHER. After figuring out what must need to be used up, look for recipes that call for those ingredients (this book's index may help!). When you select your recipes, flag the most perishable ingredients in each — for example, fresh produce, herbs, dairy products, poultry and seafood. Also look for a recipe that uses one (or more!) of those ingredients to cook for lunch or dinner another night that week. This kind of strategic meal planning will help you avoid wasting ingredients.

KEEP A RUNNING LIST. Some couples use their dry-erase board to note what they need to restock; others leverage apps or the shared note function on their phones. No matter what your preferred method of communication, make sure there is one place where you can track what you need to buy at the store. To make shopping more efficient, group items by supermarket section, e.g., dry goods, produce, meat and seafood, dairy. That way you're not grabbing your milk and then your pasta and then doubling back to dairy for the cheese.

Meal planning can seem daunting. Try these formulas:

Days of the Week Assign each night its own category. Think Meatless Mondays, Taco Tuesdays, Wine + Pasta Wednesdays and so on.

Meal-Prep MVPs Prioritize batch-friendly recipes, then devote one day to cooking.

Recipe Roulette Feeling adventurous? Eyes closed, thumb through Weeknight Winners (starting on page 32) and try a new dish.

THE NEWLYWED COOKBOOK 19

Go Shopping

Next up, the grocery store, where having a strong game plan (don't forget your list!) is essential.

SHOP AROUND. Going to just one supermarket may end up costing you in the long run, because retailers often charge different prices for the same goods. Make a mental note of prices as you go to different grocery stores, then plan where you will shop for what. Try shopping local too: Hitting up the farmers' market together can turn a weekly chore into a fun date. And consider online shopping, especially for bulk items — you may unlock additional discounts like subscribe-and-save.

THINK OUTSIDE THE PACKAGE. Cooking for two? Buy exactly what you need — no more, no less. Instead of selecting a bag of green beans or a container of mushrooms, go to the loose produce bins and pick however much of each ingredient you need. In the bakery section, look to buy a demi baguette or individual sandwich rolls. The supermarket's salad bar is a great place to grab just a few grape tomatoes or cucumber slices or a cup of peas.

MAKE FRIENDS WITH THE STAFF. The folks who work at your grocery store can help you out. At the butcher counter, ask for the cut you want as well as the exact amount you need to avoid waste. In the produce section, ask if it's OK to break off a nub of fresh ginger or take a few bananas instead of buying the whole bunch. If you don't see something you're looking for, ask: There might be more in the back, or if it's an item you use frequently but that isn't in stock, the manager might be able to special-order it for you.

LOOK FOR THE DEALS. There are deals hiding all over your market. One of our go-to spots: The odds-and-ends bin in the cheese section, where stores stock unusually sized pieces of cheese, sometimes at a discounted rate. Always opt for a whole piece so you can prep it based on the recipe.

SPLURGE (AND SAVE!) STRATEGICALLY. Sometimes it makes sense to spend more. For example, a can of tomato paste costs less than a tube but will last in the fridge for a fraction of the time. (A can typically keeps for five days, whereas a tube can be refrigerated for up to eight weeks.)

"DOUBLE DATE." Constantly finding that certain items are more cost-effective when bought in bulk, but there's no way you can use that much? Ask another couple if they want to team up to shop with you and divvy up the goods. You can split the cost, share the savings and all make better use of the ingredients.

20 THE NEWLYWED COOKBOOK

SHOP SMARTER | SETTLING IN

Maximize Your Groceries

Once you're home with your bags, take a few steps to extend your food's life. This process starts as soon as you get home and ends with a fridge (and freezer) full of food that will make your cooking-and-eating life much easier.

THINK FIRST-IN, FIRST-OUT. Stock each shelf of your fridge, freezer or pantry as if you worked at a supermarket. When unpacking your shopping bags, always put the newest items behind what's already on the shelf; that way you will reach for the older things first.

PREP WHAT YOU CAN. Depending on what you're cooking, each week's meal prep can be quite different. It might include chopping vegetables for a week's worth of meals, cooking a big pot of beans or a double batch of rice, roasting meat to use in several different dishes or putting together ingredients to cook later. If you're new to meal prepping, you might want to start with prep for two to three days' worth of meals. Many people do their meal prep over the weekend, but you can use any spare time you have to get ahead.

PACK IT UP. Let cooked food cool down; then select your containers. You can use plastic or glass ones (as long as they have airtight lids) or resealable plastic freezer bags. Quart-size mason jars are great for soups and stews, though be sure not to fill them to the top, as liquids expand when they freeze and could cause the jars to crack.

DIVIDE AND CONQUER. It's helpful to divide your food into portions before freezing so you can defrost only what you need at any given point. Individual pieces of food can be wrapped tightly in plastic wrap and then in aluminum foil or placed in a resealable freezer bag.

LABEL EVERYTHING. You think you'll remember what it is, but you probably won't. To make sure you know what's what, use a chef trick: With a permanent marker, write the name of the dish and the date on a piece of masking tape, then affix it to your container before you put it in the freezer. You can do the same thing with prepped ingredients you stash in the fridge.

Reimagine Leftovers

PIZZA PARTY
Keep dough in the freezer (or stock up on shelf-stable crusts) so you'll always be ready to whip up a pie. Whenever your fridge is full of random ingredients, plan a pizza night—choose a movie and pop open a bottle of wine, then get creative with topping combos.

GAME ON
Bring your favorite cooking competition shows to your kitchen. Here are the rules: You and your partner must use at least two high-priority ingredients each (think: anything on the verge of going bad) to create an appetizer in 30 minutes. The cook of the best-tasting dish gets out of dish duty for the evening.

LET'S DO LUNCH
Grab a container of greens or cook a batch of rice or quinoa so you'll have a base ready for salads and grain bowls. Top with last night's leftovers; repeat (and eat) all week.

THE NEWLYWED COOKBOOK 21

Prioritize Your Pantry

With a well-stocked pantry, a quick meal is never far away. Everyone's definition of "pantry essential" is different, and yours will depends on a variety of factors including the type of food you love to cook, your budget and how much space you have. The list here is deep and wide, so choose what feels essential to you and build from there.

CANNED GOODS

Beans Keep a variety around — black beans, cannellini beans, chickpeas, kidney beans and pinto beans — so you'll always be ready to make chili, soup, tacos, salads and all sorts of dips. If you're the kind of cook who thinks ahead, you might want to consider dried beans: They require soaking, but you can find a wider variety of dried beans than canned ones.

Tomatoes Choose the kind that makes the most sense depending on what you like to cook; the Test Kitchen likes to keep both 14-ounce and 28-ounce cans of whole and diced tomatoes on hand. They're a go-to for pasta sauce, soups and much more. Grab a jar of oil-packed sun-dried tomatoes and a few cans of fire-roasted tomatoes too. They are full of flavor and make great shortcut ingredients.

Tomato paste Opt for a tube instead of a can, as the easy-to-squeeze container will last longer after opening (store in the fridge).

Marinara sauce With a few jars of pasta sauce and boxes of pasta in your pantry, you'll always have an option for a fast dinner. But marinara can do so much more, from deglazing a pan to serving as a simmer sauce for poached eggs or the base of a chili.

Salsa It's for more than chips! Spoon it over chicken breasts, steak or fish or stir it into scrambled eggs.

Broth It's a go-to for soups, of course, but this rich liquid also adds flavor to sauces and sautés and is a must for deglazing a skillet to make a simple pan sauce. For more flavorful rice, swap in broth for water. Choose chicken, beef, fish or vegetable broth: There are many brands available, so try a few to find your favorite.

Bouillon paste A jar of a concentrate such as Better Than Bouillon takes up less room than a few boxes or cans of broth. You can stir a teaspoon directly into dishes while cooking or mix it with water first. Keep it in the fridge after opening.

Vegetables Having a supply of shelf-stable cans and jars of artichokes, beets, peas, corn, hominy, water chestnuts and pumpkin puree means you can incorporate produce into your meals with just the opening of a lid (and maybe a quick rinse).

Roasted red peppers These tender, charred, lightly sweet peppers make a delightful addition to sandwiches, sauces, pastas and dips.

Chipotles in adobo Packed in adobo sauce — a tangy puree of tomatoes, vinegar and spices — these spicy smoked peppers add zip to dishes. Chop or puree the chiles to add a smoky hit to chilis, soups and sauces, or stir in a little adobo sauce for a similar effect. If you don't use the whole can, dollop tablespoonfuls of the chiles and sauce on a baking sheet lined with parchment paper and freeze; then, once frozen, transfer to a freezer bag.

Tinned seafood Canned tuna and salmon deserve a spot in your pantry, but consider stocking other kinds too. Options like marinated octopus and mussels are great to crack open as a fun party app. Other types, like smoked trout, mackerel and chopped clams, are perfect for adding to mixed greens or eating on toast. Anchovies will add depth of flavor to sauces and salad dressings.

Pickles Stock up on an assortment to pile on sandwiches, use in mayo-based salads, arrange on cheese boards or simply snack on. The options extend way beyond bread-and-butter and dill: Little gherkins and corinchons are great for nibbles, and pepperoncini adds zip to pizza and pasta (the brine is a great ingredient too).

LIQUIDS & SPREADS

Olive oil and vegetable oils
Have a few types of oils you rotate through frequently (unlike wine, oils do not get better with age!). Olive oil, avocado oil and vegetable oil are go-tos for cooking; canola and peanut oils work for deep-frying. Spend a little more on an extra virgin olive oil to drizzle onto finished dishes and mix into dressings.

Vinegars This is a large category, so you'll likely want an array of options. A splash can add much-needed acidity to a dish. Some starter vinegar varieties to have on hand: red wine, white wine, balsamic, apple cider and rice.

Sesame oil You'll find two types, plain and toasted. Plain is neutral and can be used in cooking, while toasted offers an intense nutty flavor that's great in salad dressing.

Soy Sauce Use this umami-packed sauce on vegetables or rice, add it to marinades or put a splash in soups, stews and sauces to add depth. Gluten-free? Pick up a bottle of tamari instead.

Coconut Milk This versatile dairy-free ingredient works in both savory and sweet dishes. Simmer your favorite protein in it for an easy curry (its mildness cuts heat), swap it in for milk in a smoothie or use it in desserts. Choose light or full-fat.

Nut and seed butters: Think of peanut, almond, cashew and sunflower butters and tahini (made from sesame seeds) as ingredients to be incorporated into sauces and baked goods, though they're great for snacking and sandwiches too.

GRAINS, PASTAS, LEGUMES & ROOT VEGETABLES

Rice This is a core pantry staple, and there are many options. Stock the types that fit your cooking style. Always on our shelf: brown rice (it takes about 50 minutes to cook, so make a big batch on the weekend — it keeps for a week in the fridge or three months in the freezer), basmati rice, long-grain white rice and Arborio rice.

Quinoa This ancient grain is gluten-free and a complete protein. Add it to pilafs, grain bowls, salads and even baked goods. To bring out its nuttiness, toast it in a dry skillet until it is fragrant before cooking.

Polenta A tube of precooked polenta makes for one of the simplest sides. Just slice and sauté or broil with a sprinkle of cheese. Soft polenta (cornmeal) is a tasty base for chicken, pork chops or sausage and peppers. For a vegetarian main, cook polenta with vegetable stock, then top with roasted or sautéed mushrooms.

Oats Old-fashioned oats are the most versatile kind — they're great for making meatloaf, apple crisp and of course a warm breakfast.

Panko These Japanese breadcrumbs bring crunch. Use them to coat fish, chicken, pork or vegetables like zucchini before baking or frying. You can also toast panko in a skillet and stir in some Parmesan for an easy and delicious topping for pastas, vegetables and casseroles.

Pasta Have a variety of shapes around to keep life interesting. Some shapes are better suited to specific recipes: Wider strands like pappardelle and fettuccine can stand up to heartier sauces like bolognese, while shorter pastas (e.g., orecchiette and shells) can capture small bits of ingredients so you can get a bite of everything in each forkful. Grain-free and legume-based pastas offer a fiber-rich gluten-free alternative.

Couscous This tiny pasta looks like a grain and cooks in 5 minutes flat: Simply add the right ratio of boiling water, cover with a lid and let sit, then fluff with a fork. Israeli or pearl couscous is slightly larger and requires a cooking technique that more closely resembles the way other pasta is prepared.

Noodles Stock up on a variety, and you'll be ready to make many different dishes. Dried ramen works as a complete meal if you opt for instant, or you can ditch the seasoning packet and use the noodles in cold salads and stir-fries. Vermicelli and flat rice noodles are great for stir-fries, soups and pad thai. Hearty soba noodles, made with buckwheat flour, add a delicious nutty flavor to broth or can be enjoyed cold. And there are many more — experiment to see which ones you love most.

Root vegetables Here is your reminder to designate some space for storing produce that's best kept in a cool, dark place (think potatoes, sweet potatoes, onions, garlic and shallots).

Lentils Red lentils cook in about 15 minutes, and green or brown lentils cook in less than an hour (with no presoaking!). Try them as a warm salad tossed with chopped veggies; mix with leftover cooked rice for a tasty complete-protein pilaf; or simmer them in a soup. A big batch of lentils is also great for meal prepping, because lentils hold up well in the fridge.

BAKING STAPLES

All-purpose flour A key ingredient in cakes, cookies and other desserts, flour can be found in many savory dishes as well as used for tasks such as dredging proteins, thickening sauces and making a roux. To preserve its freshness, store it in an airtight container. You can also stock your pantry with other types of flour, from '00' pizza flour and bread flour to whole wheat flour and cake flour.

Granulated sugar A spoonful adds sweetness to both meals and desserts. This is the most common type of sugar and is referred to simply as "sugar" in many recipes; "granulated" is usually specified only when other forms of sugar are also called for.

Brown sugar Susceptible to drying out and hardening, this form of sugar — granulated sugar mixed with molasses — is best kept in an airtight container.

Confectioners' sugar This fine, powdery sugar is made with finely ground granulated sugar that has been mixed with cornstarch to prevent it from clumping or melting into baked goods. It can be dusted on powdered donuts, French toast or lemon bars or turned into a delicious frosting or icing.

Baking soda and baking powder While each helps baked goods rise, there is good reason to keep both on hand. Baking soda is sodium bicarbonate and requires an acidic ingredient (e.g. buttermilk) to activate it. Baking powder is actually baking soda with a weak acid, similar to cream of tartar, already mixed in. Some recipes even call for both.

Salt It's not just for baking: You'll want to keep kosher salt on hand for cooking too (it's a staple in our Test Kitchen). For sprinkling, try flaky sea salt, harvested from evaporated seawater, which adds a nice finishing touch to dishes.

Vanilla extract A popular ingredient in many baked goods, this liquid is made by soaking vanilla beans in a solution of alcohol and water. Our Test Kitchen suggests splurging on pure vanilla extract, which delivers better flavor than imitation varieties.

Chocolate Stock unsweetened cocoa powder, unsweetened chocolate squares and bittersweet and semisweet chocolate chips, and you'll have the option to whip up a batch of brownies or chocolate chip cookies whenever a craving strikes.

Dried fruit With all the nutrients and soluble fiber of its fresh counterparts, dried fruit can be stored at room temperature for up to a year. Dried cranberries or cherries can add a pop of sweetness to chicken salads, while raisins are a great addition to homemade granola bars and parfaits.

DRIED HERBS & SPICES

Like the rest of your pantry, your spice cabinet will reflect what you love to cook. The list below is what our Test Kitchen always keeps in stock, but skip any you don't need and add individual spices (hello, Aleppo pepper) or spice blends (looking at you, za'atar) that you enjoy or would like to use more often.

- Allspice
- Cardamom
- Chili powder
- Cinnamon
- Cloves
- Coriander
- Cumin
- Curry powder
- Dried dill
- Dried oregano
- Dried rosemary
- Dried tarragon
- Dried thyme
- Fennel seeds
- Ginger
- Nutmeg
- Peppercorns
- Red pepper flakes

Spice Cabinet Smarts

Keep your seasonings in tip-top shape with these tricks.

- Replace herbs and spices at least every two years.

- Buy spices you don't use often in smaller amounts — you'll have less waste.

- Group spices together by type and usage on carousels, racks or designated shelves.

Fill Your Fridge

What's inside will vary from week to week, so it's important to keep track of what goes in and what comes out. You can also use your fridge to store long-lasting flavor boosters including sauces and condiments.

Vegetables Keep an eye on veggies and herbs so you can prioritize using anything that's on its way to going bad. Be sure to avoid washing veggies before putting them in the fridge.

Fruits Segregate ethylene emitters like apples and cantaloupes from produce sensitive to the gas such as lettuce and parsley.

Eggs These breakfast staples have many culinary purposes: They help bind ingredients, thicken sauces, give volume to batters and more.

Dairy items While milk and yogurt may be mainstays, you'll likely rotate through others such as sour cream, buttermilk and kefir depending on your meal plan.

Cheeses For sandwiches, salads, pastas and more, you'll want to have a variety of cheeses on hand including Cheddar, Parmesan and feta. Opt for a whole block so you'll have the freedom to slice or grate.

Olives Use them to upgrade all sorts of dishes, including sauces, relishes and pastas. Unexpected guests? Pull out a jar of marinated olives and serve with a cheese plate for an almost-instant app.

Capers Add a pop of briny flavor to sauces and dressings. Their salty sharpness also perks up fish, pasta and chicken dishes.

Jams, chutneys and marmalades The sugars in these fruit spreads caramelize during cooking, so they are great as fuss-free glazes. Slather them onto pork or poultry before grilling.

Mustards Dijon, honey, whole grain, spicy brown, yellow — there's a whole world of mustards out there, so experiment and find the ones you prefer.

Ketchup This accompaniment for fries, burgers or nuggets can also be mixed with Worcestershire sauce, vinegar and brown sugar to make barbecue sauce or a meatloaf glaze.

Mayonnaise Not just for swiping on sandwiches and stirring into tuna salad, creamy mayo is a go-to for dips, a must for deviled eggs and a great way to promote beautiful browning on chicken and even grilled cheese sandwiches.

Miso This fermented paste made from soybeans lasts a while in the fridge, and a spoonful lends umami flavor to dressings, sauces, marinades and more.

Chile pastes Stock a few types, including gochujang, harissa and sambal oelek, as each offers a different flavor and heat level.

Curry pastes A convenient shortcut, store-bought red, yellow or green curry paste makes a flavorful base for soups and curries.

Hot sauces Whether fiery habanero or mild jalapeño, chili crisp or salsa macha, your style of cooking and your heat tolerance will lead you to the right bottles.

Worcestershire sauce It adds delicious savory flavor to stews, stocks, braises and of course Bloody Marys!

SHOP SMARTER | SETTLING IN

Stock Your Freezer

With low temperatures that help extend the life of ingredients and create a safe environment for long-term storage, a properly packed freezer provides plenty of flexibility.

Big-batch dinners Make large portions of soups, stews and sauces and freeze for nights when you're pressed for time. Wrap items in individual portions, labeled and dated, for quick meals later.

Set a Date

Schedule an annual check-in so you and your partner can pause and reflect on what you have been eating, cooking and buying. Throughout your marriage, your eating styles will change as schedules shift, finances fluctuate, and taste buds adjust — not to mention if your family grows. This yearly review will give you a chance to take inventory of what's working and consider things you might like to change for the upcoming 365 days.

Bacon This morning favorite lasts longer in the freezer (at least a few months). Cut the stack of slices in half and freeze the bacon in two portions so it'll be easier to thaw.

Bread Freezing bread is especially handy in the summer, when hot temps can cause it to go moldy quickly. Freezing is also great for artisan bread from the farmers' market, which otherwise doesn't last as long as the store-bought kind. Slices can go straight from the freezer to the toaster — no need to thaw first.

Vegetables and fruits Picked at their peak and flash-frozen, frozen fruits and veggies are just as nutritious as their fresh counterparts if not more so. Buy packages of peas, spinach, corn, strawberries, raspberries, blueberries and peaches to have on hand year-round.

Shrimp Since most shellfish in the grocer's seafood case has previously been frozen and thawed, stow a bag from the frozen aisle in your home. Streamline prep by choosing shelled, deveined shrimp.

Dumplings, pierogies and ravioli With these shortcut ingredients in the freezer, you can cook a complete dinner in next to no time.

Fries and potato tots: Frozen spuds make for a tasty app or snack, especially if you have an air fryer. They also come in handy as a quick side to pair with burgers, chicken or steak and as a fun casserole or hot dish topping.

Nuts and seeds Freezing slows the deterioration of the oil in nuts and seeds so they will take longer to go rancid. When they go on sale, squirrel away almonds, cashews, pecans, pepitas, pistachios, sesame seeds and walnuts for up to a year.

Cookie dough Make a batch of it (chocolate chip is our go-to) and freeze scoops until firm, then transfer to a resealable freezer bag. When you need a little treat, bake a few straight from frozen.

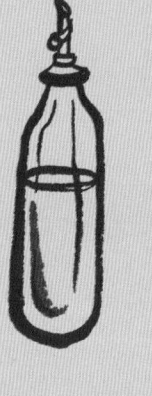

DIY It

Within minutes you can blend, whisk or stir up from-scratch sauces, spreads and dressings to stash in the fridge that will jazz up your weekly meals.

Basic Teriyaki Sauce

In a small saucepan, combine ½ cup **sake**, ½ cup **mirin**, ½ cup **reduced-sodium soy sauce** and 1 tablespoon **sugar,** stirring occasionally, until sugar dissolves, 3 to 5 minutes. Continue simmering gently until the mixture thickens slightly and coats the back of a spoon, 12 to 15 minutes more. Makes about 1 cup.

Use it
- Marinate chicken or tofu for about 30 minutes, then grill and brush with extra sauce during the last 5 minutes of cooking.
- Toss with vegetables and roast for candylike caramelization.
- Drizzle onto a burger and top with a slice of seared pineapple.

Classic Pesto

In a food processor, pulse 3 cups **fresh basil leaves**, ⅓ cup grated **Parmesan**, ¼ cup toasted **pine nuts**, 2 teaspoons grated **lemon zest** plus 2 teaspoons **lemon juice**, 1 grated clove **garlic**, ½ teaspoon **kosher salt** and ½ cup **extra virgin olive oil** and process until almost smooth. Use immediately, or freeze in ice cube trays and then transfer to a freezer-safe container for up to 3 months. Makes about 1 cup.

Use it
- Spread on toast and top with a fried egg.
- Add a dollop to a bowl of your favorite chicken or egg salad.
- Swirl into minestrone or other chunky vegetable soup.
- Roast new potatoes and toss them in pesto while warm. (About ¼ cup per pound of potatoes is a good ratio, but you can start with less and add more to taste.)

Carrot-Ginger Sauce

In a mini food processor, process 1 medium **carrot** (peeled and chopped), one 1-inch piece **fresh ginger** (peeled and chopped), ¼ cup **canola oil** and 2 tablespoons each **white miso** and **rice vinegar** until smooth, 1 minute. Makes ½ cup.

Use it
- Toss with shredded cabbage, cooked rice noodles or chopped romaine lettuce for a quick side.
- Spoon over grilled shrimp and vegetables.
- Mix with shredded chicken for a next-level chicken salad. Consider adding some chopped roasted cashews or peanuts.

Homestyle Italian Dressing

In a blender, puree 3 tablespoons **white wine vinegar**, 1 tablespoon **red wine vinegar**, 1 clove **garlic**, ½ tablespoon **fresh thyme**, 2 teaspoons **Dijon mustard**, 1 teaspoon **agave** or **honey**, 6 leaves fresh **basil** and ¼ teaspoon each **kosher salt** and **pepper** until smooth. With blender on high speed, gradually pour in ⅔ cup **canola oil** or **olive oil**, then stir in ½ teaspoon **red pepper flakes** and ¼ teaspoon **dried oregano**. Makes about 1 cup.

Use it
- Marinate chicken breasts or thighs or steak in the dressing for about 30 minutes, then grill, saute or broil.
- For a quick side or an easy lunch, toss with a cooked grain like rice, quinoa or farro, then add a handful of chopped herbs and some cubed or crumbled cheese. Add some protein to make it a meal.
- Make it the dressing for potato salad, coleslaw or tuna salad. You can just use the dressing or mix it with mayo.

Creamy Feta Sauce

In a mini food processor, puree ½ cup **milk**, 4 ounces **feta**, crumbled (⅔ cup), 1 teaspoon **lemon zest**, 2 tablespoons **fresh lemon juice**, and ¼ teaspoon each **kosher salt** and **pepper** until smooth, 2 minutes. Makes 1 cup.

Use it

- Drizzle over sliced tomato.
- Use as a dip for cucumbers and radishes.
- Spoon over grilled zucchini, bell peppers and other grilled veggies.
- Serve with poached or baked salmon.

Sweet and Spicy Gochujang

In a medium bowl, whisk together ¼ cup **gochujang**, 2 tablespoons reduced-sodium **soy sauce**, 2 tablespoons **rice vinegar**, 1 tablespoon **canola oil**, 1 tablespoon **honey** and 2 teaspoons **toasted sesame oil** until smooth. Makes ½ cup.

Use it

- Drizzle on roasted chicken, pork or steak.
- Use as a glaze to baste grilled salmon, shrimp and meats.
- Stir into rice and farro.

Green Olive Dressing

In a mini food processor, process ½ cup **pitted Castelvetrano olives**, ¼ cup **olive oil**, 1 tablespoon **fresh lemon juice**, ½ teaspoon **Dijon mustard** and 1 clove **garlic** until smooth, 2 minutes. Fold in 2 tablespoons chopped **flat-leaf parsley** and 1 teaspoon **nutritional yeast**. Makes ½ cup.

Use it

- Spoon over chicken and fish.
- Layer into a sandwich with your favorite cold cuts.
- Spoon over roasted potatoes, carrots or fennel.

Tangy Tahini Sauce

In a medium bowl, whisk together ½ cup **tahini**, 2 tablespoons **white wine vinegar**, 1 teaspoon **pure maple syrup**, ½ teaspoon **kosher salt**, ¼ teaspoon **pepper** and ¼ cup **water**. If needed, whisk in more water, 1 tablespoon at a time, until creamy. Makes ¾ cup.

Use it

- Drizzle on roasted sweet potatoes or carrots.
- Spoon over roasted chicken and pork.
- Drizzle over chopped lettuce or sliced cucumbers.

Mojo-Style Sauce

In a blender, blend 1½ cups **cilantro leaves and tender stems**, ¼ cup **fresh orange juice**, ¼ cup **olive oil**, 2 tablespoons **fresh lime juice**, ½ teaspoon **kosher salt**, ¼ teaspoon **red pepper flakes**, 1 small **shallot** (chopped) and 1 small clove **garlic** until homogenous but still bright green, 30 seconds. Makes ¾ cup.

Use it

- Marinate a whole chicken (cut into pieces) for up to 1½ hours before grilling.
- Use as a dip for fried chicken, roasted chicken and shrimp.
- Make your favorite turkey or chicken sandwich and use as a punchy dip as you eat.

PART 2

Weeknight Winners

Skip the "What's for dinner tonight?" text or phone call in the midafternoon. These speedy and simple recipes offer something for every night of the week and can be whipped up in 45 minutes or less (plus, they are pretty tasty!).

Chicken Dinners

- 37 Smoky Chicken Thighs on Baby Romaine
- 39 Tandoori-Spiced Cauliflower Chicken Flatbreads
- 41 Skillet Balsamic Chicken
- 43 Moroccan-Spiced Skillet Chicken & Couscous
- 45 Paprika Chicken with Crispy Chickpeas & Tomatoes
- 47 Crispy Chicken Salad
- 49 Grilled Chicken Caprese
- 51 Slow Cooker Chicken Pozole Verde
- 53 Chicken Paprikash
- 55 Za'atar Chicken with Whipped Feta

Meaty Mains

- 57 Aleppo Grilled Steak with Farro Salad
- 59 Saucy Pizza Beans
- 61 Air-Fried Steak Fajitas
- 63 Sheet Pan BBQ Beef Nachos
- 65 Mustard-Glazed Pork Chops
- 67 Roasted Sausages & Vegetables
- 69 Steak with Beans & Roasted Broccolini
- 71 Pork Meatball Banh Mi Bowls
- 73 Five-Spice Steak & Broccoli
- 75 Sheet Pan Gnocchi with Sausage & Green Beans

Noodle Night

- 77 Three-Cheese Summer Skillet Lasagna
- 79 Chilled Ramen Salad
- 81 Rigatoni with Sausage-Style Turkey & Arugula
- 83 Red Lentil Bolognese
- 85 Sesame Noodles
- 87 Rigatoni alla Norma
- 89 Chicken Francese Pasta
- 91 Steak & Rice Noodle Bowls
- 93 Creamy Kale Pasta
- 95 Inside-Out Pork Dumplings

Seafood Suppers

- 97 Seared Salmon with Charred Green Beans
- 99 Green Curry Shrimp
- 101 Classic Tuna Melt
- 103 Crab Cakes with Creamy Sauce
- 105 Manhattan Clam Chowder
- 107 Fish & Chips
- 109 Seared Salmon with Spiced Sweet Potatoes
- 111 California Roll Salad
- 113 Baked Feta Shrimp
- 115 Herby Salmon Burgers

Plant-Powered Plates

- 117 Smoky Black Bean & Quinoa Soup
- 119 Adobo-Glazed Portobello Tacos
- 121 Green Goddess Sandwiches
- 123 Butternut Squash Curry
- 125 Sticky Tofu Bowl
- 127 Shakshuka
- 129 Air-Fried Falafel Salad
- 131 Black Bean Burgers
- 133 Palak Paneer
- 135 Onion Flatbread

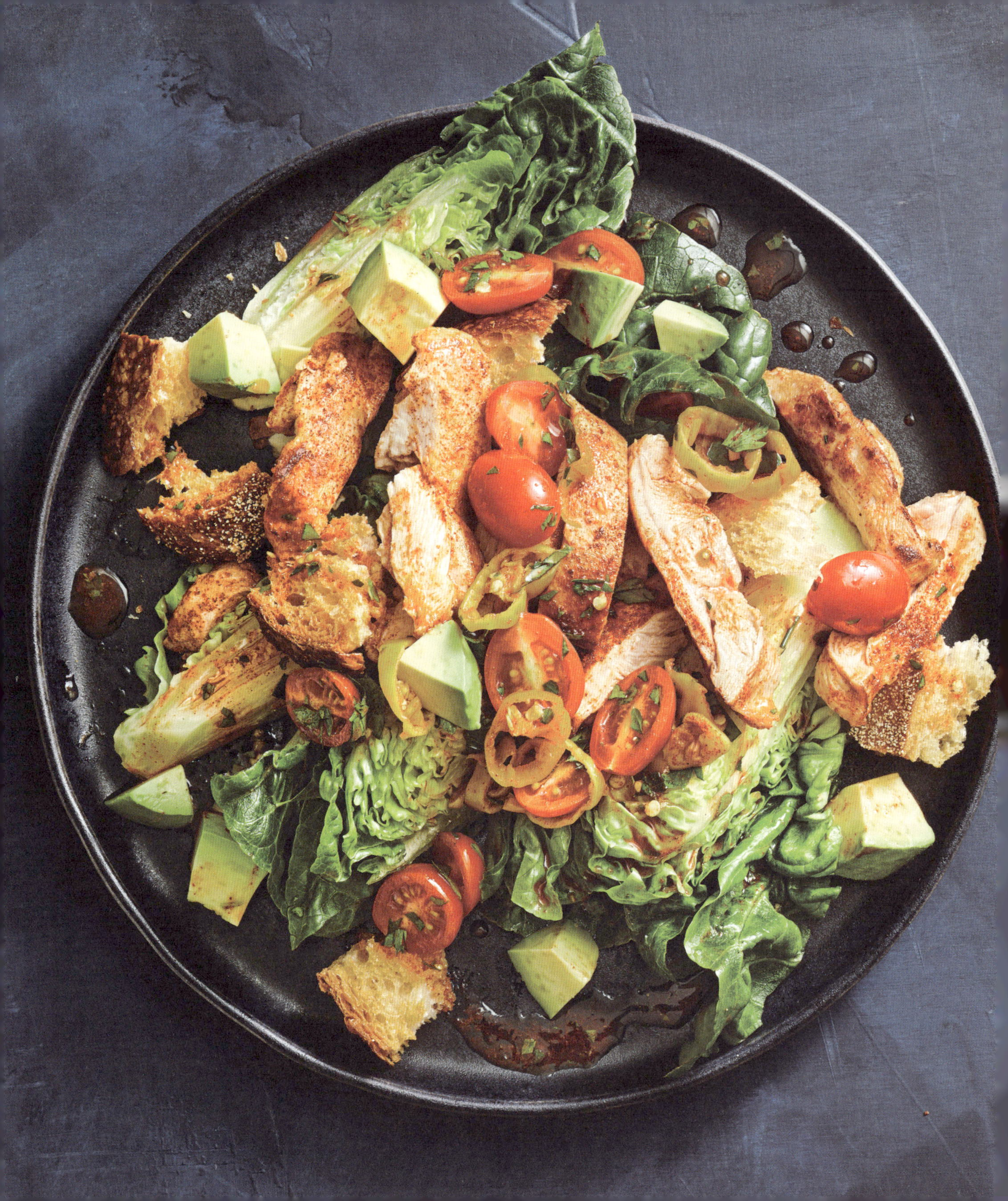

Smoky Chicken Thighs on Baby Romaine

⅓ cup fresh lemon juice

⅓ cup plus 2 teaspoons olive oil, divided

3 large cloves garlic, grated

1¾ teaspoons smoked paprika, divided

Kosher salt

4 5-ounce boneless, skinless chicken thighs

3 slices sourdough bread

1 pint cherry or grape tomatoes, halved

2 jarred pepperoncini peppers, sliced

¼ cup flat-leaf parsley, chopped

4 heads baby romaine or Little Gem lettuce, halved, or quartered if large

1 avocado, diced

Serves 4 | Active time 20 minutes | Total time 40 minutes (includes marinating)

Smoked paprika lends pizzazz to a simple garlicky vinaigrette that is used both to marinate chicken and to dress an herb-flecked tomato salad. Pile everything on a bed of lettuce, and a flavorful, feel-good dinner is served.

1. In a medium bowl, whisk together the lemon juice, ⅓ cup of oil, the garlic, 1½ teaspoons of smoked paprika and ½ teaspoon of salt. Transfer ¼ cup of the dressing to a resealable bag, add the chicken and marinate at least 20 minutes, up to 2 hours; reserve the remaining dressing.

2. Meanwhile, toast the bread until golden brown, then tear it into pieces and set it aside.

3. Heat the remaining 2 teaspoons of oil in a large skillet on medium. Remove the chicken from the marinade, season it with ¼ teaspoon of salt and cook it until golden brown, 4 to 5 minutes per side. Transfer the chicken to a cutting board, sprinkle with the remaining ¼ teaspoon of smoked paprika and let rest 5 minutes, then slice.

4. To the reserved dressing, add the tomatoes, pepperoncini and parsley and toss to combine.

5. Arrange the lettuce on plates and top with torn sourdough and then with the tomato mixture, avocado and sliced chicken.

Love Notes

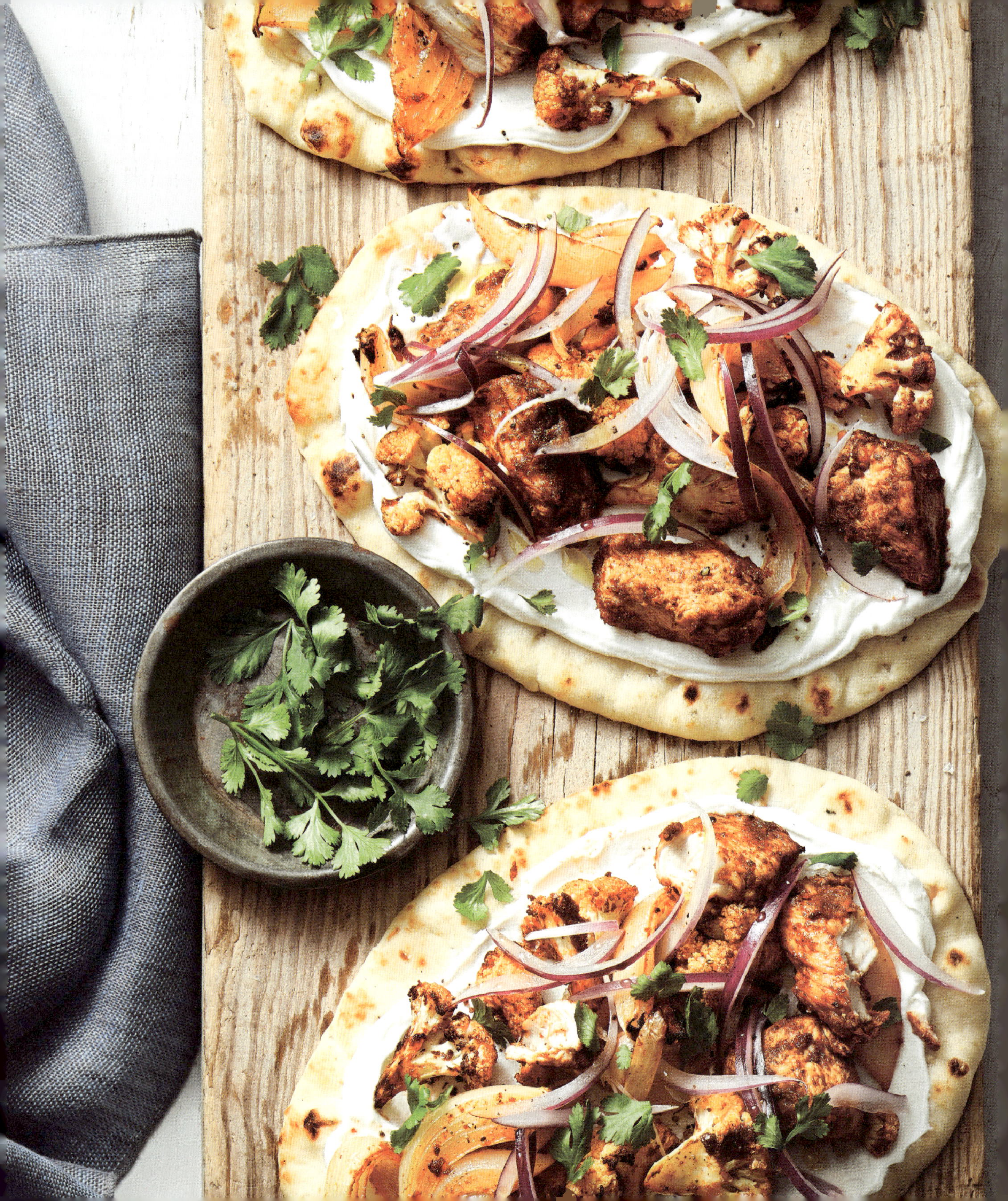

CHICKEN DINNERS | **WEEKNIGHT**

Tandoori-Spiced Cauliflower Chicken Flatbreads

- 1 small red onion, thinly sliced
- 1½ teaspoons paprika
- 1½ teaspoons ground coriander
- 1½ teaspoons ground cumin
- 1 teaspoon smoked paprika
- ¼ teaspoon cayenne pepper
- ¼ teaspoon dry mustard powder
- ⅛ teaspoon ground cardamom
- Kosher salt
- 3 tablespoons olive oil
- 1 tablespoon tomato paste
- 2 cloves garlic, grated
- 2 teaspoons grated fresh ginger
- 1½ pounds cauliflower, trimmed and cut into small florets
- 12 ounces boneless, skinless chicken breasts, cut into 2-inch cubes
- 1 small yellow onion, cut into ½-inch-thick wedges
- 1 tablespoon fresh lemon juice
- 4 pieces naan or flatbread, warmed
- ½ cup Greek yogurt or labneh
- Cilantro leaves, for serving

Serves 4 | Active time 20 minutes | Total time 40 minutes

Streamline post-dinner cleanup by making a delicious feast that dirties only your air fryer and a bowl. Plus, these flatbreads, featuring perfectly charred chicken and cauliflower seasoned with a robust spice mix inspired by tandoori masala, are easy to assemble.

1. Place the red onion in a small bowl, cover it with cold water and let it sit.

2. In a large bowl, combine the paprika, coriander, cumin, smoked paprika, cayenne, mustard and cardamom and 1 teaspoon salt. Stir in the oil, tomato paste, garlic and ginger. Add the cauliflower and toss to coat, then add the chicken and toss; let it sit for 15 minutes.

3. Heat an air fryer to 375°F. Pick out the chicken and transfer it to a second bowl. Add the onion to the cauliflower mixture and toss to combine. Air-fry the cauliflower mixture in a single layer, shaking the basket halfway through, until slightly charred and browned, 14 minutes. Transfer to a plate. Air-fry the chicken until it is cooked through, 8 minutes. Transfer to a plate.

4. Meanwhile, drain the red onion, then toss it with lemon juice and ¼ teaspoon of salt.

5. Spread the naan with yogurt. Top with the chicken and vegetables, then the red onion. Sprinkle with cilantro if desired.

Love Notes

THE NEWLYWED COOKBOOK

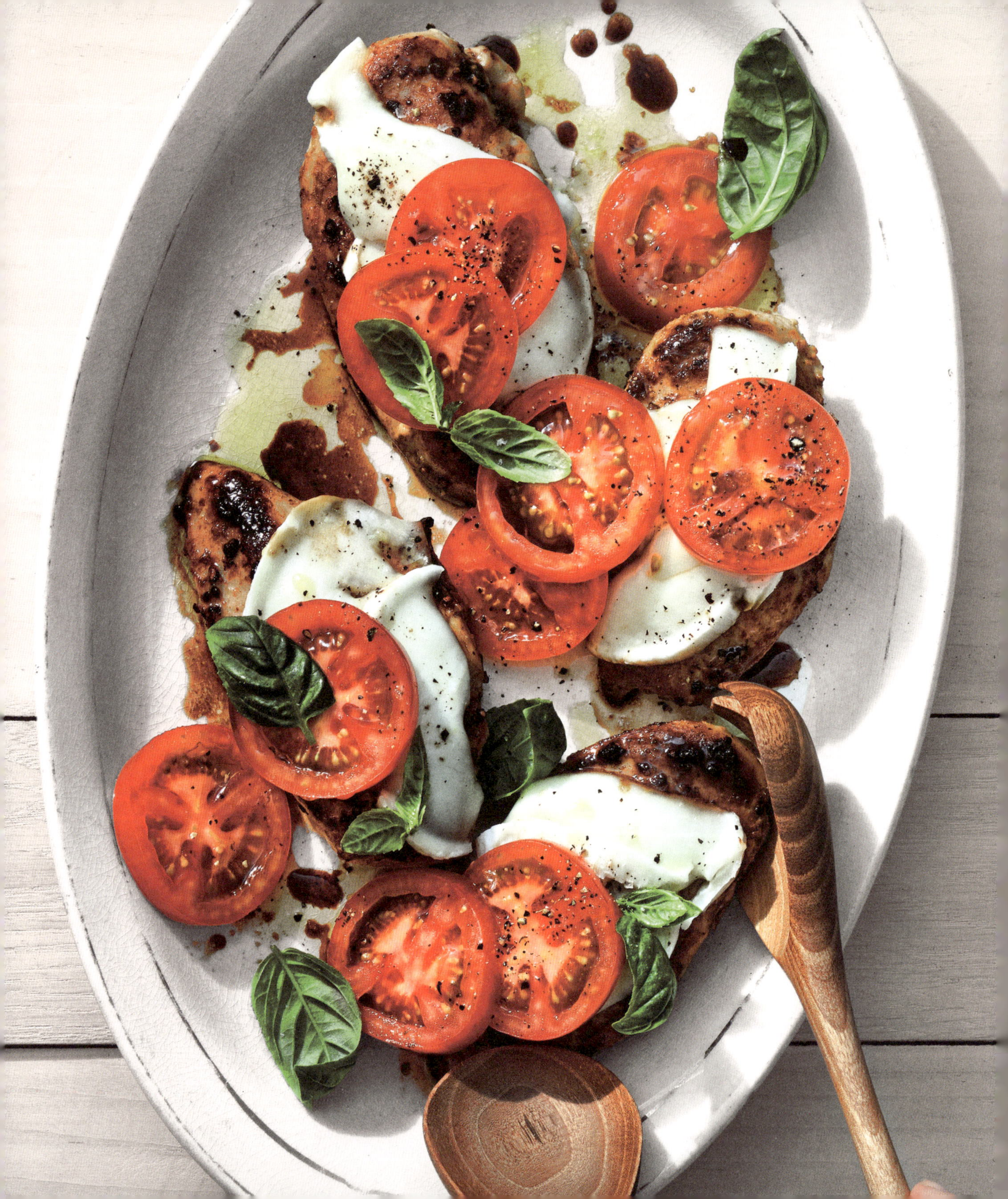

CHICKEN DINNERS | **WEEKNIGHT**

Skillet Balsamic Chicken

- 1 tablespoon olive oil
- 4 6-ounce boneless, skinless chicken breasts
- Kosher salt and pepper
- ¼ cup balsamic vinegar
- 6 ounces fresh mozzarella, sliced
- 1 to 2 heirloom tomatoes, sliced
- ¼ cup fresh basil leaves

Serves 4 | Active time 20 minutes | Total time 30 minutes

This five-ingredient dish not only is delicious but also boasts your new flavor-maker technique: simmering balsamic vinegar until it's syrupy and then turning the chicken to to coat it and transform each bite.

1. Heat the oven to 400°F. Heat the oil in a large ovenproof skillet on medium-high. Season the chicken with ½ teaspoon of salt and ¼ teaspoon of pepper and cook until deep golden brown on one side, 4 to 5 minutes.

2. Flip the chicken and cook 1 minute. Reduce the heat to medium, add the balsamic vinegar and gently simmer until slightly thickened and syrupy, 1 to 2 minutes. Transfer the skillet to the oven and roast 10 minutes.

3. Turn the chicken to coat in vinegar, top with the mozzarella and roast until the chicken registers 165°F on an instant-read thermometer and the cheese begins to melt, about 2 minutes.

4. Serve topped with tomatoes and basil leaves and sprinkle with salt and pepper. Drizzle with any additional balsamic glaze from the skillet.

Love Notes

THE NEWLYWED COOKBOOK

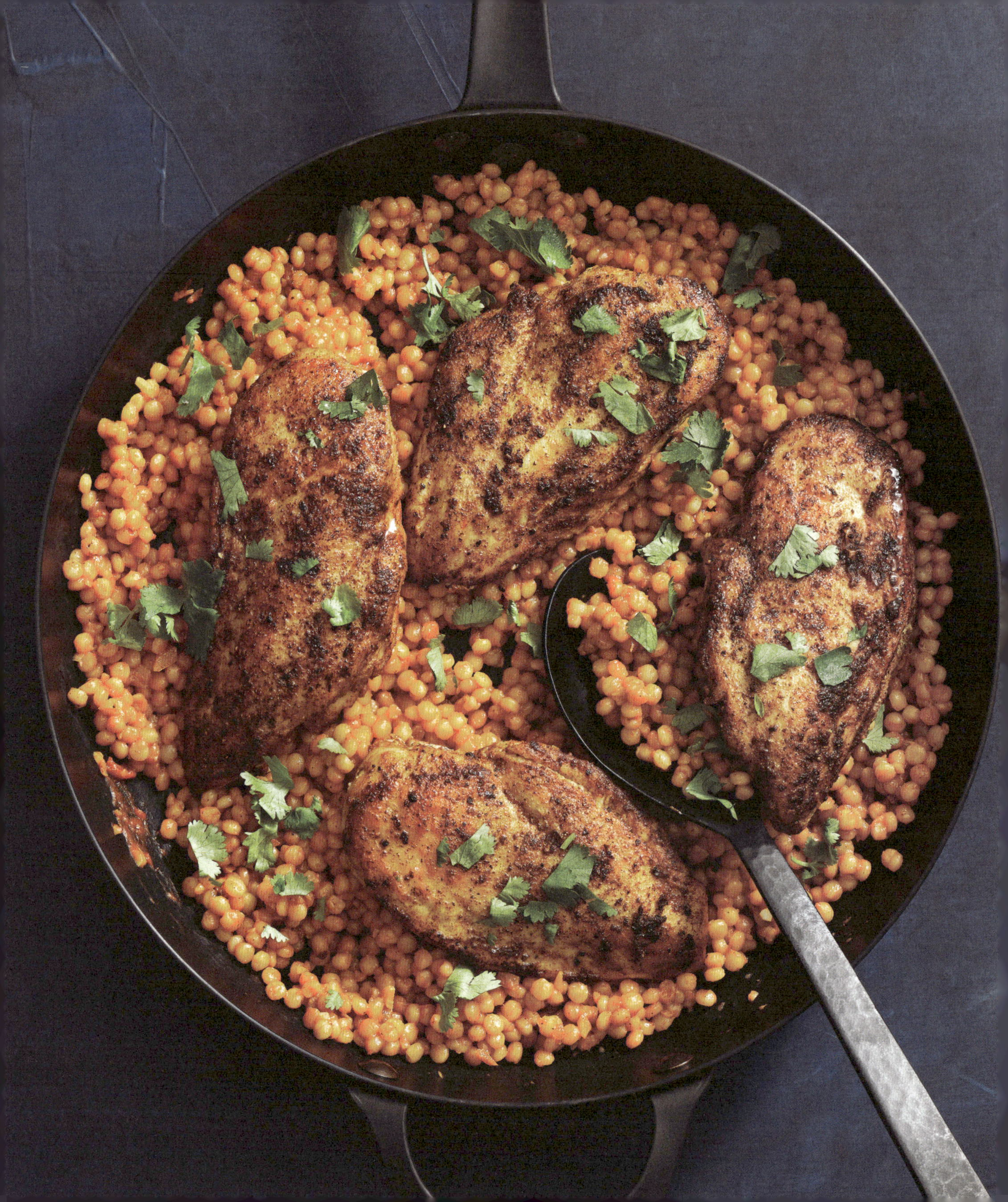

CHICKEN DINNERS | **WEEKNIGHT**

Moroccan-Spiced Skillet Chicken & Couscous

Serves 4 | Active time 20 minutes | Total time 30 minutes

Cozy up with this skillet chicken dinner that gets a complex flavor from preserved lemon rind, smoked paprika and ras el hanout — a warm, earthy multi-spice mix (think baking spices with a lovely floral note) used in North African cooking.

- 4 6-ounce boneless, skinless chicken breasts
- 3 tablespoons olive oil, divided
- 1 tablepsoon ras el hanout
- Kosher salt and pepper
- 2 large cloves garlic, finely chopped
- Rind from ¼ preserved lemon, pulp scraped and discarded, finely chopped (2 tablespoons)
- 2 tablespoons tomato paste
- ½ teaspoon smoked paprika
- 1 cup quick-cooking pearl couscous
- 1½ teaspoons chicken bouillon base (we use Better Than Bouillon) whisked into 1½ cups water
- ½ cup cilantro, chopped

1. Place the chicken in a large bowl and toss with 1 tablespoon of oil, then the ras el hanout and ¼ teaspoon each of salt and pepper to coat.

2. Heat 1 tablespoon of oil in a large, deep skillet or Dutch oven on medium. Add the chicken and cook, undisturbed, until golden brown, 7 to 8 minutes. Flip and cook until the other side is golden brown, 2 to 3 minutes; transfer to a plate (the chicken will finish cooking in step 4).

3. Add the remaining tablespoon of oil to the skillet along with the garlic and preserved lemon rind and cook, stirring constantly, 30 seconds. Add the tomato paste and smoked paprika; cook, stirring constantly, 1 minute.

4. Add the couscous and stir to coat. Stir in the bouillon mixture and bring to a boil. Nestle the chicken, darker side up, in the couscous and add any juices from the plate. Cover, reduce heat and simmer until the couscous has absorbed most of the liquid and the chicken is cooked through, 14 to 15 minutes. Serve sprinkled with cilantro.

MIND YOUR BLEND

The ingredients of ras el hanout can vary. If yours does not have cumin or cinnamon, add 1 teaspoon ground cumin and ¼ teaspoon cinnamon to the recipe when adding paprika.

Love Notes

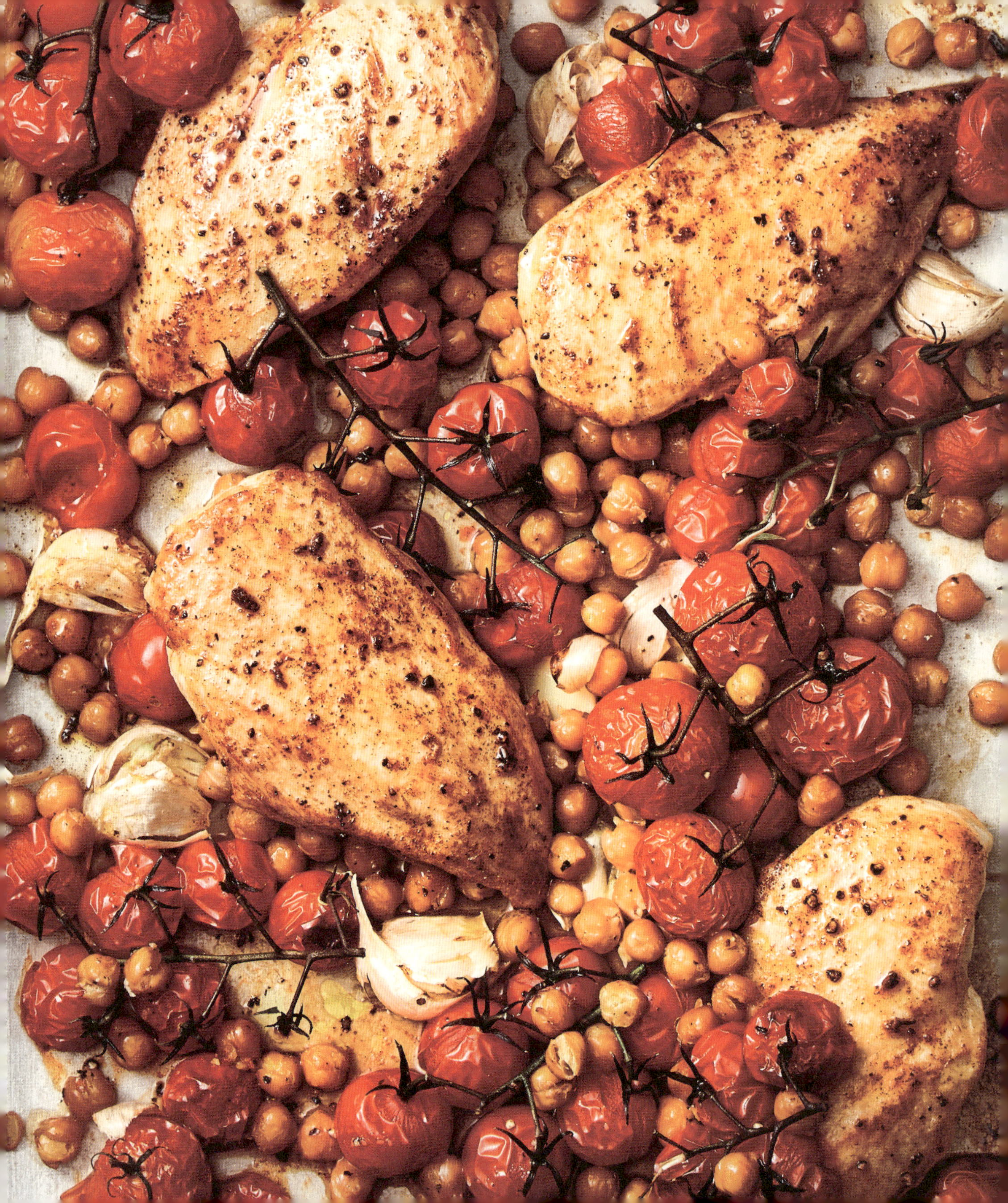

Paprika Chicken with Crispy Chickpeas & Tomatoes

- 12 ounces cherry or grape tomatoes
- 8 cloves garlic, smashed, in their skins
- 1 15-ounce can chickpeas, rinsed
- 3 tablespoons olive oil, divided
- Kosher salt and pepper
- 4 6-ounce boneless, skinless chicken breasts
- 2 teaspoons paprika

Serves 4 | Active time 10 minutes | Total time 20 minutes

Juicy tomatoes and a ton of garlic create a built-in sauce for spiced chicken while everything roasts on one sheet pan. Easy, right?

1. Heat the oven to 425°F. On a rimmed baking sheet, toss the tomatoes, garlic and chickpeas with 2 tablespoons of oil and ¼ teaspoon each of salt and pepper. Roast 10 minutes.

2. Meanwhile, heat the remaining tablespoon of oil in a large skillet on medium. Season the chicken with paprika and ½ teaspoon each of salt and pepper and cook until golden brown on one side, 5 to 6 minutes. Flip and cook 1 minute more.

3. Transfer the chicken to the baking sheet, nestling it in with the tomatoes and chickpeas, and roast until cooked through, 6 minutes more. Before serving, discard the garlic skins.

MEAL PREP MAGIC
Consider this week's lunches covered. Grab a second sheet pan, cook up a double batch and store leftovers in airtight containers. To serve, slice the chicken and toss everything with mixed greens plus a drizzle of olive oil.

Love Notes

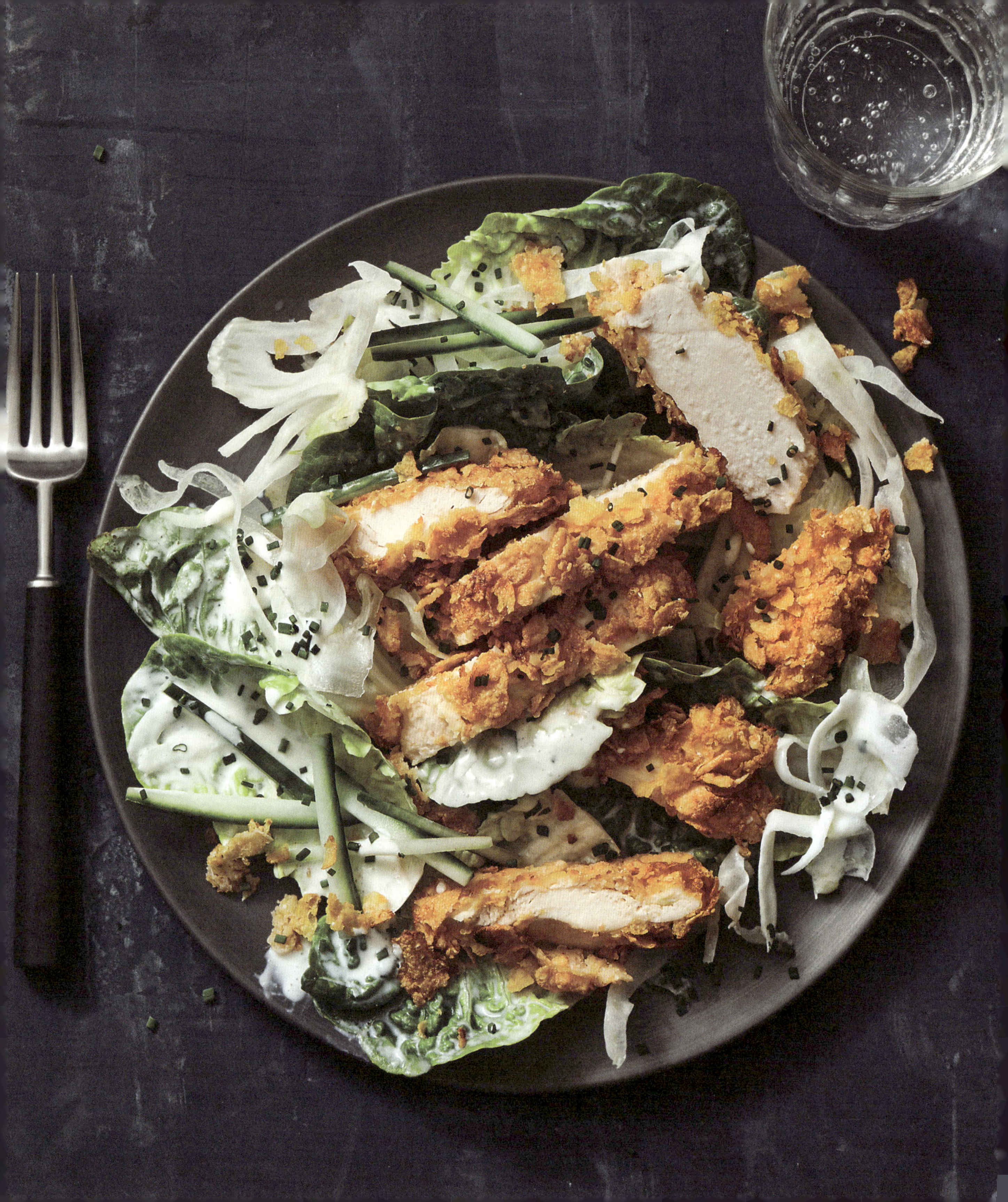

CHICKEN DINNERS | **WEEKNIGHT**

Crispy Chicken Salad

- 4 cups cornflakes, slightly crushed
- ½ cup buttermilk, divided
- 4 5- to 6-ounce boneless, skinless chicken breasts (about 1½ pounds)
- ½ teaspoon cayenne
- Kosher salt and pepper
- ¼ cup sour cream
- 1½ tablespoons white wine vinegar
- 1 teaspoon Dijon mustard
- 1 tablespoon fresh tarragon, chopped
- 6 cups torn Little Gem or green leaf lettuce
- ½ medium bulb fennel, cored and thinly sliced
- 1 small seedless cucumber, cut into matchsticks
- 2 tablespoons chopped fresh chives

Serves 4 | Active time 15 minutes | Total time 35 minutes

Lighten things up with a plate of greens that isn't short on flavor. Buttermilk does double duty: First it is used to adhere crushed cornflakes, creating an irresistibly crisp coating on baked—not fried!—chicken. Then some is used to make a creamy, tangy dressing.

1. Heat the oven to 400°F. Line a rimmed baking sheet with nonstick foil. Place the cornflakes in a shallow bowl.

2. Using ¼ cup of the buttermilk, brush the chicken breasts on all sides, then season with the cayenne, ½ teaspoon of salt and ¼ teaspoon of pepper. Coat the chicken in cornflakes, pressing gently to help them adhere, and place on the prepared baking sheet. Bake until the chicken is cooked through, 15 to 20 minutes. Slice if desired.

3. Meanwhile, in a large bowl, whisk together the sour cream, vinegar and mustard; the remaining ¼ cup of buttermilk; and ¼ teaspoon each of salt and pepper, then stir in the tarragon. Add the lettuce and toss to coat, then fold in the fennel and cucumber. Serve with the chicken and sprinkle with the chives.

BEYOND BREADCRUMBS

When you're breading meat for baking or frying, you don't have to use just breadcrumbs. Here, cornflakes create a super-crisp crust, but crushed crackers, potato chips and pretzels are also fun options.

Love Notes

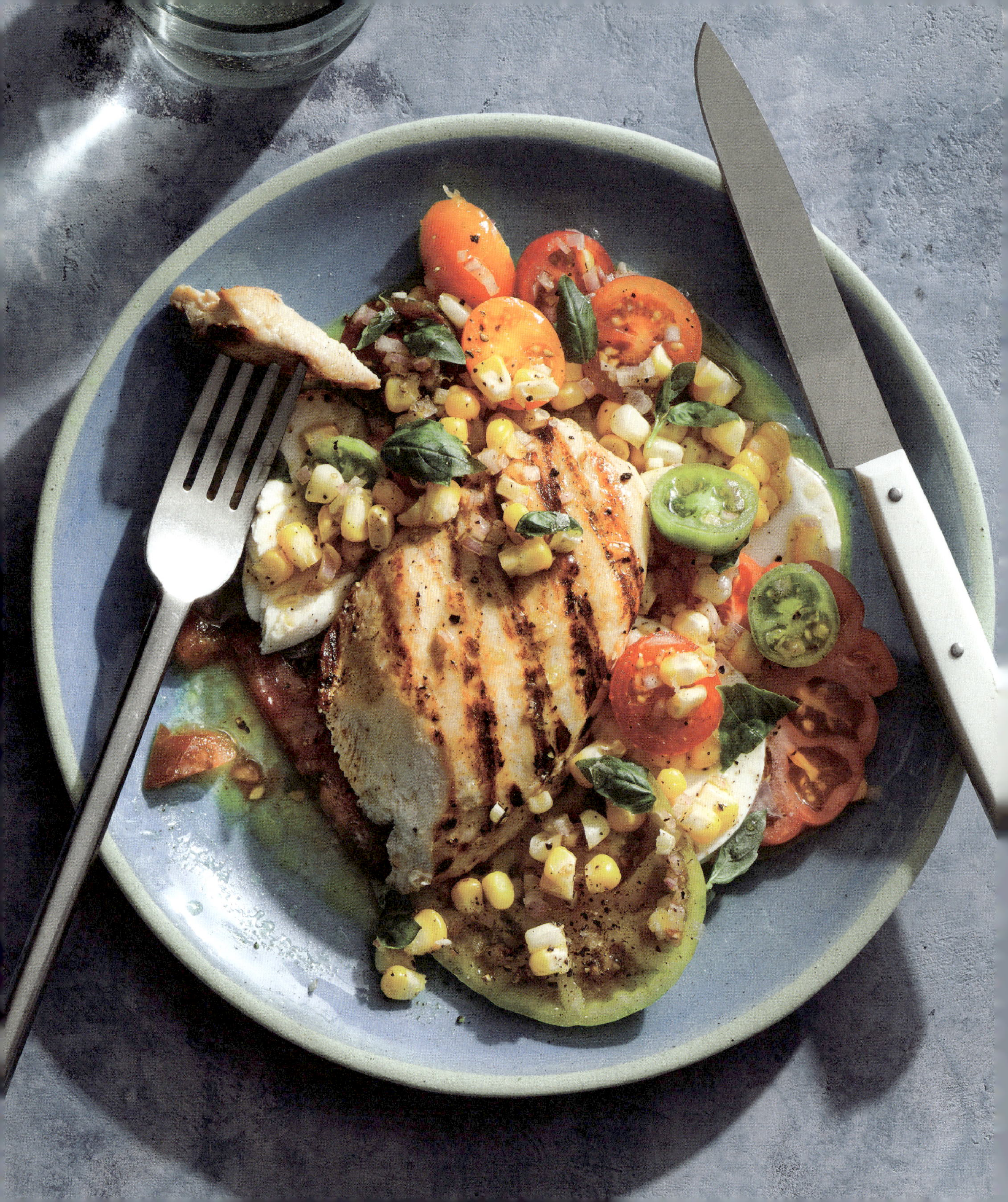

Grilled Chicken Caprese

Serves 4 | Active time 20 minutes | Total time 20 minutes

Canola oil, for grill grates

1 tablespoon red wine vinegar

3 tablespoon plus 2 teaspoons olive oil, divided

Kosher salt and pepper

1 small shallot, finely chopped

1 cup corn kernels (from 1 large ear, or frozen and thawed)

1 pint mixed-color grape or cherry tomatoes, halved

4 6-ounce boneless, skinless chicken breasts

2 pounds mixed-color medium and large tomatoes, sliced

6 ounces fresh mozzarella, sliced

¼ cup small fresh basil leaves

Spend the night outside! Fire up the grill to turn the Italian tomato, basil and mozzarella salad into a protein-packed complete meal.

1. Heat a grill to medium-high. Clean the grill and lightly oil it with canola oil. In a medium bowl, whisk together the vinegar, 3 tablespoons of the olive oil and ½ teaspoon each of salt and pepper; stir in the shallot. Add the corn and the grape tomatoes and toss to combine; set aside.

2. Rub the chicken with the remaining 2 teaspoons of oil; season with ½ teaspoon of salt and ¼ teaspoon of pepper; and grill until cooked through, 4 to 6 minutes per side.

3. Arrange the chicken, sliced tomatoes and mozzarella on a platter. Spoon the corn mixture and any juices from the bowl over the chicken, then sprinkle with the basil.

STRETCH THE SEASON
To make this dish year-round, omit the medium and large tomatoes and double the amount of cherry tomatoes, which are consistently tasty and available. You can also make the chicken on the stovetop in a skillet or a grill pan.

Love Notes

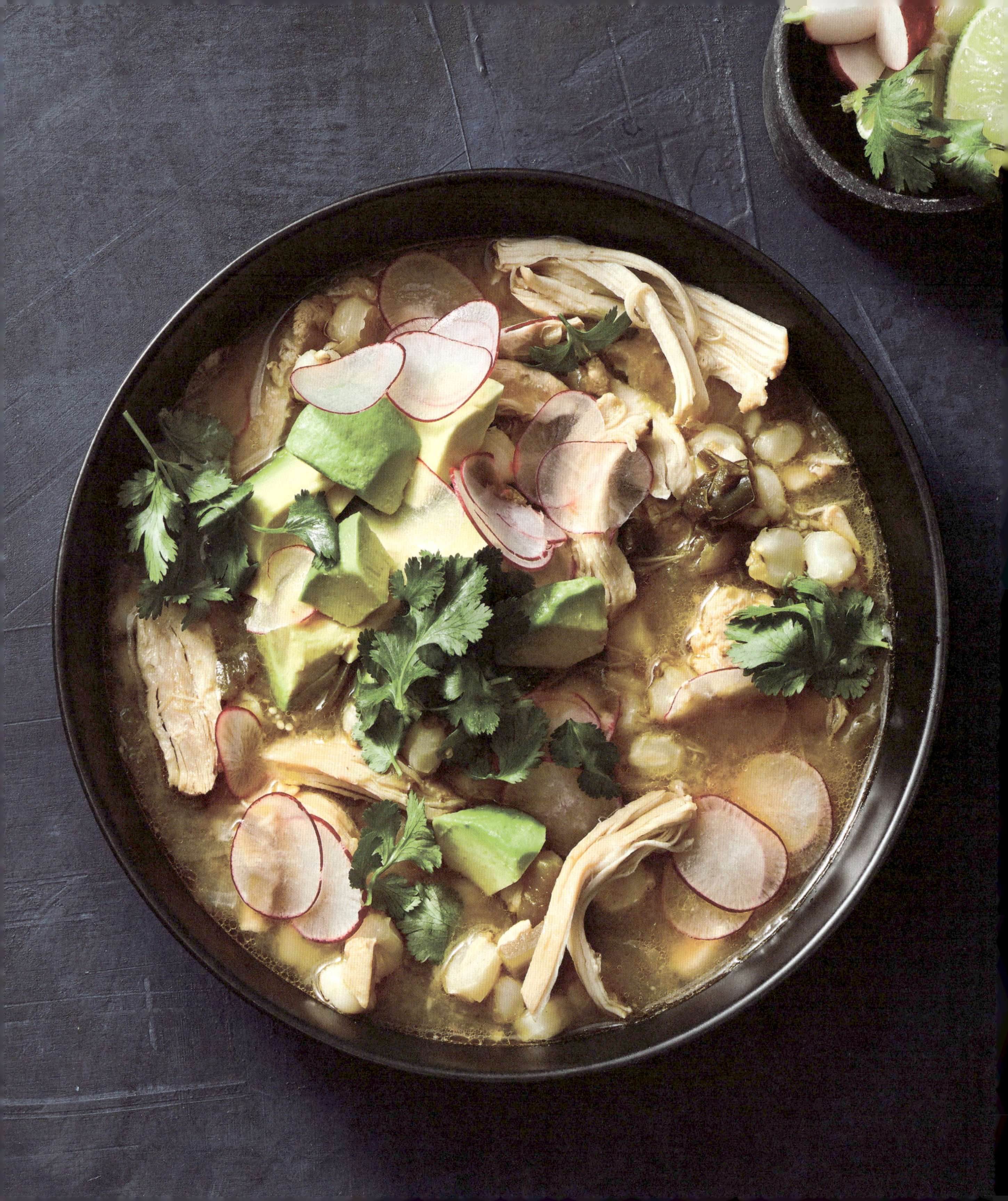

Slow Cooker Chicken Pozole Verde

Serves 4 to 6 | Active time 15 minutes | Total time 4 hours 15 minutes

- 2 ounces beer
- 1 tablespoon low-sodium chicken bouillon base (we use Better Than Bouillon)
- 2 teaspoons ground cumin
- Kosher salt and pepper
- 1½ pounds boneless, skinless chicken thighs, trimmed
- 12 ounces tomatillos, cut into ½-inch pieces
- 4 cloves garlic, finely chopped
- 1 onion, finely chopped
- 1 poblano, cut into ¼-inch pieces
- ½ small bunch cilantro, plus leaves for serving
- 1 28-ounce can hominy, rinsed
- ¼ cup fresh lime juice
- Avocado, radishes and lime wedges, for serving

Tomatillos, poblano peppers and cilantro bring a ton of green hues (and flavor!) to a tasty stew you can whip together in a slow cooker earlier in the day and serve effortlessly for dinner on a busy night.

1. In a 5- to 6-quart slow cooker, combine the beer, bouillon base, and cumin; 2 cups of water; and ½ teaspoon each of salt and pepper.

2. Add the chicken, tomatillos, garlic, onion, poblano and cilantro and stir to combine. Cook, covered, until the chicken pulls apart easily, 4 to 5 hours on High or 6 to 7 hours on Low.

3. Remove the cilantro from the slow cooker and discard; then, using 2 forks, break the chicken into smaller pieces. Add the hominy and cook, covered, until tender, 3 to 4 minutes. Stir in the lime juice and serve with cilantro leaves, avocado, radishes and lime wedges if desired.

MAKE AHEAD
Anticipating leftovers? Before adding the lime juice, freeze half in an airtight container for up to three months. To serve, thaw overnight in the refrigerator, then warm and top as desired.

Love Notes

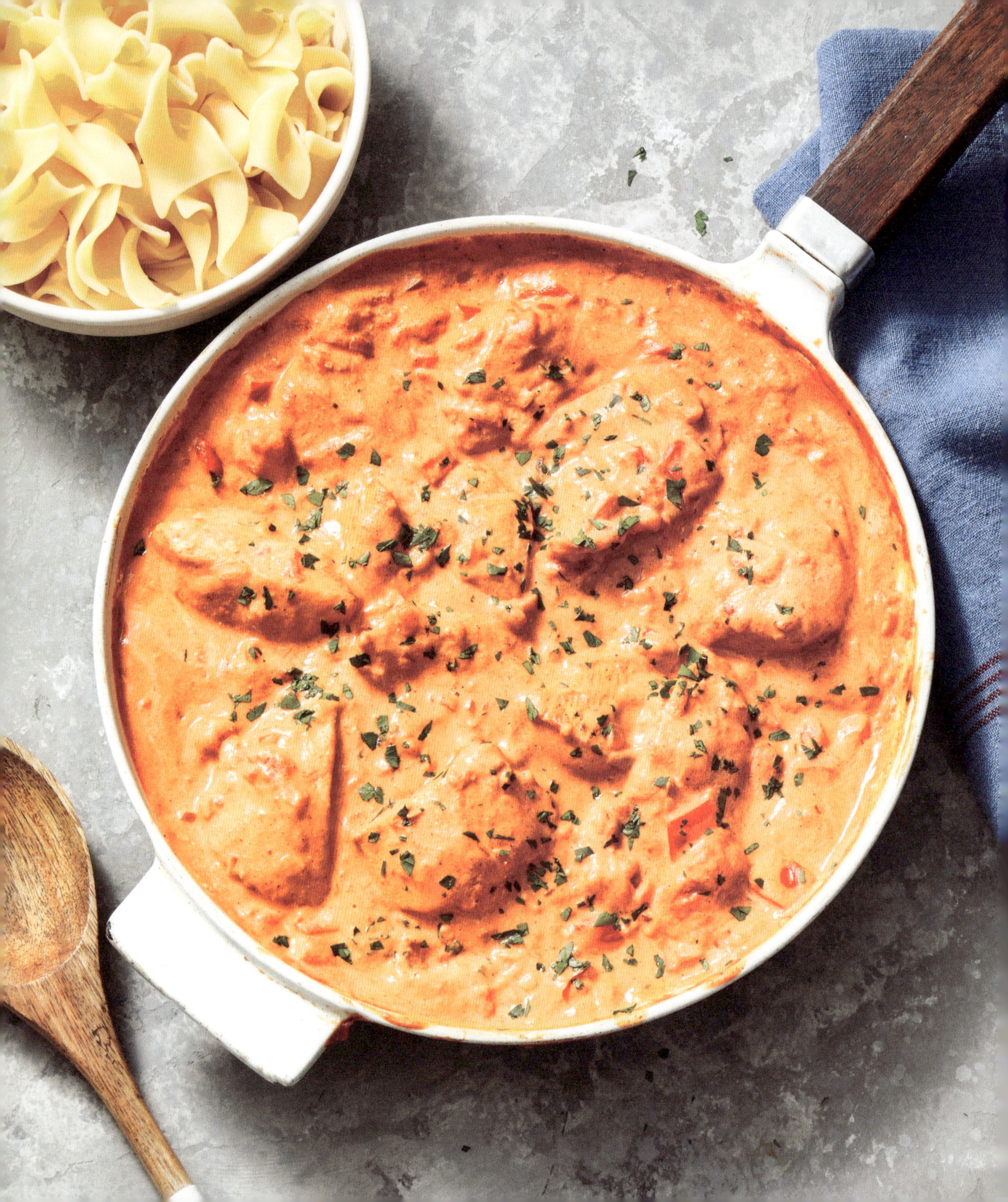

CHICKEN DINNERS | **WEEKNIGHT**

Chicken Paprikash

Serves 4 | Active time 35 minutes | Total time 35 minutes

The perfect one-dish dinner for chilly nights, this classic entree features a rich, creamy sauce seasoned with paprika. Opt for a bright, mild Hungarian sweet variety, then sizzle in oil to release its flavors.

- 3 tablespoons olive oil, divided
- 1½ pounds boneless, skinless chicken breasts, cut into 2½-inch pieces
- Kosher salt and pepper
- 1 large onion, chopped
- 1 large red pepper, seeded and cut into ¼-inch pieces
- 4 cloves garlic, finely chopped
- 3 tablespoons all-purpose flour
- 1½ tablespoons paprika (Hungarian if possible)
- 1 cup low-sodium chicken broth
- 1 14-ounce can whole tomatoes, drained and chopped
- ½ to 1 teaspoon hot sauce (optional)
- ½ cup sour cream
- Cooked egg noodles and chopped parsley, for serving

1. Heat 2 tablespoons of oil in a large skillet on medium-high. Season the chicken with ¼ teaspoon each of salt and pepper and cook until golden brown, 2 to 3 minutes per side; transfer to a plate.

2. Reduce heat to medium and add the remaining tablespoon of oil to the skillet along with the onion; cook, stirring occasionally, 5 minutes. Add the red pepper and the garlic and cook, stirring, 2 minutes.

3. Sprinkle the vegetables with flour and cook, stirring, 2 minutes. Sprinkle with paprika and cook, stirring, 1 minute. Stir in the chicken broth, then the tomatoes; simmer 5 minutes.

4. Return the chicken to the skillet along with any juices and add the hot sauce (if using), then simmer until the chicken is cooked through, 5 to 8 minutes. Remove from the heat and stir in the sour cream. Serve over egg noodles and sprinkle with parsley.

Love Notes

THE NEWLYWED COOKBOOK

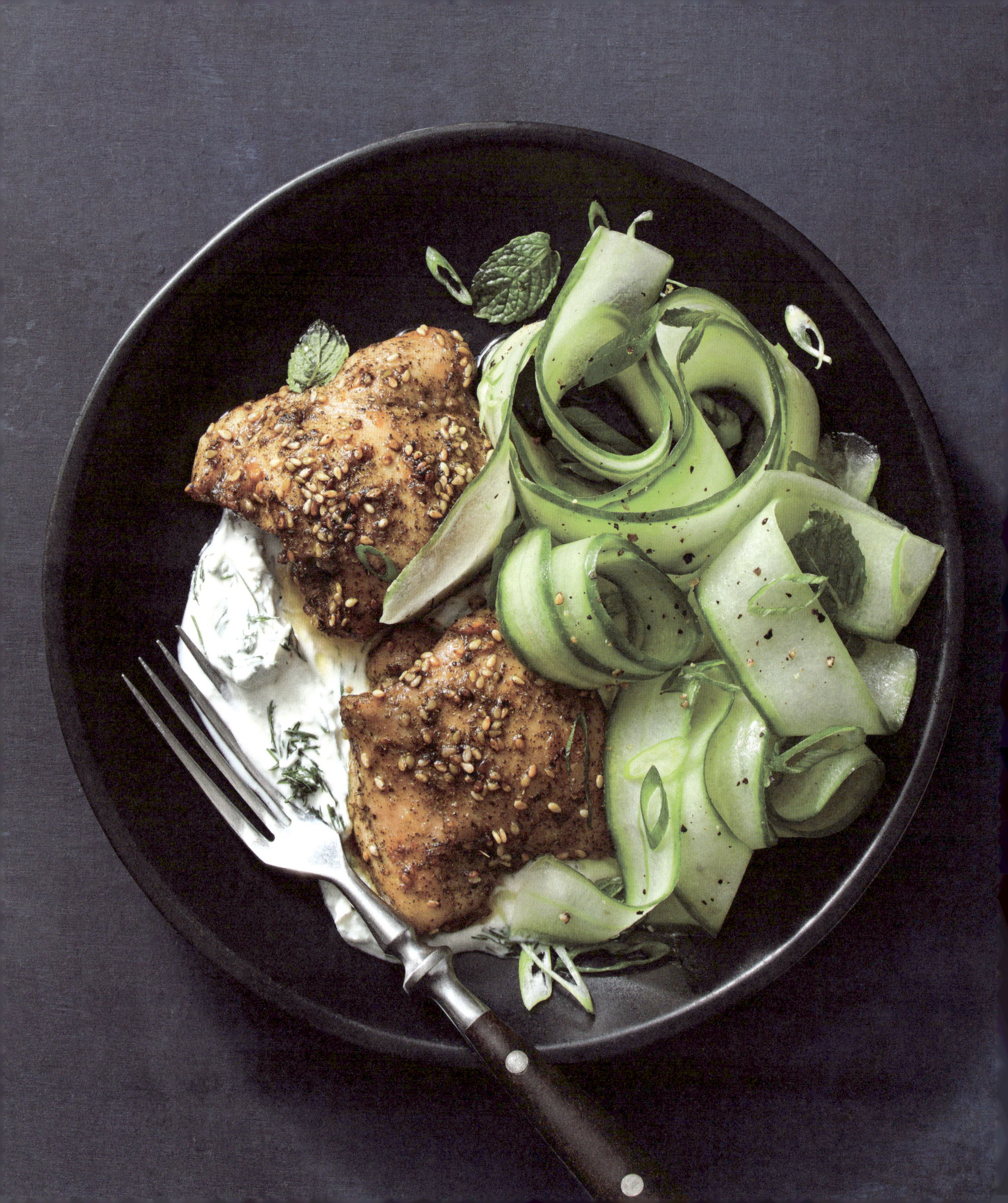

Za'atar Chicken with Whipped Feta

Serves 4 | Active time 30 minutes | Total time 30 minutes

A fragrant, herbaceous Middle Eastern spice, za'atar adds savory depth to charred chicken thighs, which pair perfectly with a creamy feta yogurt spread.

- 4 tablespoons olive oil, divided
- 2 tablespoons za'atar
- Kosher salt and pepper
- 8 small boneless, skinless chicken thighs, trimmed (about 1½ pounds)
- 2½ tablespoons lemon juice, divided, plus ½ teaspoon lemon zest
- 1 cup low-fat Greek yogurt
- 2 ounces feta cheese, crumbled
- ¼ cup dill fronds, chopped
- 1 seedless cucumber, halved crosswise and thinly shaved lengthwise with peeler
- 2 scallions, thinly sliced diagonally
- 2 tablespoons small mint leaves

1. Heat the oven to broil and arrange racks in the upper and middle positions. Brush a rimmed baking sheet with ½ tablespoon of oil.

2. In a large bowl, stir together the za'atar, 2 tablespoons of olive oil and ¼ teaspoon each of salt and pepper. Add the chicken and toss to coat. Arrange on the prepared sheet and broil on the middle rack until beginning to brown, 12 to 14 minutes. Transfer the sheet to the top rack and broil until browned and cooked through, 2 to 3 minutes more. Immediately add 1 tablespoon of lemon juice to the baking sheet and scrape up any browned bits, then flip the chicken to coat it with pan juices.

3. Meanwhile, in a food processor, puree the yogurt, feta and lemon zest, ½ tablespoon of lemon juice and ¼ teaspoon each of salt and pepper until smooth, 1 to 2 minutes. Scrape the sides of the bowl, then add the dill and pulse to combine.

4. In a large bowl, whisk together the remaining 1½ tablespoons of oil and the remaining tablespoon of lemon juice with ¼ teaspoon each of salt and pepper. Add the cucumber, scallions and mint and toss to combine. Spread the whipped feta on plates and top with the chicken and the cucumber salad.

Love Notes

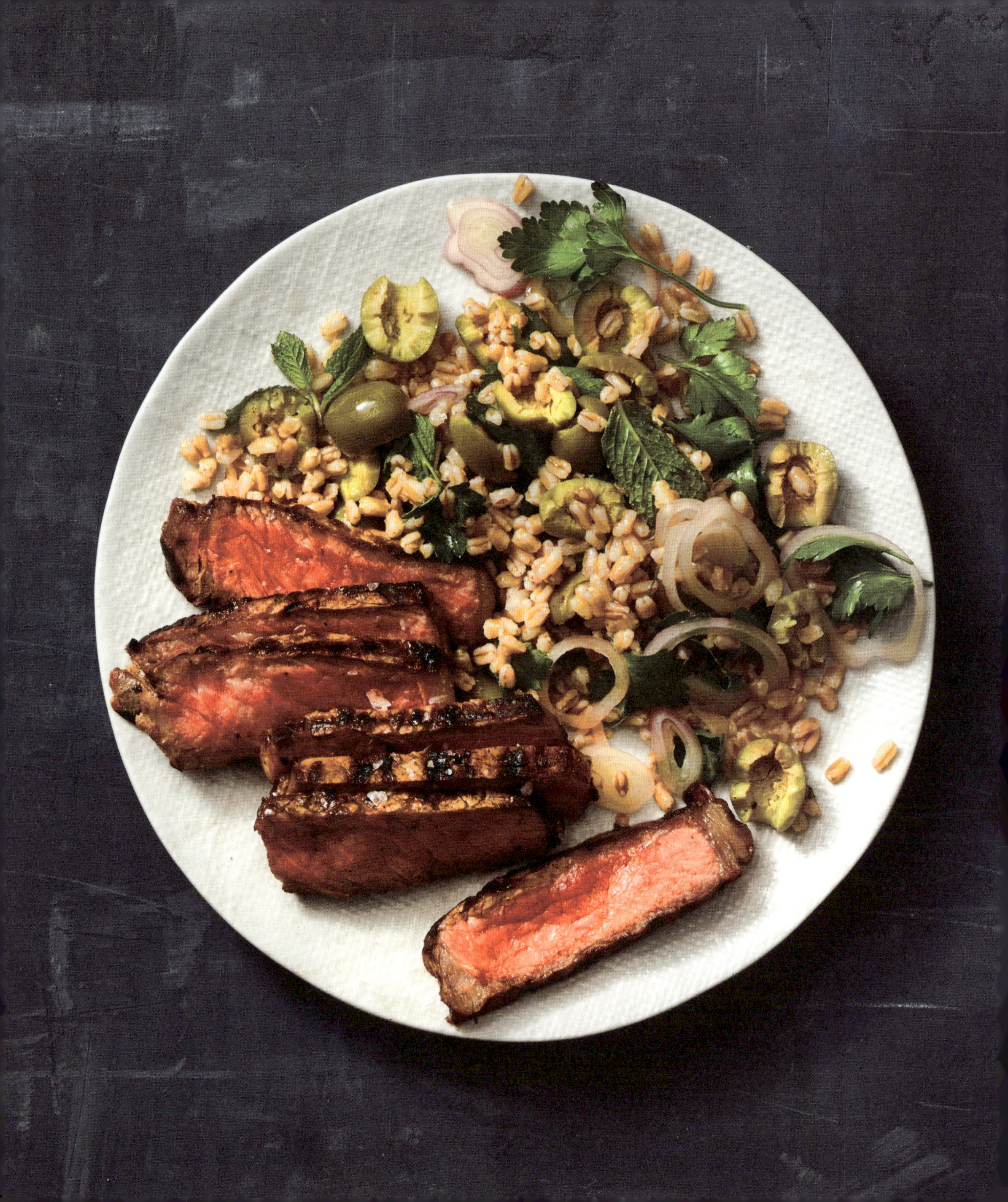

Aleppo Grilled Steak with Farro Salad

Serves 4 | Active time 25 minutes | Total time 25 minutes

- 1½ cups quick-cooking farro
- 2 12-ounce strip steaks (each about 1½ inches thick)
- ¾ teaspoon Aleppo pepper
- Kosher salt and pepper
- 2 teaspoons grated lemon zest, plus 3 tablespoons lemon juice
- 2 small shallots, thinly sliced
- 3 tablespoons olive oil
- ¾ cup pitted Castelvetrano olives, crushed and roughly chopped
- ¼ cup flat-leaf parsley, roughly chopped
- ¼ cup fresh mint, torn or roughly chopped

Consider this recipe your excuse to cook up steak on any given weeknight: It's fast and simple yet packed with flavor. No special occasion required!

1. Heat a grill to medium. Cook the farro per the package directions.

2. Season the steak with Aleppo pepper, ½ teaspoon of salt and ¼ teaspoon of pepper. Grill the steak to the desired doneness, 5 to 8 minutes per side for medium-rare. Transfer the steak to a cutting board and let it rest at least 5 minutes before slicing.

3. In a medium bowl, combine the lemon zest and juice, the shallots and ½ teaspoon each of salt and pepper; let sit for 5 minutes.

4. Stir the oil into the shallot mixture, then toss with the farro. Fold in the olives, parsley and mint and serve with the steak.

GO VEG!
For a vegetarian alternative, use Halloumi, a firm grilling cheese, in place of steak. Season slices with Aleppo pepper, then grill until lightly charred, about 20 seconds per side.

Love Notes

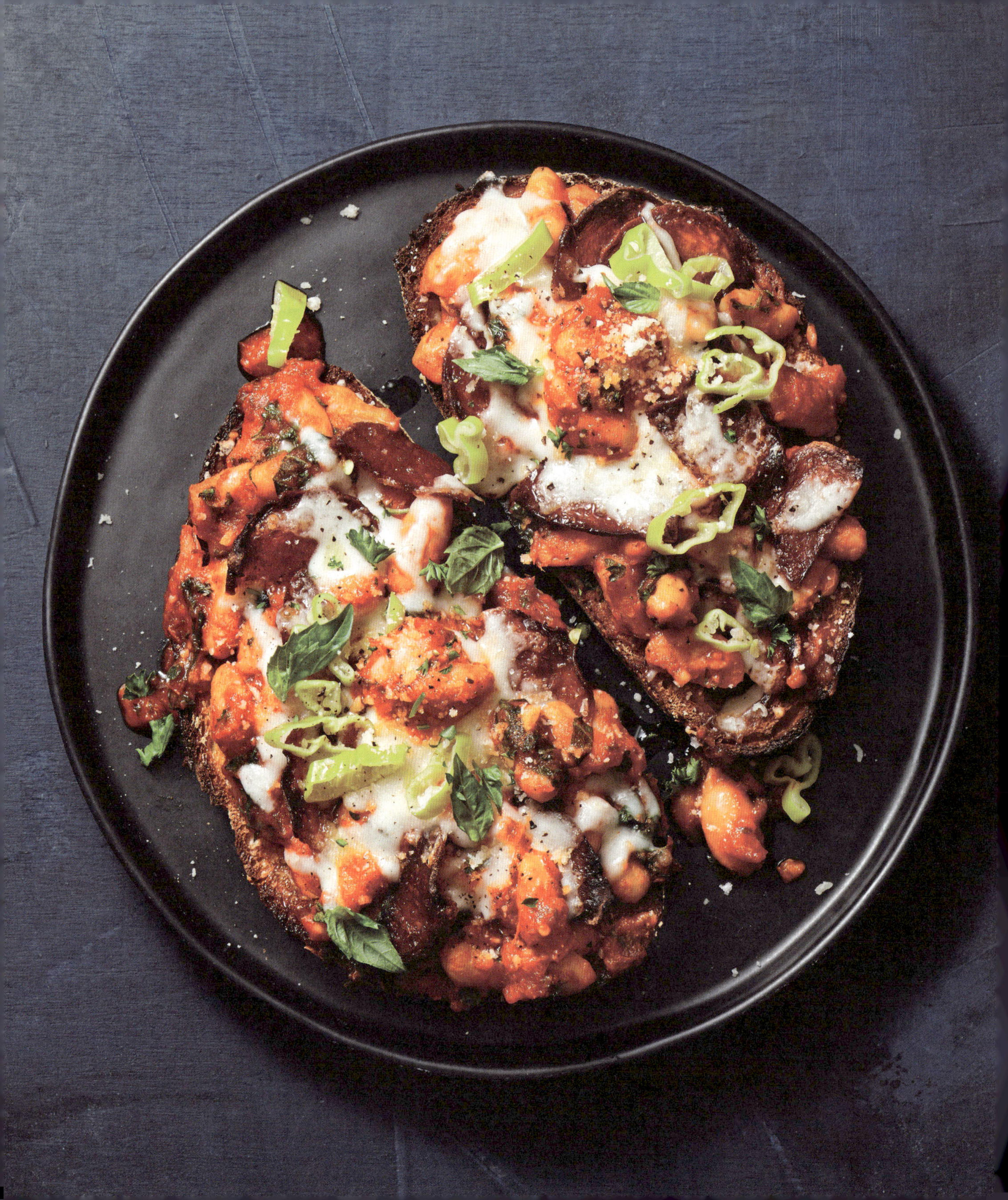

Saucy Pizza Beans

Serves 4 | **Active time 15 minutes** | **Total time 15 minutes**

- 8 slices sourdough bread
- 2 tablespoons olive oil, divided
- 2 large cloves garlic, 1 whole and 1 finely chopped
- ¼ cup grated Parmesan, plus more for serving
- 1 ounce pepperoni, sliced in half
- 1 15-ounce can cannellini beans, drained and rinsed
- 1 cup jarred marinara sauce
- 4 medium pepperoncini, thinly sliced, plus 1 tablespoon brine
- ¼ cup fresh basil leaves, chopped, plus more for serving
- 2 tablespoons flat-leaf parsley, chopped
- 6 ounces whole-milk mozzarella, coarsely shredded

Think of this dish as French bread pizza 2.0: creamy, garlicky cannellini beans, loads of sauce, crispy pepperoni and tangy pepperoncini piled high on crisp sourdough toasts.

1. Heat the broiler. Place the bread on a baking sheet and, using 1 tablespoon of the oil, brush both sides of each piece of bread. Broil, flipping once, until the bread is golden brown on both sides, 3 to 4 minutes total. Immediately rub the bread with the whole garlic clove, then sprinkle with the Parmesan cheese.

2. In a medium skillet, heat the remaining tablespoon of oil on medium. Add the pepperoni and cook until it starts to crisp, about 1 minute per side. Using a slotted spoon, transfer the pepperoni to a plate, leaving the oil in the skillet. Stir in the chopped garlic and cook 1 minute. Add the beans and warm them in the oil 1 minute. Add the marinara sauce and cook until heated through, about 2 minutes. Remove the bean mixture from the heat and stir in the pepperoncini brine, then fold in the basil and parsley.

3. Spoon the beans onto the toasts, top with the pepperoni and mozzarella and broil until the cheese melts, 1 to 2 minutes. Serve sprinkled with sliced pepperoncini and additional Parmesan and basil if desired.

BRINE TIME

In this recipe, a tablespoon of tangy pepperoncini brine perks up a can of beans. Keep that trick in mind for all the brines that are often left behind in jars. You can add them to sauces, marinades for meats (especially chicken for frying) and even cocktails.

Love Notes

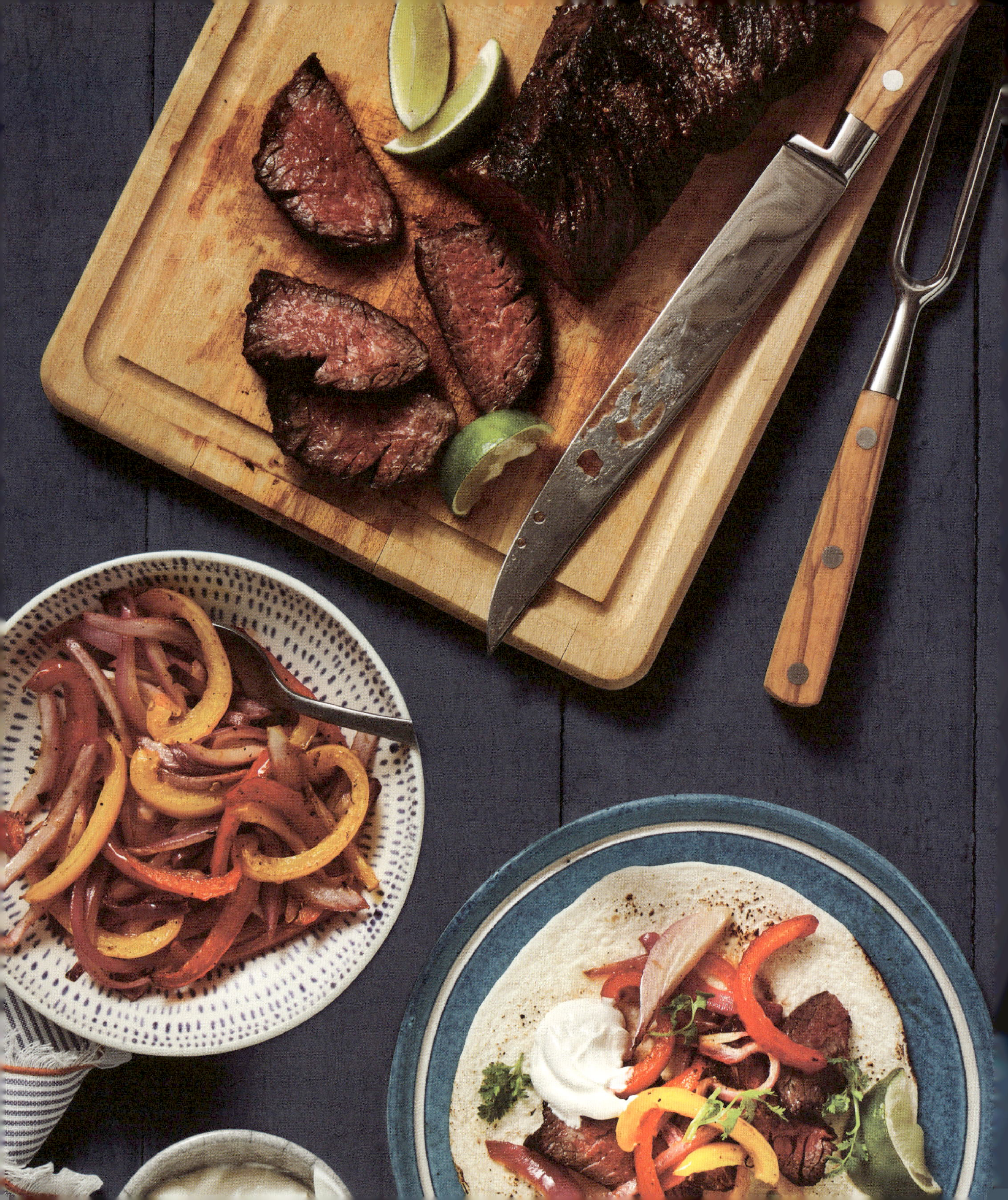

MEATY MAINS | **WEEKNIGHT**

Air-Fried Steak Fajitas

Serves 2 to 4 | Active time 15 minutes | Total time 35 minutes

Fajitas aren't just restaurant fare! With an air fryer, you can easily sizzle some up at home. Pair with a batch of margaritas.

1. In a large bowl, toss the peppers, onion, lime zest and juice and cumin, 1 tablespoon of the oil, ¼ teaspoon of the garlic, ½ teaspoon of salt and ¼ teaspoon of pepper. Air-fry at 400°F, shaking the basket occasionally, 10 minutes.

2. Meanwhile, rub the steak with the remaining 2 teaspoons of oil, then season it with ancho chile powder, the remaining ¼ teaspoon of granulated garlic and ½ teaspoon each of salt and pepper. Push the vegetables to one side of the air fryer and add the steak to the other side. Air-fry, flipping once, to the desired doneness, 10 minutes for medium-rare. Transfer the steak to a cutting board and let it rest at least 5 minutes before slicing.

3. Toss the vegetables with the cilantro. Fill the tortillas with steak and peppers, then top with sour cream, sprinkle with cilantro and serve with lime wedges if desired.

Ingredients

- 1 large red pepper, quartered lengthwise, then sliced crosswise
- 1 large yellow pepper, quartered lengthwise, then sliced crosswise
- 1 large red onion, sliced ¼-inch thick
- 2 teaspoons grated lime zest, plus 2 tablespoons lime juice, plus lime wedges for serving
- ¼ teaspoon ground cumin
- 1 tablespoon plus 2 teaspoons canola oil, divided
- ½ teaspoon granulated garlic, divided
- Kosher salt and pepper
- 12 ounces skirt steak (cut crosswise into 4-inch pieces) or hanger steak (halved)
- 1 teaspoon ancho chile powder
- ¼ cup cilantro, chopped, plus more for serving
- 8 6-inch flour tortillas, warmed
- Sour cream, for serving

Love Notes

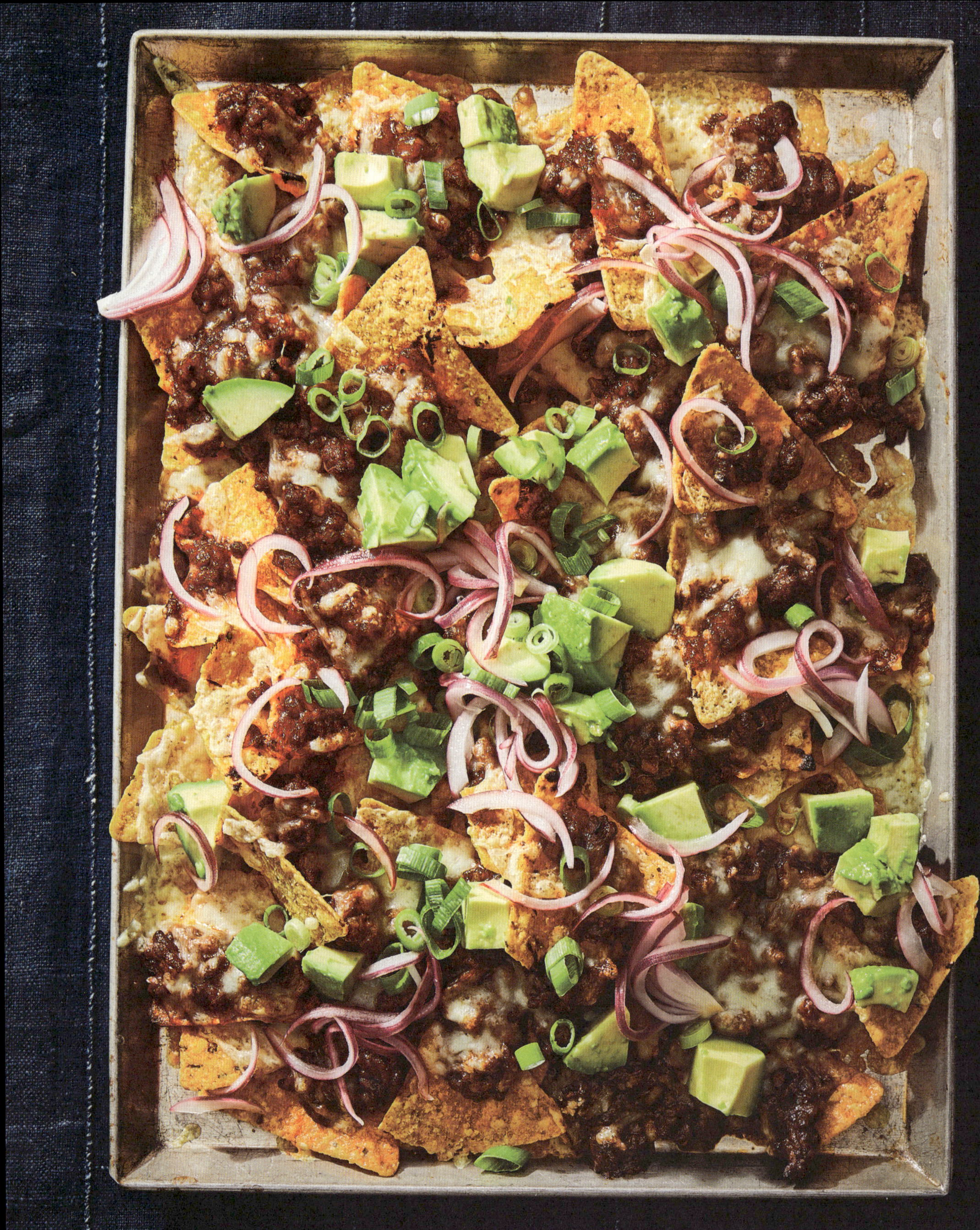

MEATY MAINS | **WEEKNIGHT**

Sheet Pan BBQ Beef Nachos

¼ small red onion, thinly sliced

2 tablespoons fresh lime juice

Kosher salt

1 tablespoon olive oil

1 large yellow onion, finely chopped

2 cloves garlic, pressed

1 pound ground beef

1 cup barbecue sauce

½ cup canned tomato sauce

6 ounces tortilla chips (about 7 cups)

8 ounces Monterey Jack cheese, coarsely grated (about 2 cups)

3 scallions, thinly sliced

1 ripe avocado, diced

Serves 4 | Active time 30 minutes | Total time 40 minutes

Whether there's a big game on tonight or you both are ready to binge an entire series together, serve up this fun meal that's ideal for eating—with your hands!—in front of the television.

1. Heat the oven to 450°F. In a small bowl, combine the red onion, the lime juice and a pinch of salt and let stand.

2. Heat the oil in a large skillet on medium. Add the yellow onion and ¼ teaspoon of salt and cook, covered, stirring occasionally, until tender, 6 to 8 minutes. Stir in the garlic and cook 1 minute.

3. Add the beef and cook, breaking up into small pieces, 5 minutes. Stir in the barbecue sauce and the tomato sauce and simmer until slightly thickened, 4 to 5 minutes.

4. On a rimmed baking sheet, toss the chips and half of the Monterey Jack. Top with the beef mixture and sprinkle the remaining cheese on top. Bake until the cheese has melted, 3 to 4 minutes.

5. Top the nachos with the scallions, avocado and pickled red onion.

Love Notes

THE NEWLYWED COOKBOOK

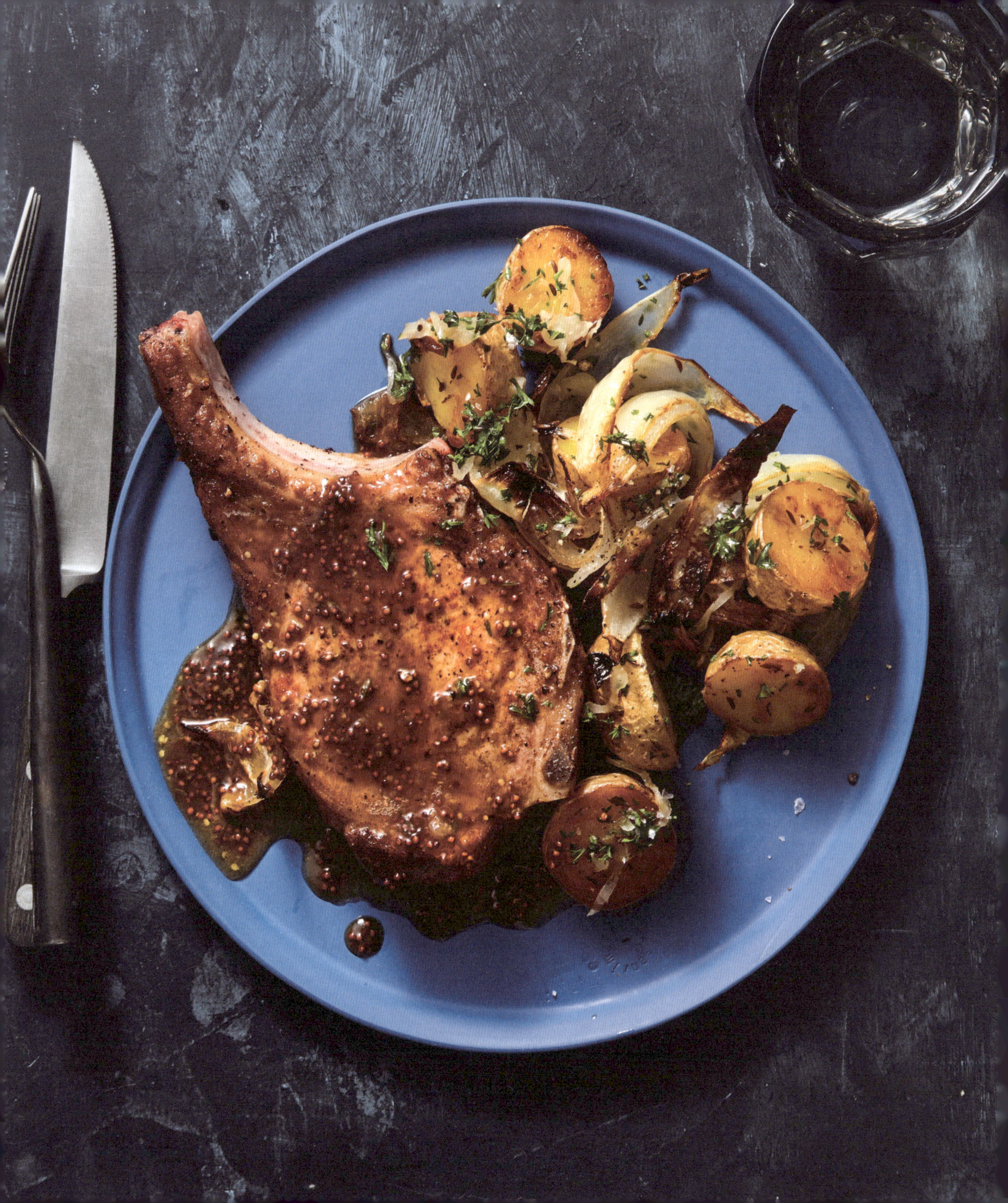

Mustard-Glazed Pork Chops

Serves 4 | **Active time 30 minutes** | **Total time 40 minutes**

- 1¾ pounds golden new potatoes, halved (quartered if large)
- 2 small onions, cut into ¼-inch-thick wedges
- 3 tablespoons olive oil, divided
- 6 sprigs fresh thyme
- Kosher salt and pepper
- ½ teaspoon caraway seeds
- 4 small bone-in pork chops (about 2½ pounds total)
- 1 cup apple cider
- 1 tablespoon whole-grain mustard
- 2 sprigs fresh thyme, broken into pieces
- ½ cup sauerkraut
- ¼ cup flat-leaf parsley, chopped

A spicy mustard sauce cuts through the richness of the pork for a well-balanced dish. Roasted potatoes and onions on the side round out the meal.

1. Heat the oven to 450°F. On a large rimmed baking sheet, toss the potatoes and onions with 2 tablespoons of oil, the thyme and ½ teaspoon each of salt and pepper, then the caraway seeds. Arrange all potatoes cut sides down and roast until golden brown and tender, 25 to 30 minutes.

2. While the vegetables are roasting, heat a large skillet on medium. Season the chops with ½ teaspoon each of salt and pepper, add 1 tablespoon of oil to the skillet and cook the chops until golden brown and just cooked through (140°F on instant-read thermometer), 7 to 9 minutes per side; transfer to the plates.

3. Drain off and discard any fat in the skillet and return to high heat. Add the cider, mustard and thyme, then reduce the heat and vigorously simmer until slightly thickened and glistening, 5 to 6 minutes. Remove from the heat.

4. Toss the caraway vegetables with sauerkraut and parsley and serve with the pork chops and pan sauce.

Love Notes

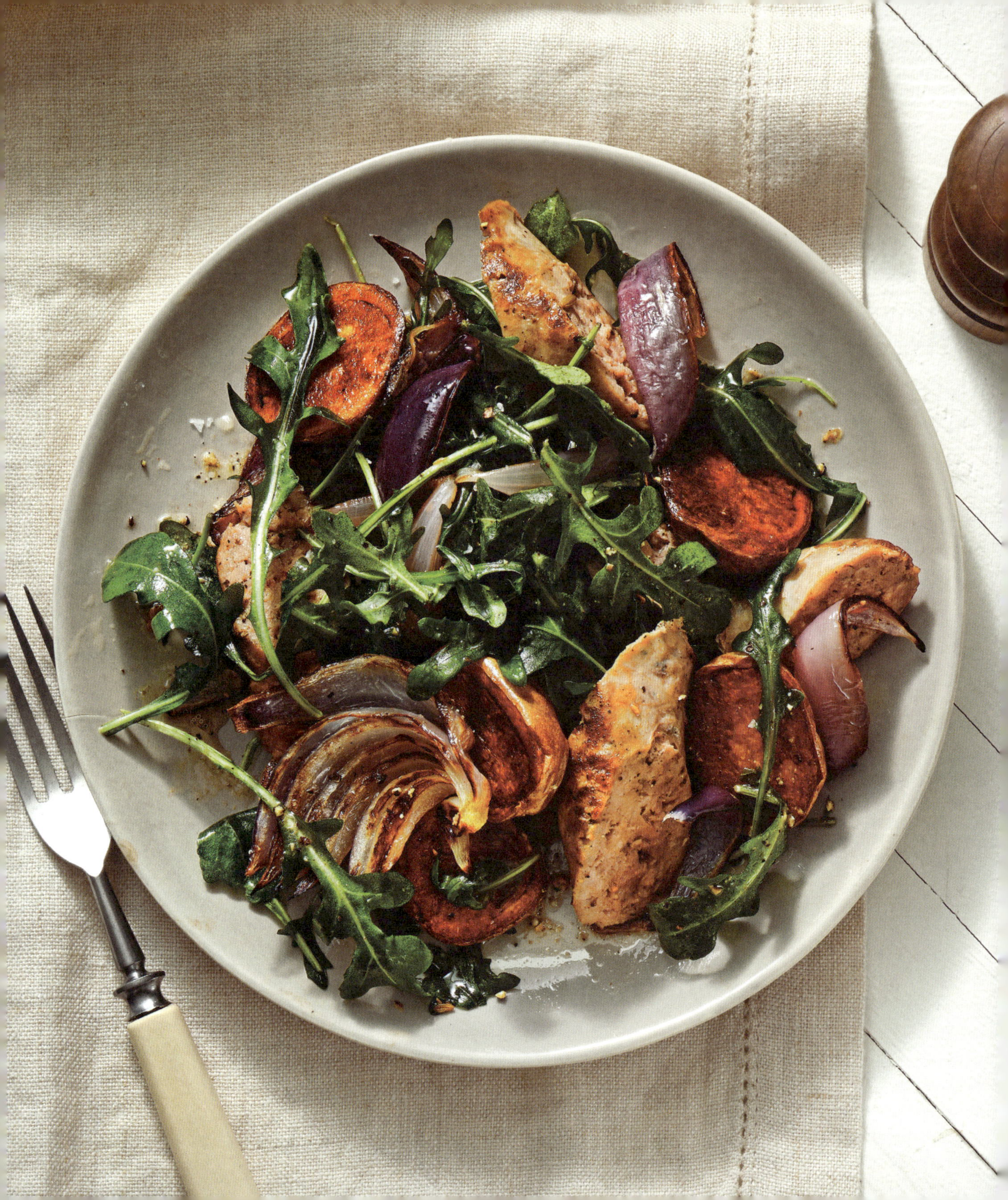

MEATY MAINS | **WEEKNIGHT**

Roasted Sausages & Vegetables

- 1½ tablespoons olive oil, divided
- 1 pound baby yellow potatoes, halved
- 2 medium red onions, cut into ½-inch-thick wedges
- 6 small links Italian sausage (about 1½ pounds)
- 2 ounces baby arugula (about 4 cups)
- 2 tablespoons Italian dressing

Serves 4 | Active time 15 minutes | Total time 40 minutes

Tender roasted onions and golden brown potatoes pair well with juicy slices of Italian sausage in this simple five-ingredient dinner perfect for busy weeknights.

1. Heat the oven to 450°F. Brush a large rimmed baking sheet with 1 tablespoon of oil; then add potatoes, cut sides down, and onions. Roast 15 minutes. Flip the onions, then continue to roast until the onions and potatoes are golden brown and tender, 10 to 14 minutes.

2. Meanwhile, heat ½ tablespoon of oil in a large ovenproof skillet on medium. Add the sausage and cook, turning occasionally, until browned, 5 to 6 minutes. Transfer the skillet to the oven along with the potatoes and roast until cooked through, 10 to 15 minutes more.

3. Scatter the arugula over the onions and potatoes, drizzle with the Italian dressing and gently toss to combine. Serve alongside the sausage, or slice sausage and gently toss together.

DO-IT-ALL DRESSING
Store-bought (or homemade!) Italian dressing can be used to marinate meat, toss into pasta salad, dip raw veggies into or drizzle over greens.

Love Notes

THE NEWLYWED COOKBOOK

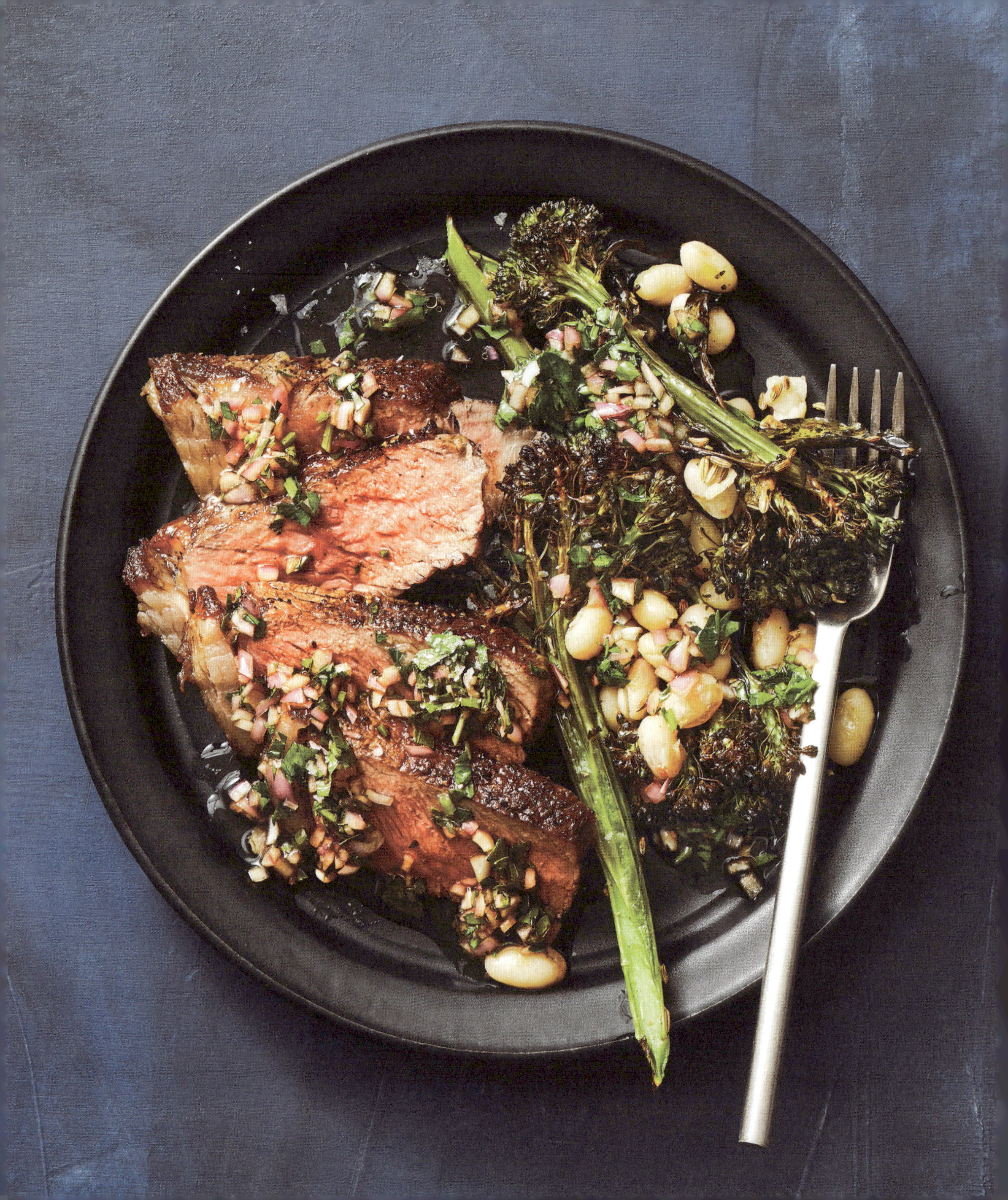

Steak with Beans & Roasted Broccolini

Serves 4 | Active time 25 minutes | Total time 25 minutes

Tender-crisp Broccolini, juicy steak and an addictive shallot and parsley relish we would happily eat by the spoonful — yes, please! To crack the fennel seeds, use a mortar and pestle, the bottom of a heavy pan or the side of a chef's knife.

1. Heat the oven to 425°F. On a large rimmed baking sheet, toss the Broccolini, garlic and fennel seeds with 2 tablespoons of oil and ½ teaspoon each of kosher salt and pepper and roast, tossing once, 9 minutes. Add the beans and roast until heated through, 2 to 3 minutes more.

2. Meanwhile, heat ½ tablespoon of oil in a large cast-iron skillet on medium-high. Season the steaks with ½ teaspoon each of kosher salt and pepper and cook, until deep brown, 3 minutes per side. Transfer the skillet to the oven along with the Broccolini and roast to the desired doneness, 4 to 5 minutes for medium. Transfer to a cutting board and let rest 5 minutes before slicing.

3. While the steak and the Broccolini cook, prepare the relish: In a small bowl, combine the vinegar, the honey and ¼ teaspoon of salt to dissolve. Mix in the shallot and let sit 5 minutes. Stir in the oil, then the parsley and any fennel seeds still on the Broccolini pan. Serve spooned over the steak and Broccolini.

FOR THE STEAK & BEANS

- 3 bunches Broccolini, trimmed and cut into large florets
- 2 large cloves garlic, roughly chopped
- 1 tablespoon fennel seeds, lightly crushed
- 2½ tablespoons olive oil, divided
- Kosher salt and pepper
- 1 15-ounce can white beans, rinsed
- 2 1½-inch-thick strip steaks, about 12 ounces each

FOR THE SHALLOT AND PARSLEY RELISH

- 3 tablespoons sherry vinegar
- 1 teaspoon honey
- Kosher salt
- 1 medium shallot, finely chopped
- 1 tablespoon olive oil
- ¼ cup flat-leaf parsley, finely chopped

Love Notes

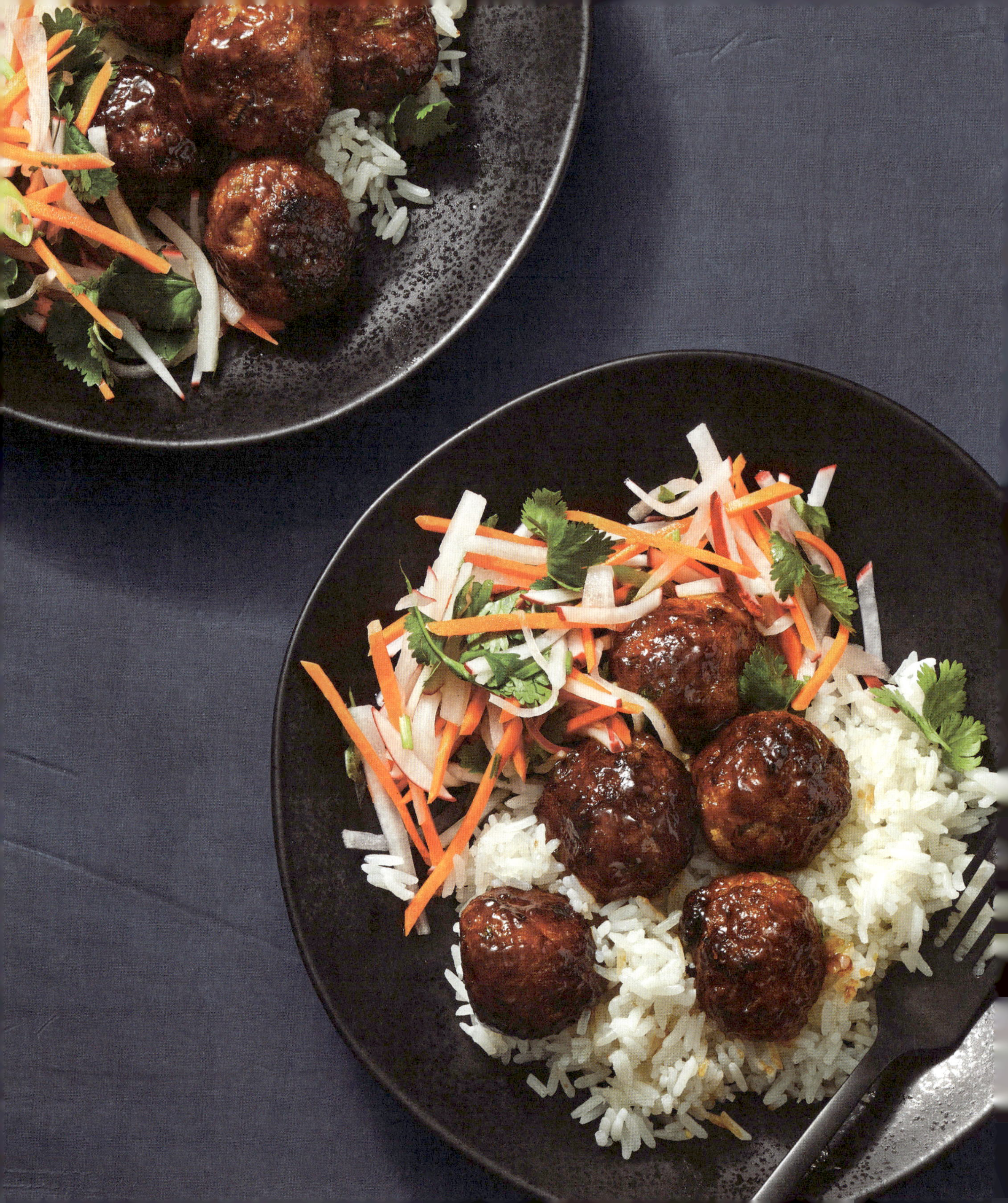

MEATY MAINS | **WEEKNIGHT**

Pork Meatball Banh Mi Bowls

Serves 4 | Active time 30 minutes | Total time 30 minutes

- 1 cup jasmine rice
- 3 scallions
- 1 large egg
- 1½ tablespoons white miso
- 1 cup panko
- 1 tablespoon grated peeled fresh ginger
- 1 large garlic clove, grated
- ½ cup cilantro, chopped and divided
- 1 pound ground pork
- ¼ cup hoisin sauce
- 2 teaspoon plus ¼ cup rice vinegar, divided
- ½ teaspoon sugar
- Kosher salt
- 7 ounces daikon, scrubbed and cut into matchsticks
- 7 ounces carrots, scrubbed and cut into matchsticks
- 4 radishes, cut into matchsticks

Sweet and savory, these hoisin-glazed meatballs paired with a tangy carrot-radish salad evoke the flavors of the beloved Vietnamese sandwich.

1. Cook the rice per the package directions. Arrange the oven rock 6 inches from the broiler and heat the broiler. Line a rimmed baking sheet with nonstick foil.

2. Thinly slice the dark green scallion tops and set aside. Finely chop the scallion white and light green parts. In a medium bowl, whisk together the egg and the miso, then stir in the panko. Stir in the ginger, the garlic, the finely chopped scallions and half of the cilantro. Add the pork and mix until just combined.

3. Shape the mixture into 20 balls (about 2 tablespoons each) and place on a prepared baking sheet. Broil until cooked through, 8 to 12 minutes.

4. In a large bowl, stir together the hoisin sauce and 2 teaspoons of the vinegar; add the cooked meatballs and gently toss to coat.

5. While the meatballs are cooking, in a separate bowl, whisk together the sugar, the remaining ¼ cup vinegar and ¼ teaspoon of kosher salt. Add the daikon, carrot and radishes and toss to combine, then toss with the remaining cilantro and sliced scallion greens. Serve over the rice and meatballs.

MAKE THE CUT
For bite-size vegetable strips, either use a julienne peeler or thinly slice them crosswise on a mandoline, stack slices and thinly cut lengthwise.

Love Notes

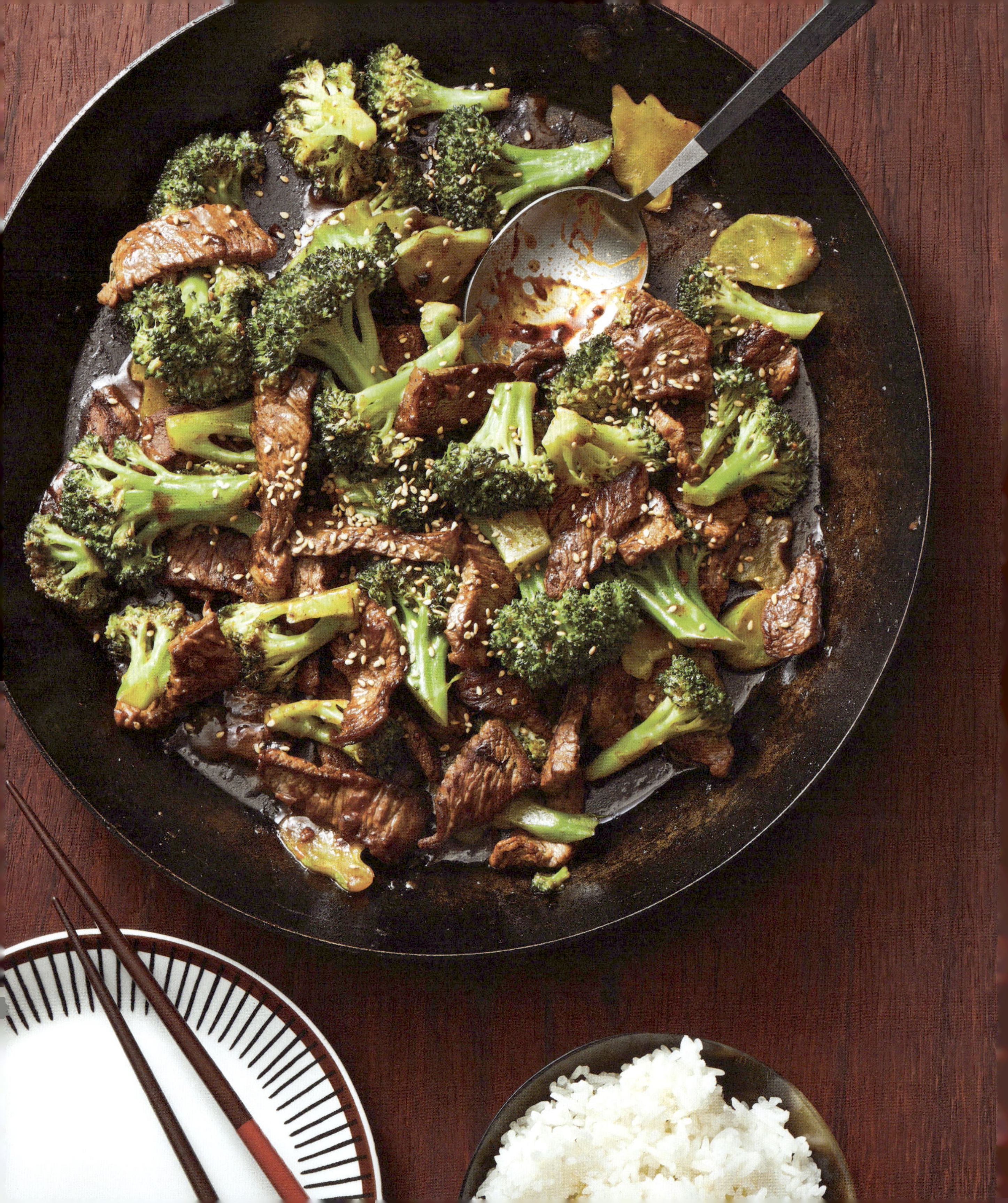

MEATY MAINS | WEEKNIGHT

Five-Spice Steak & Broccoli

Serves 4 | Active time 30 minutes | Total time 30 minutes

- 1 cup long-grain white rice
- 1¼ pounds broccoli, cut into florets, stems peeled and sliced crosswise
- 1 pound sirloin steak, halved lengthwise and thinly sliced crosswise
- 1 teaspoon Chinese five-spice powder
- Kosher salt and pepper
- 2 tablespoons canola oil, divided
- 1 tablespoon chili black bean sauce
- Sesame seeds, for serving

Sliced sirloin is seasoned with an aromatic Chinese five-spice powder and cooked, then tossed with chili black bean paste and tender-crisp broccoli for savory, feel-good oomph.

1. Cook the rice per the package directions.

2. Meanwhile, in a large skillet, bring ½ cup of water to a simmer. Add the broccoli and cook, covered, until bright green and barely tender, 4 to 5 minutes. Transfer the broccoli to a plate and wipe out the skillet.

3. In a medium bowl, toss the steak, the five-spice powder and ½ teaspoon each of salt and pepper to coat. Add 1 tablespoon of canola oil to the skillet and heat on medium-high. In batches, cook the steak in a single layer until browned, 2 minutes per side. Transfer to a bowl.

4. Reduce the heat to medium and add the remaining tablespoon of oil to the skillet, then the chili black bean sauce; cook, stirring, until fragrant, 1 minute. Return the steak and any juices to the skillet along with ¼ cup of water and cook, tossing, until coated in the sauce, 30 seconds. Fold in the broccoli. Serve over rice. Sprinkle with the sesame seeds if desired.

Love Notes

THE NEWLYWED COOKBOOK 73

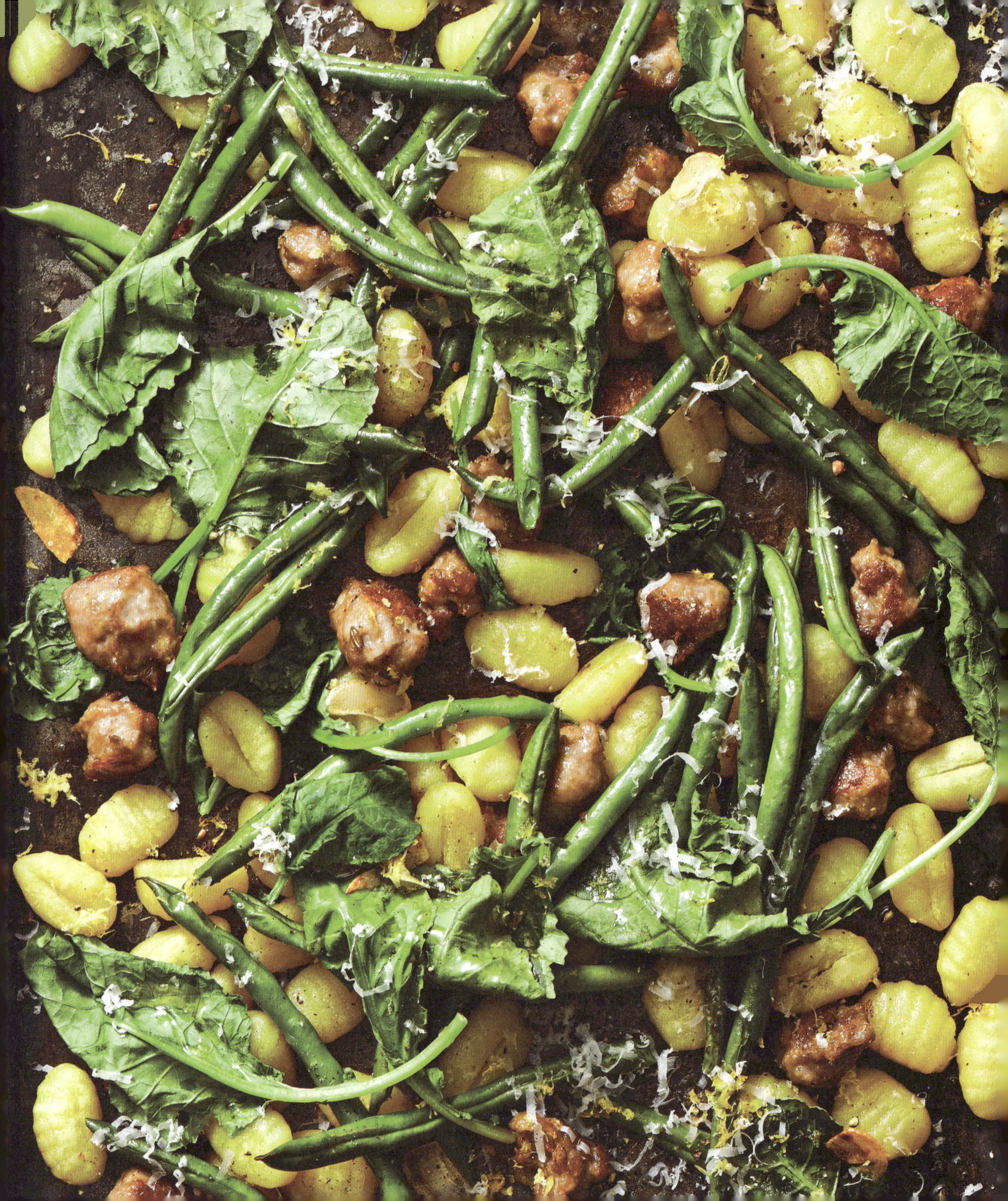

MEATY MAINS | **WEEKNIGHT**

Sheet Pan Gnocchi with Sausage & Green Beans

Serves 4 | Active time 15 minutes | Total time 30 minutes

No need to boil a pot of water! Instead, cook the gnocchi on a sheet pan with the Italian sausage, green beans and baby kale so the potato-based pasta gets golden and crispy on the outside and tender on the inside.

1. Heat the oven to 425°F. On a large rimmed baking sheet, toss the gnocchi with 1½ tablespoons of the oil and ½ teaspoon of black pepper, then arrange them in an even layer. Break up the sausage into pieces, add the pieces to the baking sheet and roast for 10 minutes.

2. In a medium bowl, toss the green beans and garlic with the remaining tablespoon of oil, then the red pepper flakes and ¼ teaspoon of salt. Toss the gnocchi and sausage on the baking sheet, scatter the green bean mixture on top and roast until everything is golden brown and tender, 8 to 10 minutes more.

3. Scatter the kale on the baking sheet and roast until it wilts, about 2 minutes. Toss the gnocchi mixture with lemon zest. Serve dolloped with ricotta and sprinkled with Parmesan if desired.

- 1 17.5-ounce package shelf-stable potato gnocchi
- 2½ tablespoons olive oil, divided
- Kosher salt and black pepper
- 8 ounces Italian sausage, casings removed
- 8 ounces green beans, trimmed
- 4 cloves garlic, thinly sliced
- ½ teaspoon red pepper flakes
- 1 5-ounce package baby kale
- 1 teaspoon lemon zest
- Ricotta and grated Parmesan, for serving

SWITCH IT UP

This recipe works with all sorts of vegetables. Swap out the green beans for broccoli, cauliflower or a combination. Cut the vegetables into small florets and toss them with the sausage-gnocchi mixture, adding 1 tablespoon more oil, then roast all together.

Love Notes

THE NEWLYWED COOKBOOK 75

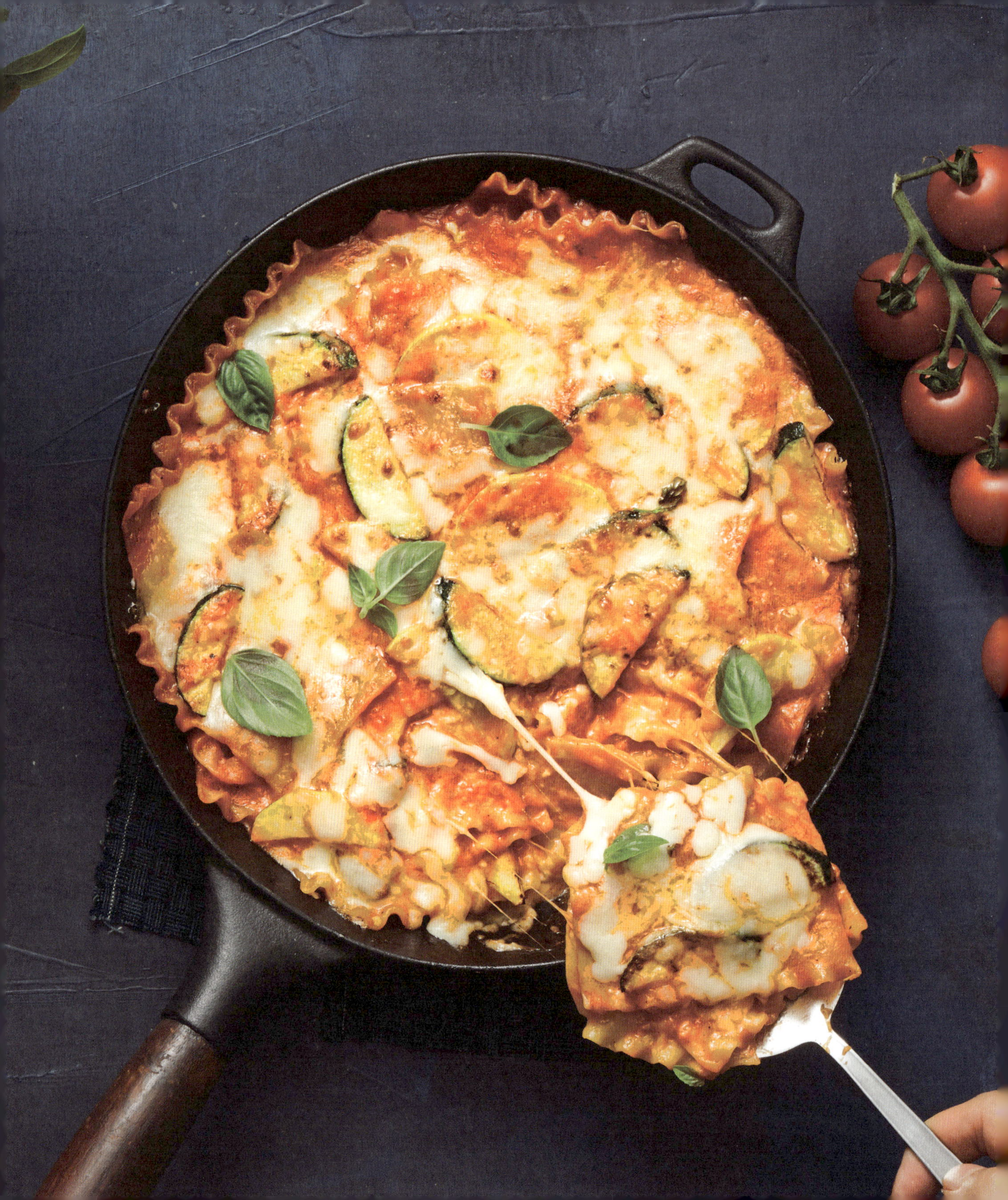

Three-Cheese Summer Skillet Lasagna

Serves 4 | Active time 30 minutes | Total time 30 minutes

- 1½ tablespoons olive oil, divided
- 2 small zucchini, cut into ¼-inch-thick half-moons
- 1 small summer squash, cut into ¼-inch-thick half-moons
- Kosher salt and pepper
- 1 small onion, finely chopped
- 2 cloves garlic, finely chopped
- ½ teaspoon red pepper flakes
- 8 lasagna noodles, broken into pieces
- 2 cups marinara sauce
- 3 cups low-sodium chicken broth
- 2 ounces cream cheese, cut into small pieces
- ½ cup chopped basil, plus more for serving
- 4 ounces mozzarella, coarsely grated (about 1 cup), divided
- 2 tablespoons grated Romano

Forget the tedious layering and long bake time involved in making a lasagna: Breaking the noodles into pieces and cooking them in the sauce on the stove makes this dish doable on a weeknight.

1. Heat 1 tablespoon of the oil in a large cast-iron skillet on medium-high. Add the zucchini and squash, season with ¼ teaspoon each of salt and pepper and cook, tossing occasionally, until the squash is light golden brown, 3 to 4 minutes. Transfer the squash to a plate.

2. Reduce the heat to medium, add the remaining ½ tablespoon of oil and the onion and cook, stirring occasionally, until the onion is tender, 4 to 5 minutes. Stir in the garlic and red pepper flakes; cook for 30 seconds more.

3. Add the noodles, marinara sauce and broth to the skillet; bring to a boil. Simmer vigorously, stirring often, until the sauce begins to reduce, 6 minutes. Lower the heat and gently simmer until the pasta is tender, 7 to 8 minutes more.

4. Meanwhile, heat the broiler. Fold in the cream cheese to melt, then the vegetables, the chopped basil and ½ cup mozzarella.

5. Sprinkle with the remaining ¾ cup mozzarella and the grated Romano and broil until golden brown, 2 to 3 minutes. Top with torn basil.

Love Notes

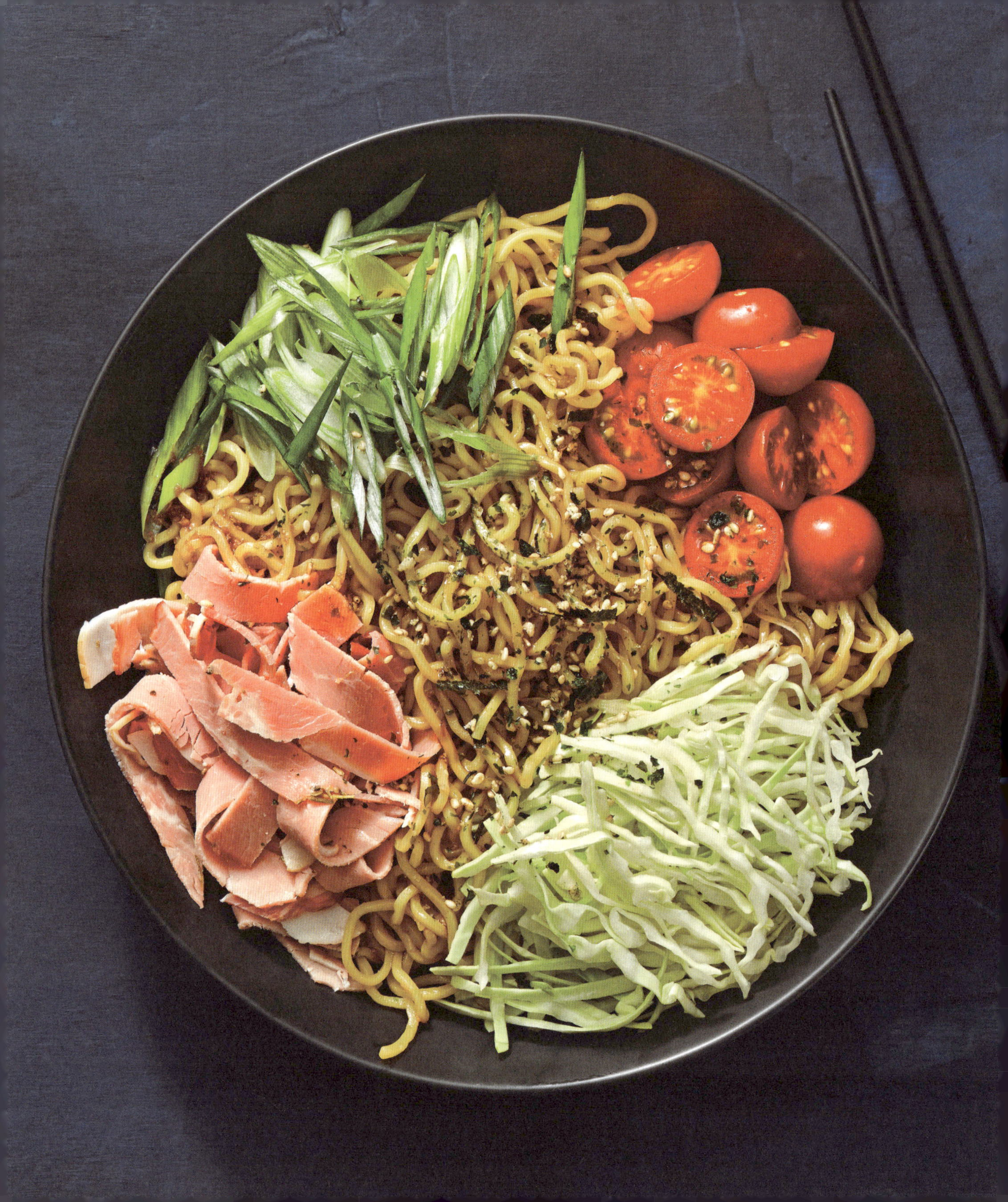

Chilled Ramen Salad

Serves 8 | **Active time 20 minutes** | **Total time 20 minutes**

Chewy noodles tossed with a gingery soy dressing are the perfect canvas for a medley of colorful toppings. Consider this hassle-free dish your go-to for those nights when you need dinner, stat.

1. Cook the ramen per the package directions. Rinse the noodles under cold water to cool, then drain well.

2. In a large bowl, whisk together the vinegar, soy sauce, sugar, sesame oil and ginger.

3. Add the noodles to the dressing and toss to coat. Divide the noodles among bowls and top with the cabbage, tomatoes, scallions and ham. Serve immediately, sprinkled with the furikake if desired.

- 12 ounces dried ramen (four 3-ounce instant ramen packages, seasoning packets saved for another use; see Tip)
- ¼ cup rice vinegar
- 3 tablespoons soy sauce
- 2 teaspoons sugar
- 1 teaspoon toasted sesame oil
- 1½ teaspoons grated peeled fresh ginger
- ½ small Savoy cabbage, cored, shaved on a mandoline
- 1 cup grape tomatoes, halved
- 2 scallions, thinly sliced
- 6 ounces sliced deli ham, cut into strips
- Furikake, for serving

POWER PACKS

Don't toss those unused seasoning packets! For a burst of flavor, sprinkle them on popcorn or add them to sauces, broth or rice.

Love Notes

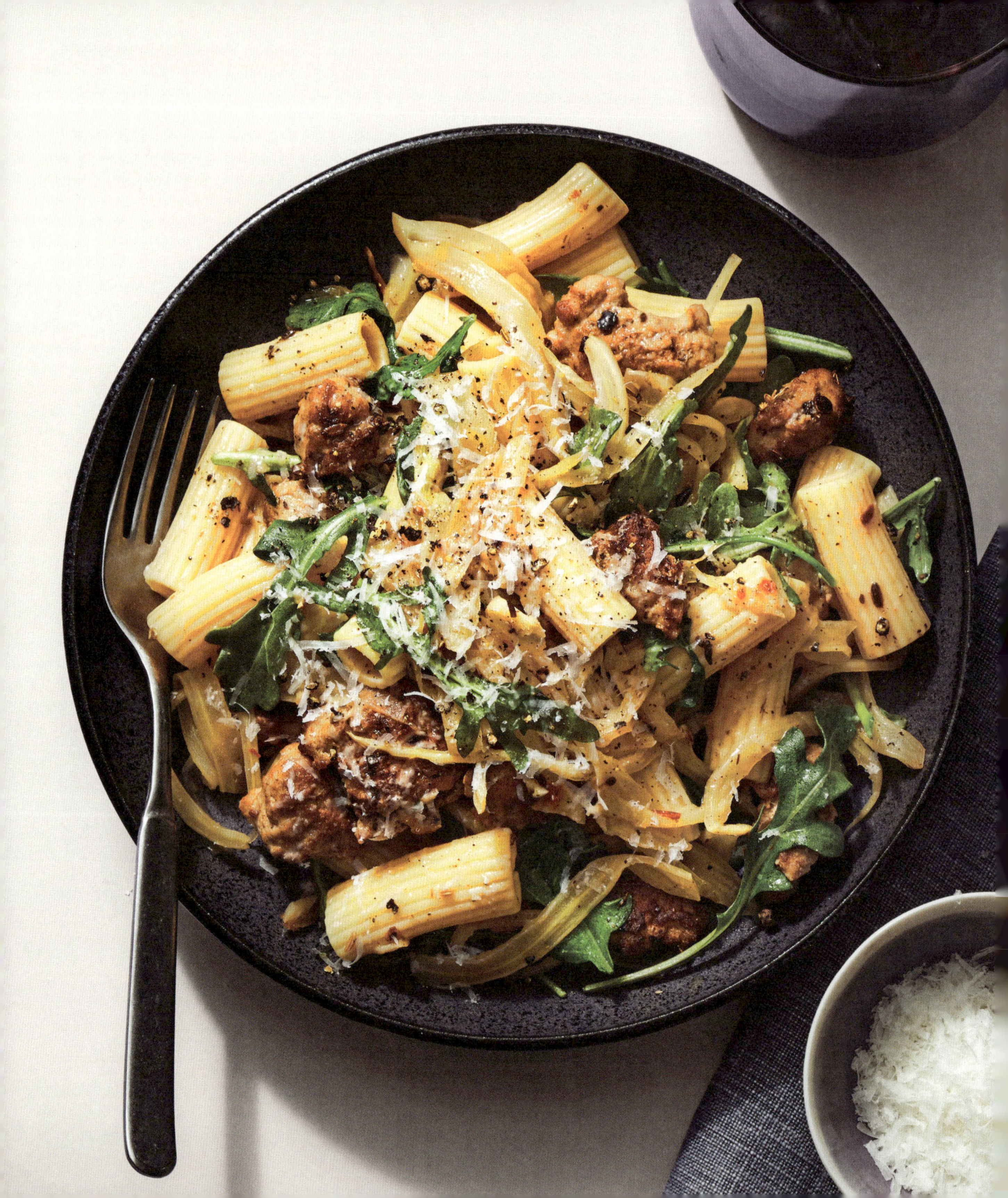

Rigatoni with Sausage-Style Turkey & Arugula

Serves 4 | Active time 25 minutes | Total time 25 minutes

- 1 pound lean ground turkey
- 2 teaspoons sweet paprika
- 4 cloves garlic, grated, divided
- 1 teaspoon red pepper flakes, divided
- Kosher salt
- 12 ounces rigatoni
- 3 tablespoons olive oil, divided
- 2 tablespoons fennel seeds, lightly crushed
- 1 large bulb fennel, cored and thinly sliced
- 2 teaspoons fresh lemon juice
- 4 cups loosely packed baby arugula
- ⅓ cup grated Pecorino Romano cheese

Lean ground turkey with robust seasoning evokes the flavor of sausage but has a better-for-you feel. Using grain-free chickpea pasta makes this dish gluten-free.

1. In a bowl, combine the turkey, the paprika, half of the garlic, ½ teaspoon of red pepper flakes and ½ teaspoon of salt until just fully mixed. (You can make and refrigerate this up to 1 day ahead.)

2. Cook the pasta per the package directions, reserving 1 cup cooking liquid before draining.

3. Meanwhile, heat 2 tablespoons of the oil in a large skillet on medium-high. Add the fennel seeds to the skillet and then quickly add bite-size pieces of sausage mixture on top, gently pressing down. Cook until the sausage is golden brown, 5 to 6 minutes. Toss and cook until just cooked through, 1 to 2 minutes more. Transfer the sausage to a plate.

4. Wipe out the skillet and heat the remaining tablespoon of oil on medium. Add the sliced fennel and ¼ teaspoon salt and cook, stirring occasionally, until the fennel is just tender, about 4 minutes. Stir in the remaining garlic and cook for 1 minute. Stir in the lemon juice, ½ cup of the reserved pasta cooking liquid and the remaining ½ teaspoon of red pepper flakes.

5. Gently fold the pasta and arugula into the fennel mixture, then half of the sausage, adding more cooking liquid if the pasta seems dry. Serve topped with the remaining sausage and the Pecorino Romano.

Love Notes

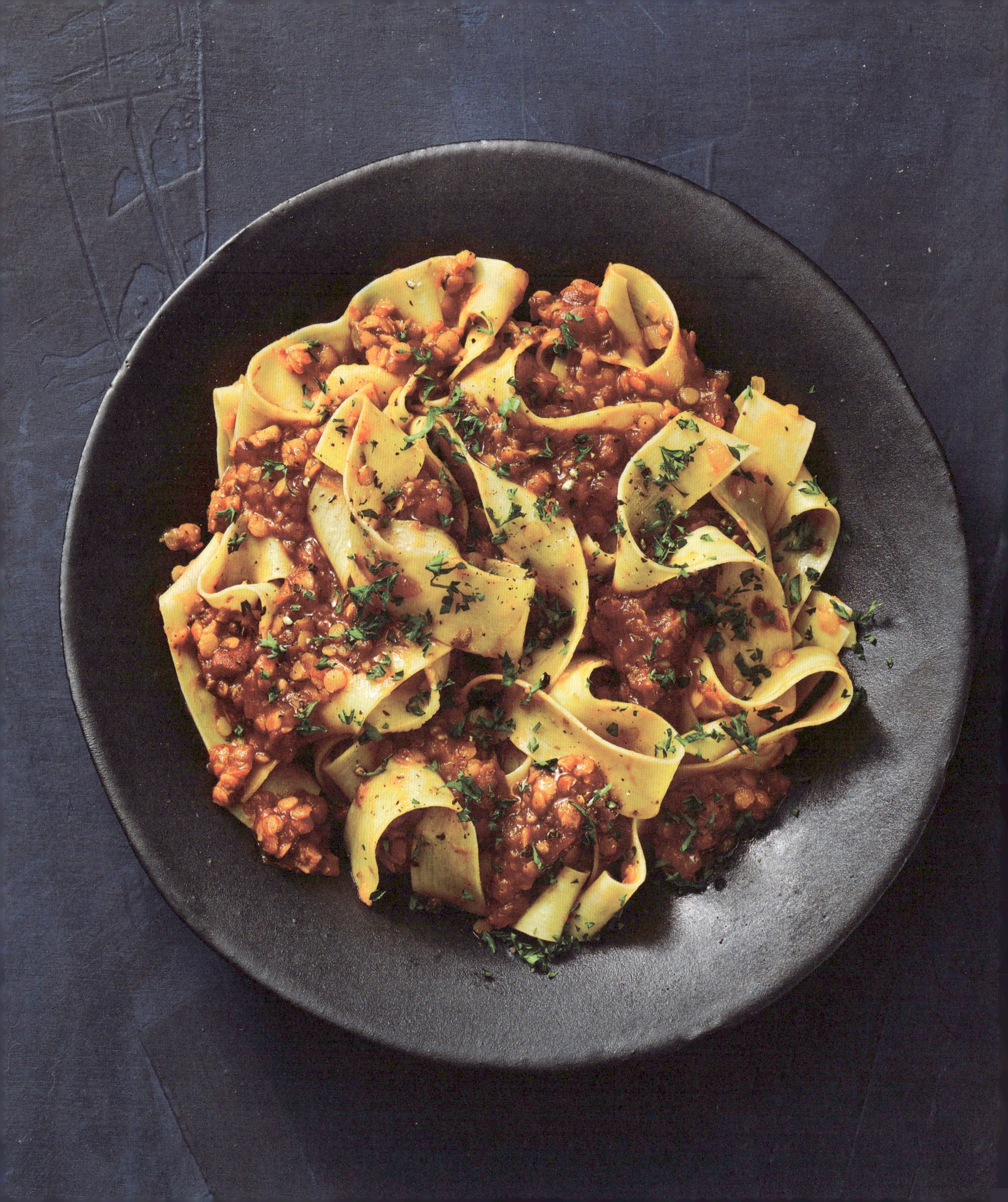

Red Lentil Bolognese

Serves 4 to 6 | Active time 20 minutes | Total time 55 minutes

This vegan dish is rich and hearty thanks to the combination of meaty mushrooms, protein-rich lentils and plant-based bouillon. Serve the sauce with pasta or polenta or on hamburger buns for a Sloppy Joe–ish experience.

- 3 tablespoons olive oil
- 1 onion, finely chopped
- Kosher salt and pepper
- 8 ounces cremini mushrooms, trimmed and chopped in a food processor
- 2 large cloves garlic, finely chopped
- ¼ to ½ teaspoon crushed red pepper
- 3 tablespoons tomato paste
- ½ cup dry white wine
- 1 cup red lentils
- 1 14.5-ounce can crushed tomatoes
- 1 tablespoon mushroom bouillon base (we used Better Than Bouillon)
- 1 pound pappardelle, linguine or fettuccine
- Chopped parsley, for serving

1. Heat the oil in a Dutch oven on medium. Add the onion, season with ½ teaspoon each of salt and pepper and cook, covered, stirring occasionally, 4 minutes. Increase the heat to medium-high, add the mushrooms and cook, stirring occasionally, until they are deep brown and beginning to stick to the pan, 8 to 10 minutes.

2. Reduce the heat to medium, stir in the garlic and crushed pepper and cook for 1 minute. Stir in the tomato paste and cook, stirring until it turns dark brown, 2 minutes. Stir in the wine, scraping up any browned bits, then stir in the lentils, the tomatoes, 2 cups of water and the bouillon. Bring the mixture to a boil, then simmer until the lentils are tender, 30 to 35 minutes.

3. Meanwhile, cook the pasta per the package directions. Serve the bolognese over the pasta, topped with parsley if desired.

GET AHEAD
This sauce isn't difficult to make, but it does need to simmer for a while. It holds well in the refrigerator and freezes well too, so it's great for a Sunday afternoon meal prep ahead of a busy week.

Love Notes

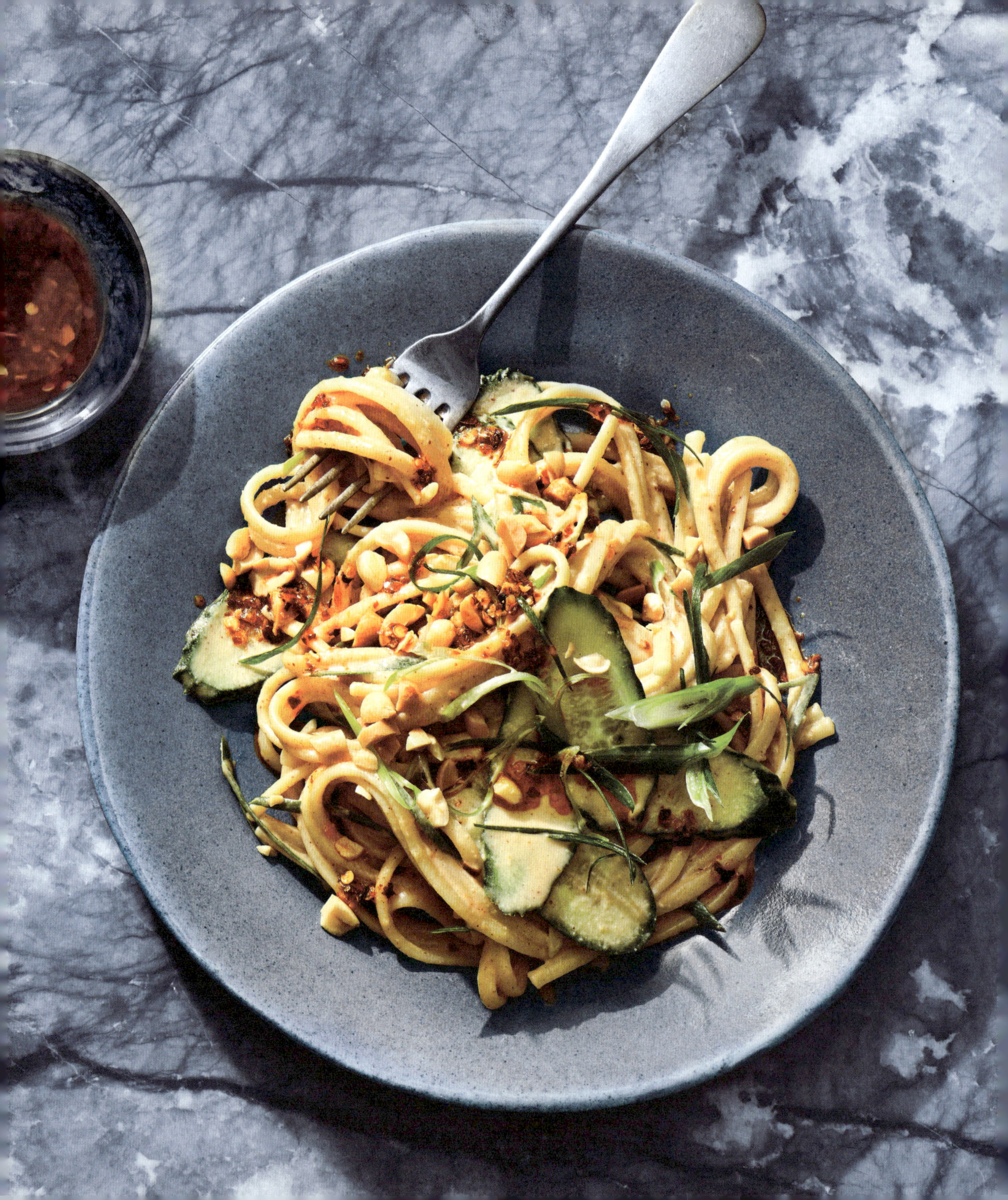

NOODLE NIGHT | WEEKNIGHT

Sesame Noodles

- 12 ounces linguine
- ⅓ cup tahini
- ¼ cup smooth natural peanut butter
- 2½ teaspoons reduced-sodium soy sauce
- 2 teaspoons chili crisp, plus more for serving
- 2 teaspoons pure maple syrup
- 1½ teaspoons rice vinegar
- 1 teaspoon toasted sesame oil
- ½ teaspoon grated ginger
- 1 clove garlic, grated
- 2 scallions, thinly sliced on bias
- 2 Persian cucumbers, thinly sliced on bias on mandoline
- Chopped roasted peanuts, for serving

Serves 8 | Active time 25 minutes | Total time 25 minutes

Peanut butter and tahini create the nutty, savory sauce for this crave-worthy noodle dish. Rinsing the noodles before tossing them in the sauce ensures a glossy, perfectly creamy coating that calls for slurping—with an extra drizzle of chili crisp if you wish.

1. Cook the pasta per the package directions 1 minute past al dente. Reserve ½ cup of the pasta cooking water, drain the pasta and rinse it under cold water to cool.

2. Meanwhile, in a large bowl, whisk the tahini, peanut butter, soy sauce, chili crisp, maple syrup, rice vinegar, sesame oil, ginger and garlic and 6 tablespoons of water until smooth. Add the rinsed pasta and toss, adding a splash of the reserved pasta water as needed, until coated.

3. Divide the pasta among bowls and top with the scallions, cucumbers, peanuts and chili crisp if desired.

Love Notes

THE NEWLYWED COOKBOOK 85

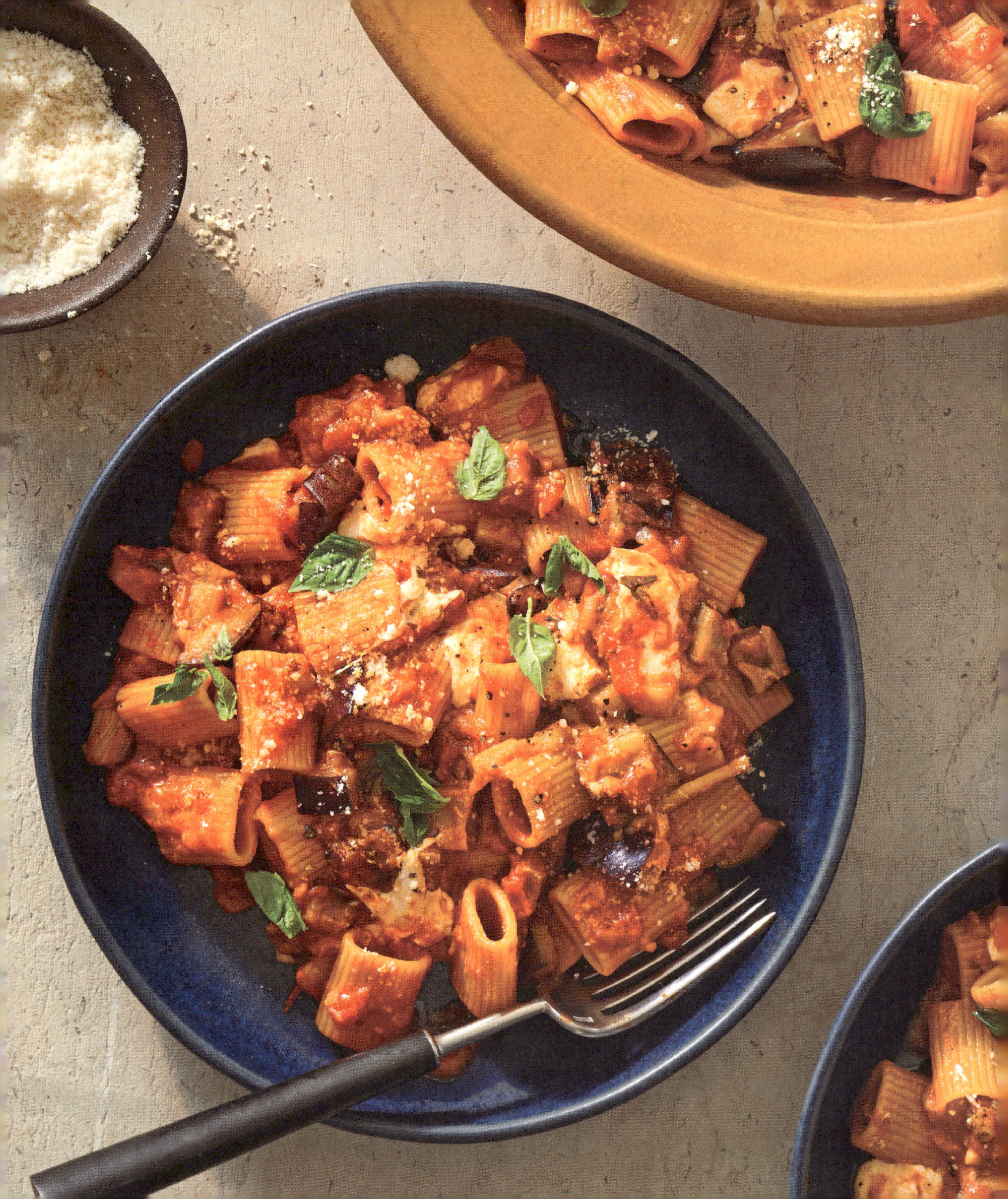

NOODLE NIGHT | **WEEKNIGHT**

Rigatoni alla Norma

Serves 8 | Active time 45 minutes | Total time 45 minutes

- 8 ounces fresh mozzarella, cut into ½-inch pieces
- 1 ¼ pounds eggplant, cut into ½-inch pieces
- ¼ cup plus 2 tablespoons olive oil, divided
- 1 large shallot, finely chopped
- 4 cloves garlic, pressed
- ¼ teaspoon red pepper flakes
- 1 cup marinara sauce
- 1 14.5-ounce can petite diced tomatoes
- 1 tablespoon vegetable bouillon base (we used Better Than Bouillon)
- 12 ounces rigatoni
- 1 Parmesan cheese rind (any you have is great), plus grated Parmesan for serving
- ½ cup basil leaves, torn

Even Nonna would approve of these cooking tricks! Adding the rigatoni right into the sauce along with a Parmesan rind means you won't need another pot and deepens the pasta's savory flavor. Folding in frozen pieces of mozzarella at the end ensures that the cheese stays intact.

1. Freeze the mozzarella until firm, at least 10 minutes. Meanwhile, heat the oven to 425°F. On a large rimmed baking sheet, toss the eggplant with ¼ cup oil. Roast 15 minutes. Toss and continue roasting until golden brown and tender, 15 to 18 minutes more.

2. Meanwhile, in a large Dutch oven, heat the remaining 2 tablespoons of oil and the shallot on medium and cook, stirring occasionally, until sizzling, 2 minutes. Stir in the garlic and the red pepper flakes. Add the marinara, the tomatoes (and their juices), the bouillon base and 3 cups water, then stir in the pasta and bring to a boil.

3. Stir in the Parmesan rind and simmer vigorously, stirring frequently, until the pasta is al dente, 12 to 15 minutes.

4. Remove the Parmesan rind, fold the eggplant and mozzarella into the pasta and serve topped with the basil and grated Parmesan if desired.

Love Notes

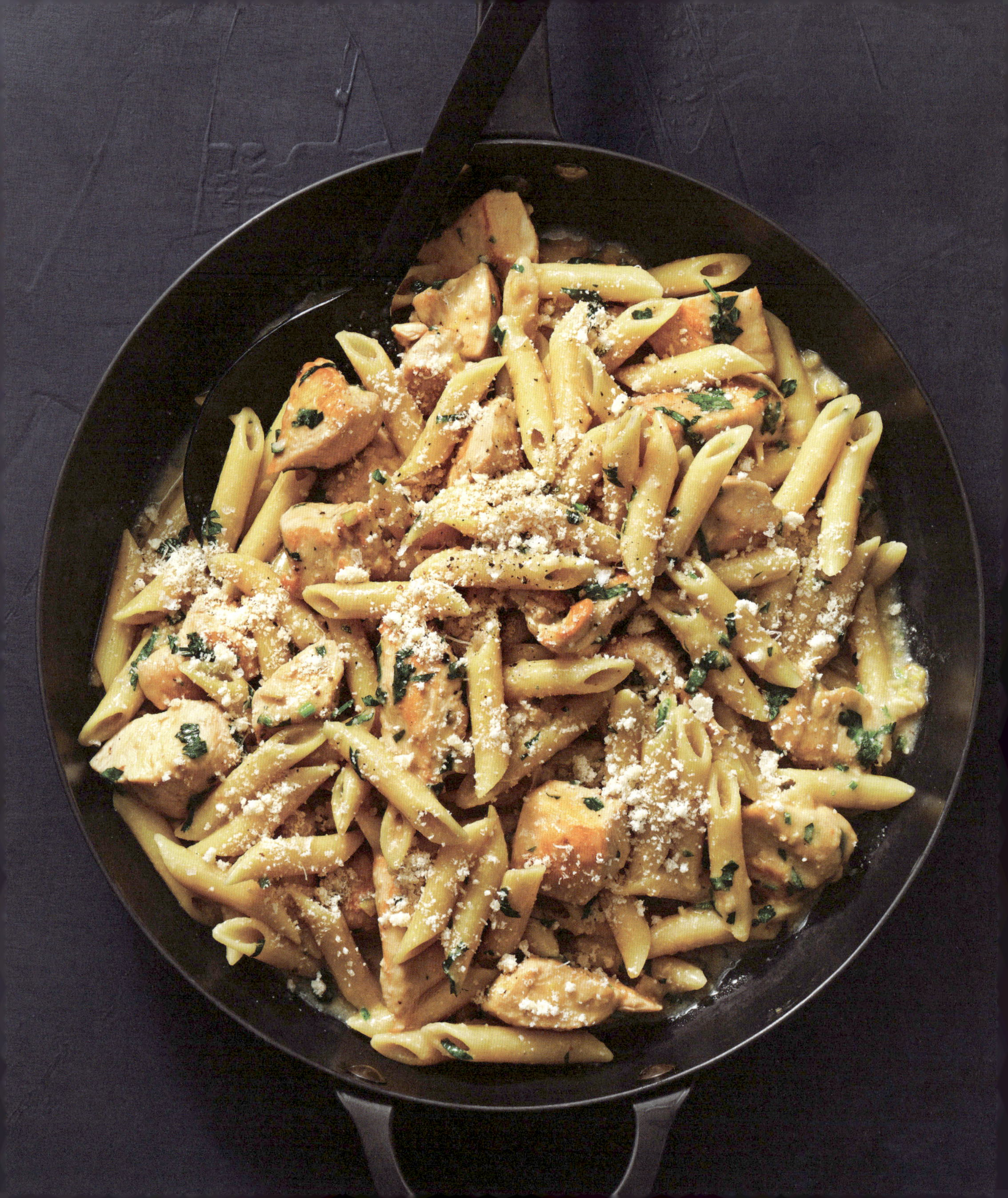

Chicken Francese Pasta

Serves 4 | Active time 30 minutes | Total time 30 minutes

Ingredients

- 1½ tablespoons plus 1 teaspoon olive oil, divided
- 1½ pounds boneless, skinless chicken breasts, cut into 1-inch pieces
- Kosher salt and pepper
- 1 small lemon, sliced and seeds removed
- ¼ cup fresh lemon juice
- ⅓ cup dry white wine
- 3½ teaspoons chicken bouillon base (we used Better Than Bouillon)
- 12 ounces penne
- 1 tablespoon unsalted butter
- 2 ounces Parmesan cheese, finely grated (¾ cup grated), divided
- ¼ cup flat-leaf parsley, roughly chopped

This one-pan pasta incorporates whole lemon slices (yep, peel and all!) that, when cooked and finely chopped, add a bright, jammy burst to the creamy, comforting dish.

1. Heat 1½ tablespoons of oil in a large high-sided skillet on medium-high. Season the chicken with ½ teaspoon each salt and pepper; cook until browned on both sides, 2 to 3 minutes per side. Transfer to a bowl.

2. Add the remaining teaspoon of oil and the lemon slices to the skillet; reduce the heat to medium and cook until browned, about 1 minute per side; transfer the lemon slices to a cutting board. Add the lemon juice to the skillet and scrape up any browned bits, then transfer to the bowl with the chicken.

3. Add the wine to the skillet and simmer 1 minute. Whisk in 3½ cups of water and the bouillon base. Add the penne and simmer, stirring occasionally, 10 minutes.

4. Return the chicken (and any juices) to the skillet and simmer until the pasta is al dente and the chicken is cooked through, 2 to 4 minutes more.

5. Finely chop the cooked lemon slices. Remove the skillet from the heat; swirl in the butter to melt. Toss with the chopped lemon and half of the Parmesan, then fold in the parsley and sprinkle with the remaining Parmesan.

PASTA PICK

Penne size can vary by brand—select one that's slender and short for the most accurate cook time.

Love Notes

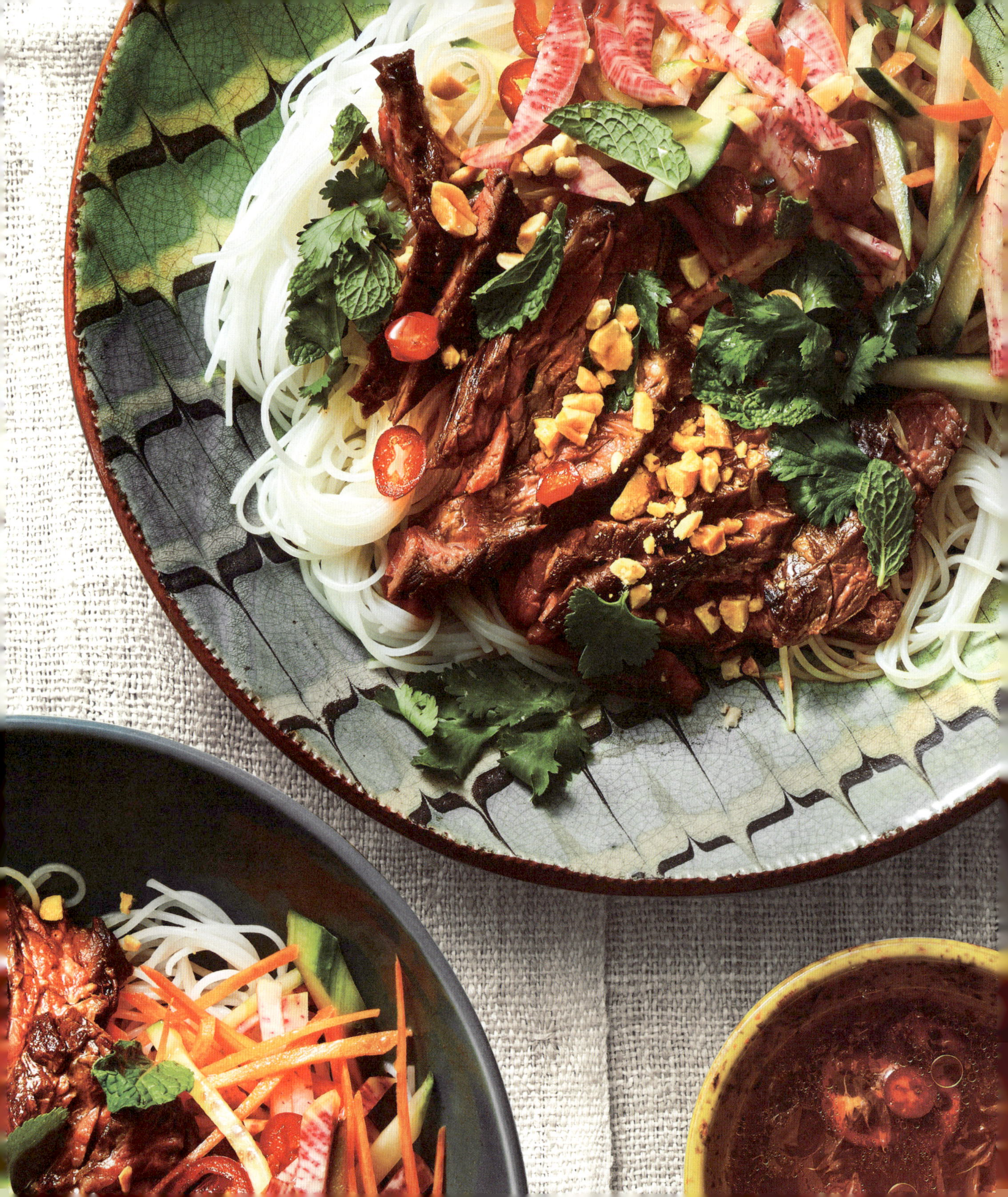

Steak & Rice Noodle Bowls

Serves 4 | Active time 20 minutes | Total time 30 minutes

- 6½ ounces rice noodles
- ¼ cup fresh lime juice (3 limes)
- 2 tablespoons plus 1 teaspoon olive oil, divided
- 2 teaspoons fish sauce
- 1 teaspoon light brown sugar
- 1 Fresno chile, thinly sliced
- 12 ounces skirt steak, cut crosswise into 5-inch pieces
- 1 large carrot
- ½ seedless cucumber
- 1 watermelon radish
- 1 cup mint leaves
- 1 cup cilantro leaves
- ¼ cup roasted and salted peanuts, chopped (optional)

Inspired by Vietnamese buns, this is a choose-your-own-adventure dinner. Set out a medley of colorful julienne veggies, grilled skirt steak, fresh herbs and a tangy-sweet dressing, and you can each dress up your bowl as you desire.

1. Heat the grill on medium-high. Cook the noodles per the package directions and drain.

2. Meanwhile, in a small bowl, combine the lime juice, 2 tablespoons of olive oil, the fish sauce, the brown sugar and the chile.

3. Rub the skirt steak with the remaining teaspoon of oil and grill to the desired doneness, 2 to 3 minutes per side for medium-rare, basting with 1 tablespoon of the dressing during the last 2 minutes of cooking. Transfer the steak to a cutting board and let rest at least 5 minutes before slicing.

4. Divide the noodles among bowls. Using a julienne peeler, julienne the carrot, cucumber and radish. Top the noodles with the vegetables, sliced steak and herbs. Serve with the remaining dressing and peanuts if desired.

Love Notes

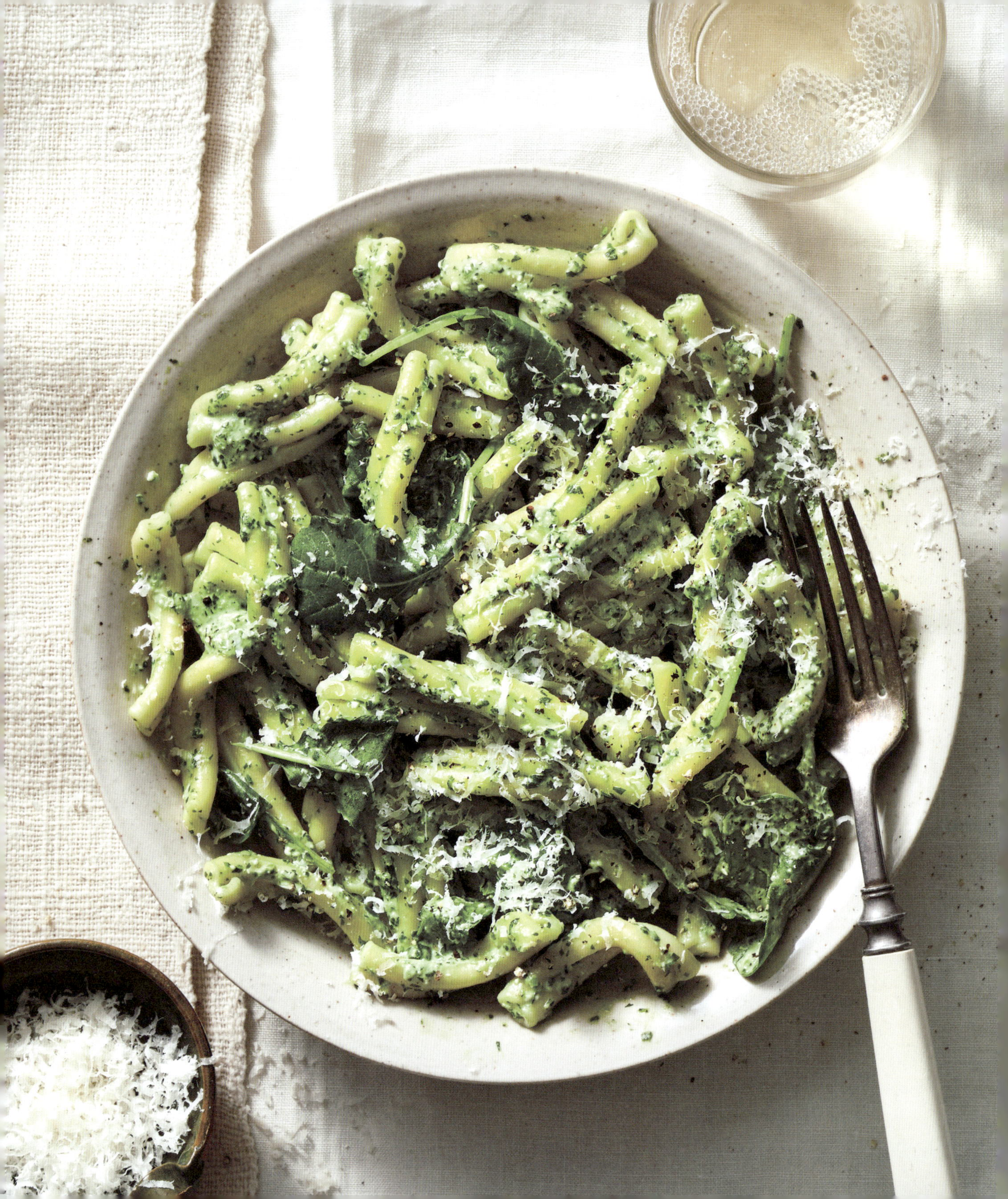

Creamy Kale Pasta

Serves 4 | Active time 25 minutes | Total time 25 minutes

- 12 ounces short pasta (like orecchiette or gemelli)
- 2 scallions, roughly chopped
- 1 5-ounce package baby kale
- ½ cup cottage cheese
- ⅓ cup grated Parmesan, plus more for serving
- Kosher salt and pepper
- 2 tablespoons extra virgin olive oil

For a super-easy nut-free take on pesto, we swapped in protein-packed cottage cheese, which adds velvety body to the sauce. Be sure to reserve some pasta cooking water to toss the kale in before serving.

1. Cook the pasta per the package directions. Reserve ½ cup of the cooking water, drain and return the pasta to the pot.

2. While the pasta cooks, in a food processor, pulse the scallions and 3 cups of kale to finely chop. Add the cottage cheese, the Parmesan and ½ teaspoon each of salt and pepper and pulse to combine.

3. Scrape down the sides and then, with the machine running, gradually add the oil and puree until smooth.

4. Toss the pasta with the sauce to coat, then toss with the remaining 3 cups of kale, adding a couple of tablespoons of the reserved pasta water as necessary to help the kale wilt. Serve topped with additional Parmesan and freshly cracked pepper.

Love Notes

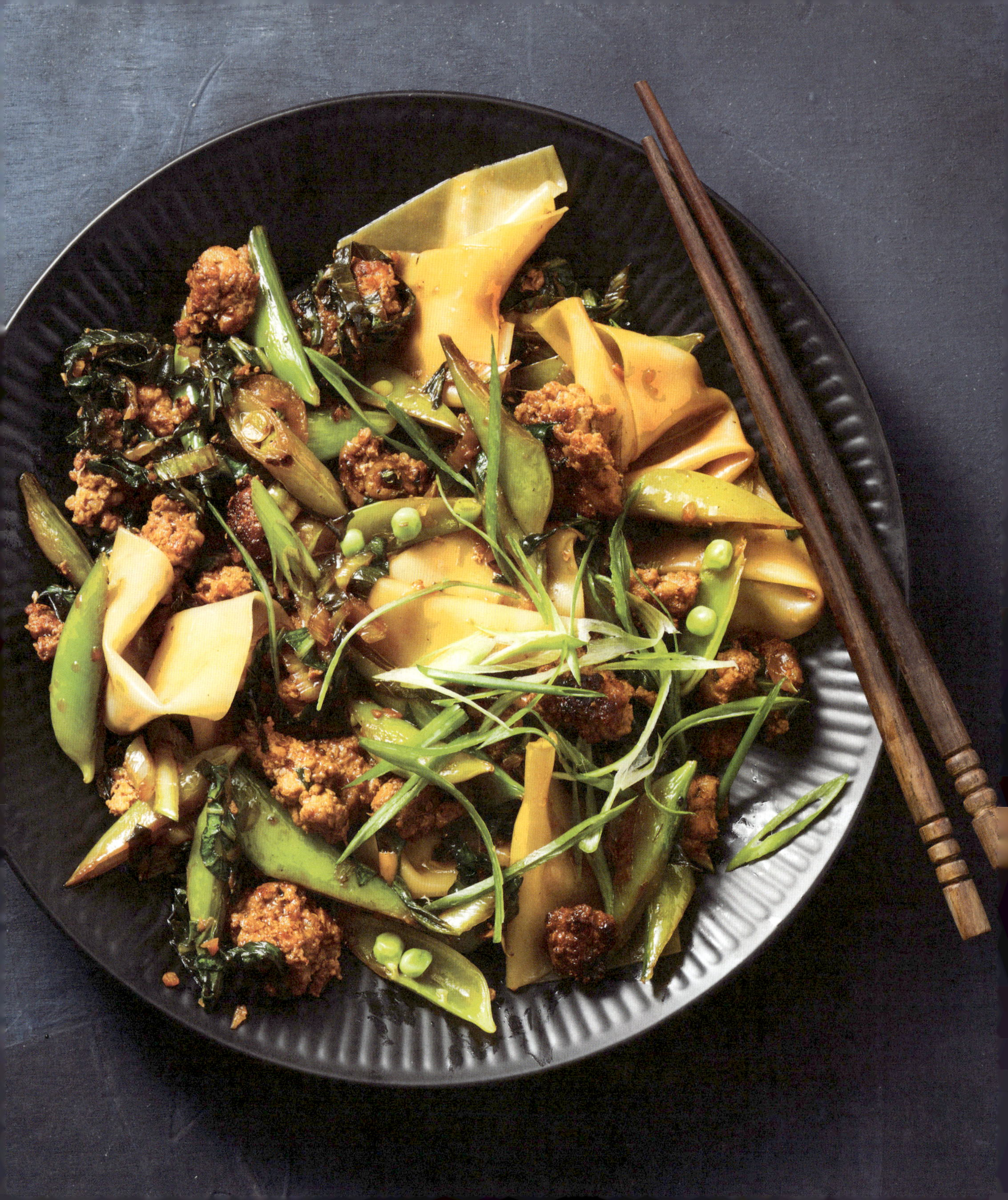

Inside-Out Pork Dumplings

Serves 4 | Active time 20 minutes | Total time 20 minutes

- 12 ounces square wonton wrappers
- 3 tablespoons reduced-sodium tamari
- 1 tablespoon rice vinegar
- 2 teaspoons pure maple syrup
- 4 cloves garlic, pressed
- 1 tablespoon grated fresh ginger
- 4 scallions, white and light green parts chopped, dark green parts thinly sliced
- 1 pound ground pork
- Pepper
- 1 tablespoon sesame oil, divided
- 4 ounces sugar snap peas, sliced
- 2 heads baby bok choy (about 4 ounces each), thinly sliced

Here's all the deliciousness of dumplings with a fraction of the work: Wonton wrappers are cooked like noodles, and the dumpling filling becomes the "sauce."

1. Bring a large pot of water to a boil. Working in stacks, halve the wonton wrappers to create noodles, then separate the wonton strips. In a small bowl, combine the tamari, rice vinegar and maple syrup; set aside.

2. In another small bowl, mix the garlic and ginger, then add scallions. In a medium bowl, mix half of the scallion mixture with the pork and ½ teaspoon pepper.

3. Heat 1 teaspoon of sesame oil in a large skillet on medium-high. Add the pork mixture, break it up and let it cook, undisturbed, until the bottom is crisp, 5 minutes. Break up and continue to cook the pork, scraping up any bits, until cooked through, 2 minutes. Drain the fat, then toss with half of the tamari mixture. Transfer the pork to a plate.

4. In the same large skillet, heat the remaining 2 teaspoons of sesame oil on medium. Add the reserved scallion mixture and sauté 15 seconds. Toss with the sugar snap peas and bok choy, then increase the heat to medium-high and sauté 2 minutes. Remove the skillet from the heat and toss the vegetables with the remaining tamari mixture.

5. Add the noodles to the boiling water, stirring to prevent them from sticking together. Cook for 1 minute, then drain and rinse them under cool water, separating the noodles. Shake off the water; toss with the vegetables, then toss with the pork mixture. Sprinkle with sliced scallion greens.

Love Notes

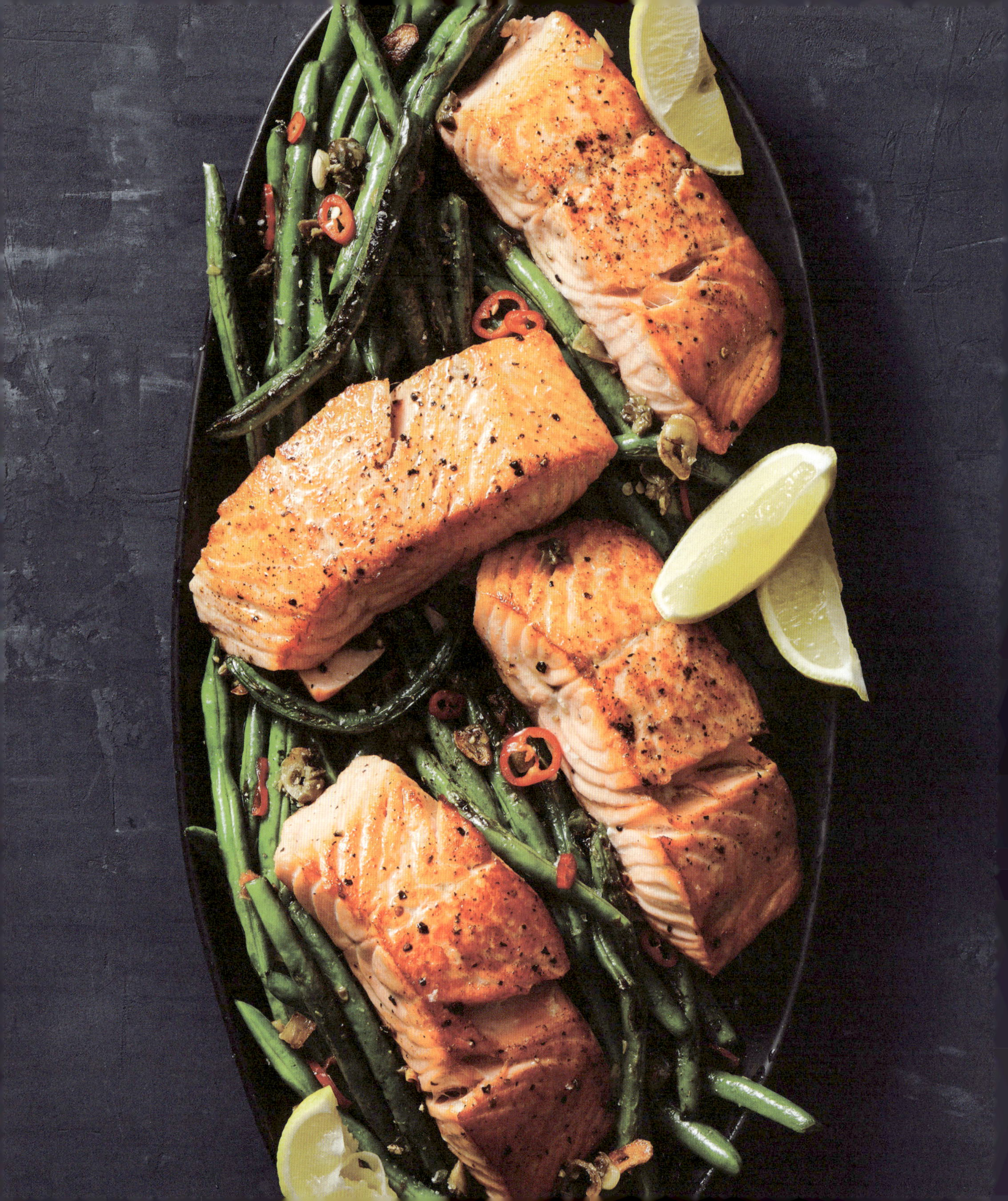

SEAFOOD SUPPERS | **WEEKNIGHT**

Seared Salmon with Charred Green Beans

Serves 4 | Active time 15 minutes | Total time 15 minutes

This 15-minute, five-ingredient supper is proof that health and convenience aren't mutually exclusive. Each serving clocks in at under 300 calories (with more than 30 grams of protein), so add roasted potatoes or cooked rice to your plate if you want something a little heartier.

- 2 tablespoons plus 2 teaspoons olive oil, divided
- 1¼ pounds skinless salmon fillet, cut into 4 portions (5 ounces each)
- Kosher salt and pepper
- 1 pound green beans, trimmed
- 4 cloves garlic, smashed and thinly sliced
- 1 small red chile, thinly sliced
- 2 tablespoons capers, drained, patted dry
- Lemon wedges, for serving

1. Heat 2 teaspoons of oil in a large skillet on medium-high. Season the salmon with ½ teaspoon each of salt and pepper, add to a skillet flesh side down, reduce heat to medium and cook until golden brown and just opaque throughout, 5 to 6 minutes per side.

2. Heat the remaining 2 tablespoons of oil in a large cast-iron skillet on medium-high. Add the green beans and cook until browned, 2½ minutes. Turn with tongs and cook until browned and just barely tender, about 3 minutes more.

3. Remove from heat and toss with ¼ teaspoon salt, then the garlic, chile and capers. Return to medium heat and cook, tossing, until the garlic is golden brown, 1 to 2 minutes. Serve with salmon and lemon wedges if desired.

CHARRED CHAMP
To dial up the delish factor of this green veg side, turn up the heat and reach for a cast-iron skillet. This pan retains high temps, helping impart a blackened flavor to food.

Love Notes

THE NEWLYWED COOKBOOK **97**

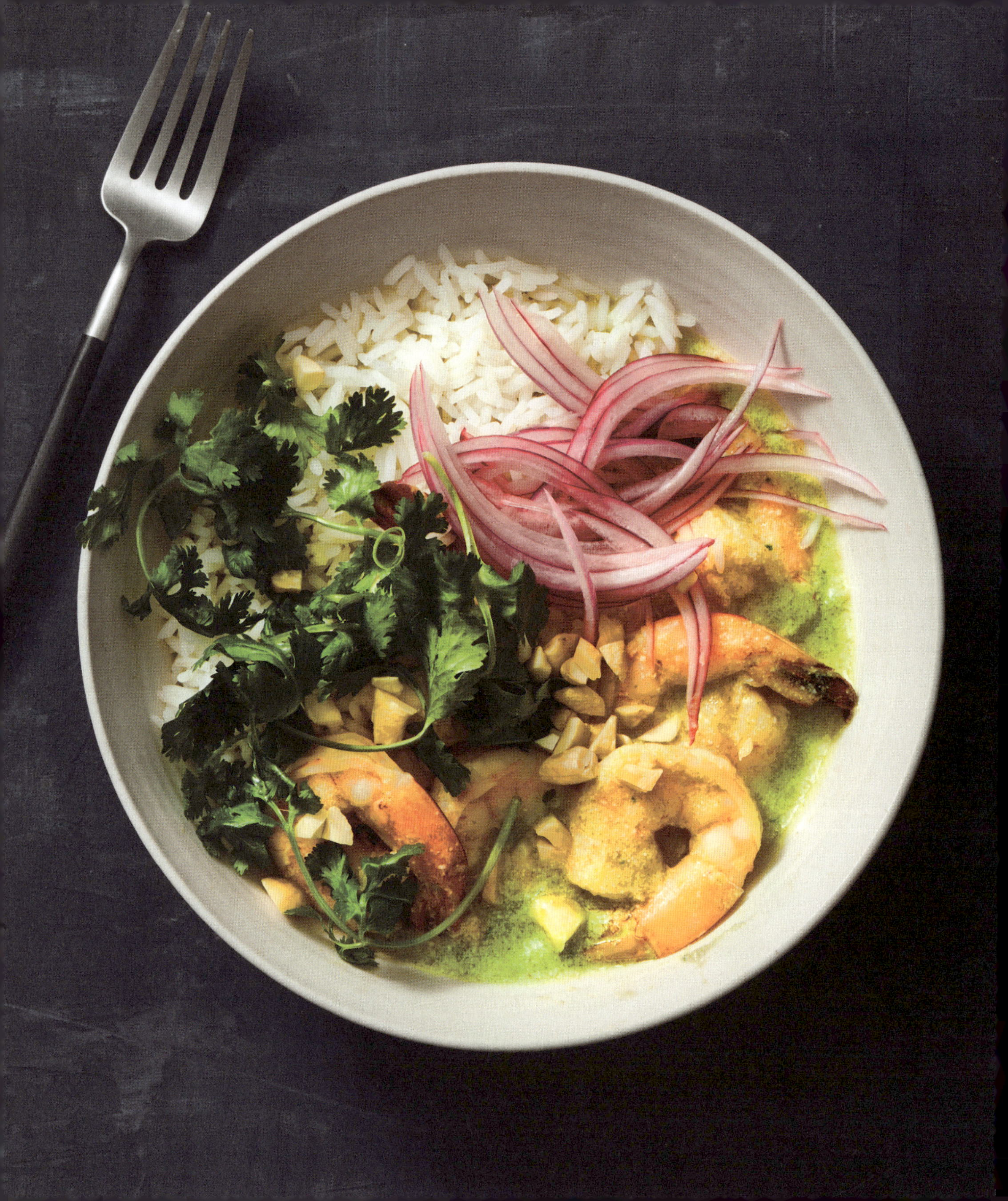

SEAFOOD SUPPERS | **WEEKNIGHT**

Green Curry Shrimp

Serves 4 | Active time 15 minutes | Total time 25 minutes

1 cup long-grain white rice

1 small red onion, thinly sliced

5 tablespoons fresh lime juice, divided, plus wedges for serving

Kosher salt

1 teaspoon olive oil

3 tablespoons Thai green curry paste

1 13.5- to 14-ounce can coconut milk

¼ bunch cilantro, trimmed and tied, plus cilantro leaves for serving

1½ pounds large shrimp, peeled and deveined

1 to 2 tablespoons fish sauce

Cashews, for sprinkling

This creamy dish doesn't need to simmer all day — Thai green curry paste adds flavor and fragrance almost instantly. Top with quick-pickled red onion before serving for a boost of brightness.

1. Cook the rice per package directions. In a small bowl, toss the onion with 2 tablespoons of lime juice and ¼ teaspoon of salt; set aside.

2. Meanwhile, heat the oil in a large saucepan on medium. Add the curry paste and cook, stirring often, until fragrant, about 3 minutes. Stir in the coconut milk and 1 cup of water, add the cilantro bunch and simmer for 5 minutes.

3. Discard the cilantro; add the shrimp and cook until the shrimp is just opaque throughout, 4 to 5 minutes. Remove the saucepan from the heat and stir in the fish sauce and the remaining 3 tablespoons of lime juice. Serve the curry over the rice, topped with cashews, pickled onion and cilantro if desired. Serve with lime wedges.

PICK YOUR PROTEIN

Shrimp is great in this recipe, but you can sub in any protein you like. Chicken or salmon would be especially good, or you could use cauliflower or tofu as a plant-based alternative.

Love Notes

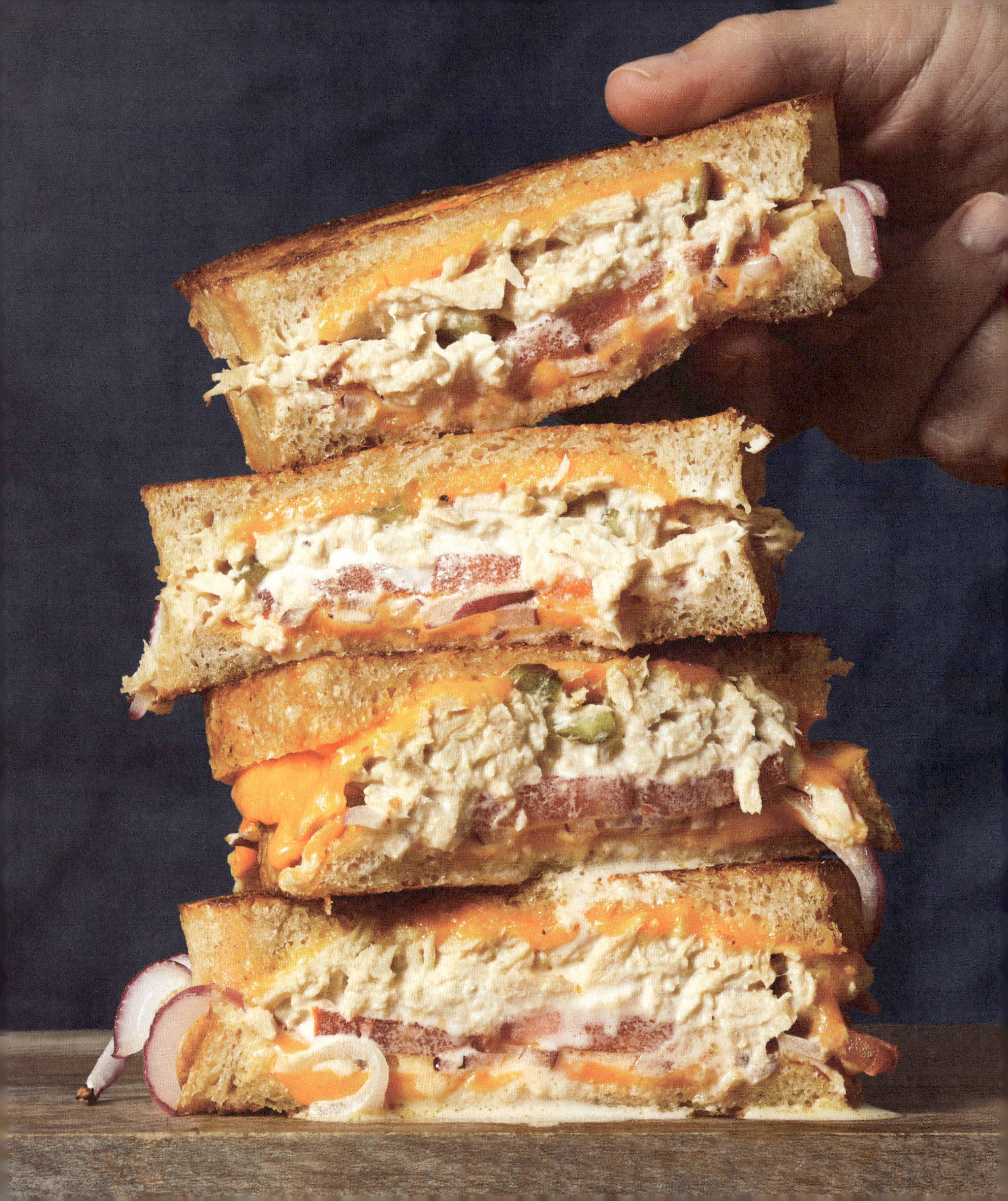

SEAFOOD SUPPERS | **WEEKNIGHT**

Classic Tuna Melt

Serves 4 | Active time 10 minutes | Total time 10 minutes

With a can or two of tuna in your pantry, you're never more than a few extra ingredients away from a seriously satisfying meal—like these creamy, cheesy sandwiches that will always hit the spot.

1. In a small bowl, whisk together the mayonnaise, lemon juice and Dijon mustard and ¼ teaspoon each of salt and pepper. Add the tuna and mix to combine, then fold in the pickle.

2. Heat a large nonstick skillet on medium. Lightly spread 1 side of the bread with mayonnaise. Turn the bread, mayonnaise side down, onto a work surface. Top 4 of the bread slices with the Cheddar, then the tuna, tomato and red onion and a second slice of Cheddar. Add the remaining bread slices, mayonnaise side up, and cook until golden brown, 2 to 3 minutes per side.

- ¼ cup mayonnaise, plus more for bread
- ½ tablespoon fresh lemon juice
- ½ tablespoon Dijon mustard
- Kosher salt and pepper
- 2 5-ounce cans solid white tuna in water, drained
- 1 small pickle, chopped
- 8 slices white bread
- 8 thin slices orange Cheddar cheese
- 1 large tomato, sliced
- ½ small red onion, thinly sliced

MAYO MAGIC
For that photo-worthy golden brown exterior, spread mayo on bread slices. The oil-based condiment doesn't burn as quickly as butter and makes for a super-crispy crust.

Love Notes

THE NEWLYWED COOKBOOK **101**

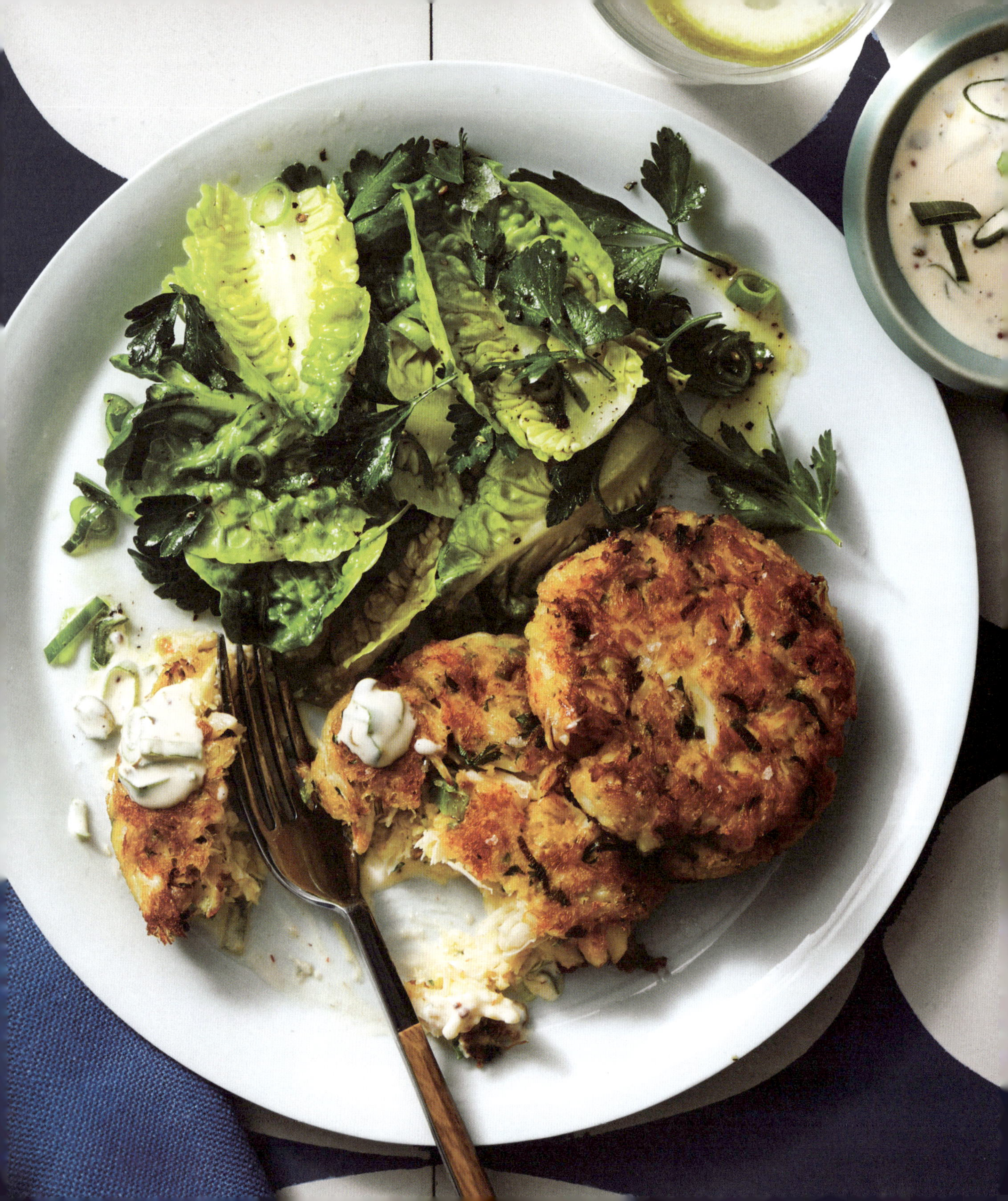

Crab Cakes with Creamy Sauce

Serves 4 | Active time 25 minutes | Total time 25 minutes, plus chilling

Turn any average weeknight into date night by uncorking a bottle of white wine and enjoying appetizers for dinner. When paired with a simple green salad, these patties transform from a starter to a stunning main.

FOR THE CREAMY SAUCE
- ¼ cup mayonnaise
- 1 tablespoon Dijon mustard
- ½ tablespoon whole-grain mustard
- 2 teaspoons lemon juice
- ¼ teaspoon hot sauce
- 1 scallion, finely chopped
- 1 tablespoon chopped capers or pickles

FOR THE CRAB CAKES
- ⅓ cup mayonnaise
- 1 large egg
- 2 tablespoons Dijon mustard
- 1 teaspoon Worcestershire sauce
- ¼ to ½ teaspoon hot sauce
- 2 scallions, finely chopped
- 2 tablespoons flat-leaf parsley, finely chopped, plus 1 cup leaves
- 2 teaspoons grated lemon zest plus 1 tablespoon lemon juice
- 2 8-ounce containers lump crab meat, picked
- ½ cup panko
- 1 tablespoon unsalted butter
- 2½ tablespoons olive oil, divided
- 2 heads Little Gem lettuce, leaves separated

1. Make the creamy sauce: In a bowl, combine mayonnaise, mustards, lemon juice, hot sauce, scallion and capers or pickles if desired. Refrigerate until ready to use.

2. Make the crab cakes: In a medium bowl, whisk together the mayonnaise, egg, mustard, Worcestershire sauce and hot sauce. Stir in the scallions, parsley and lemon zest. Add the crab and panko and mix to combine. Cover and refrigerate the mixture for 1 hour.

3. Shape the crab mixture into eight 1-inch-thick cakes. In a large nonstick skillet, heat the butter and 1 tablespoon of oil on medium. Cook the crab cakes in batches until golden brown and heated through, 3 to 4 minutes per side, adding more oil as necessary.

4. In a large bowl, toss lettuce and the remaining cup of parsley leaves with 1 tablespoon of lemon juice, the remaining 1½ tablespoons of oil and ¼ teaspoon each of salt and pepper. Serve with the crab cakes and the sauce.

Love Notes

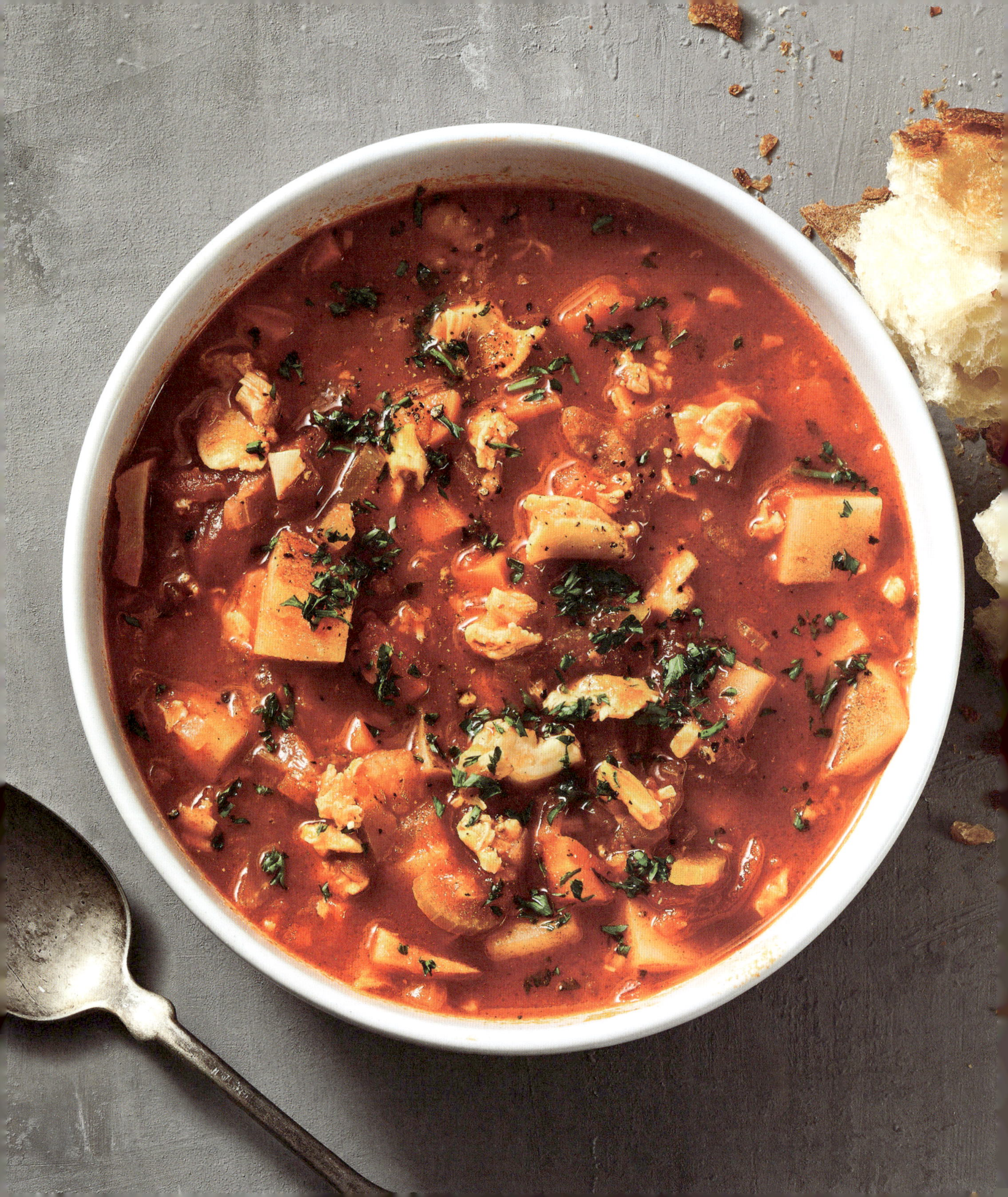

SEAFOOD SUPPERS | WEEKNIGHT

Manhattan Clam Chowder

- 2 tablespoons olive oil
- 2 stalks celery, thinly sliced
- 1 large onion, finely chopped
- 1 large carrot, cut into ¼-inch pieces
- 2 cloves garlic, finely chopped
- ½ teaspoon red pepper flakes
- 1 pound russet potatoes, cut into ½-inch pieces
- 3 sprigs thyme
- 2 8-ounce bottles clam juice
- 1 28-ounce can whole tomatoes
- ½ cup dry white wine
- 2 6.5-ounce cans chopped clams, drained
- ¼ cup flat-leaf parsley, chopped
- Crusty bread, for serving

Serves 4 | Active time 25 minutes | Total time 30 minutes

Sweet clams, bright tomatoes and white wine come together in this lighter alternative to creamy New England–style clam chowder. Stop by the bakery on your way home to pick up a baguette for dunking.

1. In a large pot or Dutch oven, heat the oil on medium. Add the celery, onion and carrot and cook, covered, stirring occasionally, until the vegetables are tender, 8 to 10 minutes. Stir in the garlic and red pepper flakes and cook for 1 minute more.

2. Add the potatoes, thyme and clam juice; the tomatoes and their juices (crushing the pieces with your hands); the white wine; and ½ cup water and bring to a boil. Reduce the heat and simmer until the potatoes are tender, 8 to 10 minutes. Stir in the clams and heat through.

3. Sprinkle with parsley and serve with bread if desired.

HAPPY AS A CLAM (JUICE)
Bottled clam juice is a great shortcut ingredient to have on hand for stews and soups. Be sure to taste for seasoning after you've added clam juice to a dish; you may not need additional salt.

Love Notes

THE NEWLYWED COOKBOOK 105

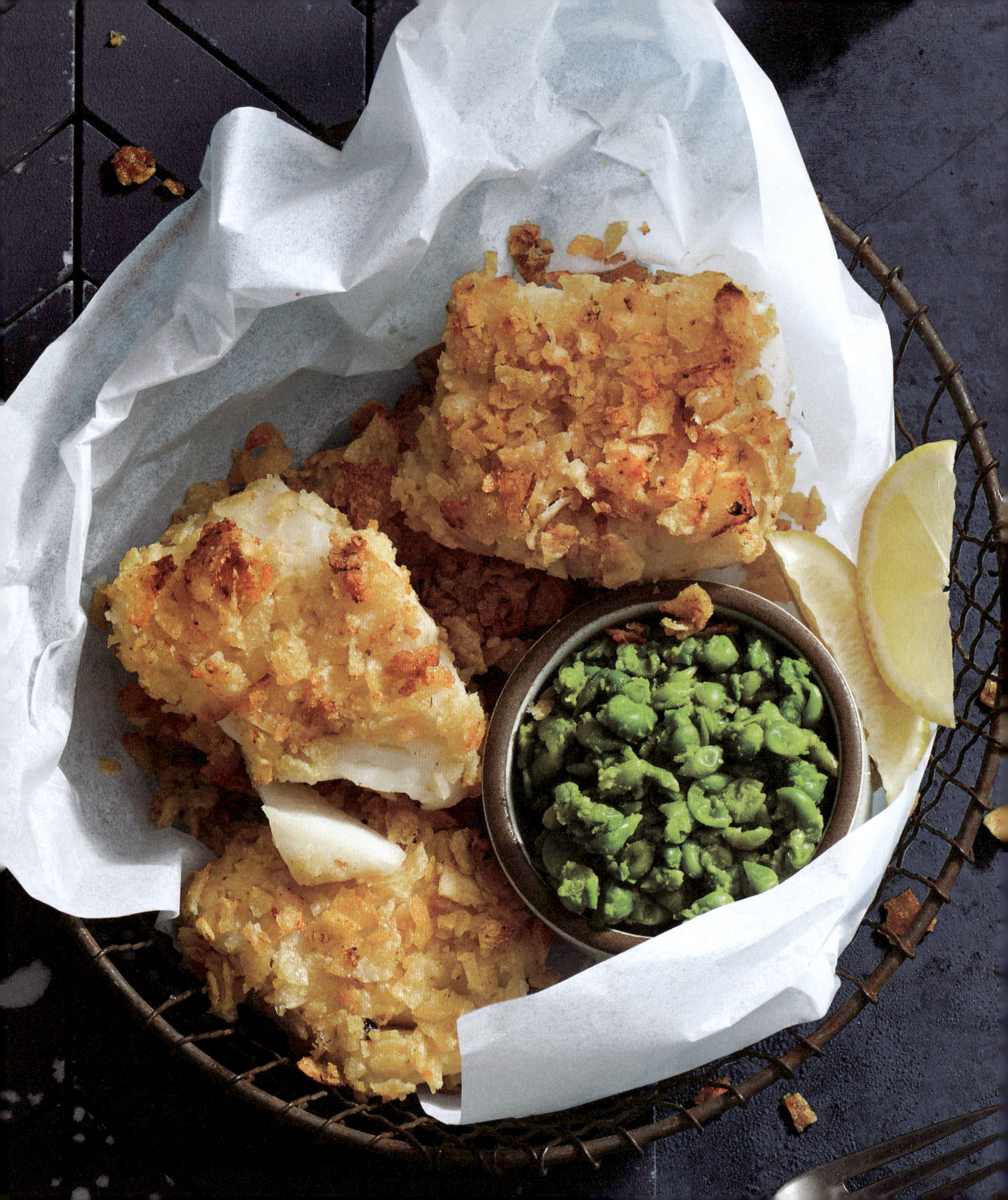

Fish & Chips

Serves 4 | Active time 20 minutes | Total time 20 minutes

- 2 large egg whites
- 2 5-ounce packages salt and vinegar potato chips (about 4 cups), crushed
- 1½ pounds cod fillets, cut into 3-inch pieces
- 1 tablespoon olive oil, plus more for spraying, divided
- 16 ounces frozen peas, thawed
- 1 teaspoon lemon zest plus 2 tablespoons lemon juice
- Kosher salt and pepper

Crushed salt and vinegar chips provide the crunchy, golden coating for cod — as well as tons of flavor — in this 20-minute (oven-free!) dinner.

1. Heat the air fryer to 400°F. In a shallow bowl, beat the egg whites and 1 tablespoon of water.

2. Place the chips in a second shallow bowl. Dip the fish in the egg whites, letting the excess drip off, then dip the fish in the crushed chips, pressing gently to help them adhere.

3. Spray the air-fryer basket with olive oil, arrange the fish in the basket and air-fry until the fish is golden brown and opaque throughout, 10 minutes.

4. Meanwhile, in a medium bowl, microwave the peas on medium power for 2 minutes. Toss with lemon zest and juice, 1 tablespoon of oil and ½ teaspoon each of salt and pepper, then mash. Serve with the fish.

OVEN OPTION
Heat the oven to 450°F. Coat the fish as directed and transfer to a large rimmed baking sheet rubbed with 1 tablespoon of oil. Roast until the fish is golden brown and opaque throughout, 10 to 12 minutes.

Love Notes

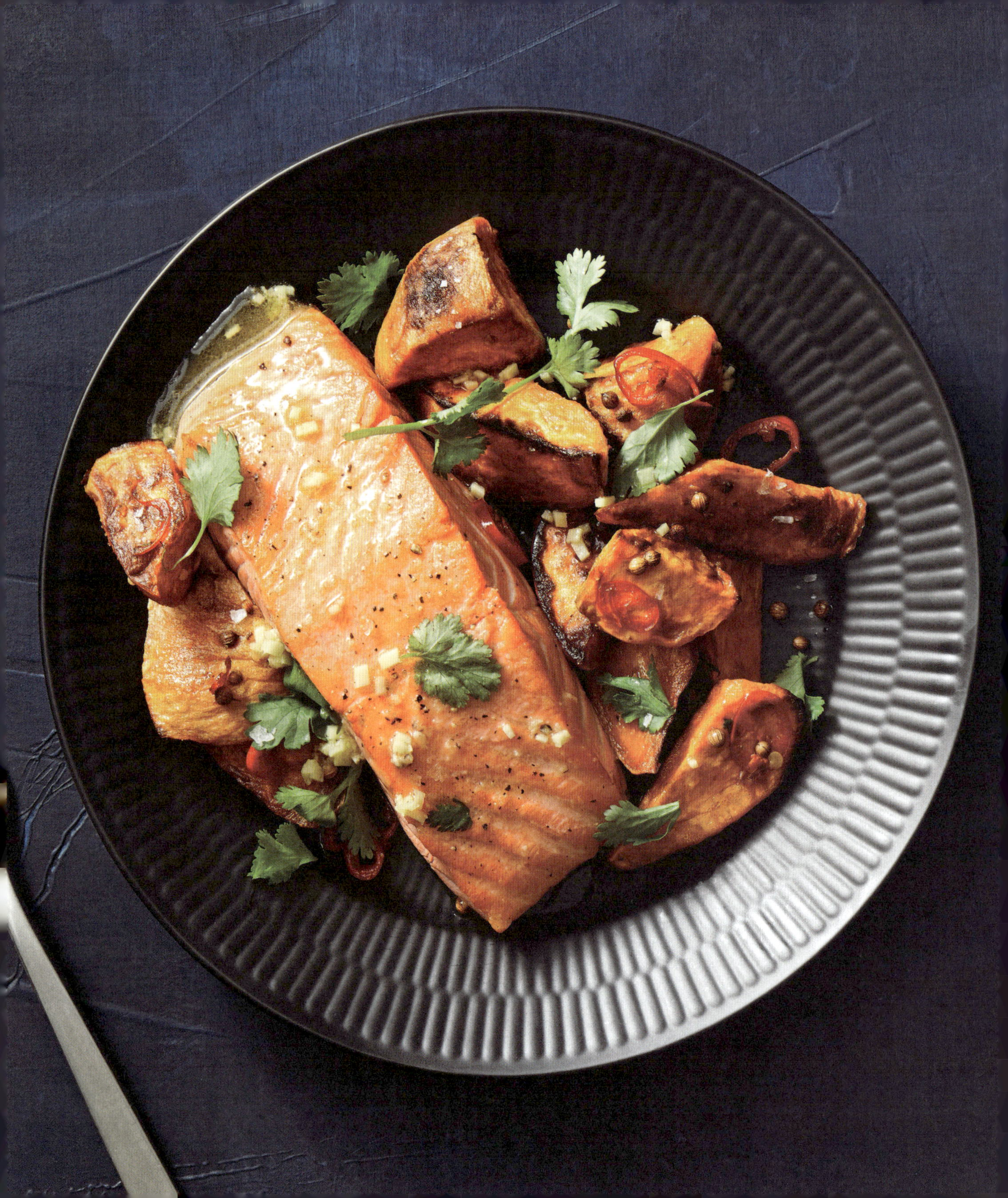

SEAFOOD SUPPERS | **WEEKNIGHT**

Seared Salmon with Spiced Sweet Potatoes

Serves 4 | Active time 15 minutes | Total time 35 minutes

This nutritious, feel-good meal—featuring salmon fillets—gets a boost of deliciousness from crushed coriander seeds, slices of red chile and a drizzle of a punchy, gingery citrus vinaigrette.

1. Heat the oven to 425°F. On a rimmed baking sheet, toss the sweet potatoes with 1 tablespoon of the oil, then toss with the coriander and chile and ½ teaspoon each of salt and pepper. Roast until the potatoes are golden brown and tender, 20 to 25 minutes.

2. Meanwhile, in a small bowl, whisk together the clementine juice, honey, ginger and vinegar and 1 tablespoon of the oil.

3. Heat the remaining tablespoon of oil in a large skillet on medium-high. Season the salmon with ½ teaspoon each of salt and pepper and cook until golden brown and just opaque throughout, 5 to 6 minutes per side. Serve with the sweet potatoes, drizzle with the vinaigrette and sprinkle with chopped cilantro leaves if desired.

- 4 small sweet potatoes (about 2 pounds), cut into 2-inch pieces
- 3 tablespoons olive oil, divided
- 1 tablespoon coriander seeds, crushed
- 1 red chile, thinly sliced
- Kosher salt and pepper
- 2 tablespoons clementine juice
- 1 teaspoon honey
- 1 teaspoon grated peeled fresh ginger
- 1 teaspoon white wine vinegar
- 1¼ pounds skinless salmon fillet, cut into 4 portions
- Chopped cilantro leaves, for serving

GINGER UP
It's not easy to peel knobby fresh ginger with a knife or a vegetable peeler. A better tool: a spoon. The edge is sharp enough to scrape off the thin ginger skin, and you won't cut yourself if it slips.

Love Notes

THE NEWLYWED COOKBOOK **109**

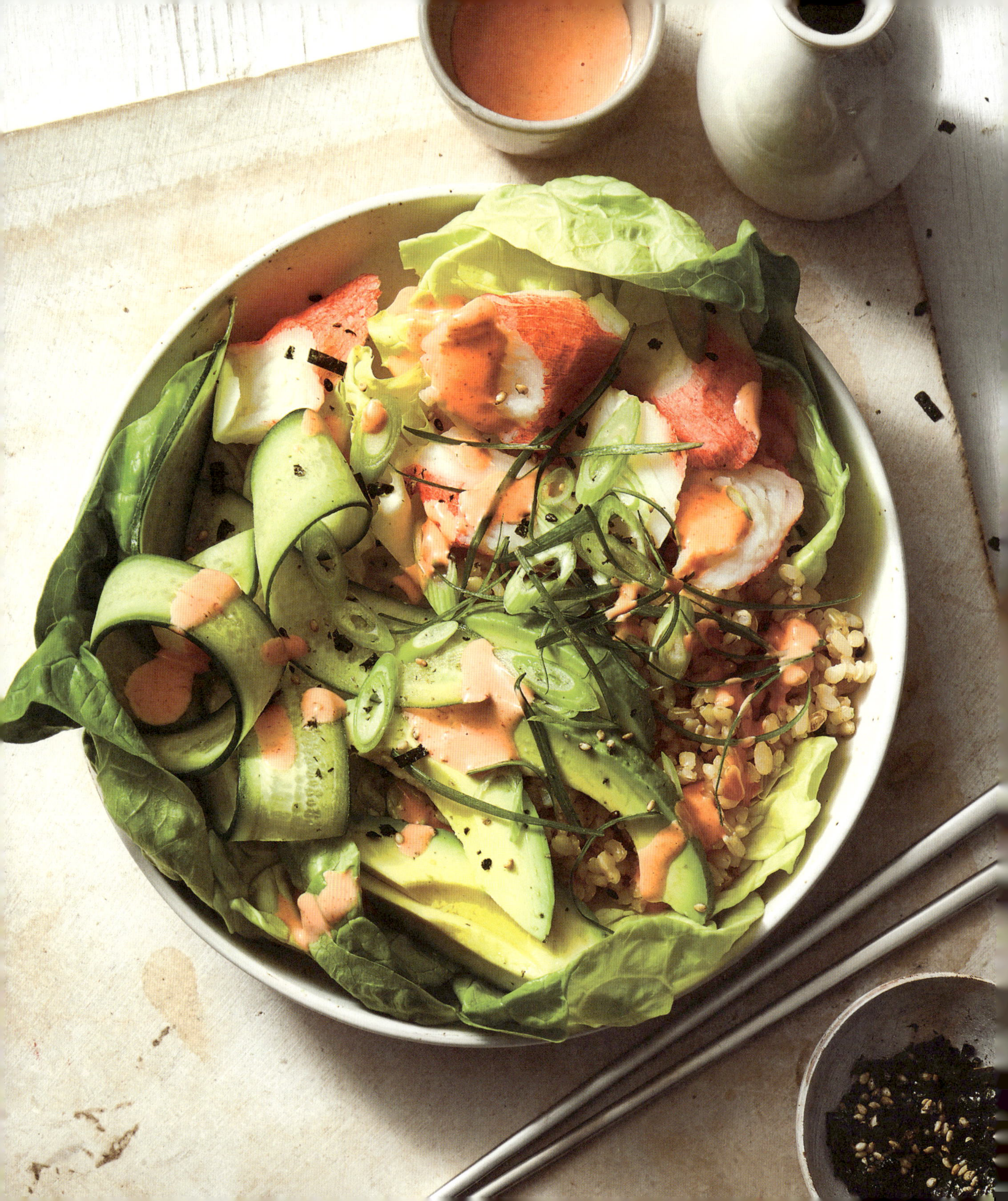

California Roll Salad

Serves 4 | Active time 15 minutes | Total time 15 minutes

- 2 tablespoons mayonnaise
- 1 tablespoon sriracha
- 1 tablespoon fresh lemon juice
- Kosher salt
- 1 to 2 heads Boston lettuce, separated into leaves
- 1½ cups cooked short-grain brown rice
- 2 Persian cucumbers, thinly sliced into ribbons
- 1 avocado, cut into pieces
- 8 ounces surimi or crabmeat
- 1 scallion, thinly sliced
- Furikake seasoning, for serving

The components of this sushi menu favorite are "unrolled" and served in a bowl topped with a drizzle of spicy mayo and furikake, a combo of sesame seeds and dried seaweed.

1. In a small bowl, whisk together the mayonnaise, sriracha and lemon juice and a pinch of salt.

2. Divide the lettuce, rice, cucumber and avocado among bowls. Top with the surimi, then drizzle with the dressing. Sprinkle with the sliced scallion and furikake if desired.

KRABBY FACTS

Surimi, also called krab or imitation crab, is often served in California rolls. It's made from fish (usually Alaskan pollack) mixed with other ingredients like starch, salt and crabmeat to make a relatively inexpensive, sustainable shellfish substitute.

Love Notes

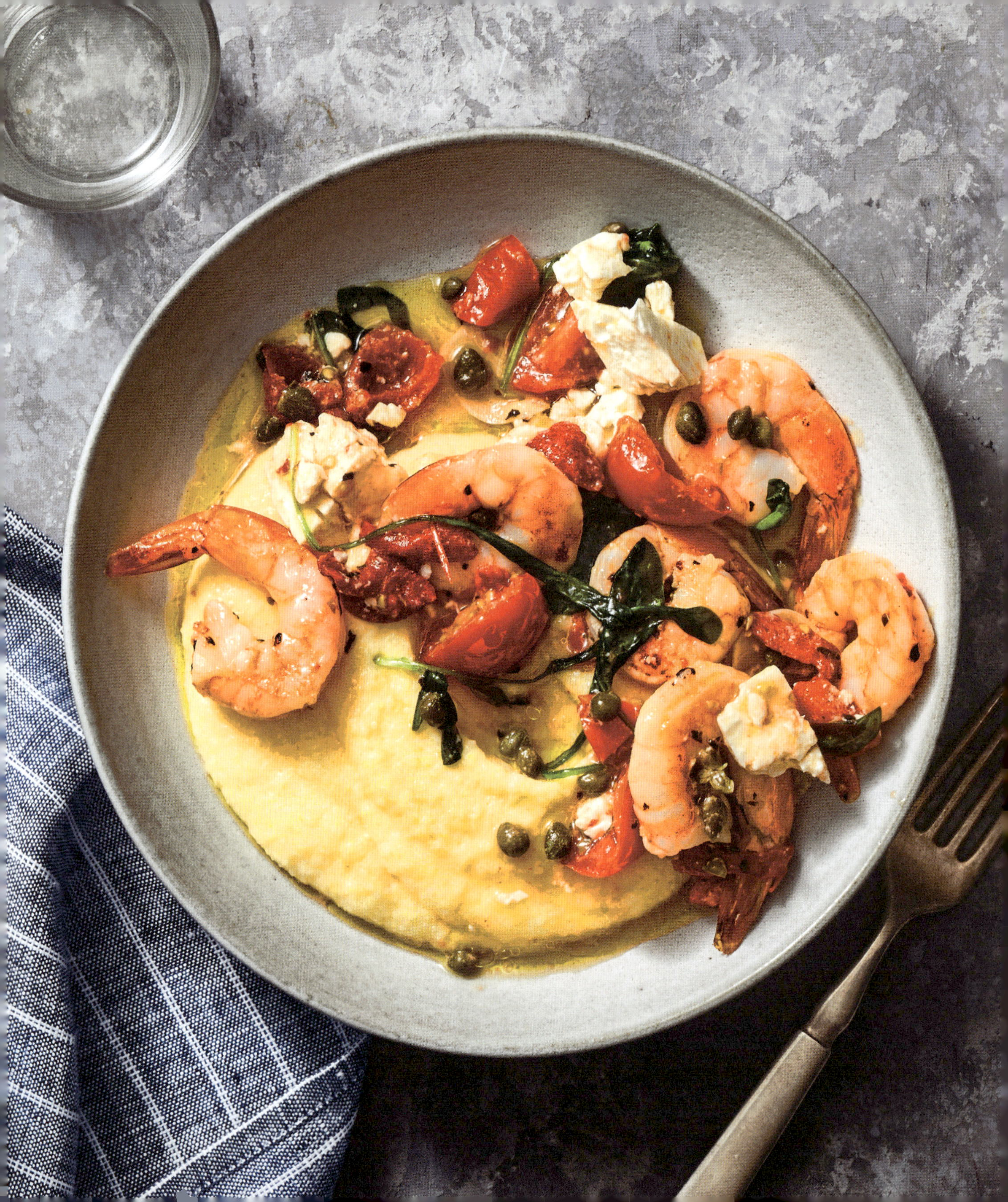

SEAFOOD SUPPERS | WEEKNIGHT

Baked Feta Shrimp

Serves 4 | Active time 20 minutes | Total time 25 minutes

Fans of the viral baked feta pasta have to try this fancy yet fast iteration. A block of feta gets roasted with peppers, capers, shrimp and juicy Campari tomatoes to create a saucy situation perfect for spooning over creamy polenta.

- 1 pound extra-large shrimp, peeled and deveined
- 2 tablespoons olive oil
- ½ teaspoon dried oregano
- Kosher salt and pepper
- 4 cloves garlic, chopped
- 6 ounces roasted red peppers, drained and cut into 1-inch pieces
- 6 small sweet red peppers (such as Peppadew), drained and chopped
- 1 tablespoon capers, drained
- 2 tablespoons dry white wine
- 4 ounces feta cheese
- 8 ounces Campari tomatoes, quartered
- 1 cup instant polenta
- 3 cups baby spinach
- Chopped parsley, for serving

1. Heat the oven to 425°F. In a 1½- to 2-quart baking dish, toss the shrimp with the oil, then the oregano and ¼ teaspoon each salt and pepper. Toss with the garlic, roasted and sweet peppers, capers and wine.

2. Nestle the feta into one corner and roast 6 minutes.

3. Gently fold in the tomatoes, making sure to leave the feta undisturbed, and continue roasting until the shrimp are opaque throughout, 5 to 7 minutes more.

4. Meanwhile, cook the polenta per the package directions.

5. Remove the shrimp from the oven and fold in the spinach just until it's beginning to wilt, leaving the feta undisturbed. Spoon the shrimp mixture over the polenta, then top with the feta and parsley.

Love Notes

THE NEWLYWED COOKBOOK

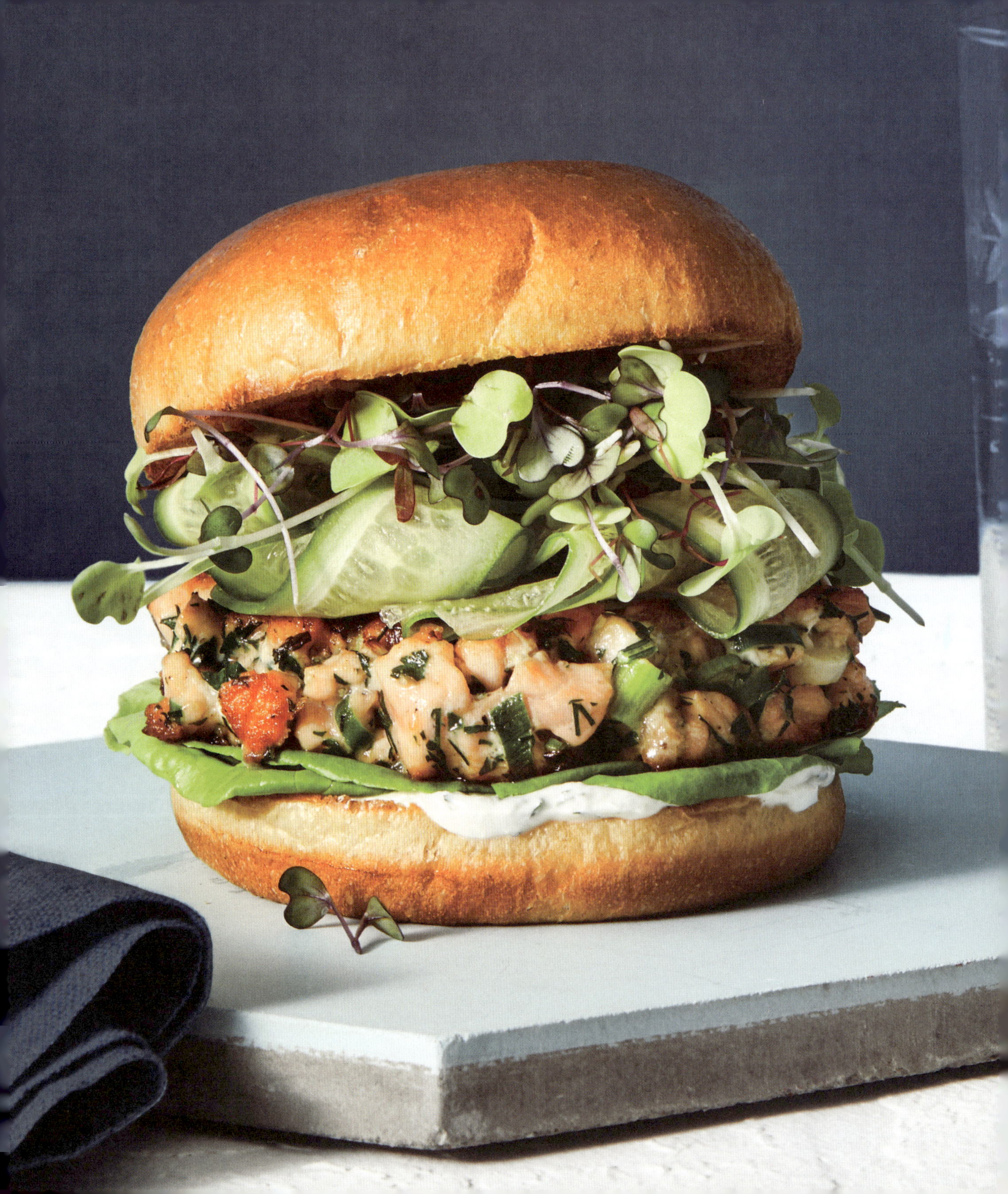

Herby Salmon Burgers

Serves 4 | Active time 30 minutes | Total time 30 minutes

- 1 large egg
- 1 pound skinless salmon fillet, finely chopped
- 2 scallions, chopped
- 3 tablespoons fresh dill, chopped and divided
- 3 tablespoons flat-leaf parsley, chopped and divided
- Kosher salt and pepper
- 1 tablespoon olive oil
- ½ cup Greek yogurt
- 1 teaspoon lemon zest plus 2 tablespoons lemon juice
- 4 brioche buns, toasted
- 8 Bibb lettuce leaves
- 2 Persian cucumbers or ½ English cucumber, shaved lengthwise
- 2 cups broccoli or radish sprouts

On burger night, think beyond beef! For the patties, swap in fresh fish mixed with lemon, dill and parsley. Then top them off with lots of bright veggies and a zingy yogurt sauce for a super-simple weeknight dinner.

1. In a medium bowl, beat the egg until frothy. Fold in the salmon, the scallions, 2 tablespoons each of dill and parsley and ¼ teaspoon each of salt and pepper.

2. In a large skillet, heat the oil on medium. Spoon four mounds of the salmon mixture (about ½ cup each) into the skillet and flatten into ½-inch-thick patties. Cook until the patties are golden brown, 2 minutes per side.

3. Meanwhile, in a small bowl, combine the yogurt, the lemon zest and juice, the remaining tablespoon of dill and parsley and ¼ teaspoon each of salt and pepper.

4. Spread the yogurt sauce on the bottom buns (about 2½ tablespoons each) and top with the lettuce, salmon patties, cucumber and sprouts; add the top buns.

Love Notes

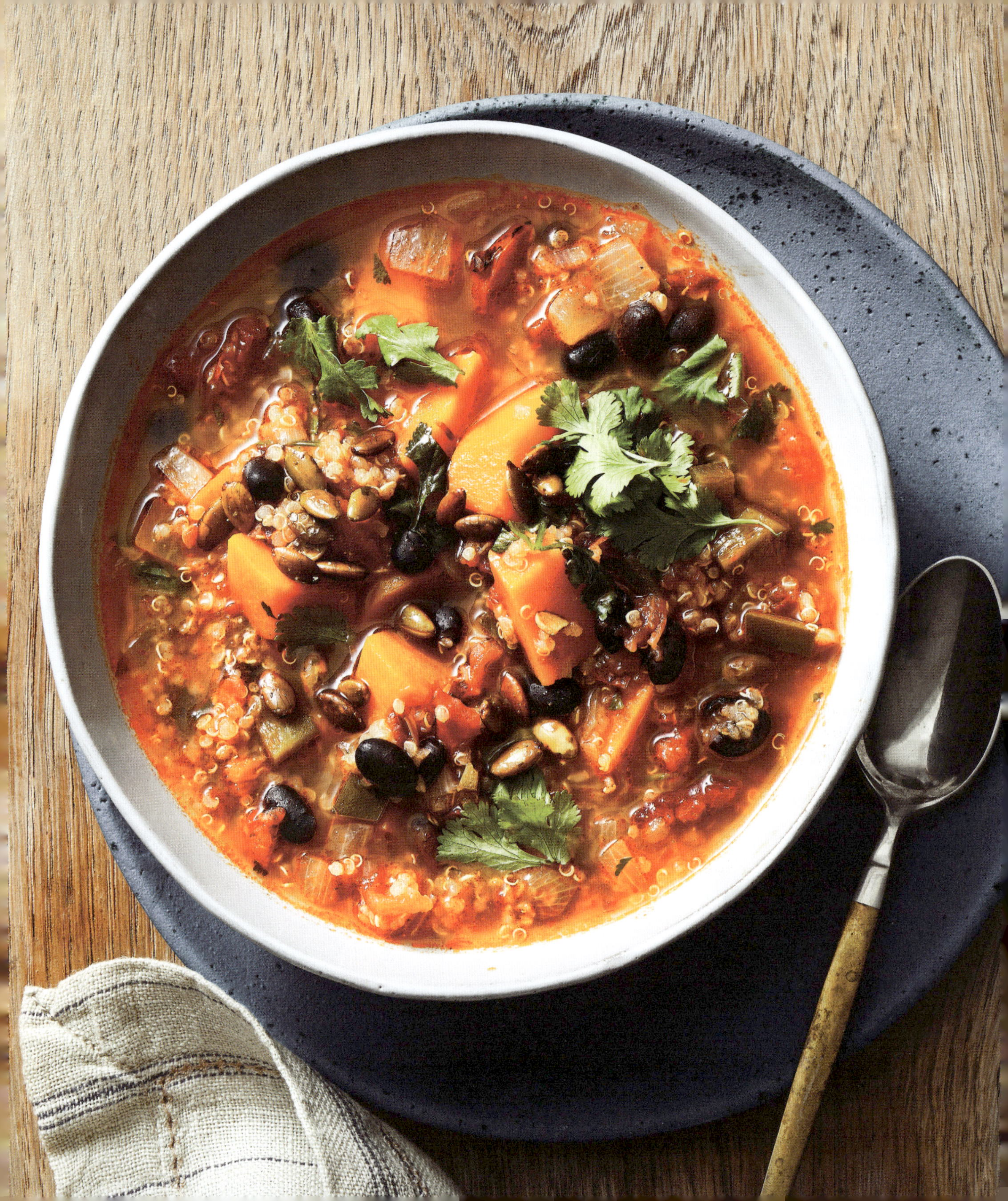

Smoky Black Bean & Quinoa Soup

Serves 4 | Active time 30 minutes | Total time 45 minutes

- 1½ tablespoons olive oil
- 1 onion, chopped
- Kosher salt
- ½ medium butternut squash (about 12 ounces), peeled and cut into ¾-inch pieces
- 1 medium poblano pepper, cut into ¼-inch pieces
- 2 cloves garlic, pressed
- 1¼ teaspoons ground cumin
- 1 canned chipotle in adobo, finely chopped, plus 1 tablespoon adobo
- 3 cups low-sodium vegetable broth
- 1 14-ounce can diced fire-roasted tomatoes
- ½ cup quinoa, rinsed
- 1 15-ounce can black beans, rinsed
- ⅓ cup cilantro, chopped, plus leaves for serving
- ⅓ cup roasted pepitas

This soup-er bowl is hearty with tender bites of butternut squash and nutty quinoa. Want an extra hit of protein? Fold in shredded chicken or cooked ground turkey when adding the black beans.

1. Heat the oil in a Dutch oven on medium. Add the onion and ½ teaspoon of salt and cook, covered, stirring occasionally, 6 minutes.

2. Add the squash and poblano and cook, stirring occasionally, 4 minutes. Stir in the garlic and cumin and cook 1 minute.

3. Stir in the chipotle and adobo, then the broth, and bring to a boil. When the edges of the pot just start bubbling, stir in the tomatoes and quinoa, reduce the heat, and simmer gently, covered, until the quinoa is tender, 12 to 14 minutes.

4. Stir the beans into the soup and cook until heated through, about 3 minutes. Stir in the cilantro and serve topped with pepitas and additional cilantro if desired.

Love Notes

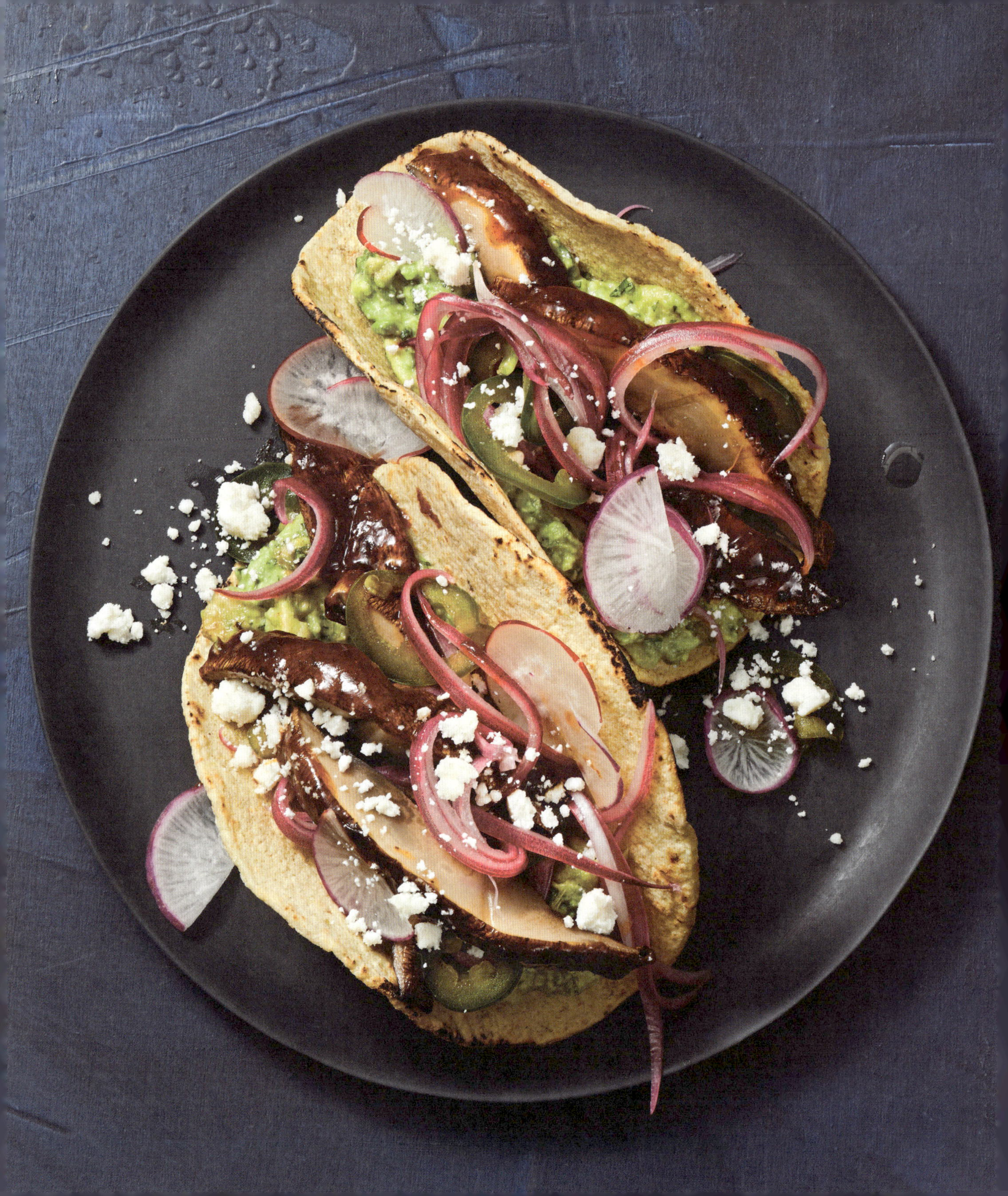

PLANT-POWERED | **WEEKNIGHT**

Adobo-Glazed Portobello Tacos

½ small red onion, thinly sliced
2½ tablespoons fresh lime juice, divided
Pinch of sugar
Kosher salt
1 jalapeño
1 avocado, halved and scooped
¼ cup cilantro leaves, finely chopped
½ cup barbecue sauce
½ tablespoon adobo sauce, plus 1 teaspoon chopped chipotle
4 portobello mushroom caps, gills removed
8 corn tortillas, warmed
3 radishes, thinly sliced
¼ cup cotija cheese

Serves 4 | Active time 15 minutes | Total time 20 minutes

A mixture of adobo sauce and barbecue sauce creates the smoky-sweet glaze for the mushrooms, and a quick-pickled red onion adds a little zip to these super-satisfying veggie tacos.

1. In a small bowl, combine the onion, 1 tablespoon of the lime juice, the sugar and a pinch of salt. Slice half of the jalapeño into thin rounds and add them to the bowl. Set aside. Finely chop the remaining jalapeño and add it to a medium bowl. Add the avocado, cilantro and the remaining 1½ tablespoons of lime juice and ½ teaspoon of salt; mash everything until creamy.

2. Heat the broiler to high. In another small bowl, stir together the barbecue sauce, adobo sauce and chopped chipotle.

3. On a rimmed baking sheet, place the portobellos cap sides down. Broil for 5 minutes. Flip, then brush the mushrooms with adobo glaze and broil until browned in spots, 2 to 3 minutes, brushing with more glaze if desired. Transfer the mushrooms to a cutting board and slice them into strips.

4. Serve the mushrooms in tortillas with the mashed avocado, radishes, pickled onion and jalapeño and cotija cheese.

THAT'S A WRAP
For soft, pliable tortillas, stack 3 or 4, bundle in a damp paper towel and microwave for 30 seconds. To slightly char (and soften) tortillas, heat them directly over a gas flame or warm in a skillet until they smell nutty and brown spots appear.

Love Notes

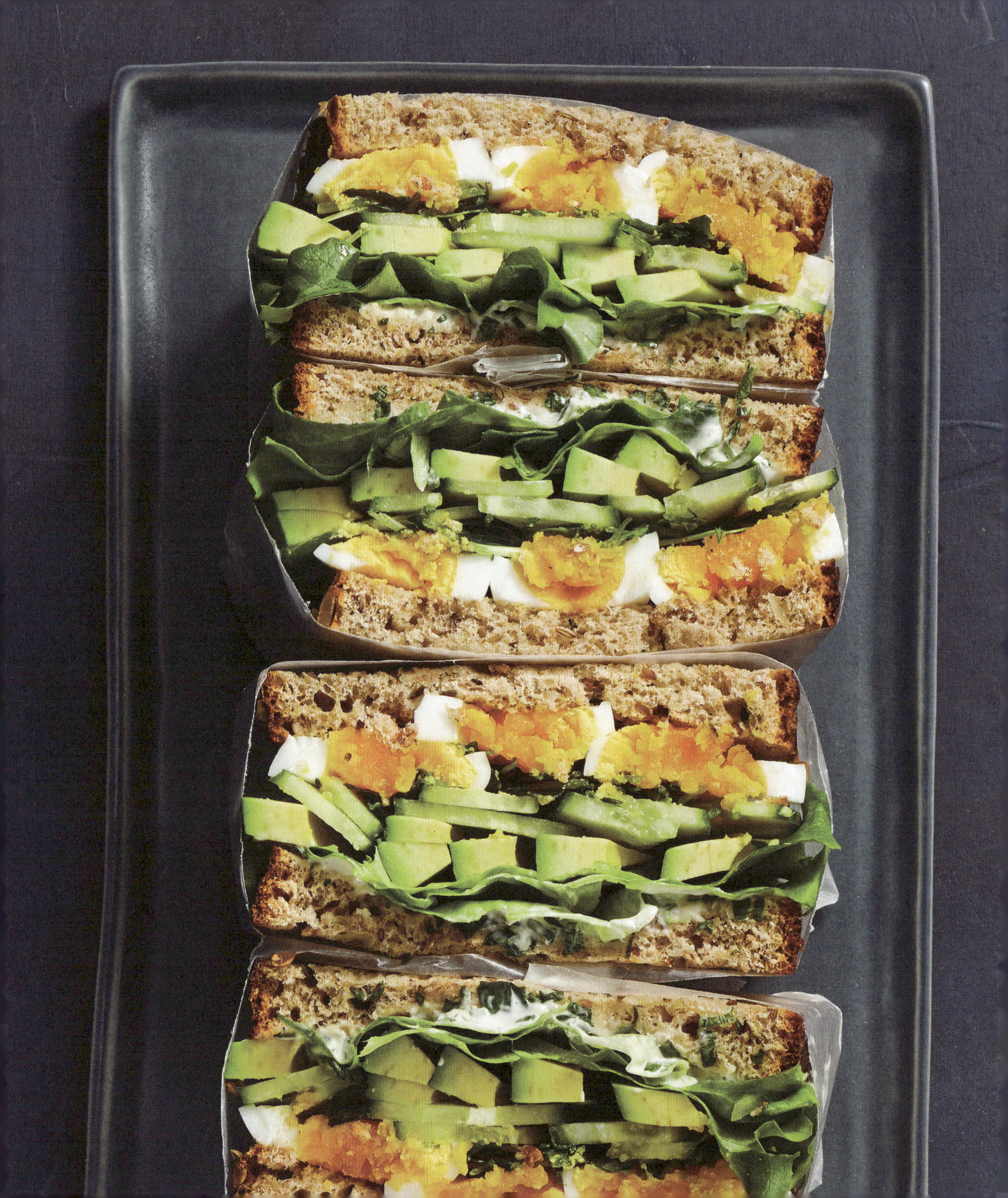

Green Goddess Sandwiches

Serves 4 | Active time 15 minutes | Total time 25 minutes

- 4 large eggs
- Ice water, for cooling
- ⅓ cup mayonnaise
- ½ tablespoon lemon juice
- ½ small clove garlic, finely grated
- Kosher salt and pepper
- ¼ cup basil, chopped
- 2 tablespoons chopped chives
- 8 slices whole-grain bread
- 2 cups salad greens or favorite lettuce
- 1 avocado, sliced
- ½ seedless cucumber, halved crosswise and thinly sliced lengthwise
- 1 cup sprouts

Inspired by green goddess dressing, this dinner-worthy stack stars a creamy basil mayo. Start by prepping the eggs in your air fryer (it's so easy!), or skip that step if you already have a stash of hard-boiled eggs in the fridge.

1. Heat an air fryer to 275°F. Place the eggs in the air-fryer basket and air-fry for 15 minutes. Immediately transfer the eggs to a bowl of ice water to cool for a few minutes, then peel and slice the eggs.

2. Meanwhile, in a small bowl, combine the mayo, lemon juice and garlic and ¼ teaspoon each of salt and pepper; fold in the basil and chives.

3. Spread the basil mayo on the bread, then create sandwiches with the lettuce, avocado, cucumber, sprouts and eggs.

GET AHEAD
Whether you air-fry or boil eggs (11 minutes), once they're cooked, transfer them to a bowl of ice water to cool. Refrigerate them in their shells for up to one week. Peel them right before using.

Love Notes

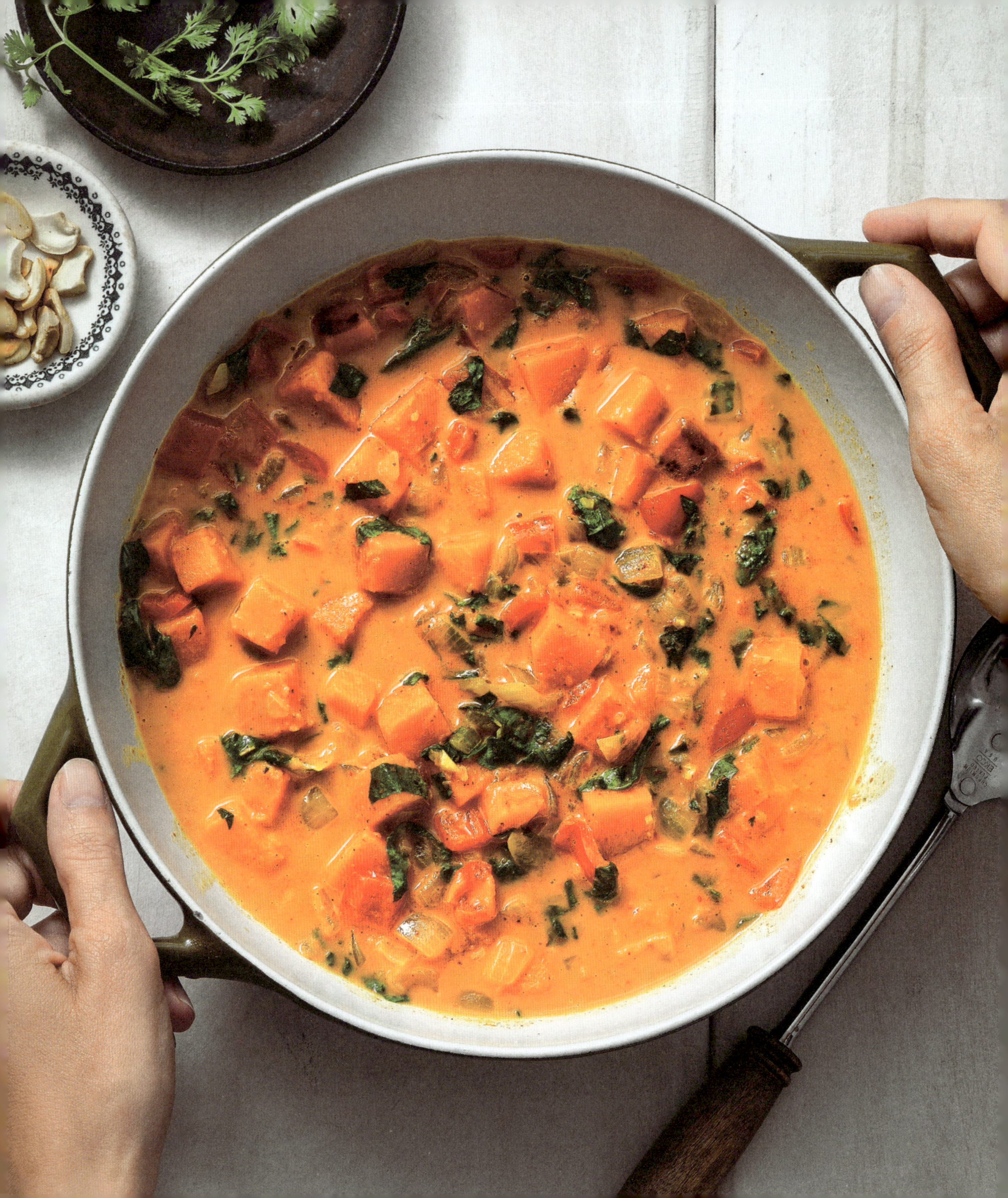

Butternut Squash Curry

Serves 4 | Active time 35 minutes | Total time 45 minutes

Cozy up with a coconut-based curry that tastes as if it has been simmering for hours. Thanks to the combination of fresh ginger, turmeric, jalapeño and mild Thai curry paste, this dish packs maximum flavor but takes just 45 minutes from start to finish.

- 1 cup long-grain white rice
- 3 tablespoons coconut or canola oil, divided
- ½ small butternut squash (about 1 pound), peeled and cut into ½-inch pieces (about 2½ cups)
- 1 onion, chopped
- 2 cloves garlic, finely chopped
- 1 tablespoon grated peeled fresh ginger
- 3 tablespoons yellow Thai curry paste
- 1 13.5-ounce can light coconut milk
- 1 jalapeño, halved
- ½ teaspoon ground turmeric
- 1 red pepper, seeded and cut into ½-inch pieces
- 2 tablespoons lime juice, plus lime wedges for serving
- 1 tablespoon soy sauce
- 3 cups baby spinach, chopped
- Chopped cashews and cilantro, for serving

1. Cook the rice per the package directions. Meanwhile, heat 2 tablespoons of the oil in a large skillet (or medium Dutch oven) on medium. Add the squash and cook, tossing occasionally, until the squash is golden brown and beginning to soften, 4 to 6 minutes; transfer to a plate.

2. Add the remaining tablespoon of oil along with the onion to the skillet and cook for 6 minutes. Stir in the garlic and ginger; cook for 2 minutes more. Add the curry paste and cook, stirring, 1 minute.

3. Add the coconut milk, jalapeño and turmeric and bring to a simmer. Add the red pepper and squash and simmer until the squash is just tender, about 15 minutes. Remove from the heat and remove and discard the jalapeño. Stir in the lime juice and soy sauce, then fold in the spinach to wilt. Serve the curry over rice and sprinkle with cashews and cilantro if desired.

Love Notes

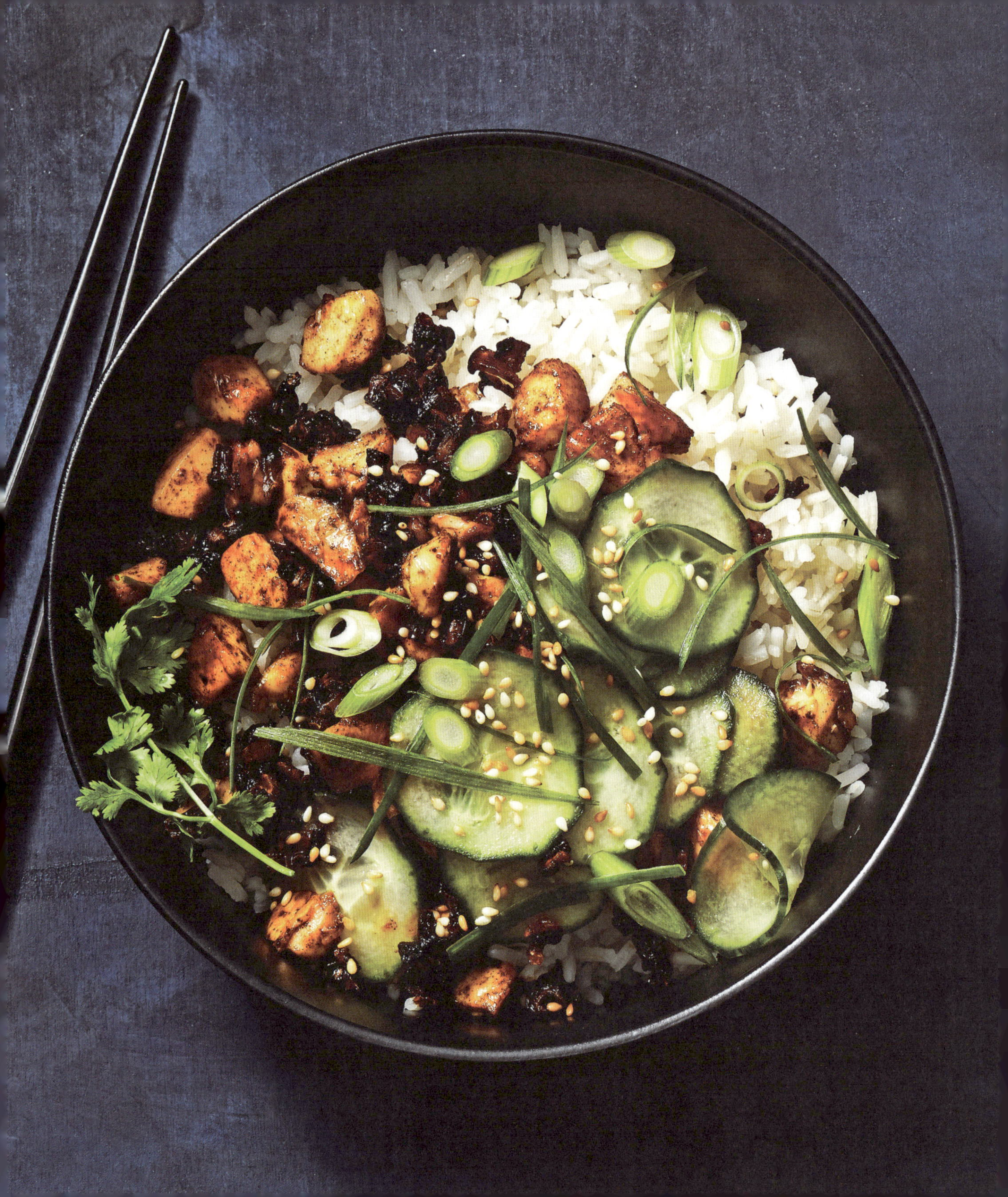

Sticky Tofu Bowl

Serves 4 | Active time 25 minutes | Total time 25 minutes

- 1 cup rice
- 12 ounces extra-firm silken tofu
- 4 tablespoons oil, divided
- 1 teaspoon Chinese five-spice powder
- Kosher salt
- 1 small English cucumber, thinly sliced
- 1½ tablespoons rice vinegar
- 8 ounces shiitake mushrooms, stemmed and cut into ¼-inch pieces
- ¼ cup reduced-sodium soy sauce
- 1 tablespoon dark brown sugar
- 2 teaspoons chili garlic sauce
- Sliced scallions, sesame seeds and cilantro, for serving

The plant-based protein contains all nine essential amino acids and easily absorbs the flavors of this balanced sweet-salty sauce.

1. Heat the oven to 450°F. Cook the rice per the package directions.

2. Gently pat the tofu dry with paper towels. On a rimmed baking sheet, break the tofu into small pieces. Drizzle with 2 tablespoons of the oil, then season with the five-spice powder and ¼ teaspoon of salt and gently toss to combine. Arrange in an even layer on the baking sheet and roast for 10 minutes.

3. Meanwhile, in a bowl, toss the cucumber with the vinegar and ¼ teaspoon of salt. Set aside.

4. In a medium bowl, toss the mushrooms with the remaining 2 tablespoons oil and ¼ teaspoon of salt and scatter over the tofu, then gently mix to combine. Continue roasting until the tofu is golden brown and crisp, 8 to 10 minutes more.

5. In the same bowl, whisk together the soy sauce, sugar and chili garlic sauce. Pour the mixture over the tofu and roast until slightly sticky, 2 minutes.

6. Serve the tofu and mushrooms over the rice along with the cucumber, scallions, sesame seeds and cilantro.

Love Notes

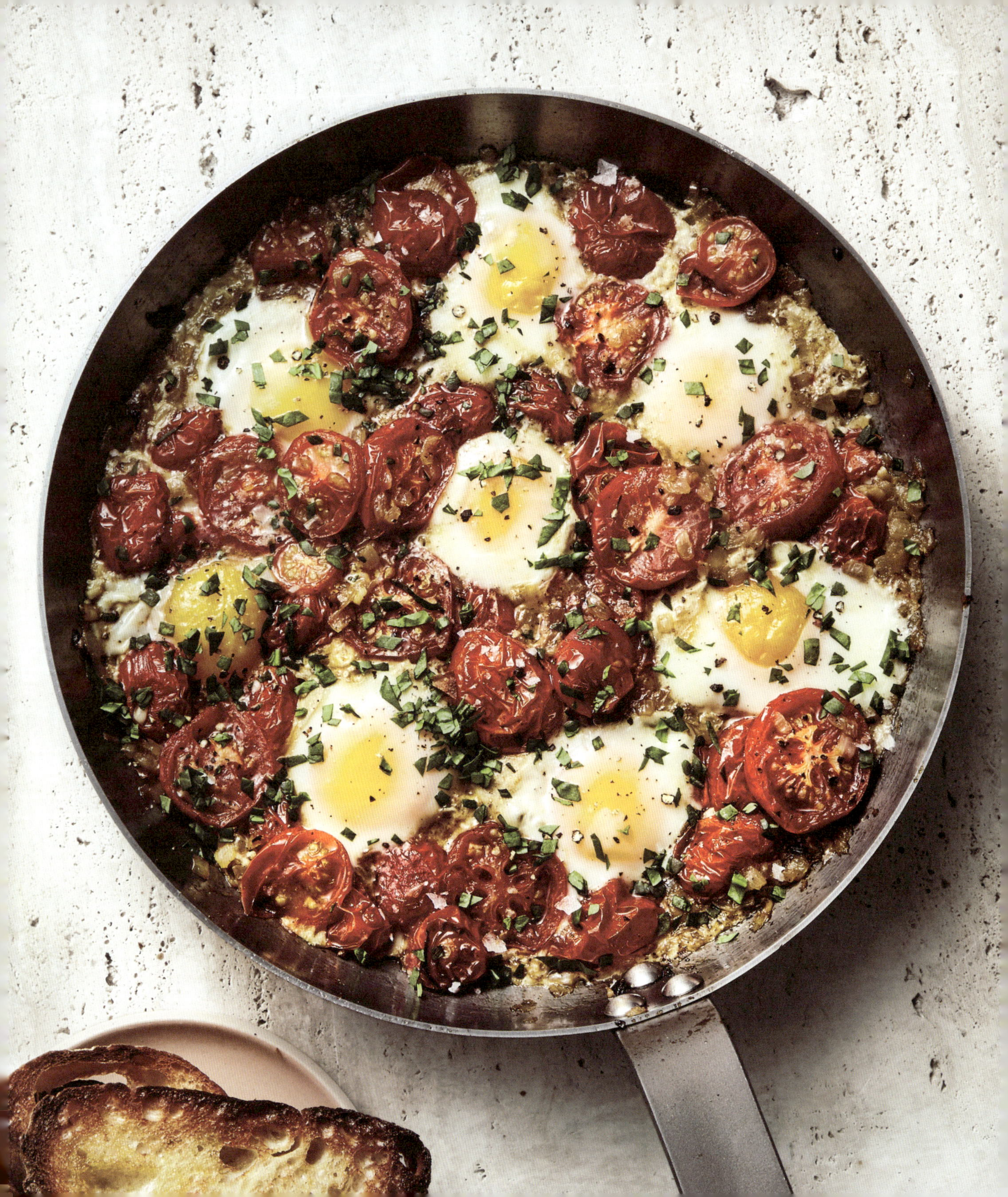

PLANT-POWERED | **WEEKNIGHT**

Shakshuka

Serves 4 | Active time 15 minutes | Total time 35 minutes

- 2 tablespoons olive oil
- 1 yellow onion, finely chopped
- 1 clove garlic, finely chopped
- 1 teaspoon ground cumin
- Kosher salt and pepper
- 1 pound tomatoes, halved if large
- 8 large eggs
- ¼ cup baby spinach, finely chopped
- Toasted baguette, for serving

Delicious at any time of day, this simple one-skillet meal doesn't require many ingredients and can be switched up according to the veggies you have on hand. Don't forget to serve it with crusty bread—perfect for sopping up every last bit.

1. Heat the oven to 400°F. Heat the oil in a large oven-safe skillet on medium. Add the onion and sauté until golden brown and tender, 8 minutes. Stir in the garlic and cumin and ½ teaspoon each of salt and pepper and cook 1 minute.

2. Stir in the tomatoes, transfer to the oven and roast 10 minutes. Stir, then make 8 small wells in the vegetable mixture and carefully crack 1 egg into each. Bake the eggs to desired doneness, 7 to 8 minutes for slightly runny yolks. Sprinkle with the spinach and, if desired, serve with toasted baguette slices.

Love Notes

THE NEWLYWED COOKBOOK

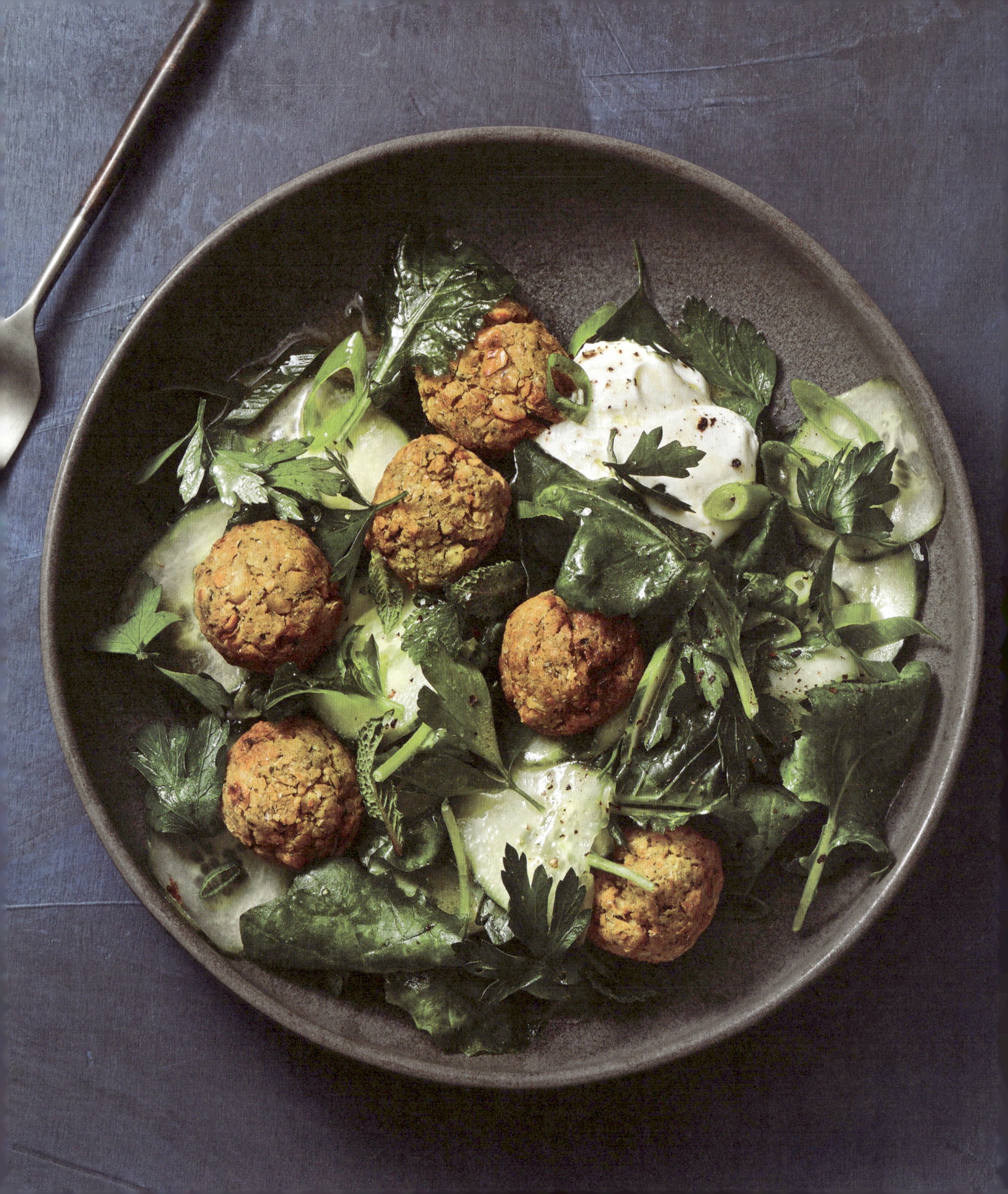

PLANT-POWERED | **WEEKNIGHT**

Air-Fried Falafel Salad

Serves 4 | **Active time 15 minutes** | **Total time 35 minutes**

- 2 cloves garlic
- 4 scallions, whites and greens thinly sliced and separated
- 6½ cups baby kale, divided
- 2 15-ounce cans chickpeas, drained and rinsed
- 1 teaspoon grated lemon zest, plus 2 tablespoons lemon juice
- 2 tablespoons all-purpose flour
- 1 teaspoon ground cumin
- 1 teaspoon ground coriander
- Kosher salt
- 4 tablespoons olive oil, divided, plus more for basket
- ½ English cucumber, thinly sliced on bias
- ½ cup fresh parsley leaves
- ¼ cup fresh mint leaves
- Greek yogurt, for serving

Homemade falafel in half an hour without the hassle of deep-frying? You heard that right! Skip the pita too and serve these crisp falafel balls over a refreshing cucumber-herb salad.

1. In a food processor, pulse the garlic, the scallion whites and ½ cup baby kale until very finely chopped. Add the chickpeas, lemon zest, flour, cumin and coriander and ½ teaspoon of salt and pulse until the mixture is combined and the chickpeas are coarsely chopped. Form the mixture into 24 two-tablespoon balls.

2. Heat an air fryer to 325°F. Brush the insert or basket with oil and add 12 falafel balls. Air-fry for 15 minutes. Brush the falafel with 1 tablespoon of the oil and increase the air-fryer temperature to 400°F. Air-fry until deeply golden, 4 minutes more. Repeat with the remaining falafel.

3. In a large bowl, whisk together the lemon juice and the remaining 2 tablespoons of olive oil. Add the cucumbers and let marinate for 5 minutes. Toss with the remaining 6 cups of baby kale; the parsley, mint leaves and scallion greens; and ½ teaspoon salt. Top with the falafel and a dollop of yogurt.

Love Notes

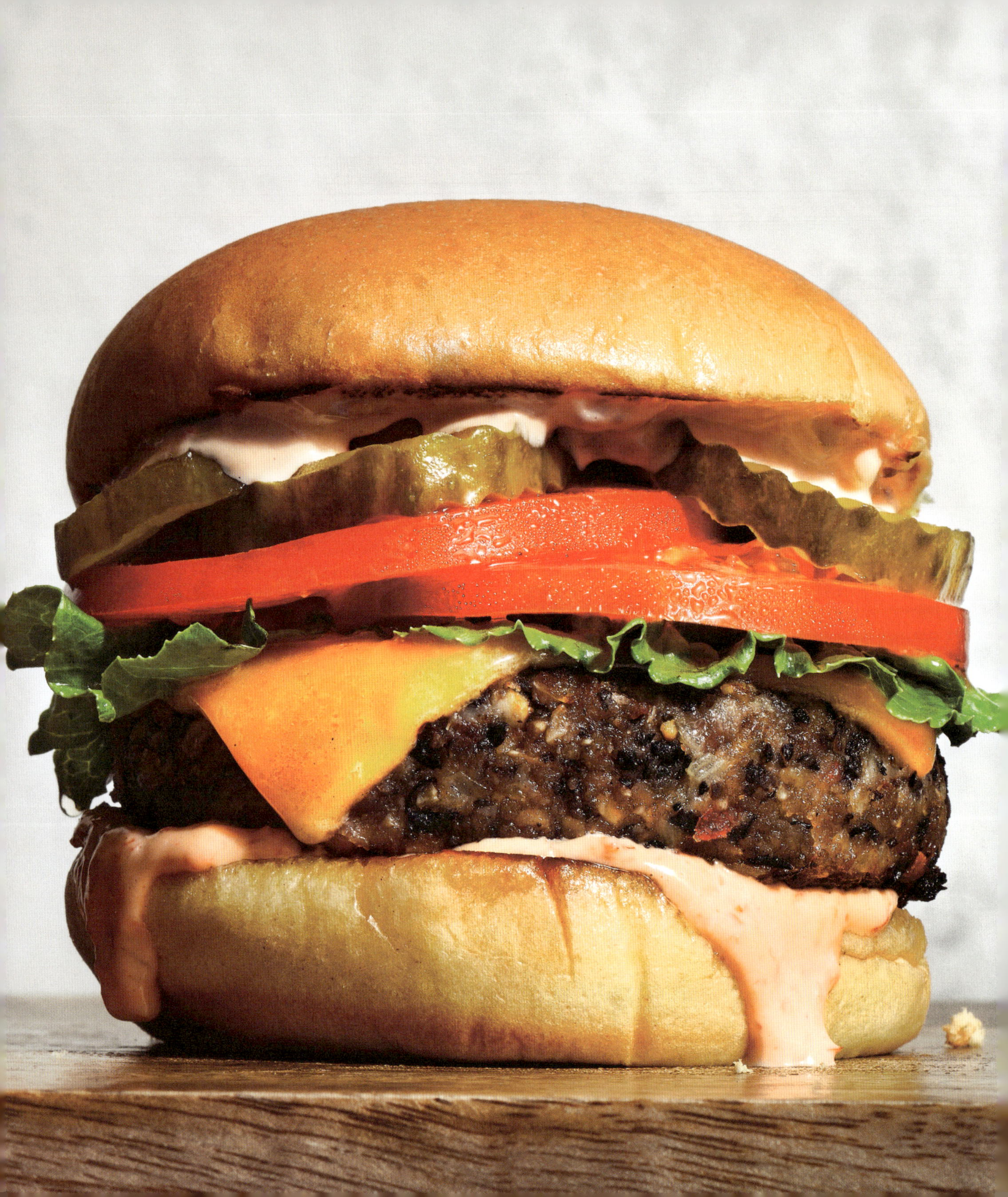

PLANT-POWERED | **WEEKNIGHT**

Black Bean Burgers

Serves 4 | Active time 1 hour | Total time 1 hour, plus chilling

- 2 15.5-ounce cans black beans, rinsed and patted dry
- 1 tablespoon olive oil, plus more for brushing
- 1 medium onion, chopped
- ¾ cup raw cashews
- Kosher salt and pepper
- 3 cloves garlic, finely chopped
- 2 tablespoons plus 2 teaspoons sambal oelek, divided
- 1 ounce whole-milk mozzarella, shredded (¼ cup)
- 1 large egg, beaten
- ¾ cup panko
- ½ cup plus 2 tablespoons mayonnaise, divided
- 8 potato rolls, split
- Sliced Cheddar cheese, tomatoes, pickles and lettuce leaves, for serving

Loaded with roasted black beans, cashews, sambal and a handful of shredded mozz, these patties boast intense savory flavor in each bite — and best of all, they can be made in advance and frozen, then later grilled.

1. Heat the oven to 350°F. Place the black beans in a single layer on a large rimmed baking sheet and bake until the beans are dry and mostly split open, 20 to 22 minutes.

2. Meanwhile, heat the oil in a large skillet on medium. Add the onion and the cashews and ¼ teaspoon each of salt and pepper and cook, stirring occasionally, until the onion is just tender, 5 to 6 minutes. Stir in the garlic and cook 1 minute. Add 2 tablespoons of sambal and cook, stirring, until fragrant, about 30 seconds. Remove from the heat and let cool 5 minutes.

3. Transfer the cashew-onion mixture to a food processor and pulse until the nuts are finely chopped. Add the beans and pulse until finely chopped. Transfer the mixture to a large bowl; add mozzarella, egg, panko, 2 tablespoons of mayo and ¼ teaspoon each of salt and pepper; gently fold the mixture until it is combined and holds together.

4. Form the mixture into eight ½-inch-thick patties (about 3.5 ounces each) and place on a parchment-lined baking sheet. Freeze until firm, 1 to 2 hours.

5. When ready to cook, heat the grill to medium. In a small bowl, stir together the remaining ½ cup of mayo and 2 teaspoons of sambal. Using 1 tablespoon of oil, brush both sides of the burgers and grill, covered, until cooked through and grill marks appear, 3 to 5 minutes per side, topping with the cheese during the last minute of cooking if desired. Grill the buns if desired and spread with the sambal mayo, then fill with patties, lettuce, tomatoes and pickles if desired.

Love Notes

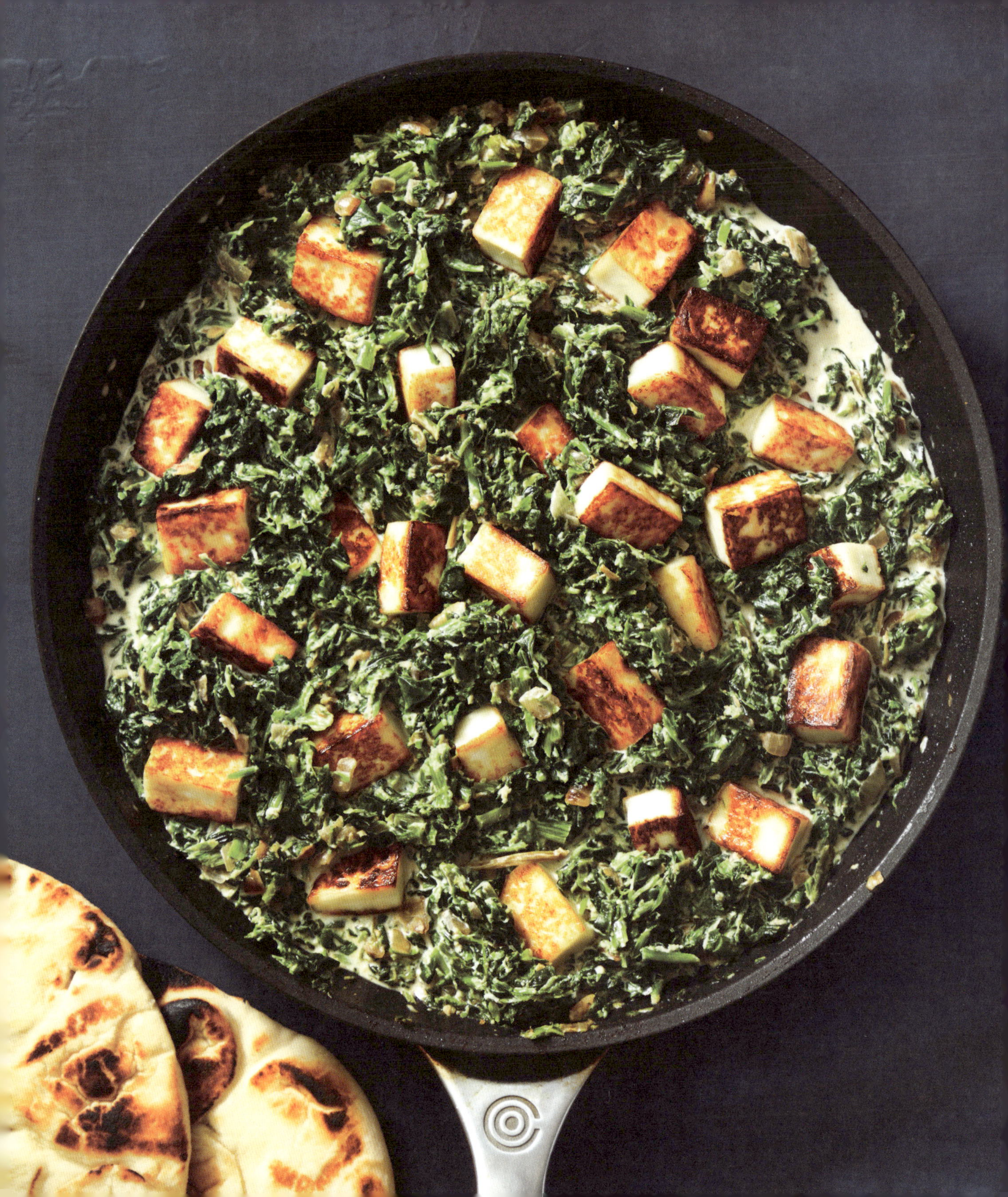

PLANT-POWERED | **WEEKNIGHT**

Palak Paneer

Serves 4 | Active time 30 minutes | Total time 30 minutes

- 1 cup basmati rice
- 3 tablespoons canola oil, divided
- 12 ounces paneer, cut into ¾-inch pieces
- 1½ teaspoons garam masala, divided
- 1¾ teaspoons ground coriander, divided
- Kosher salt and pepper
- 1 large onion, chopped
- 1 tablespoon finely grated fresh ginger
- 2 large cloves garlic, finely grated
- ½ serrano chile, seeded and finely chopped
- 1 teaspoon ground cumin
- 1 teaspoon vegetable bouillon base (we used Better Than Bouillon)
- 2 16-ounce packages frozen chopped spinach, thawed and squeezed of excess liquid
- 1 cup heavy cream
- Warm naan, for serving

While saag paneer uses a mix of leafy greens (like spinach, mustard greens and fenugreek, among others), palak paneer is made with just spinach. Here we use frozen chopped spinach to cut down on prep time and cost without skimping on flavor. Don't forget the rice and naan!

1. Cook the rice per the package directions. Heat 1 tablespoon of oil in a large nonstick skillet on medium. In a large bowl, toss the paneer with 1 tablespoon of oil, ½ teaspoon of garam masala, ¼ teaspoon of ground coriander and ¼ teaspoon of salt. Add the paneer and cook undisturbed until golden brown on the bottom, 2 to 4 minutes. Toss, then continue to cook until golden brown on the other side, 2 to 3 minutes more. Transfer the paneer to a plate.

2. Add 1 tablespoon of oil to the skillet and heat on medium. Add the onion and ¼ teaspoon each of salt and pepper and cook, covered, stirring occasionally, until beginning to soften, 5 minutes. Add the ginger, garlic and serrano and cook, stirring, 1 minute. Add the remaining 1½ teaspoons of ground coriander and teaspoon of garam masala and the ground cumin and cook, stirring, 1 minute more.

3. Whisk the vegetable bouillon base into 1 cup of warm water and add to a skillet along with spinach and ¼ teaspoon salt. Cover and cook, stirring occasionally, until the spinach is very soft, 6 minutes. Remove from the heat, then stir in the heavy cream until incorporated. Fold in the paneer. Serve with the rice and naan.

Love Notes

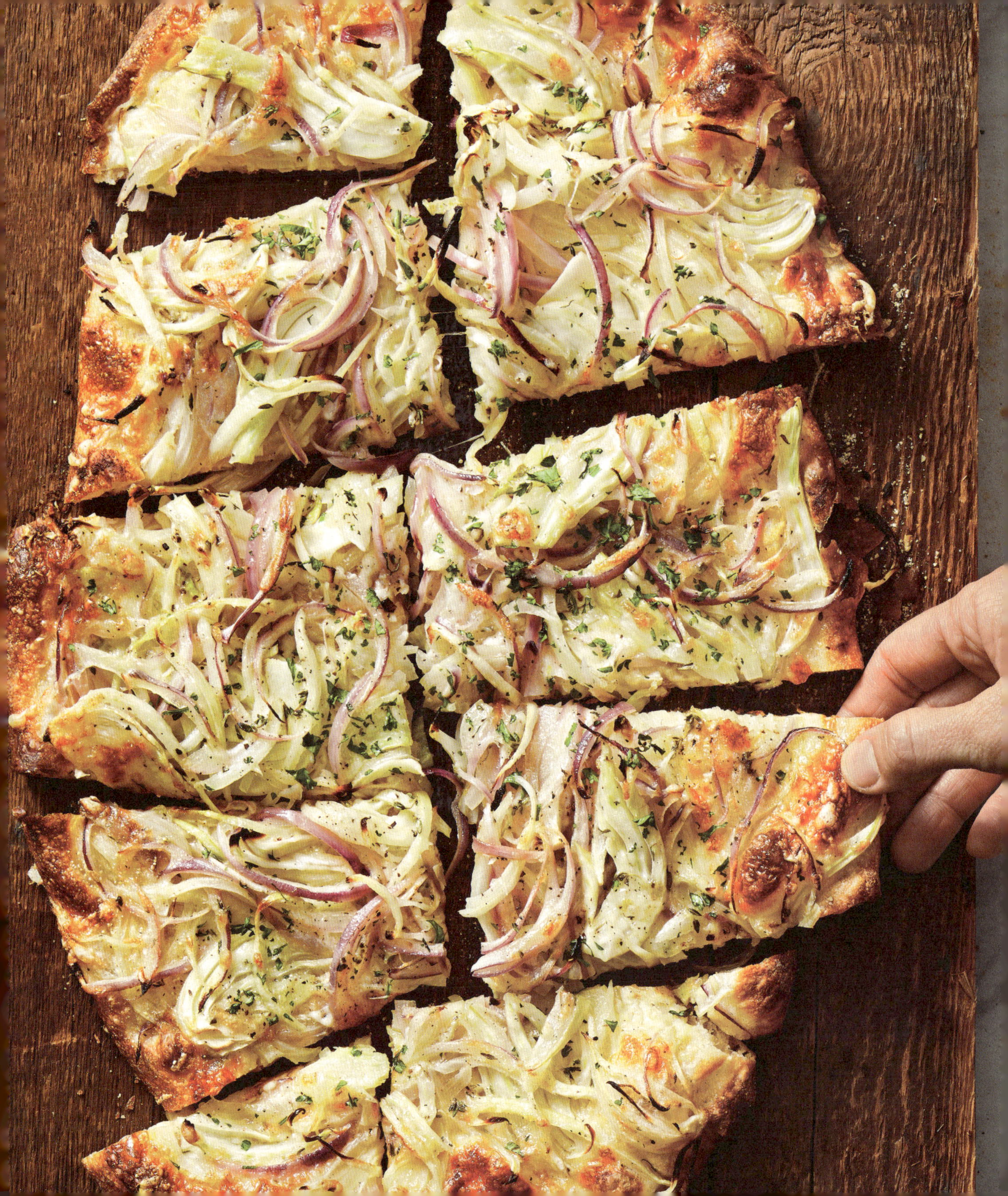

Onion Flatbread

Serves 4 to 6 | **Active time 15 minutes** | **Total time 30 minutes**

Flour, for surface

1 pound pizza dough, at room temperature

Cornmeal, for baking sheet

1½ tablespoons Dijon mustard

4 ounces thinly sliced provolone cheese

1 small yellow onion, thinly sliced

1 small red onion, thinly sliced

1 small bulb fennel, cored and thinly sliced

2 teaspoons fresh thyme leaves

1½ tablespoons olive oil

Kosher salt and pepper

2 ounces fontina cheese, coarsely grated

Finely chopped flat-leaf parsley, for serving

Store-bought pizza dough provides the start to so many simple dinners that go beyond your average cheese pie—like this flatbread featuring fennel and onions that sweeten up as they roast.

1. Heat the oven to 500°F (if you can't heat the oven this high without broiling, heat it to 475°F).

2. On a lightly floured surface, shape the pizza dough into a 14-inch oval. Place on a cornmeal-dusted or parchment-lined baking sheet. Spread with the mustard, then top with the provolone.

3. In a large bowl, toss the onions, fennel, thyme and oil and ½ teaspoon each of salt and pepper; fold in the fontina. Scatter onion mixture over the dough and bake until the crust is golden brown and the vegetables are just tender, 10 to 12 minutes. Sprinkle with the parsley before serving.

Love Notes

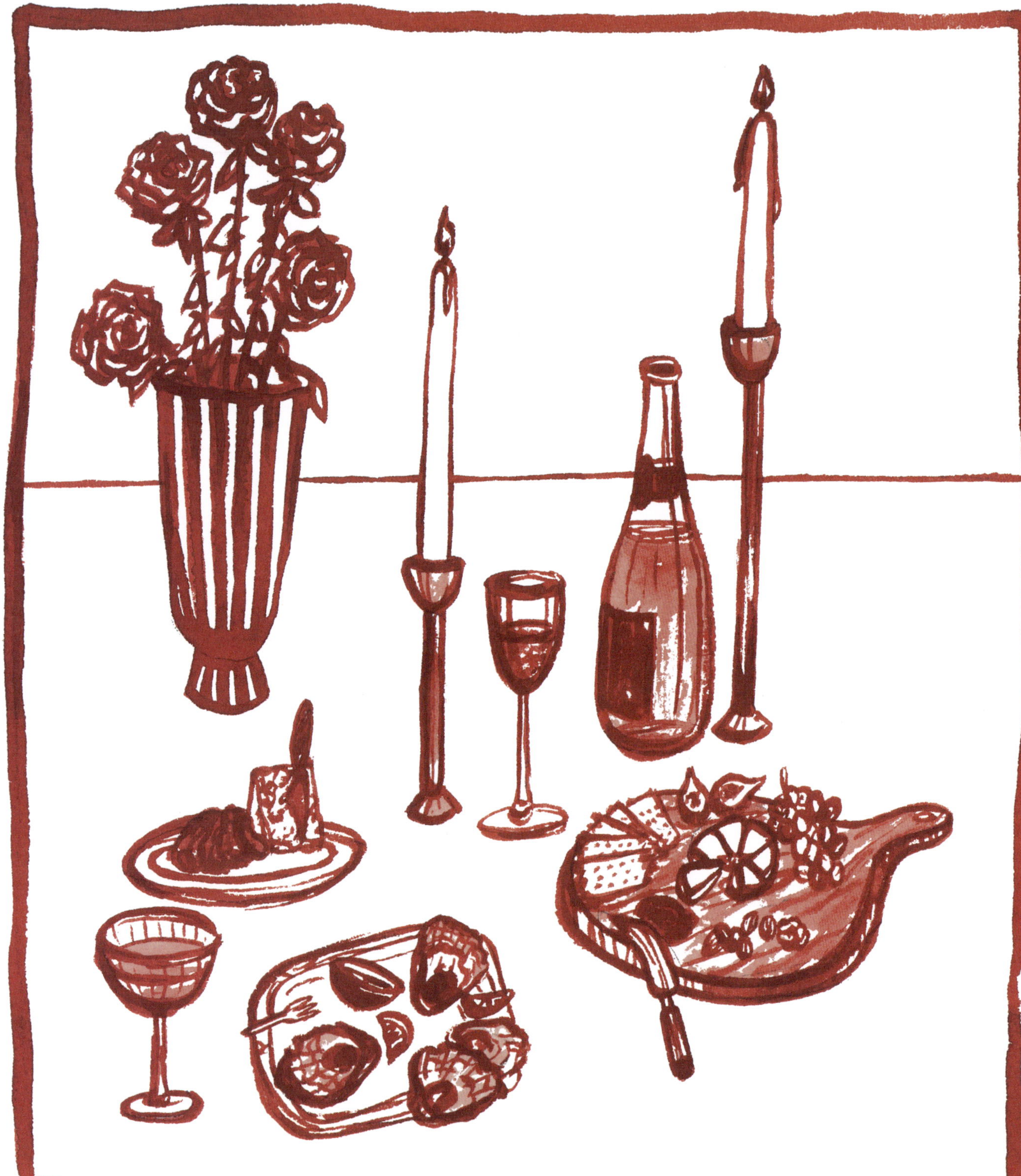

PART 3

Easy Entertaining

Your marriage will be full of fun reasons to gather around the table—date nights in, low-key hangouts, fancy dinner parties, family gatherings, you name it. These easy-to-pull-off menus will help you turn any celebration into something truly special (and delicious!).

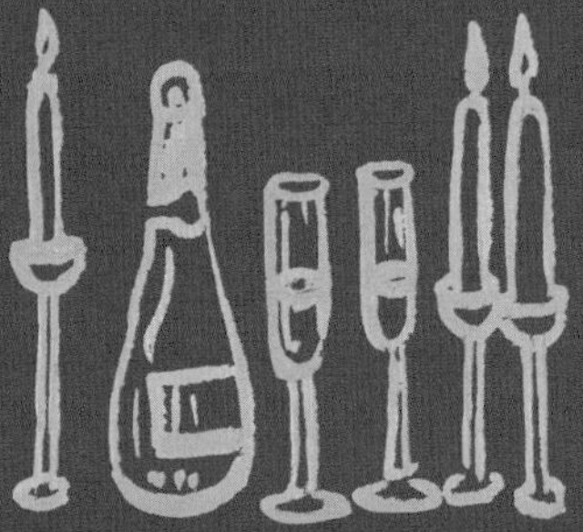

Date Night In

141 Steak au Poivre with Rosemary Roasted Carrot Salad

143 Shrimp Scampi

145 Sautéed Mushrooms & Creamy Polenta

147 Tomato-Poached Cod with Olives & Capers

149 Roasted Pork Chops & Pears

151 Smoky Mussels Pomodoro

153 You Married Me Chicken

155 Ice Cream Float

157 Crispy Tortilla Bowls with Strawberries & Cream

159 Peanut Butter Molten Chocolate Cakes

161 Tiramisu Dip

Game Day

163 Skillet Cheeseburger Hot Dish

165 Sheet Pan Chicken Suizas Nachos

167 Queso Fundito with Roasted Mushrooms

169 Spiced Snack Mix

171 Buffalo Chicken Pizza

173 Creamy Cannoli Dip

VIP Dinner Party

175 Creamy Cauliflower Soup with Almond-Thyme Gremolata

177 Shaved Fennel & Celery Salad

179 Short Ribs with Creamy Polenta

181 Chicken à l'Orange

183 Lemon & Thyme Pear Tart with Apricot Glaze

Brunch for a Bunch

185 Sheet Pan Asparagus Frittata

187 Tomato & Scallion Cream Cheese Bagel Bake

189 Sriracha-Maple Bacon

191 Best Ever Granola

193 Raisin-Walnut Coffee Cake

Fire Up the Grill

195 Steak & Grilled Peppers with Chimichurri

197 Grilled Sweet Potatoes with Mint-Chile Relish

199 Double Mustard–Marinated Chicken Drumsticks

201 Grilled Halloumi Salad

203 Arayes

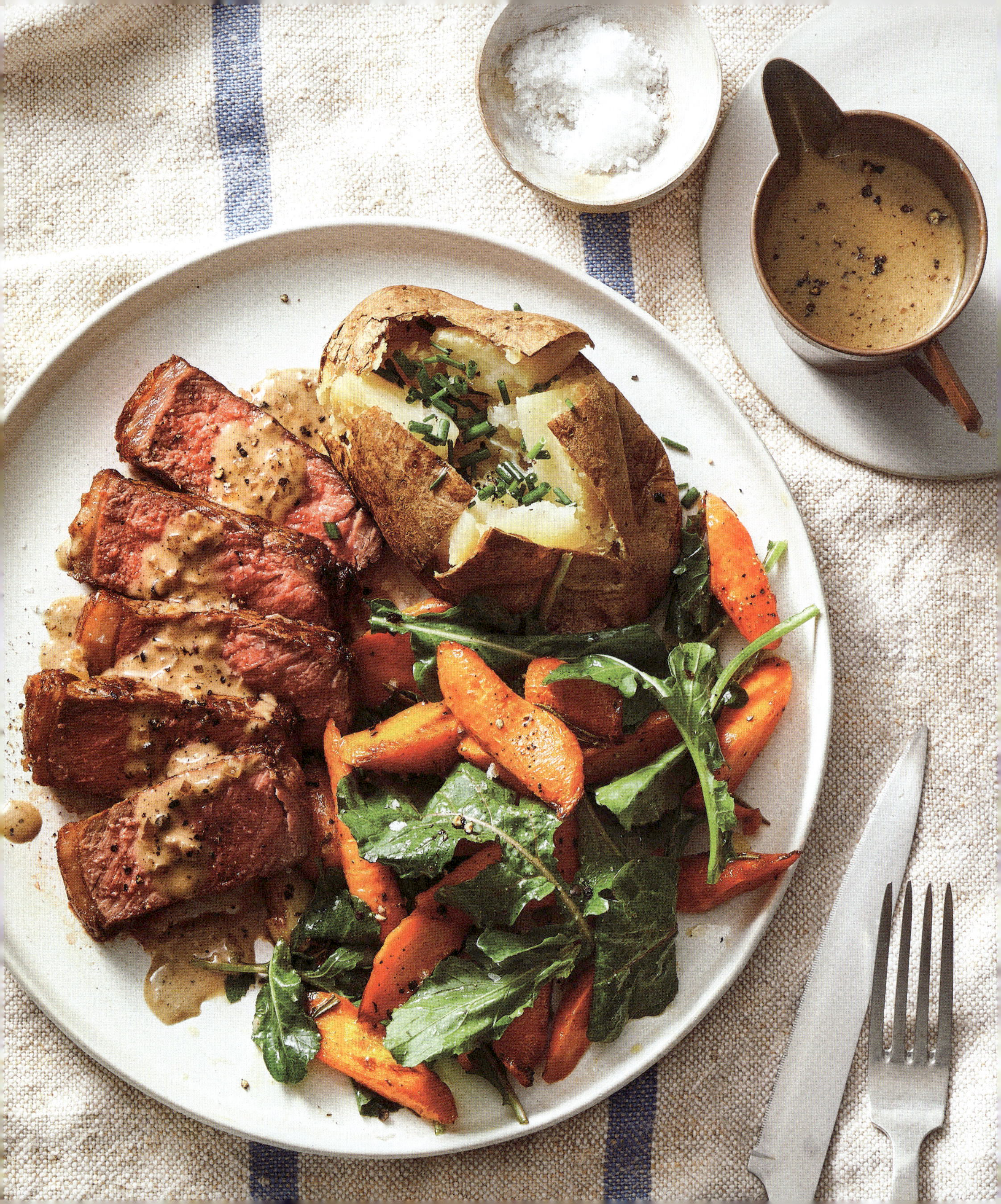

DATE NIGHT IN | **ENTERTAINING**

Steak au Poivre with Rosemary Roasted Carrot Salad

Serves 2 | **Active time 35 minutes** | **Total time 40 minutes**

Enjoy a fancy steakhouse dinner in the comfort of your own home. To crush peppercorns, use a pepper mill on the coarse setting or a mortar and pestle.

1. Make the salad: Heat the oven to 425°F. On a rimmed baking sheet, toss the carrots, garlic and rosemary with 1 tablespoon of oil, then ½ teaspoon each of salt and pepper. Arrange in a single layer; add the lemon, cut side down, to 1 corner; and roast until the carrots are just tender, 15 to 20 minutes. Let cool on the pan 10 minutes.

2. Make the steak: Heat the oil in a large skillet on medium-high. Season the steak with ½ teaspoon of salt and crushed peppercorns. Cook until well browned on each side, about 4 minutes. Transfer to a rimmed baking sheet and roast in the oven along with the carrots until an instant-read thermometer registers 125°F for medium-rare, 12 to 15 minutes. Transfer to a cutting board and let rest at least 5 minutes before slicing.

3. Meanwhile, pour off any fat from the skillet. Add the butter, the shallot and any peppercorns left over from seasoning and sauté on medium until tender, about 2 minutes. Add the cognac and cook, stirring, 1 minute, until reduced. Add the chicken broth and simmer 1 minute. Whisk in the crème fraîche and the mustard and simmer until slightly thickened, 5 to 6 minutes. Season with salt if desired.

4. Squeeze 1 tablespoon of roasted lemon juice into a large bowl. Stir in the remaining 2 teaspoons oil and a pinch each of salt and pepper. Toss with the arugula and then the carrots. Serve the sliced steak with carrot salad and baked potatoes, if desired, then spoon sauce over the steak.

FOR ROSEMARY ROASTED CARROT SALAD

- 12 ounces carrots (about 5 medium), cut into pieces
- 2 cloves garlic, smashed and peeled
- 1 tablespoon fresh rosemary, chopped
- 1 tablespoon plus 2 teaspoons olive oil, divided
- Kosher salt and pepper
- ½ lemon
- 1 small bunch arugula, thick stems discarded
- Baked potatoes, for serving, if desired

FOR STEAK AU POIVRE

- 1 tablespoon olive oil
- 1 12-ounce strip steak (about 1½ inches thick)
- Kosher salt
- 1 tablespoon black peppercorns, coarsely crushed
- 1 tablespoon unsalted butter
- 1 large shallot, finely chopped
- 2 tablespoons cognac
- ⅓ cup low-sodium chicken broth
- ½ cup crème fraîche
- 1 teaspoon Dijon mustard

Love Notes

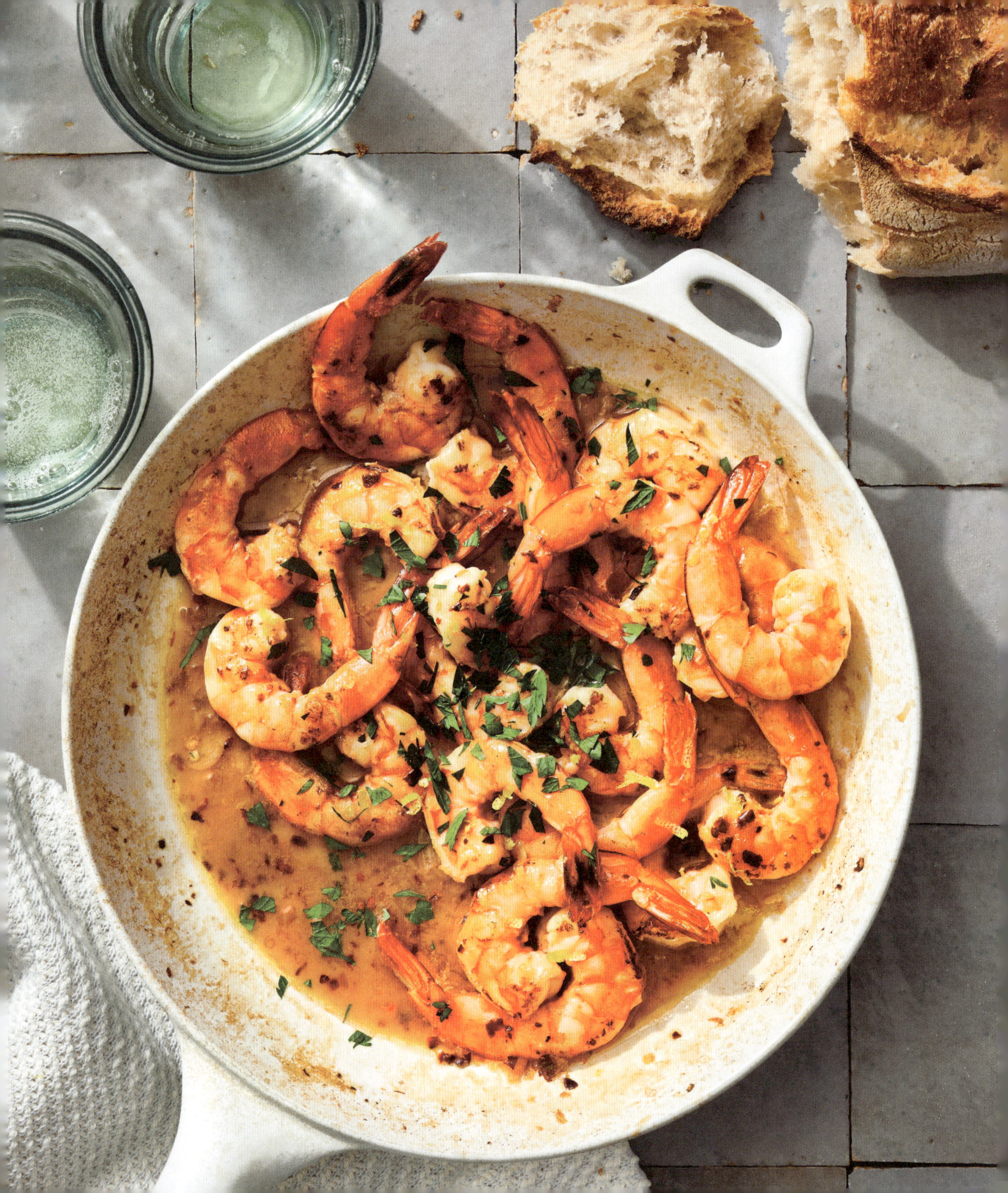

Shrimp Scampi

Serves 2 | Active time 30 minutes | Total time 30 minutes

- ¾ pound medium peeled and deveined shrimp (38 to 40)
- Kosher salt and pepper
- 2 tablespoons olive oil, divided
- 2 tablespoons unsalted butter, divided
- 1 shallot, finely chopped
- ¼ teaspoon red pepper flakes
- 2 large cloves garlic, thinly sliced
- ¾ cup dry white wine
- 1 teaspoon lemon zest, plus 2 tablespoons lemon juice
- 2 tablespoons flat-leaf parsley, chopped
- ½ baguette or small country bread, warmed

Fact: Juicy shrimp love a buttery, garlicky white wine sauce—even more so when it's brightened with lemon and a sprinkle of red pepper flakes. Serve this dish with crusty bread to soak up every last bit of sauce and a glass of crisp white wine.

1. Pat the shrimp dry, then toss in a bowl with ¼ teaspoon of salt. Heat 1 tablespoon of oil in a large skillet on medium-high. Add the shrimp and cook 2 minutes, then flip and cook 1 minute. Transfer to a plate (the shrimp will finish cooking later).

2. Reduce the heat to medium and add 1 tablespoon of butter and the remaining tablespoon of oil, then add the shallot and the red pepper flakes and cook, stirring, 1 minute. Add the garlic and cook, stirring, until golden brown, 1 to 2 minutes.

3. Add the wine and simmer, scraping up any browned bits, until reduced by half, 3 to 4 minutes. Stir in the lemon zest and juice, ⅛ teaspoon each salt and pepper and the remaining tablespoon of butter and simmer until slightly reduced, 1 to 2 minutes.

4. Return the shrimp to the skillet and cook until heated through, 1 minute. Sprinkle with parsley and serve immediately with crusty bread.

PASTA NIGHT
Cook linguine per package directions, then drain and transfer to a large bowl and toss with 2 tablespoons of lemon juice. Set aside. When ready to serve, top pasta with shrimp and drizzle on pan juices.

Love Notes

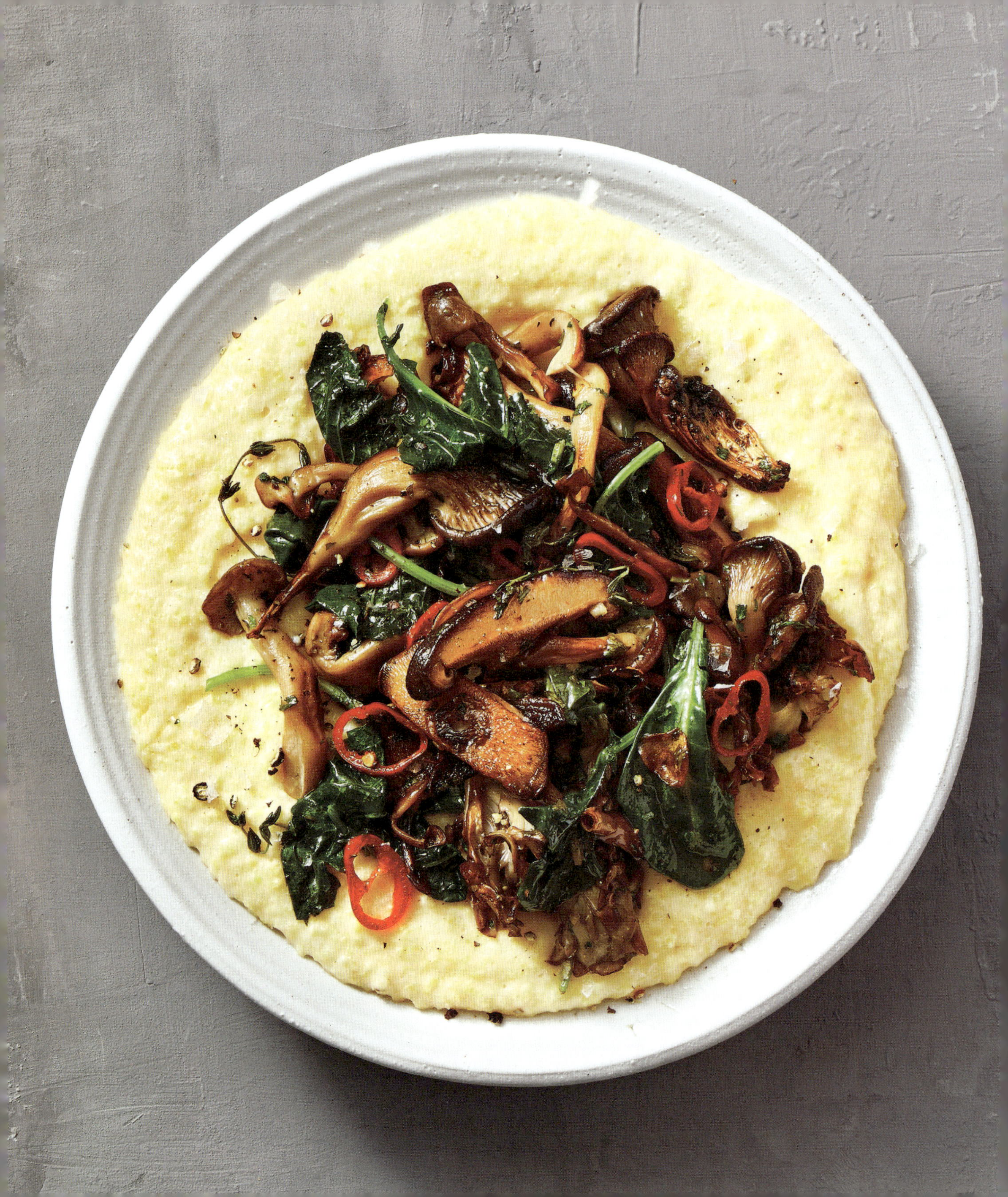

Sautéed Mushrooms & Creamy Polenta

Serves 2 | Active time 30 minutes | Total time 30 minutes

- 1½ tablespoons olive oil
- 12 ounces mixed mushrooms (such as oyster, shiitake, maitake, beech, cremini), torn, quartered or sliced
- 1 clove garlic, finely chopped
- ½ red chile, thinly sliced
- Kosher salt and pepper
- 1 cup whole milk
- 1 tablespoon unsalted butter
- 2 ounces instant polenta (about heaping ⅓ cup)
- 2 tablespoons finely grated Pecorino Romano cheese
- 2 tablespoons finely grated Parmesan cheese, plus more for serving
- 1 teaspoon red wine vinegar
- 2 tablespoons flat-leaf parsley, chopped
- 1 cup baby kale

It's always good to have a go-to vegetarian recipe in your back pocket, and this elegant dish is actually really easy to make. Hearty, garlicky mushrooms top ultra-creamy polenta for a big bowl of delicious comfort.

1. Heat the oil in a large skillet on medium-high. Add the mushrooms and cook, tossing occasionally, until golden brown, 6 to 8 minutes. In the last 2 minutes of cooking, add the garlic and chile and ¼ teaspoon each of salt and pepper, tossing to cook; remove from the heat and set aside.

2. Meanwhile, prepare the polenta: In a medium saucepan, bring the milk, the butter and ¼ teaspoon of salt to a boil. Whisk in the polenta. Reduce the heat (the mixture will sputter) and gently simmer, stirring constantly, until the mixture is thick and creamy and pulls away from the sides of the pan, 3 to 4 minutes. Remove from the heat and stir in the cheeses (if the polenta seems too thick, stir in 1 to 3 tablespoons of water).

3. Return the mushrooms to low heat, add the vinegar and toss to combine, then toss with the parsley. Add the kale and cook, tossing until just wilted, 1 minute. Serve the mushrooms and kale over the polenta with additional Parmesan if desired.

Love Notes

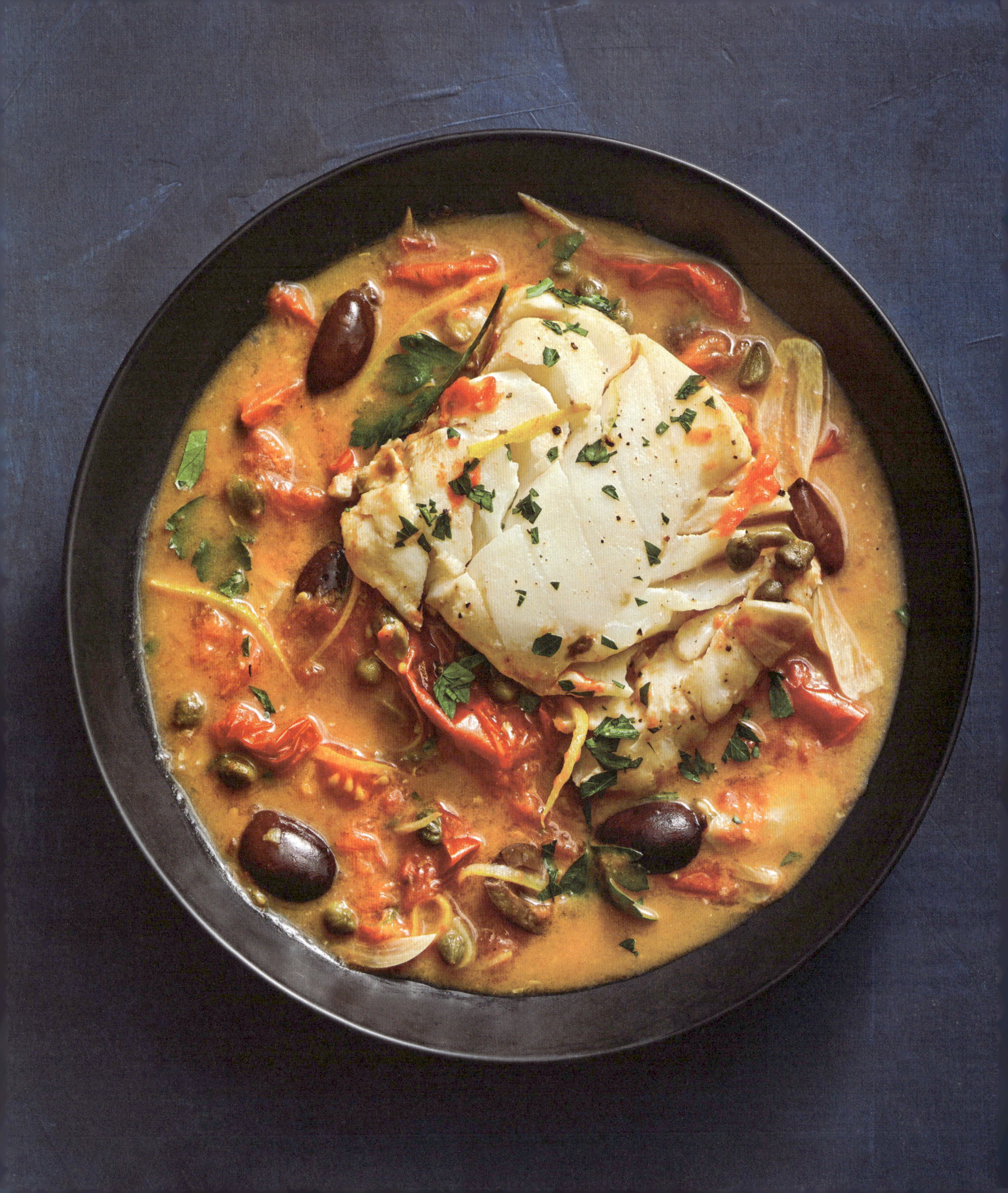

DATE NIGHT IN | **ENTERTAINING**

Tomato-Poached Cod with Olives & Capers

Serves 2 | Active time 10 minutes | Total time 20 minutes

This light one-skillet dish features flaky poached cod simmered with just a bit of rosé, which means you and your date get to enjoy the rest of the bottle with your meal. Cheers!

1. In a medium skillet on medium, heat the oil, garlic, capers and lemon zest, stirring occasionally, until the garlic is lightly golden brown, about 2 minutes.

2. Add the wine and simmer 2 minutes. Stir in the tomatoes, the olives and ¼ teaspoon each of salt and pepper.

3. Nestle the fish in the tomatoes and simmer, covering the skillet during the last 3 minutes of cooking, until the cod is opaque throughout, 6 to 8 minutes. Sprinkle with the parsley just before serving if desired.

- 2 tablespoons olive oil
- 1 clove garlic, thinly sliced
- ½ tablespoon capers, rinsed
- 1 small strip lemon zest, thinly sliced
- ½ cup dry rosé (preferably from Southern France or Italy)
- 6 ounces Campari tomatoes, quartered
- 2 tablespoons pitted kalamata olives, halved
- Kosher salt and pepper
- 2 6-ounce skinless cod fillets
- Chopped parsley, for serving

Love Notes

THE NEWLYWED COOKBOOK **147**

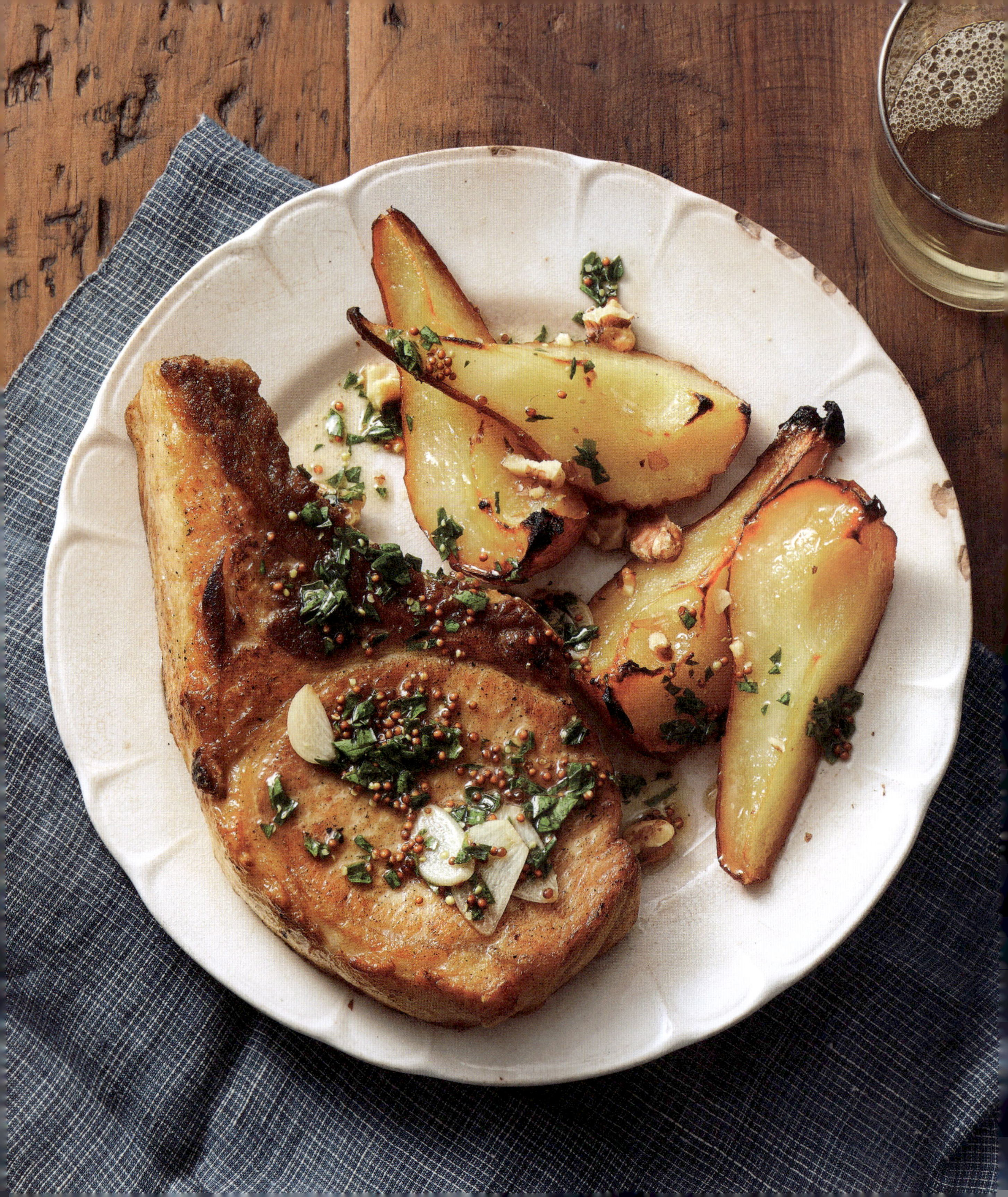

Roasted Pork Chops & Pears

Serves 2 | Active time 20 minutes | Total time 30 minutes

- 2 Bosc pears, cored and quartered
- 1½ tablespoons olive oil, divided
- Kosher salt and pepper
- 2 small bone-in rib pork chops
- 1 tablespoon maple syrup
- 1 clove garlic, sliced
- ⅓ cup dry white wine
- ½ tablespoon whole-grain mustard
- ¼ cup flat-leaf parsley, chopped
- ¼ cup walnuts, toasted
- Sautéed kale, for serving

Deciding on a date night in doesn't mean sacrificing a special meal. Wow your significant other by tucking pork chops in between maple-sweetened pears, then roasting the whole thing and topping it off with walnuts and herbs.

1. Heat the oven to 425°F. On a large rimmed baking sheet, toss the pears with 1 tablespoon of oil and a pinch each of salt and pepper and roast 10 minutes.

2. Meanwhile, heat the remaining ½ tablespoon of oil in a medium skillet on medium-high. Season the pork chops with ¼ teaspoon each of salt and pepper and cook until golden brown, 2 to 3 minutes per side.

3. Toss the pears with the syrup, then transfer the chops to a baking sheet, nestling them among the pears, and roast until the chops are just cooked through and the pears are golden brown and tender, 5 to 6 minutes more.

4. While the pears and the pork are roasting, return a skillet to medium heat. Add the garlic and cook, stirring, 1 minute. Add the wine and simmer 2 minutes, then remove from the heat and stir in the mustard, then the parsley.

5. Transfer the pork to plates and toss the pears with the walnuts. Serve with the pork chops and spoon the pan sauce over the top. Serve with the sautéed kale if desired.

A CUT ABOVE
Bone-in pork chops are often juicier and more flavorful than their boneless counterparts, which can be prone to drying out when cooked at high temps.

Love Notes

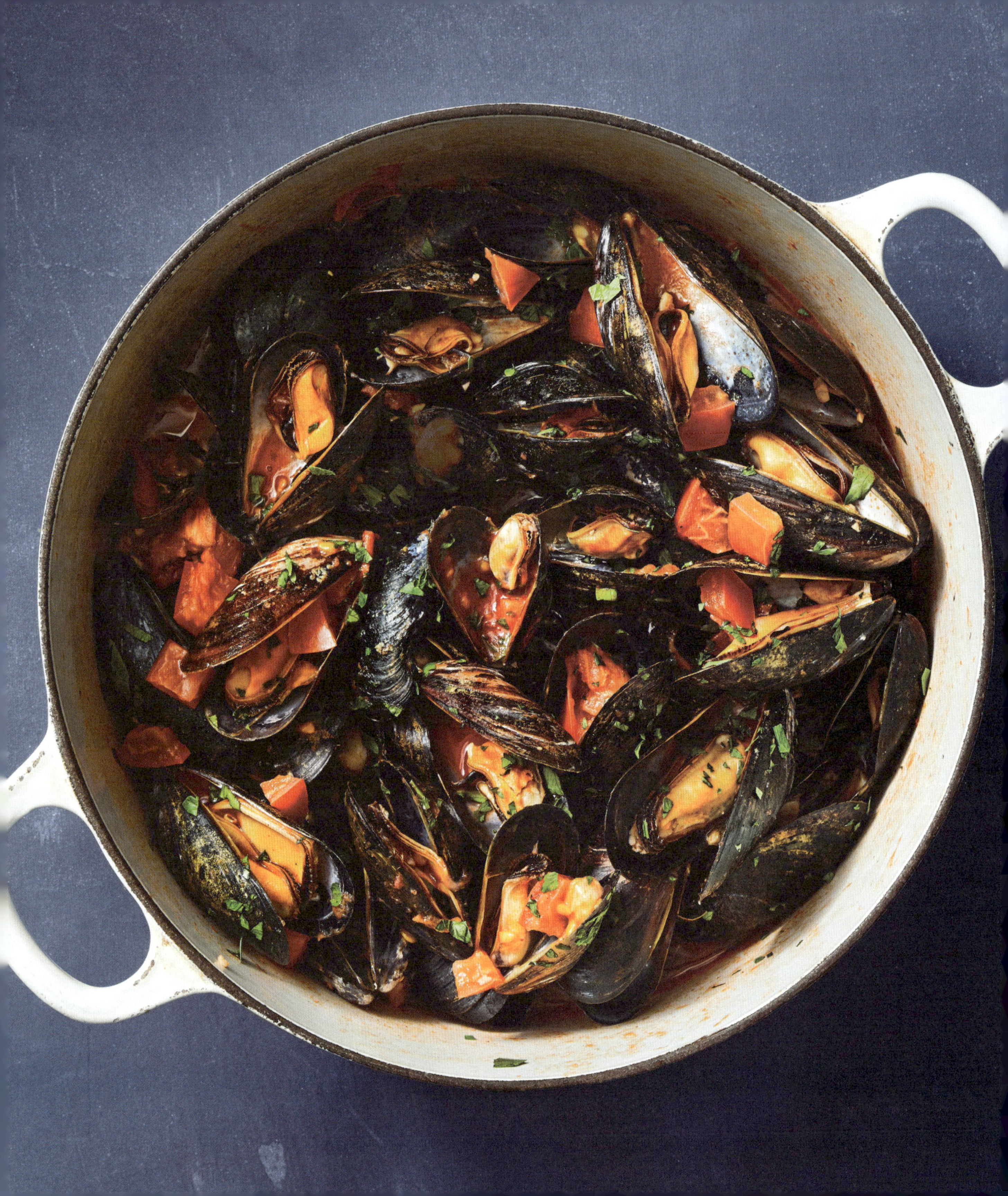

DATE NIGHT IN | **ENTERTAINING**

Smoky Mussels Pomodoro

- 2 tablespoons olive oil
- 2 cloves garlic, finely chopped
- 1 tablespoon tomato paste
- ¼ teaspoon smoked paprika
- ½ cup dry white wine
- Kosher salt
- 1 pound mussels, scrubbed and debearded
- 2 plum tomatoes, chopped
- Chopped parsley and crusty bread, for serving

Serves 2 | Active time 25 minutes | Total time 25 minutes

Mussels may look complicated to make, but this main is both simple and impressive. Plus, sharing a loaf of crusty bread to sop up the paprika-wine sauce gives you a wonderful excuse to cozy up together.

1. Heat the oil in a small Dutch oven on medium. Add the garlic and cook, stirring, 1 minute. Stir in the tomato paste and cook, stirring, 2 minutes. Stir in the paprika and cook 1 minute.

2. Add the wine and cook, stirring and scraping up any browned bits, and then bring to a vigorous simmer.

3. Stir in ¼ teaspoon of salt, then add the mussels and simmer, covered, until the mussels begin to open, about 3 minutes.

4. Add the tomatoes and simmer, covered, until nearly all the mussels have opened, 2 to 3 minutes. Discard any unopened mussels. Serve sprinkled with the parsley and with the crusty bread for dipping if desired.

GOOD, CLEAN FUN
To prep mussels, place them in a colander. Under cold running water, scrub off any sand, barnacles, mud or seaweed. Discard any with cracked shells or that are open (and don't close when gently tapped).

Love Notes

THE NEWLYWED COOKBOOK **151**

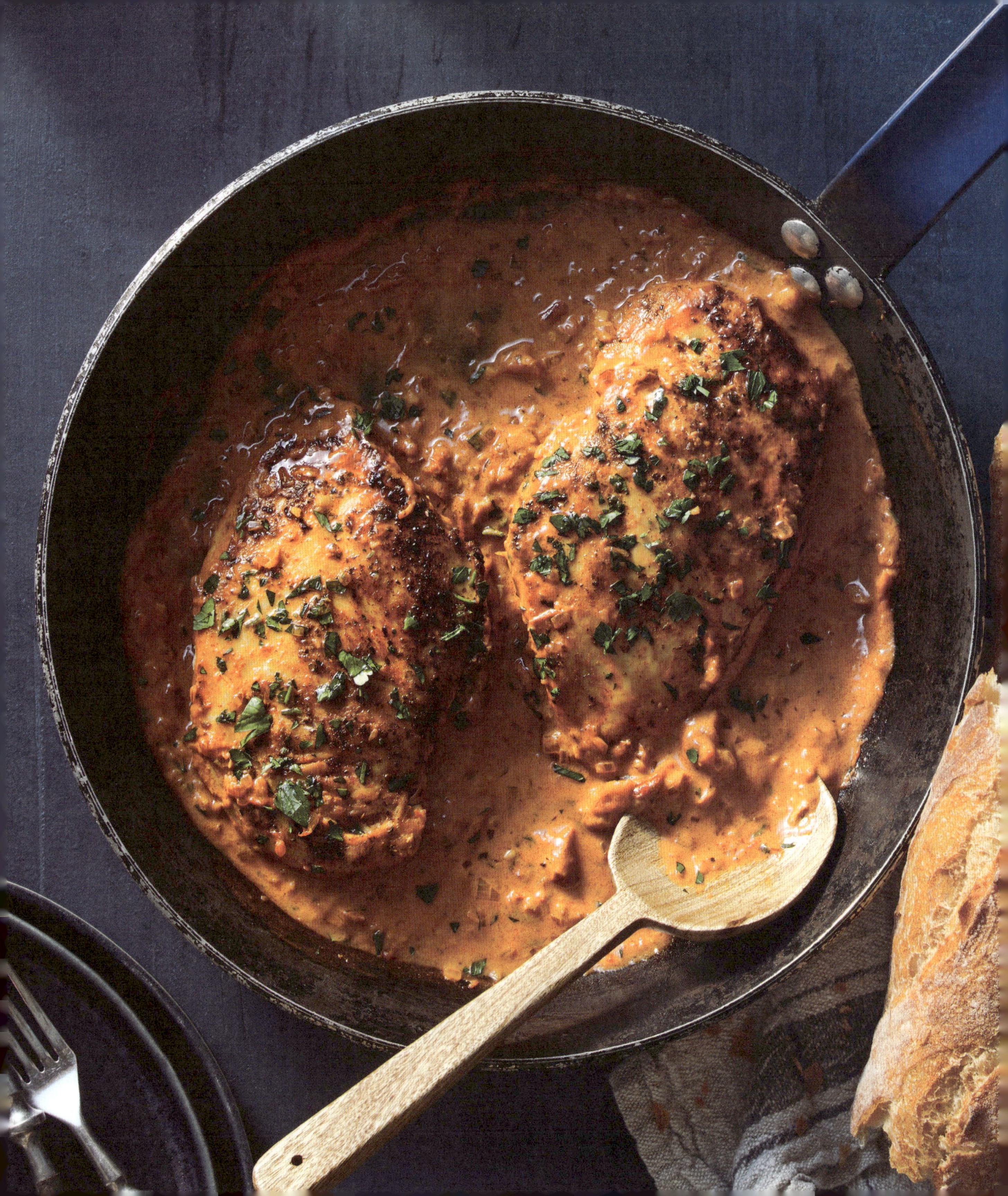

You Married Me Chicken

Serves 2 | Active time 30 minutes | Total time 30 minutes

- ½ teaspoon paprika
- ½ teaspoon Italian seasoning
- Kosher salt and pepper
- 2 6-ounce boneless, skinless chicken breasts, pounded ½ inch thick
- 1½ tablespoons olive oil, divided
- 1 medium shallot, finely chopped
- 2 cloves garlic, finely chopped
- 1 tablespoon tomato paste
- ¼ cup dry white wine
- ½ teaspoon low-sodium chicken bouillon base (we used Better Than Bouillon)
- 2 tablespoons oil-packed sun-dried tomatoes, chopped
- 2 tablespoons cold cream cheese, cut or torn into small pieces
- 3 tablespoons flat-leaf parsley leaves, roughly chopped
- Baguette, for serving

If you're looking for a chicken dinner that will make jaws drop, reach for this viral recipe. Chicken breasts are seared until golden brown, then nestled into the dreamiest decadent cream sauce studded with sun-dried tomatoes.

1. In a small bowl, stir together the paprika, the Italian seasoning and ¼ teaspoon each of salt and pepper; sprinkle over the chicken breasts on both sides.

2. Heat 1 tablespoon of oil in a large skillet on medium. Cook the chicken until golden brown and mostly cooked through, 3 to 4 minutes per side. Transfer to a plate. Reduce heat to medium-low. Add the remaining ½ tablespoon of oil to the skillet, then the shallot and garlic, and cook, covered, stirring often, until tender, 4 to 5 minutes.

3. Add the tomato paste and cook, stirring, until deepened in color, 1 to 2 minutes. Increase the heat to medium, add the wine and cook, scraping the bottom of the pan, until most of the liquid evaporates.

4. In a measuring cup, whisk the bouillon base with ½ cup of water, then whisk into a skillet along with the sun-dried tomatoes. Bring to a boil, then reduce the heat to a gentle simmer. Whisk in the cream cheese until fully incorporated, then return the chicken (along with any juices from plate) to the skillet. Cover and cook until the chicken is cooked through, 1 to 2 minutes. Sprinkle with parsley and serve with a baguette.

Love Notes

1783
PREMIUM MIXERS
SICILIAN LEMON
CLUB SODA
6.32 FL OZ (187 mL)

DATE NIGHT IN | **ENTERTAINING**

Ice Cream Float

- 6 tablespoons soda or cocktail syrup, divided
- 4 tablespoons half-and-half, divided
- Club soda
- Vanilla ice cream
- Whipped cream, for serving (optional)

Serves 2 | Active time 5 minutes | Total time 5 minutes

Cap your evening in a fun way—with a retro treat that will transport you to an old-school soda shop. Simply mix and match your favorite flavors of syrup and ice cream to find your ideal combo.

1. In each of 2 tall glasses, stir together 3 tablespoons of syrup and 2 tablespoons of half-and-half.

2. Add enough soda so it comes about ¾ of the way up the glass. Add 2 scoops of ice cream, then top with whipped cream if desired.

SWITCH IT UP
We developed this with vanilla ice cream, but it was also delicious with chocolate and coffee. Try a combo for a black and white or a twist on mocha.

Love Notes

THE NEWLYWED COOKBOOK 155

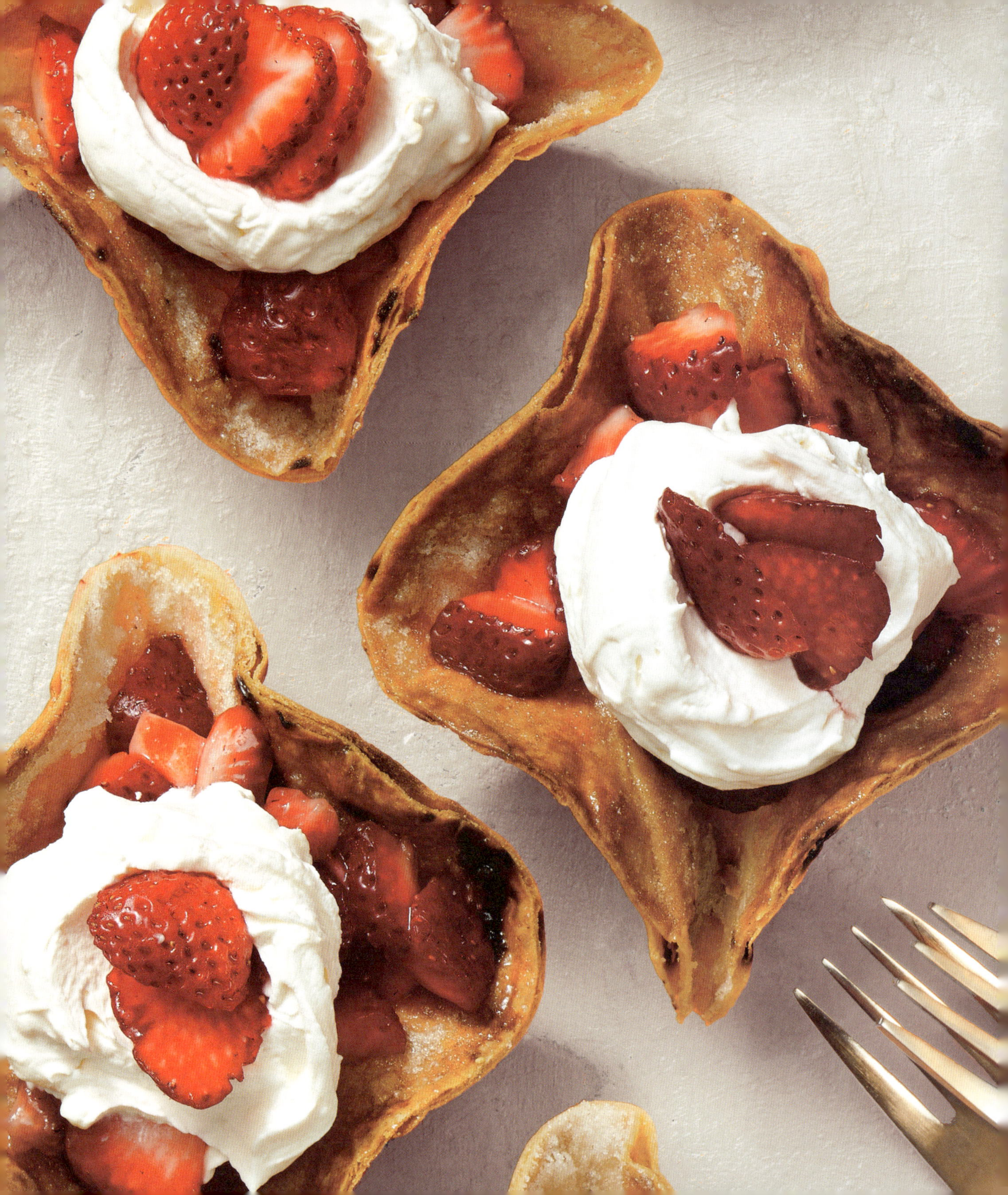

DATE NIGHT IN | **ENTERTAINING**

Crispy Tortilla Bowls with Strawberries & Cream

- 2 8-inch flour tortillas
- Melted unsalted butter, for brushing
- 2 teaspoons sugar, divided
- 8 ounces strawberries
- ¼ cup cold heavy cream
- 1 ounce mascarpone cheese
- Pinch grated lemon zest

Serves 2 | Active time 25 minutes | Total time 25 minutes

Yes, tortillas can be sweet! Pop them into muffin pans to bake into crispy sugar-coated shells, then fill them with fresh, juicy strawberries and a homemade whipped cream.

1. Heat the oven to 375°F. Using a 5-inch round cutter or sharp knife, cut the tortillas into 5-inch rounds. Brush 1 side of each round with the melted butter and sprinkle with ⅛ teaspoon of sugar.

2. Invert a 12-cup muffin pan and nestle each tortilla (sugared side up) between 4 muffin cups, shaping corners evenly between the grooves. Bake until golden brown, 11 to 14 minutes. Let cool.

3. Meanwhile, hull and chop all but 2 strawberries and transfer to a bowl. Sprinkle with 1 teaspoon of sugar and toss to combine; let sit, tossing occasionally, until ready to use.

4. In a second bowl, using an electric mixer, beat the cream, mascarpone and lemon zest and the remaining ¾ teaspoon of sugar on medium-high just until stiff peaks form, 1½ to 2 minutes. Refrigerate until ready to use.

5. To serve, divide the chopped strawberries among the tortilla bowls, then top with whipped cream. Slice or halve the remaining strawberries and arrange them on top.

FUN WITH FRIENDS
Make a bunch of tortilla shells for your next get-together, then set out different toppings. Ask friends to bring their favorite ice cream flavors for a DIY sundae party.

Love Notes

THE NEWLYWED COOKBOOK **157**

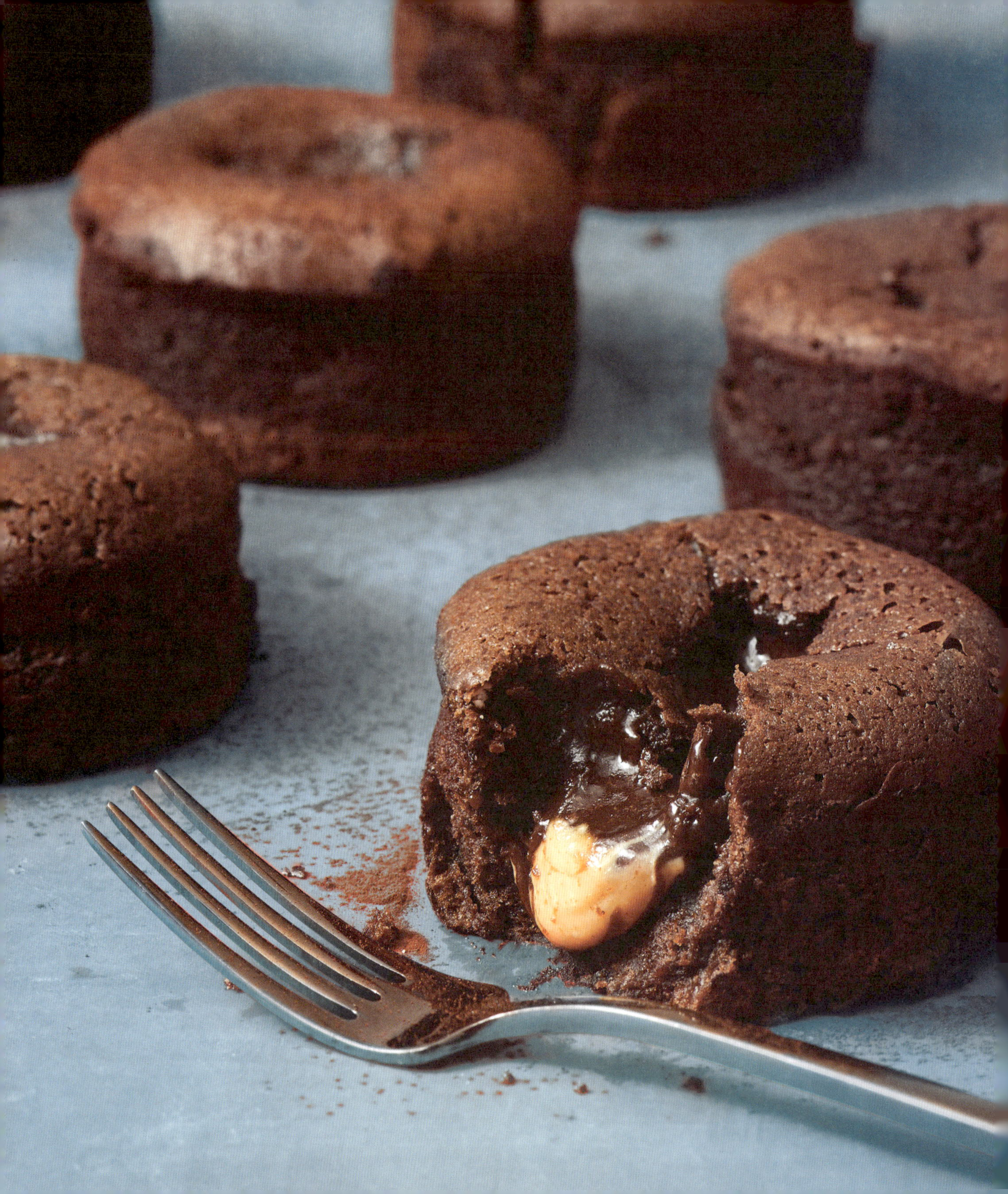

DATE NIGHT IN | **ENTERTAINING**

Peanut Butter Molten Chocolate Cakes

Serves 6 | Active time 25 minutes | Total time 45 minutes

Is there a more perfect pairing than peanut butter and chocolate? This rich dessert brings together everyone's favorite duo into one ooey, gooey treat. To create the "molten" center, slightly underbake the cakes.

- ¾ cup unsalted butter (1½ sticks), cut into pieces, plus more for greasing
- ⅓ cup granulated sugar, plus more for dusting
- 6 ounces semisweet chocolate chips
- 3 large eggs plus 3 yolks, at room temperature
- 1 teaspoon pure vanilla extract
- ¼ teaspoon kosher salt
- ⅓ cup all-purpose flour
- 1 tablespoon unsweetened cocoa powder, plus more for dusting
- ½ teaspoon baking powder
- ⅓ cup creamy peanut butter (not natural type)
- 3 tablespoons confectioners' sugar

1. Heat the oven to 450°F. In a medium saucepan, bring 1 inch of water to a simmer. Butter six 6-ounce ramekins and dust with granulated sugar.

2. Combine the chocolate chips and the butter in a large heatproof bowl and place the bowl over (but not in) simmering water to gently melt, stirring occasionally, until smooth. Remove the bowl from the heat and let cool slightly.

3. Meanwhile, in a medium bowl, whisk together the granulated sugar, eggs, yolks, vanilla and salt until well combined. In a small bowl, whisk together the flour, cocoa powder and baking powder. Add the egg mixture to the chocolate mixture and whisk until combined; add the flour mixture and gently whisk until the batter is smooth. Divide half of the batter among prepared ramekins.

4. In a second small bowl, stir together the peanut butter and confectioners' sugar until combined. Scoop 1 tablespoon into each half-filled ramekin. Cover with the remaining chocolate batter, dividing among the ramekins. Place on a rimmed baking sheet.

5. Bake until the sides of the cakes are set and the centers are still slightly gooey, 11 to 13 minutes. Let the cakes cool 2 minutes, then loosen the edges in each ramekin with a small offset spatula. Using a kitchen towel, carefully invert each onto a plate to serve. Dust with additional cocoa powder if desired.

SAVE SOME FOR LATER
Stash unbaked cakes in the freezer for up to 2 weeks, then pop them into a 450°F oven for 15 minutes.

Love Notes

THE NEWLYWED COOKBOOK **159**

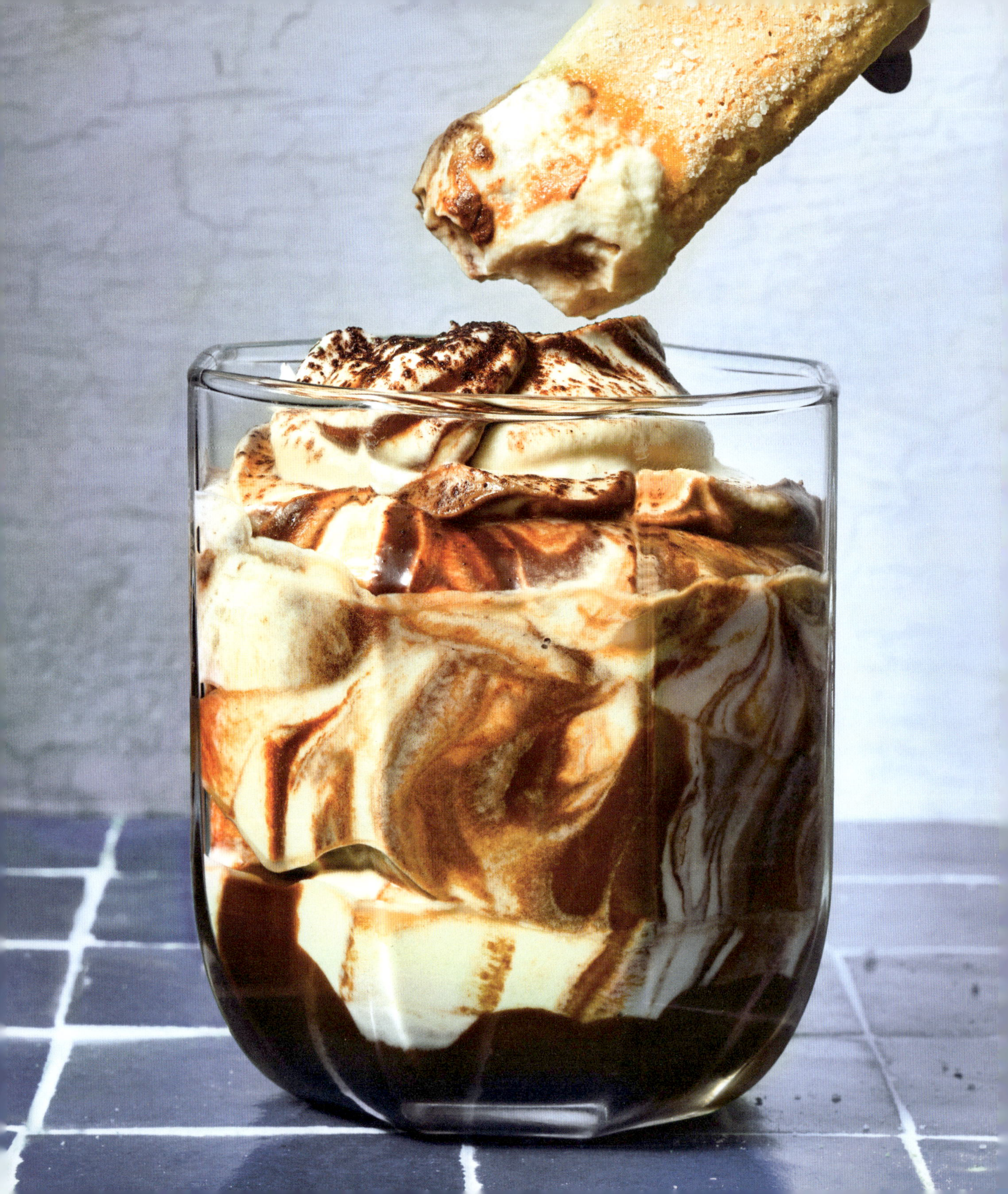

Tiramisu Dip

Serves 6 | Active time 15 minutes | Total time 25 minutes

- 3 ounces bittersweet chocolate, finely chopped
- 1½ cups heavy cream, divided
- ¼ cup Kahlua
- 8 ounces mascarpone
- ½ cup confectioners' sugar
- ½ teaspoon instant espresso powder
- ½ teaspoon pure vanilla extract
- Kosher salt
- Unsweetened cocoa powder, for dusting
- Ladyfingers, for dipping

Classic tiramisu requires hours of chilling, but this spoonable version is ready in a fraction of the time. Using real mascarpone (Italian cream cheese) and Kahlua coffee liqueur gives it that authentic taste.

1. Place the chopped chocolate in a medium bowl. In a small saucepan, combine ¼ cup of heavy cream and the Kahlua and heat on medium until simmering, 3 to 4 minutes (or microwave in a bowl until hot, about 1 minute). Pour the cream mixture over the chocolate, let sit 5 minutes, then stir until smooth. Refrigerate until cool but still pourable, 10 to 15 minutes.

2. Meanwhile, in a stand mixer fitted with a whisk attachment on medium, beat the mascarpone, confectioners' sugar, espresso powder and vanilla and a pinch of salt until smooth and creamy, 1 to 2 minutes.

3. Gradually add the remaining 1¼ cups of heavy cream and beat until stiff peaks form, 2 to 3 minutes.

4. Divide the tiramisu dip among glasses, layering with the chocolate sauce and gently folding to swirl. Dust with the cocoa powder and serve with the ladyfingers. Alternatively, in a large bowl, fold the chocolate sauce into the dip and serve family-style.

Love Notes

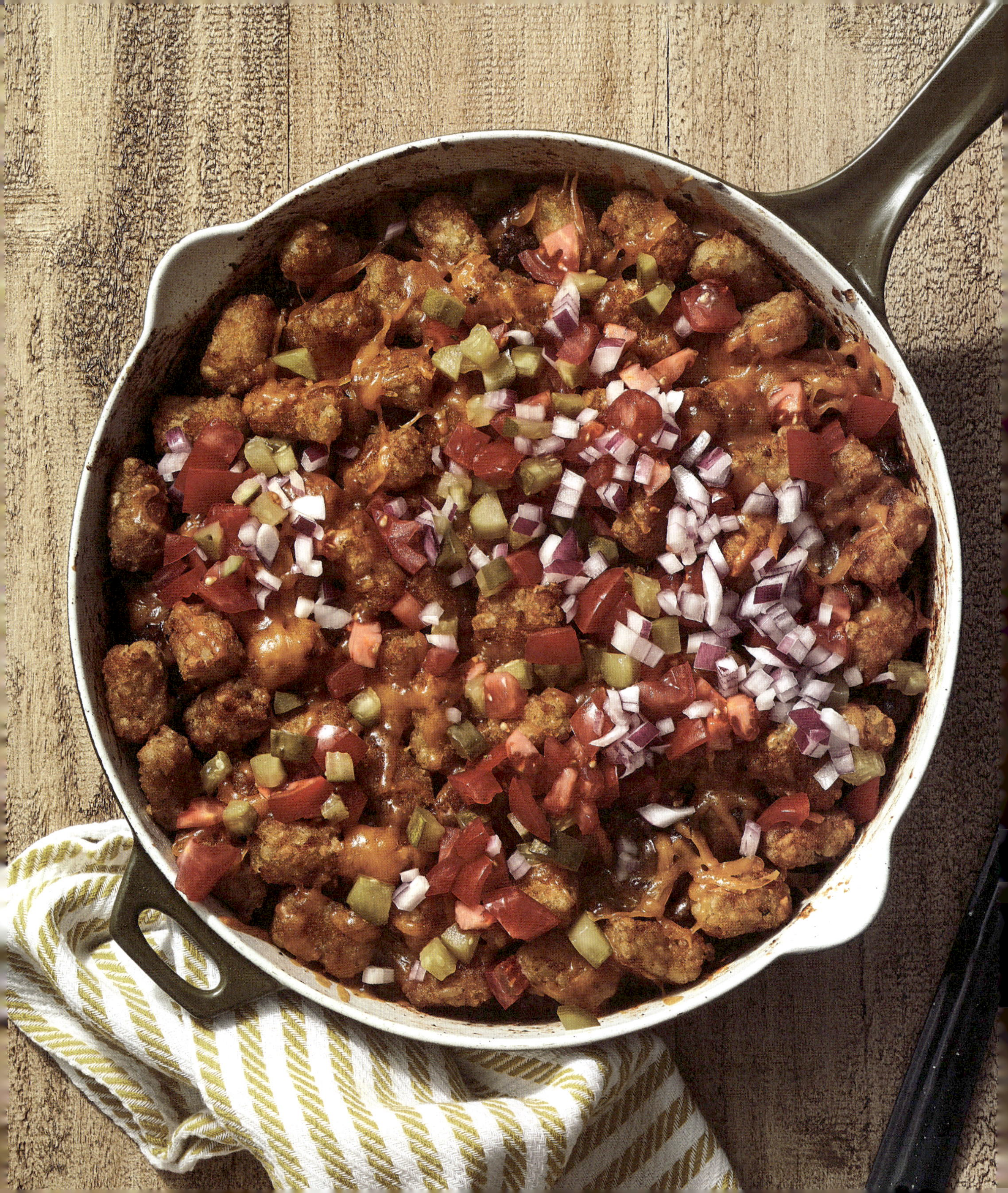

GAME DAY | **ENTERTAINING**

Skillet Cheeseburger Hot Dish

Serves 6 | Active time 25 minutes | Total time 45 minutes

- 1 28-ounce bag frozen potato tots
- 1 medium red onion, chopped and divided
- 3 tablespoons pickle brine, divided, plus 6 pickle chips, chopped
- 1 tablespoon olive oil
- 1½ pounds 90% lean ground beef
- 2 teaspoons steak seasoning
- 3 tablespoons tomato paste
- 2 tablespoons all-purpose flour
- 1½ teaspoons beef bouillon base (we used Better Than Bouillon Roasted Beef) mixed with 1½ cups warm water
- 6 ounces Cheddar cheese, coarsely grated (1½ cups) and divided
- ¼ cup mayonnaise
- 3 tablespoons ketchup
- 1 tablespoon yellow mustard
- 4 Campari tomatoes, chopped

Layers of crispy tots, melty cheese and tasty spiced beef? Yes, please! This take on an iconic Minnesotan comfort food will be a slam dunk at your gathering.

1. Heat the oven to 425°F. Place the tots on a rimmed baking sheet and bake until browned and crispy, 25 to 30 minutes.

2. In a small bowl, combine half of the onion with 2 tablespoons of pickle brine. Let sit, tossing occasionally, until ready to use.

3. Meanwhile, heat the oil in a large cast-iron skillet on medium. Add the remaining onion and saute until tender and golden, 6 to 7 minutes. Add the beef and the steak seasoning and cook, breaking up meat, until no longer pink, 5 to 6 minutes.

4. Add the tomato paste and cook, stirring continuously, until caramelized and darkened in color, 2 to 3 minutes. Sprinkle with flour and cook, stirring, 1 minute. Gradually add the bouillon mixture and simmer, stirring occasionally, until slightly thickened, 3 to 5 minutes; remove from heat.

5. Sprinkle with 1 cup of cheese and top with the tots, then add the remaining ½ cup of cheese. Bake until the cheese is melted and the mixture is bubbling, 5 to 6 minutes.

6. Meanwhile, in a small bowl, whisk together the mayonnaise, ketchup and mustard and the remaining 1 tablespoon pickle brine.

7. Drain the pickled onions, then scatter over the tots along with the tomatoes and pickles. Serve with the special sauce on the side.

Love Notes

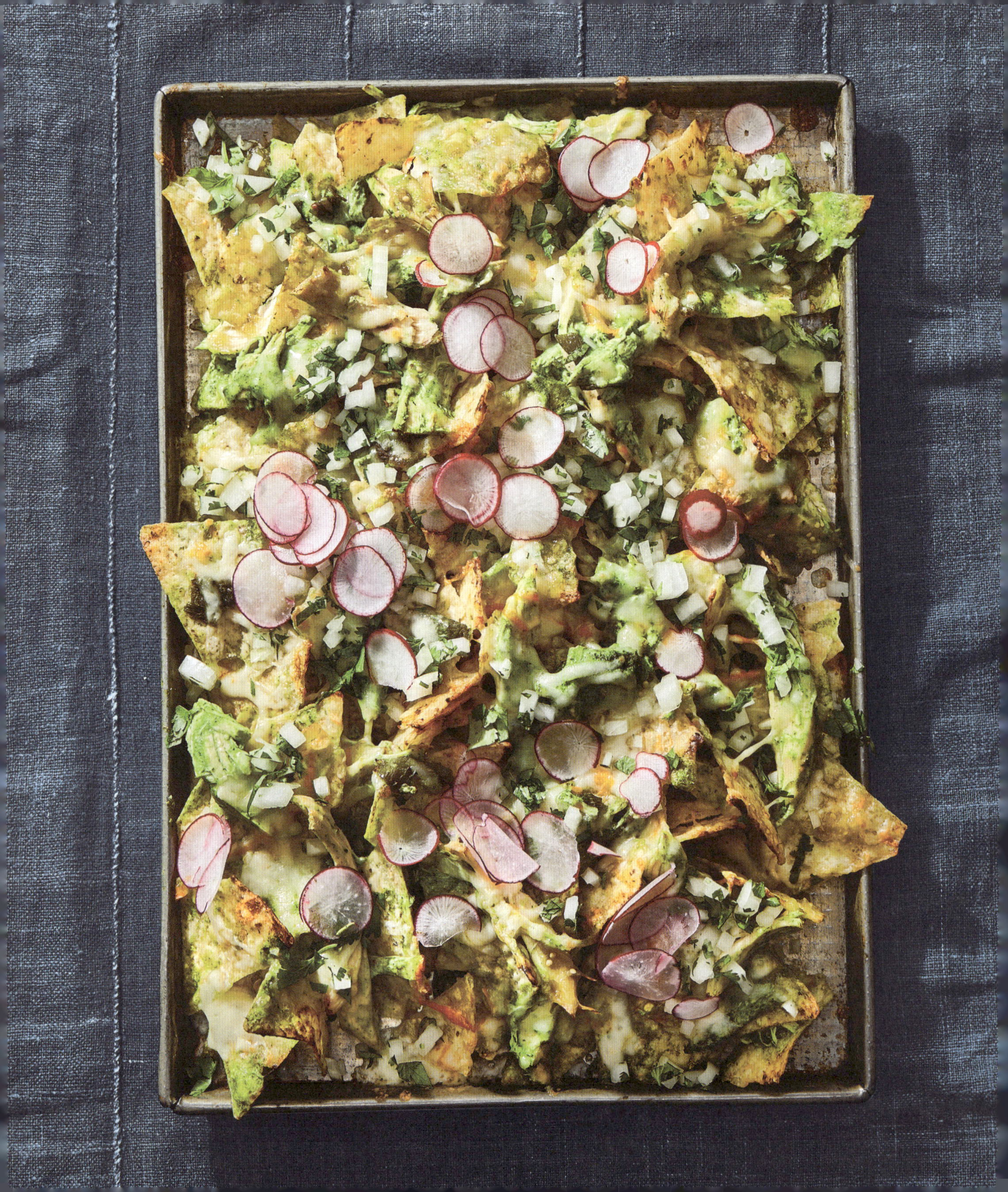

GAME DAY | ENTERTAINING

Sheet Pan Chicken Suizas Nachos

Serves 6 | Active time 20 minutes | Total time 35 minutes

- 1 large poblano pepper, halved and seeded
- ½ cup prepared salsa verde
- 2 tablespoons sour cream
- 2½ cups fresh cilantro, divided
- 2½ cups shredded white-meat rotisserie chicken
- 6 ounces tortilla chips (about 7 cups)
- 8 ounces Muenster cheese, coarsely grated (about 2 cups)
- ¼ small white onion, finely chopped
- 4 small radishes, thinly sliced

Nachos and game day make for a winning combo. Finishing touches like fresh cilantro, chopped onions and sliced radishes score this easy app an extra point.

1. Heat the broiler. Arrange the poblano, cut sides down, on a rimmed baking sheet and broil until charred, 3 to 5 minutes. Transfer to a bowl, cover and let stand 5 minutes. Use a paper towel to remove the skins, then cut the peppers into ¼-inch pieces.

2. Reduce the oven temperature to 450°F. In a blender, puree the salsa verde, the sour cream and 2 cups cilantro until smooth. Toss with the chicken to coat.

3. On the same baking sheet, toss the chicken with the chips, half of the Muenster and the chopped poblano. Sprinkle the remaining cheese on top. Bake until the cheese has melted and the chicken is hot, 6 to 7 minutes.

4. Chop the remaining ½ cup of cilantro and toss with the onion. Scatter the onion mixture and radishes over the nachos.

YOUR GAME PLAN
For fully loaded bites every time, toss the chips with the cheese and heavier toppings instead of simply layering them on the sheet pan. No naked chips here!

Love Notes

THE NEWLYWED COOKBOOK **165**

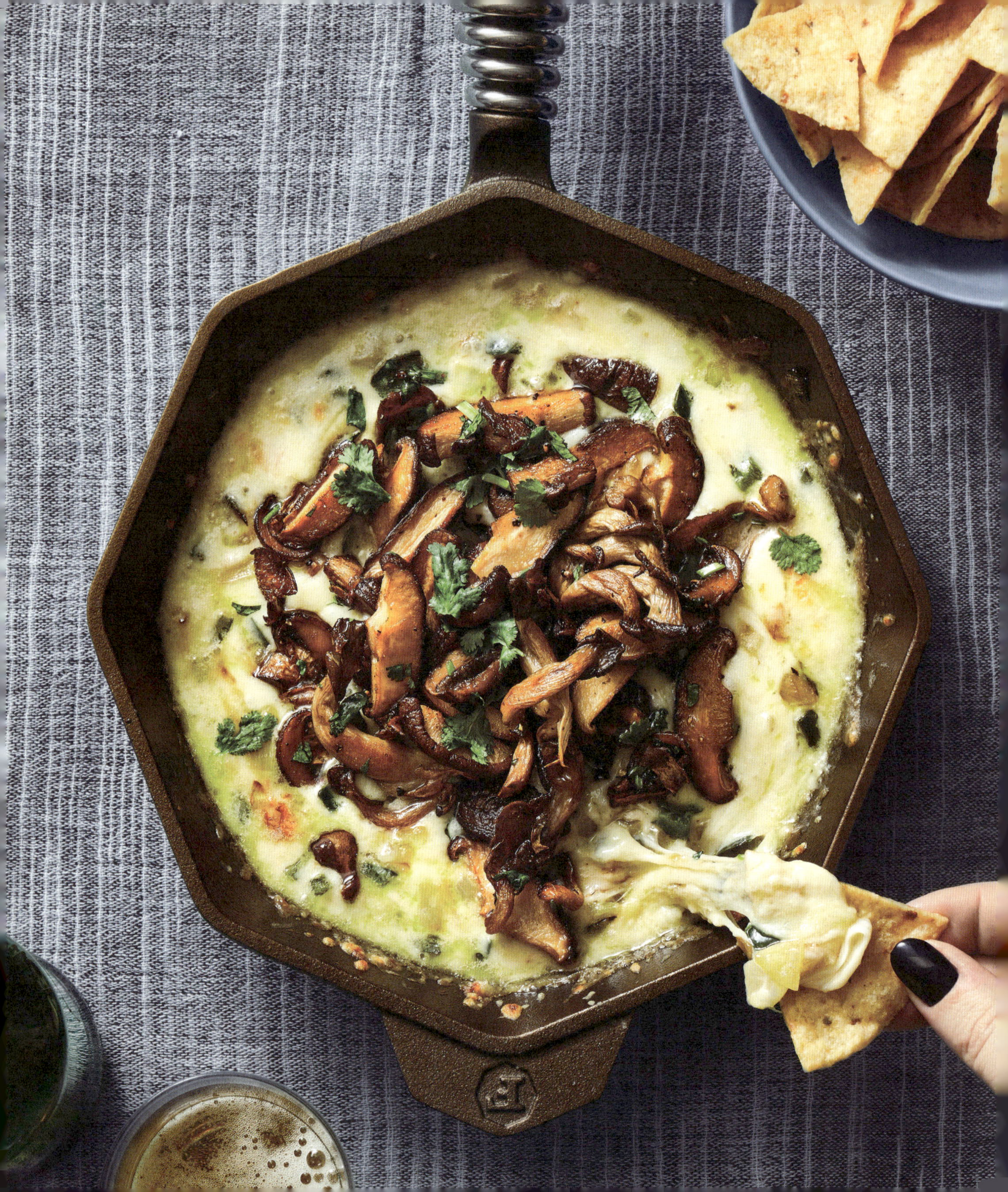

GAME DAY | ENTERTAINING

Queso Fundido with Roasted Mushrooms

Serves 6 | Active time 25 minutes | Total time 30 minutes

You'll want to grab extra-sturdy tortilla chips and dig into this swoon-worthy poblano-studded melted cheese right away.

1. Heat the oven to 425°F. On a rimmed baking sheet, toss the mushrooms with 1½ tablespoons of oil and ¼ teaspoon each of salt and pepper. Spread the mushrooms in a single layer and roast until golden, 13 to 15 minutes.

2. Meanwhile, heat the remaining ½ tablespoon of oil in an 8-inch cast-iron skillet on medium. Add the garlic and cook, stirring, until sizzling and fragrant, about 45 seconds. Add the poblano, the onion and ¼ teaspoon of salt and cook, stirring, until the onion is translucent and the poblano is tender, 5 to 6 minutes.

3. Remove from the heat, add both cheeses and fold to combine (it's OK if the cheese starts to melt in the pan). Carefully transfer the skillet to the oven and bake until the cheese is melted, 4 to 5 minutes. Fold the cilantro into the mushrooms and spoon over the queso fundido. Serve immediately with tortilla chips for scooping.

- 8 ounces mixed mushrooms, trimmed and sliced (we used cremini, oyster and shiitake)
- 2 tablespoons olive oil, divided
- Kosher salt and pepper
- 1 clove garlic, minced
- ½ poblano pepper, seeded and chopped
- ½ small onion, chopped
- 8 ounces Oaxaca cheese, coarsely grated (about 2 heaping cups)
- 4 ounces pepper Jack cheese, coarsely grated (about 1 heaping cup)
- 2 tablespoons chopped cilantro leaves
- Tortilla chips, for serving

Love Notes

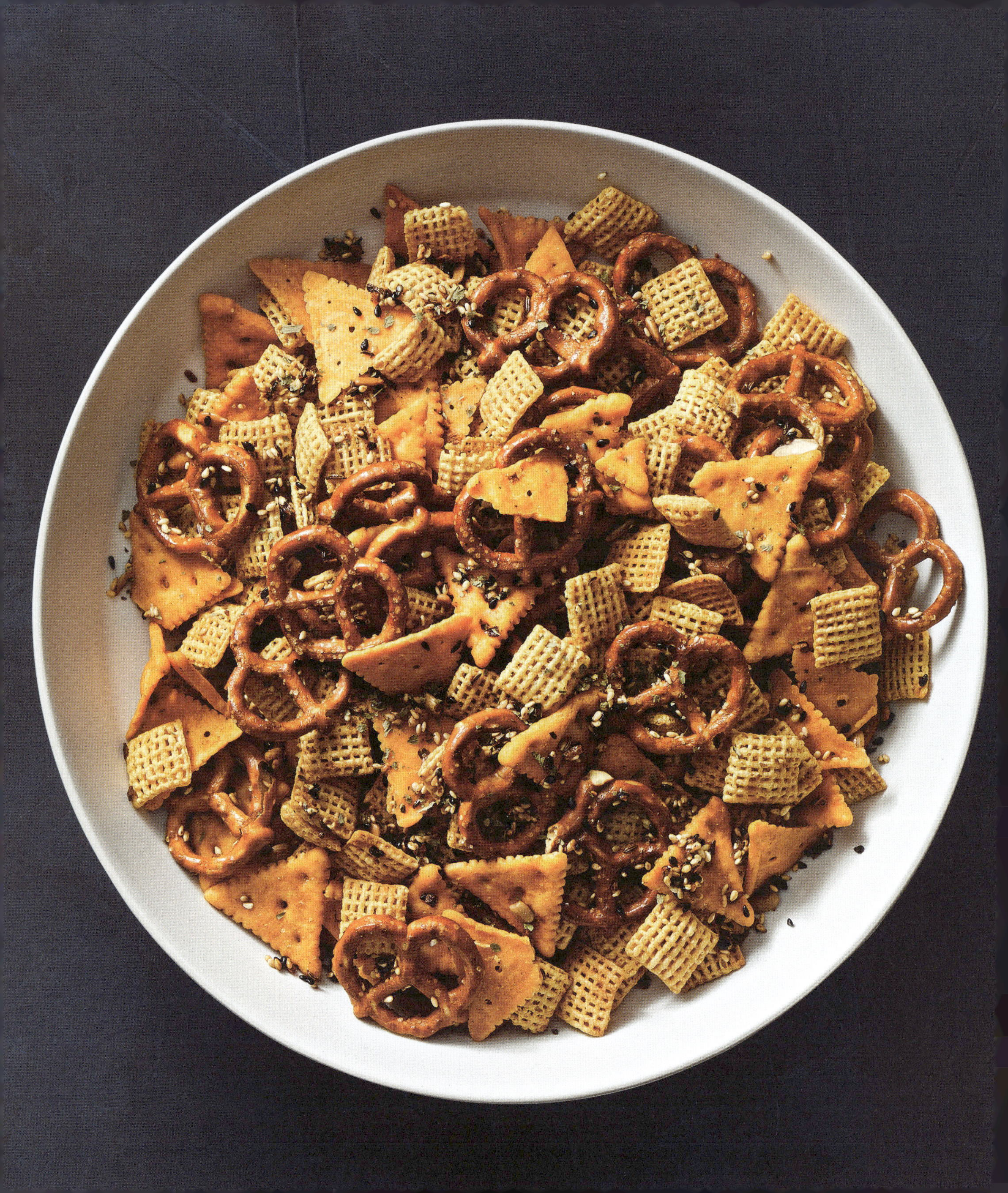

GAME DAY | **ENTERTAINING**

Spiced Snack Mix

- 3½ cups mini pretzels
- 2 cups toasted corn squares cereal (we used Corn Chex)
- 2 cups cheese crackers
- 6 tablespoons unsalted butter, melted
- ¼ cup sunflower seeds
- 2 tablespoons sesame seeds
- 1 tablespoon black sesame seeds
- 1 tablespoon dried minced onion
- 1 teaspoon caraway seeds
- 1 teaspoon dried parsley
- ½ teaspoon cracked black pepper

Makes 8 cups | Active time 10 minutes | Total time 30 minutes

This party favorite is deliciously salty and savory, and customizable too! Try grated Parmesan and Romano cheeses and extra cracked pepper instead of sesame seeds or a pinch of ground cumin and smoked paprika instead of caraway seeds.

1. Heat the oven to 300°F. Line 2 large rimmed baking sheets with parchment paper.

2. In a large bowl, toss the pretzels, cereal and crackers with melted butter to coat, then toss with the sunflower seeds, sesame seeds, onion, caraway seeds, parsley and pepper.

3. Arrange the mixture in an even layer on prepared baking sheets and bake, tossing once, until lightly toasted in spots, about 20 minutes. Let cool, then serve or store in an airtight container up to 1 week.

CRUNCH TIME
Make this snack in an air fryer: Heat to 300°F. Working in batches, if needed, arrange the mixture in an even layer and air-fry for about 30 minutes, shaking basket halfway through.

Love Notes

THE NEWLYWED COOKBOOK

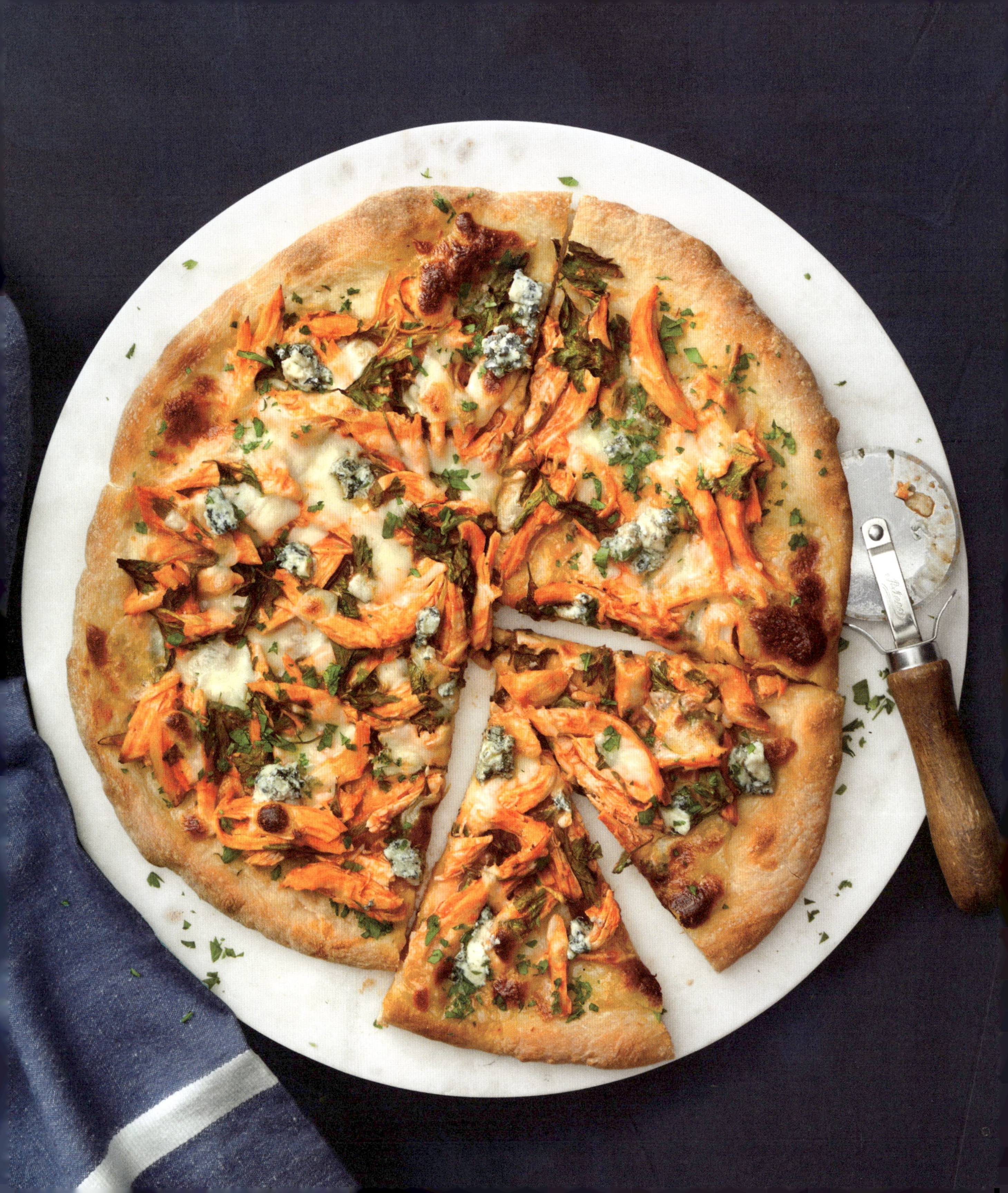

Buffalo Chicken Pizza

Cornmeal and flour, for dusting
1 pound pizza dough
2 cups shredded cooked chicken
½ cup cayenne pepper sauce (we used Frank's)
1 sliced scallion
1 cup flat-leaf parsley leaves, plus chopped for serving
1¼ cups shredded mozzarella
1¼ cups crumbled blue cheese

Serves 6 | Active time 15 minutes | Total time 30 minutes

Can't decide between wings and pizza? How about both? Use rotisserie chicken as a shortcut in this pie that subs in the signature hot sauce for marinara.

1. Heat the oven to 475°F. Sprinkle a baking sheet with cornmeal.

2. On a lightly floured surface, shape the pizza dough into a 14-inch circle or oval and place on the prepared sheet.

3. Toss the chicken with cayenne pepper sauce. Fold in the scallion and parsley leaves. Scatter over the pizza dough and sprinkle with the shredded mozzarella.

4. Bake until the crust is golden brown, 12 to 15 minutes. Sprinkle with the crumbled blue cheese and chopped parsley.

Love Notes

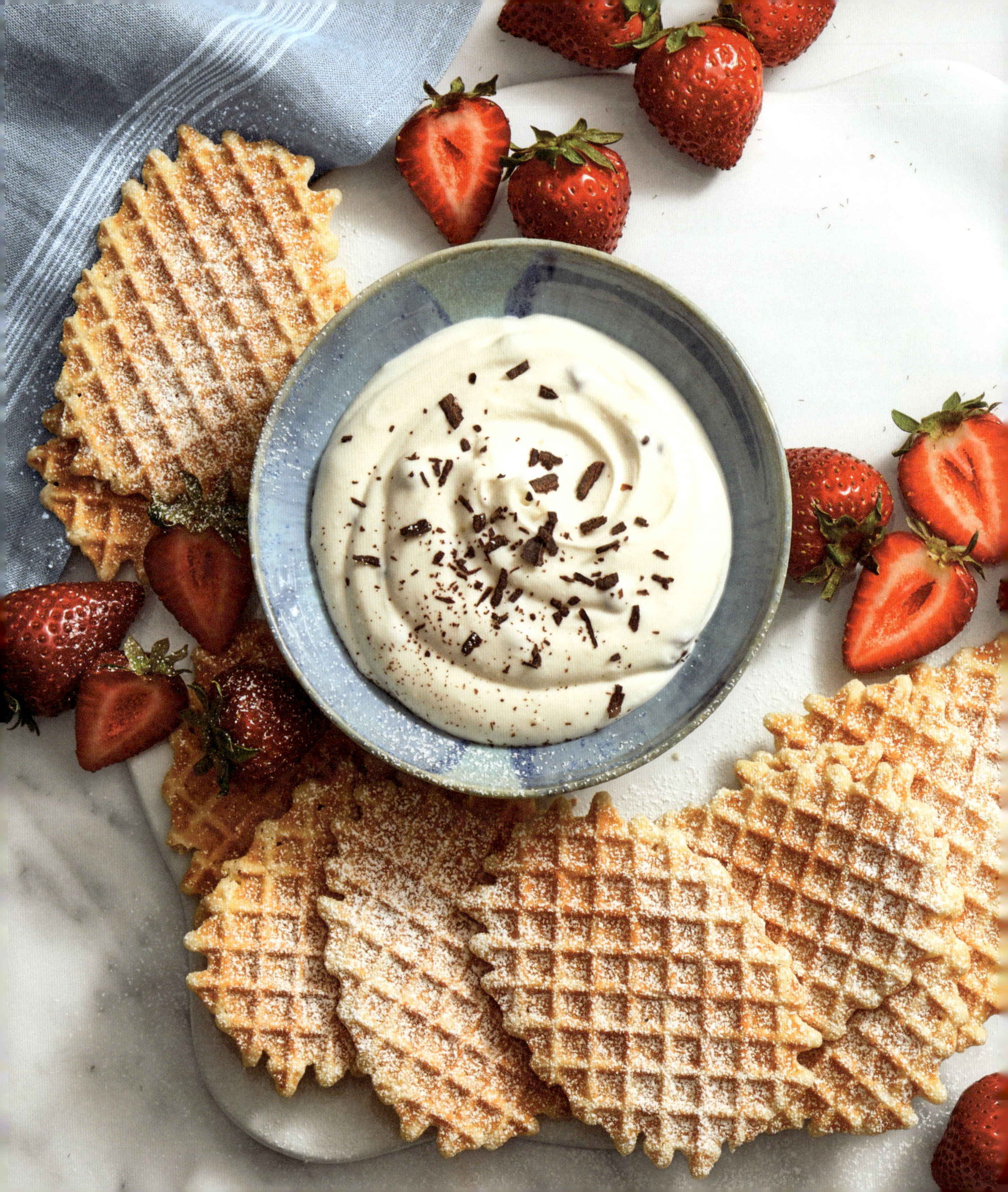

GAME DAY | **ENTERTAINING**

Creamy Cannoli Dip

| 16 ounces whole-milk ricotta
| 8 ounces mascarpone
| ½ cup confectioners' sugar
| 1 teaspoon pure vanilla extract
| 1 teaspoon grated fresh lemon zest
| Kosher salt
| 1 to 2 tablespoons heavy cream, if needed
| ½ cup mini chocolate chips, plus more for serving
| Strawberries and waffle cookies, for dipping

Serves 6 | Active time 10 minutes | Total time 1 hour 10 minutes

Transform the decadent Italian treat into a party-ready dip that everyone will love. Serve with plenty of waffle cookies and fruit for dunking.

1. Place the ricotta in a fine-mesh strainer or cheesecloth set over a bowl and let it sit for at least 1 hour at room temperature or refrigerate up to overnight.

2. In a food processor (a blender won't work), puree the drained ricotta, the mascarpone, the sugar, the vanilla, the lemon zest and a pinch of salt until smooth, adding the cream only if needed to loosen the dip. Transfer to a bowl and fold in the chocolate chips. Serve with the strawberries and cookies and sprinkle with the chocolate chips if desired.

3. Transfer the dip to a bowl and fold in the chocolate chips. Serve with the strawberries and cookies and sprinkle with the chocolate chips if desired.

TASTY TOPPER

This creamy dip is also great spooned over toasted pound cake or eaten in a bowl with a medley of fresh berries.

Love Notes

THE NEWLYWED COOKBOOK **173**

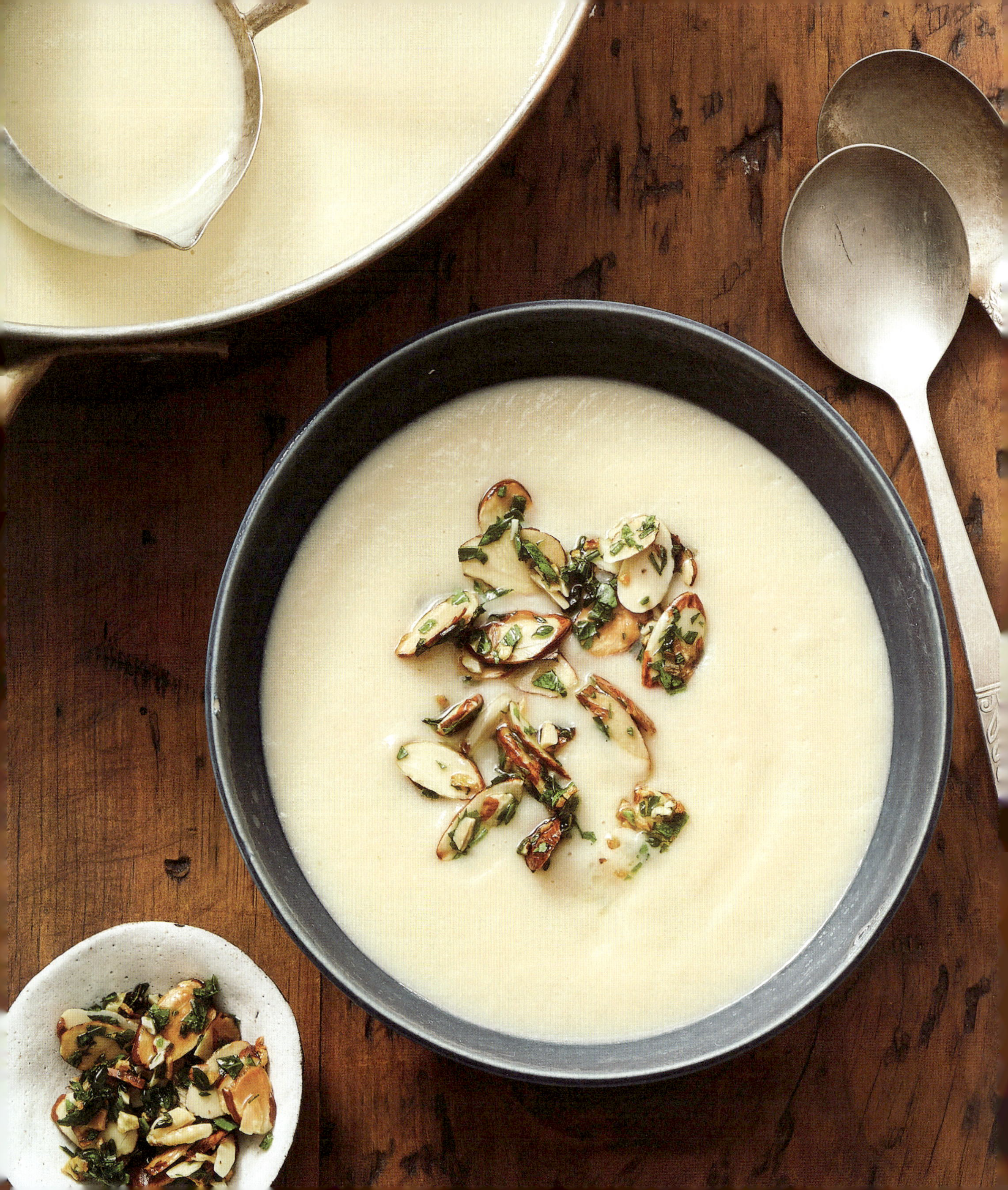

VIP DINNER PARTY | **ENTERTAINING**

Creamy Cauliflower Soup with Almond-Thyme Gremolata

FOR SOUP

- 1 tablespoon olive oil
- 1 tablespoon unsalted butter
- 1 large leek (white and light green parts only), cut into half-moons
- 1 white onion, chopped
- 1 stalk celery, chopped
- 2 cloves garlic, chopped
- 1 medium head cauliflower (about 2 pounds), cored and sliced
- 4 cups low-sodium chicken or vegetable broth
- ½ cup heavy cream

FOR TOPPING

- ½ tablespoon olive oil
- 1 clove garlic, finely chopped
- 1 teaspoon fresh thyme leaves
- ½ cup sliced almonds, toasted
- ¼ cup flat-leaf parsley, chopped
- 2 tablespoons chopped chives

Serves 6 | Active time 45 minutes | Total time 45 minutes

This elegant starter is surprisingly simple to make and even easier to prep ahead—just reheat when ready to serve, then sprinkle on the herby gremolata topping for a bit of crunch.

1. Make the soup: Heat the oil and butter in a large pot on medium. Add the leek, onion and celery and cook, covered, stirring occasionally, until very tender (but not browned), 10 to 12 minutes. Stir in the garlic and cook 1 minute.

2. Add the cauliflower and broth and bring to a simmer. Simmer 10 minutes. Add the cream and gently simmer until the cauliflower is very tender, 6 to 8 minutes more. Using an immersion blender (or a standard blender, in batches), puree until very smooth.

3. Make the topping: In a small skillet, heat the oil, garlic and thyme on medium until the garlic sizzles around the edges and begins to turn golden brown, about 2 minutes. Remove from the heat and toss with the almonds, then the parsley and chives. Makes 1 cup. Serve over the soup.

Love Notes

THE NEWLYWED COOKBOOK 175

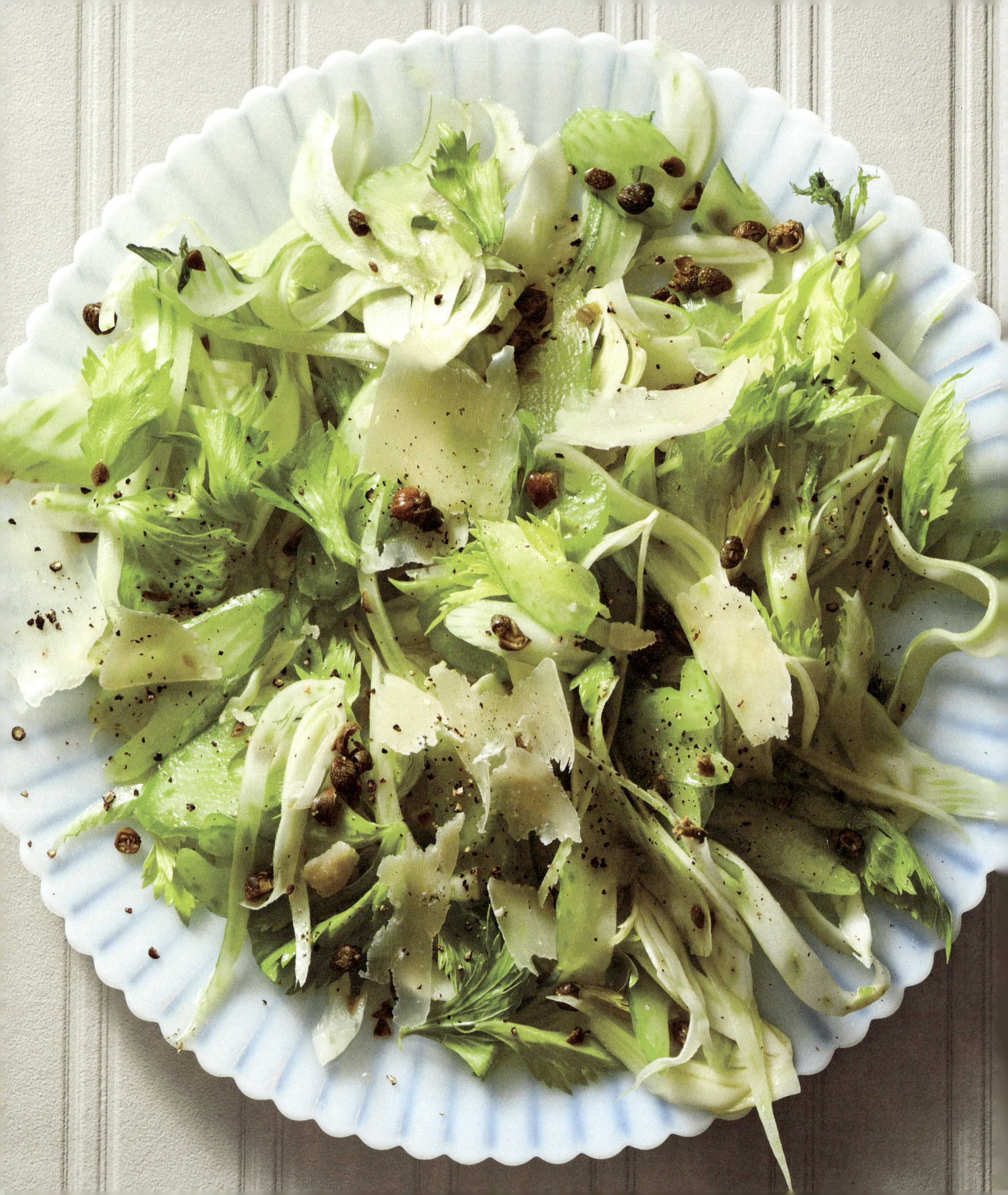

VIP DINNER PARTY | **ENTERTAINING**

Shaved Fennel & Celery Salad

| 2 tablespoons olive oil
| 1½ tablespoons fresh lemon juice
| ½ teaspoon honey
| ½ teaspoon Dijon mustard
| Kosher salt and pepper
| 2 bulbs fennel, cored and thinly sliced on mandoline
| 3 ribs celery, thinly sliced on bias
| ¼ cup celery leaves
| 2 tablespoons capers, rinsed and chopped
| 2 ounces Parmesan cheese, shaved (3 tablespoons)

Serves 4 to 6 | Active time 20 minutes | Total time 20 minutes

Round out your dinner party menu with this light and refreshing salad that can be served as an appetizer or a side. Thinly sliced fennel and celery get a boost of flavor from chopped capers, Parmesan and an irresistible honey-Dijon vinaigrette.

1. In a large bowl, whisk together the oil, lemon juice, honey and Dijon mustard and ½ teaspoon each of salt and pepper to combine.

2. Add the fennel, celery, celery leaves, capers and Parmesan and toss to combine.

SWITCH IT UP!
Keep this homemade honey-Dijon vinaigrette recipe handy. It can be drizzled over romaine or mixed greens and can even double as a marinade for chicken or pork (20 minutes max).

Love Notes

THE NEWLYWED COOKBOOK

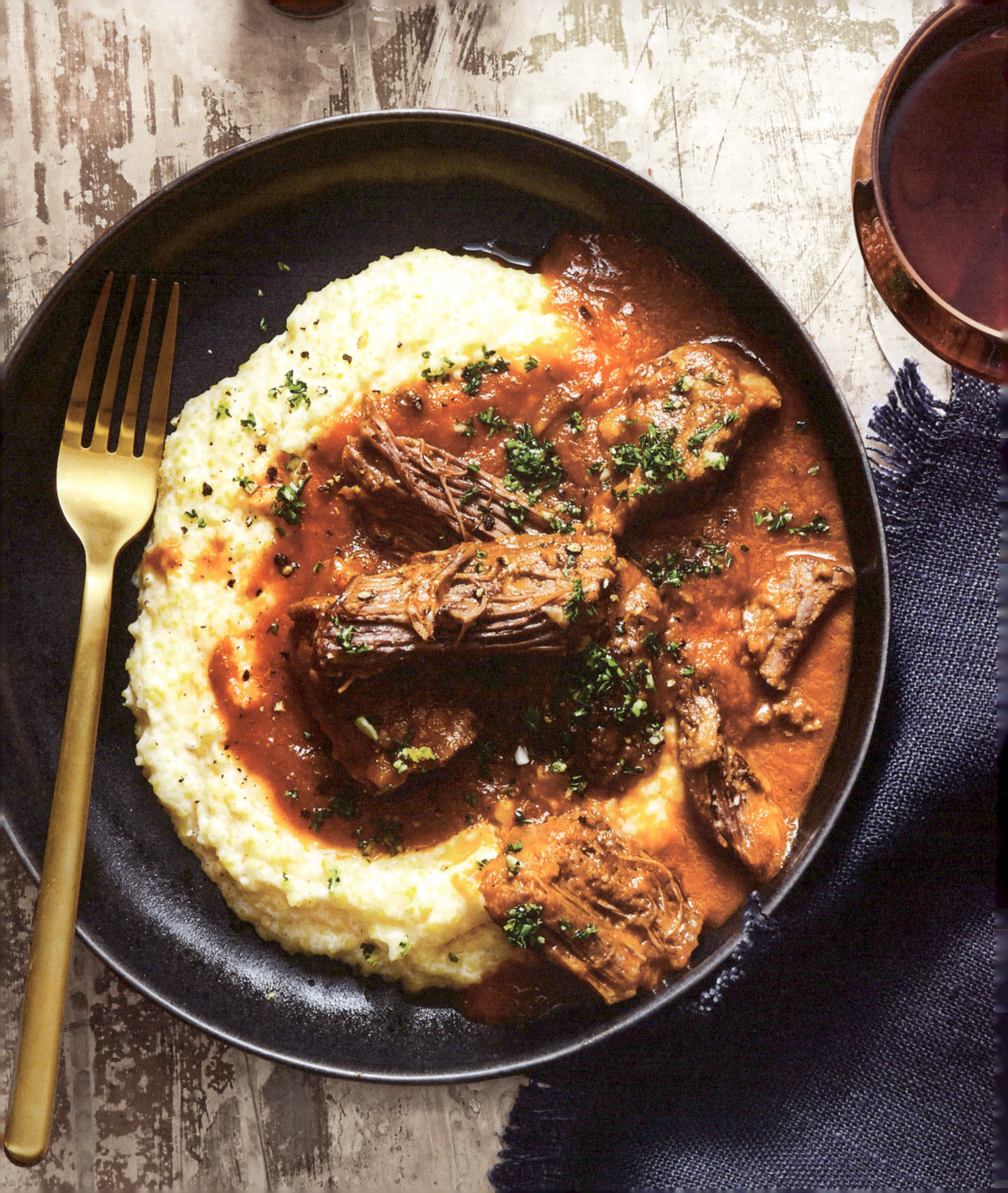

VIP DINNER PARTY | **ENTERTAINING**

Short Ribs with Creamy Polenta

Serves 4 to 6 | Active time 40 minutes | Total time 1 hour 50 minutes

The registry-favorite multicooker handles all the heavy lifting to produce tender, restaurant-worthy braised short ribs, giving you more time to ready the sides.

FOR SHORT RIBS
- 1 pound bone-in beef short ribs
- Kosher salt and pepper
- 2 tablespoons olive oil, plus more if needed
- 1 small carrot, chopped
- 1 small stalk celery, chopped
- 1 medium onion, chopped
- 1 clove garlic, pressed
- ½ tablespoon tomato paste
- 6 tablespoons dry red wine
- ½ cup canned crushed tomatoes
- ¼ to ½ teaspoon Worcestershire sauce
- 1 small sprig fresh rosemary
- 1 small sprig fresh thyme
- ¼ cup low-sodium chicken broth

FOR CREAMY POLENTA
- 1 cup whole milk
- 1 tablespoon unsalted butter
- ⅓ cup polenta
- 2 tablespoons finely grated pecorino cheese
- 1 tablespoon chopped fresh parsley
- 1 tablespoon grated lemon zest
- 1 small clove garlic, finely chopped

1. Make the short ribs: Pat the short ribs dry and season with a pinch each of salt and pepper. Set a multicooker (like an Instant Pot) to Sauté. Add the oil and cook the ribs, turning occasionally and adding more oil if needed, about 6 minutes; transfer to a bowl.

2. Add the carrot, celery, onion and garlic to a multicooker and cook, stirring often, until just tender, 6 to 8 minutes. Push the vegetables to the edges of the pot, add the tomato paste to the center and cook without stirring until browned, 1 to 2 minutes.

3. Add the wine and simmer until reduced, about 15 minutes. Stir in the crushed tomatoes, Worcestershire sauce, rosemary, thyme, broth and short ribs along with any juices from the bowl. Press Cancel. Lock the lid and cook on high pressure 35 minutes. Use the natural-release method for 10 minutes, then release any remaining pressure.

4. Transfer the short ribs (and any loose bones) to a second bowl; discard the rosemary and thyme. Skim off and discard any fat from the liquid. Using an immersion blender (or a standard blender), puree the sauce until smooth. Shred the meat into large chunks, discarding bones, and stir it back into the sauce.

5. Make the polenta: In a small saucepan, bring the milk, the butter and ¼ teaspoon of salt to a boil. Whisk in the polenta and cook, stirring constantly, until the mixture is thick and creamy and comes away from the side of the pan, 3 to 4 minutes. Stir in the cheese and, if it is too thick, 3 to 4 tablespoons water.

6. In a small bowl, mix the parsley, lemon zest and garlic. Serve the short ribs and sauce over the polenta, then sprinkle with the topping.

Love Notes

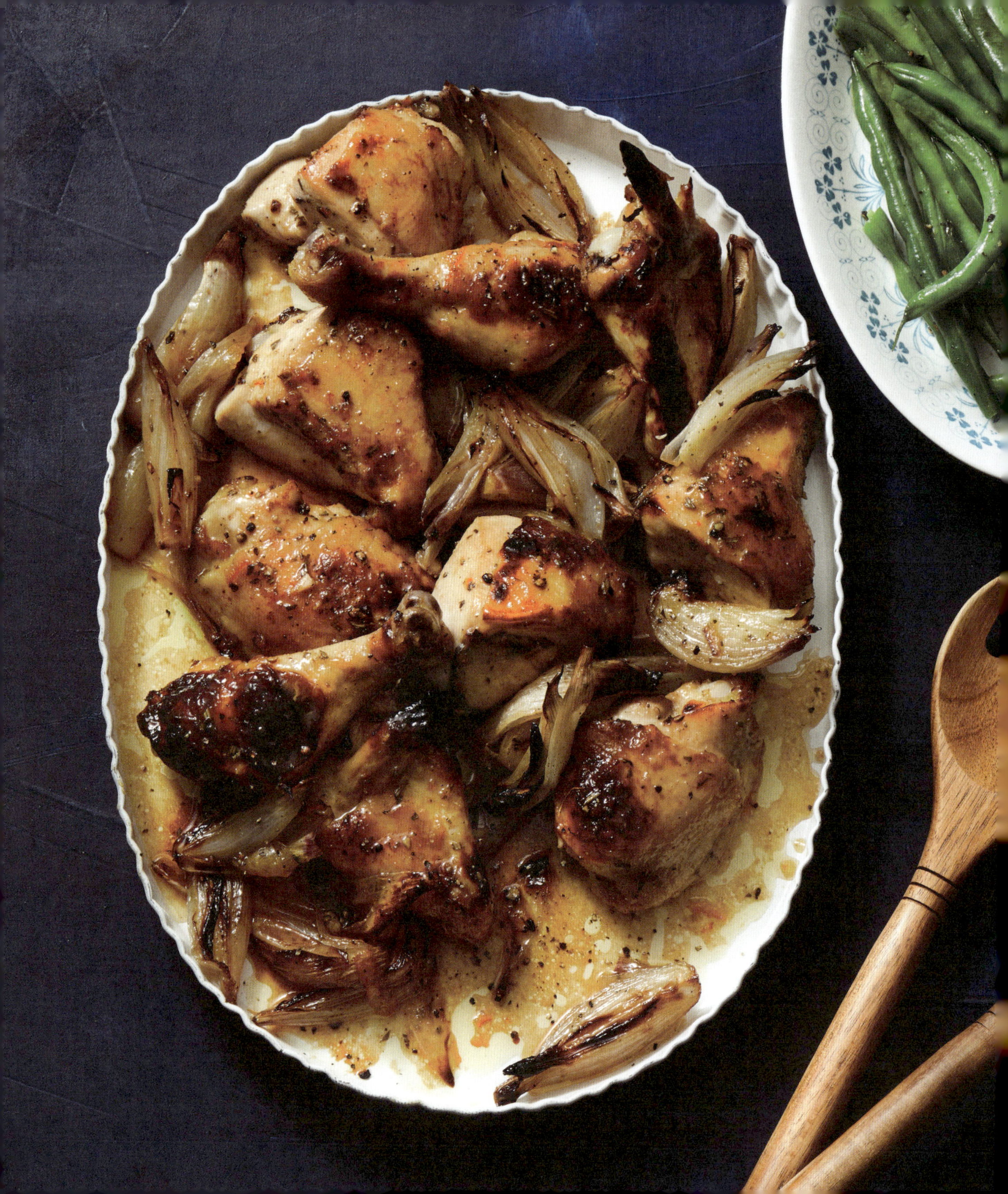

VIP DINNER PARTY | **ENTERTAINING**

Chicken à l'Orange

- 8 shallots, peeled and halved lengthwise (quartered if large)
- 2 tablespoons olive oil, divided
- Kosher salt and pepper
- 1 3- to 3½-pound whole chicken
- ½ cup orange marmalade
- 1 tablespoon white wine vinegar
- 1 tablespoon fresh rosemary, chopped
- 1 pound green beans, trimmed

Serves 4 to 6 | Active time 25 minutes | Total time 45 minutes

Paris-taught chef Julia Child helped bring French cooking, like the dinner-party favorite duck à l'orange, to America. Our updated version swaps in roast chicken for the duck and uses marmalade for its orange flair.

1. Heat the oven to 425°F. In a large, shallow roasting pan, toss the shallots with 1 tablespoon of oil and ¼ teaspoon each of salt and pepper.

2. Cut the chicken into 10 pieces (2 drumsticks, 2 thighs, 2 wings and 2 breasts—each halved). In a large bowl, whisk together the marmalade, vinegar and rosemary; the remaining tablespoon of oil; and ¼ teaspoon each of salt and pepper. Add the chicken and toss to coat.

3. Place the chicken mixture in a roasting pan, nestling the pieces among the shallots. Roast until the chicken is browned and cooked through and the shallots are golden brown and tender, 25 to 35 minutes.

4. Meanwhile, fill a large Dutch oven or saucepan with 1½ inches of water, then fit with a steamer basket (the water should be below the base of the basket) and bring to a simmer. Place the green beans in the basket, then cover and steam until crisp tender, 4 to 6 minutes. Serve with the chicken and shallots.

Love Notes

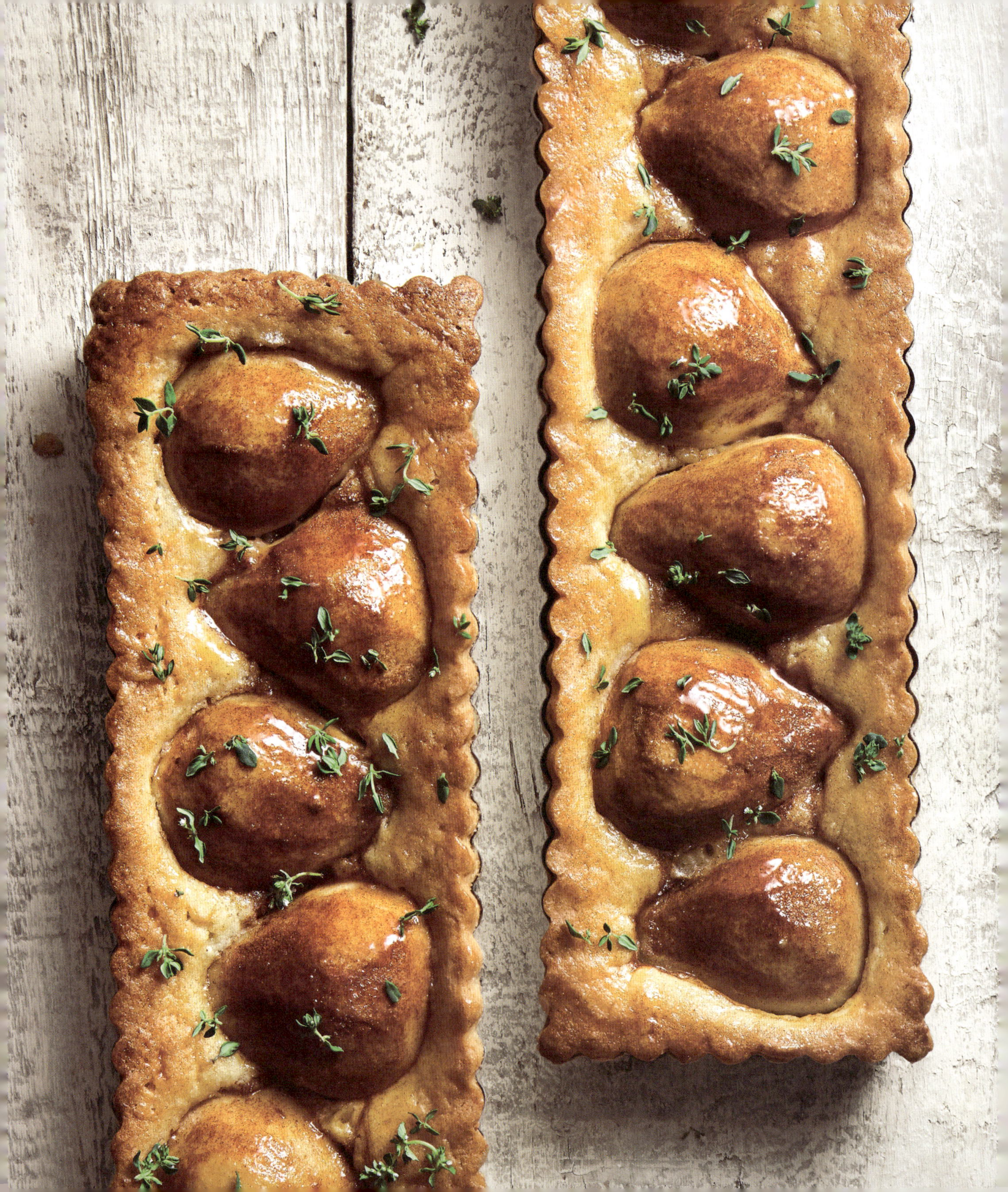

VIP DINNER PARTY | **ENTERTAINING**

Lemon & Thyme Pear Tart with Apricot Glaze

- 1 lemon
- 1 cup all-purpose flour
- ¼ teaspoon baking powder
- ¼ teaspoon kosher salt
- ½ cup (1 stick) unsalted butter, at room temperature
- ½ cup plus 1 tablespoon sugar
- 1 large egg
- 3 small Bartlett pears, peeled, halved and cored
- ¼ teaspoon ground cinnamon
- ¼ teaspoon ground ginger
- 2 tablespoons apricot preserves
- 4 fresh thyme sprigs, torn into small pieces

Serves 6 | Active time 25 minutes | Total time 1 hour 30 minutes

End the meal with something extra impressive! With a glossy apricot glaze, this tart offers the perfect balance of sweetness and tanginess.

1. Heat the oven to 350°F. Lightly coat a 14-inch by 4-inch tart pan or a 9-inch round tart pan with a removable bottom with nonstick cooking spray. From a lemon, grate ½ teaspoon of zest and squeeze 1 tablespoon of juice; set the juice aside. In a medium bowl, whisk together the flour, lemon zest, baking powder and salt.

2. In a large bowl, with an electric mixer on medium speed, beat the butter and ½ cup sugar until light and fluffy, about 3 minutes. Reduce the speed to low; beat in the egg. Gradually add the flour mixture, mixing until incorporated (the dough will be very soft).

3. Transfer the dough to the prepared tart pan; with floured fingers, push the dough evenly into the bottom and up the sides of the pan.

4. Arrange the pear halves, cut sides down, alternating top to bottom. Sprinkle with the cinnamon, the ginger and the remaining 1 tablespoon sugar. Bake until the crust is golden brown, 55 to 65 minutes; let cool on a wire rack.

5. In a small bowl, combine the apricot preserves and the lemon juice. Microwave 30 seconds or until bubbling; mix to combine. Brush gently over the entire tart; sprinkle with the thyme to serve.

NO TART PAN? NO PROBLEM
While a fluted tart pan with a removable bottom is ideal for this kind of tart, you can also use a standard pie plate. Just be sure to push the crust evenly into the bottom and only ½ inch above that on the sides.

Love Notes

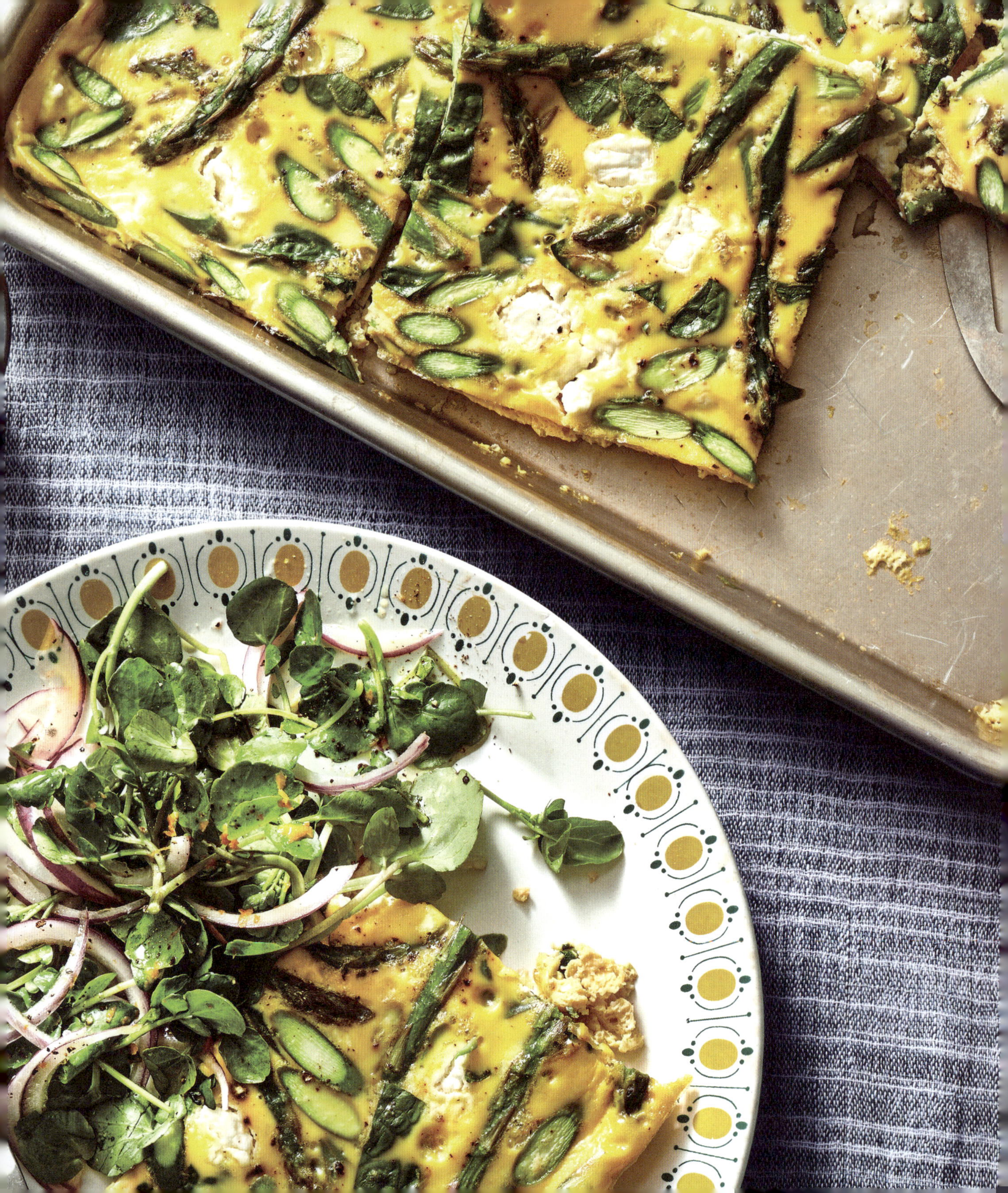

Sheet Pan Asparagus Frittata

Olive oil, for greasing
1 pound asparagus, trimmed
12 large eggs
1 cup milk
2 teaspoons Dijon mustard
Kosher salt and pepper
2 cups baby spinach, chopped
2½ ounces goat cheese, crumbled (½ cup)

Serves 6 | Active time 15 minutes | Total time 40 minutes plus resting

This feed-a-party breakfast dish is as simple as it is showstopping. Just pour the asparagus and egg mixture into a rimmed baking sheet and pop it in the oven, and — voilà! You'll spend less time doing dishes and more time with friends.

1. Heat the oven to 375°F. Lightly oil (with about 1 teaspoon of oil) a rimmed baking sheet.

2. Slice the asparagus ends on bias ¼ inch thick, leaving the top 4 inches of each spear intact, then halve each lengthwise (or quarter them if they are thick).

3. In a large bowl, whisk together the eggs, milk and Dijon mustard, 1 teaspoon of salt and ½ teaspoon of pepper. Stir in the spinach and the bias-cut asparagus, then pour into a prepared baking sheet. Scatter the top with the asparagus spears and goat cheese.

4. Bake, rotating the pan halfway through, until the eggs are puffed and the middle no longer jiggles, 20 to 22 minutes. Let rest 5 minutes before slicing.

EXTRA SLICES?
Stack them between pieces of parchment and freeze in an airtight container for up to 2 months. To reheat, remove parchment, wrap in a damp paper towel and microwave on High until warmed through, 1 minute and 30 seconds.

Love Notes

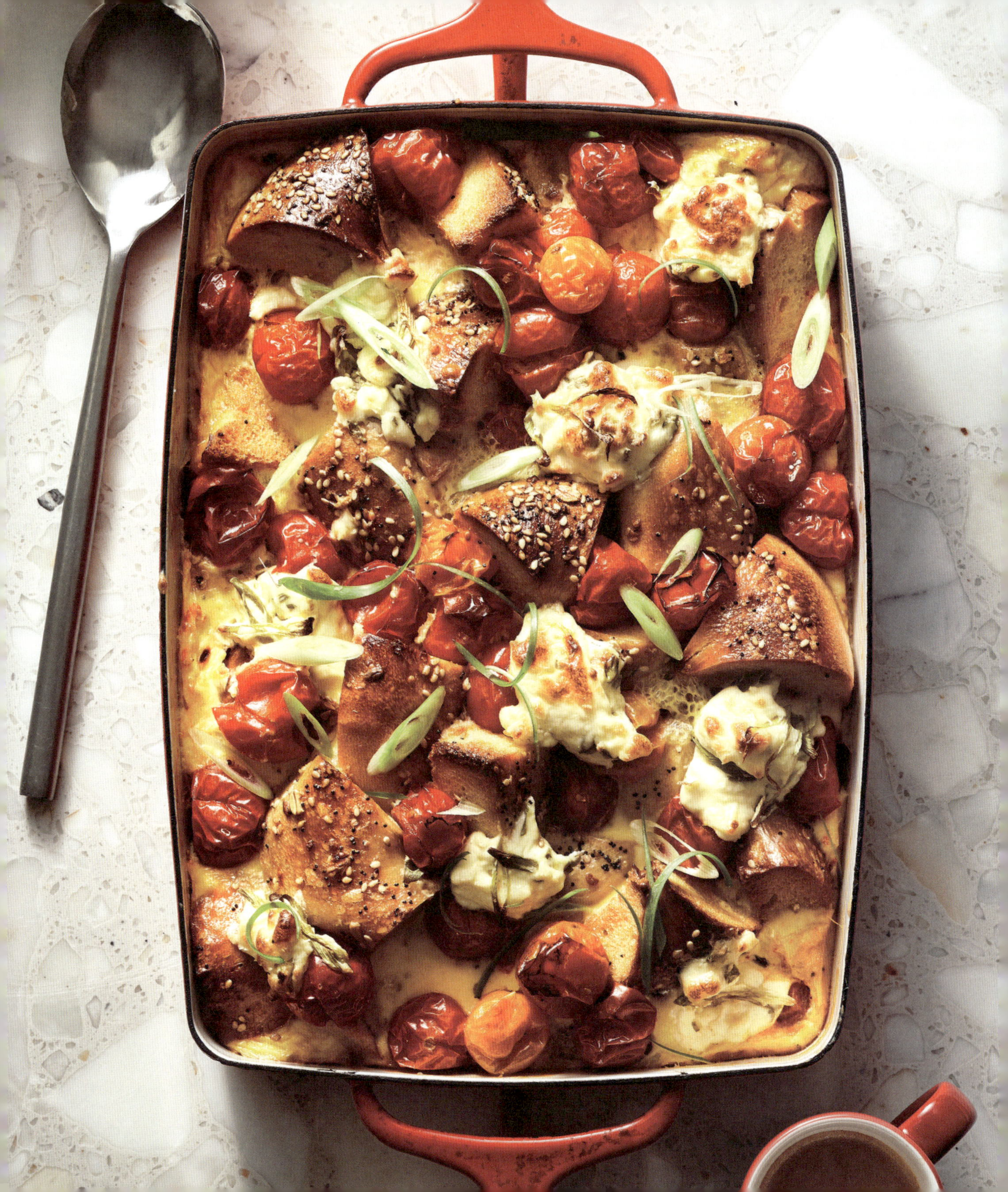

Tomato & Scallion Cream Cheese Bagel Bake

Serves 6 | Active time 15 minutes | Total time 1 hour 10 minutes

- 2 12-ounce packages grape tomatoes
- 2 tablespoons olive oil, plus more for the dish
- Kosher salt and pepper
- 3 everything bagels (about 12.5 ounces), split and cut into 1½-inch pieces
- 6 large eggs
- 1½ cups whole milk
- 4 ounces scallion cream cheese
- Sliced scallions, for serving

With just a few ingredients, you can cook up a crowd-pleasing casserole that offers a clever twist on a morning staple. Pre-toasting the bagels will keep them from getting soggy while baking.

1. Heat the oven to 400°F. On a small rimmed baking sheet, toss the grape tomatoes with the olive oil, ½ teaspoon of kosher salt and ¼ teaspoon of pepper. Roast until beginning to reduce, 25 to 30 minutes.

2. Arrange the everything bagel pieces on a large rimmed baking sheet and toast in the oven along with the tomatoes until lightly golden brown, 8 to 10 minutes.

3. Meanwhile, oil a shallow 2½- to 3-quart baking dish. In a large bowl, whisk together the eggs, the milk and ½ teaspoon each of salt and pepper. Toss with the toasted bagels; let sit, tossing occasionally, at least 15 minutes.

4. Reduce the oven temperature to 350°F. Fold the tomatoes into the bagel mixture, transfer to the prepared dish and dot with the scallion cream cheese. Bake until set and a knife inserted into the center comes out clean, 40 to 45 minutes. Scatter the sliced scallions on top if desired.

MAKE IT AHEAD
Assemble this casserole the night before, then pop it into the fridge while you sleep. In the morning, leave it on the counter as your oven comes to temperature, then cook as instructed above.

Love Notes

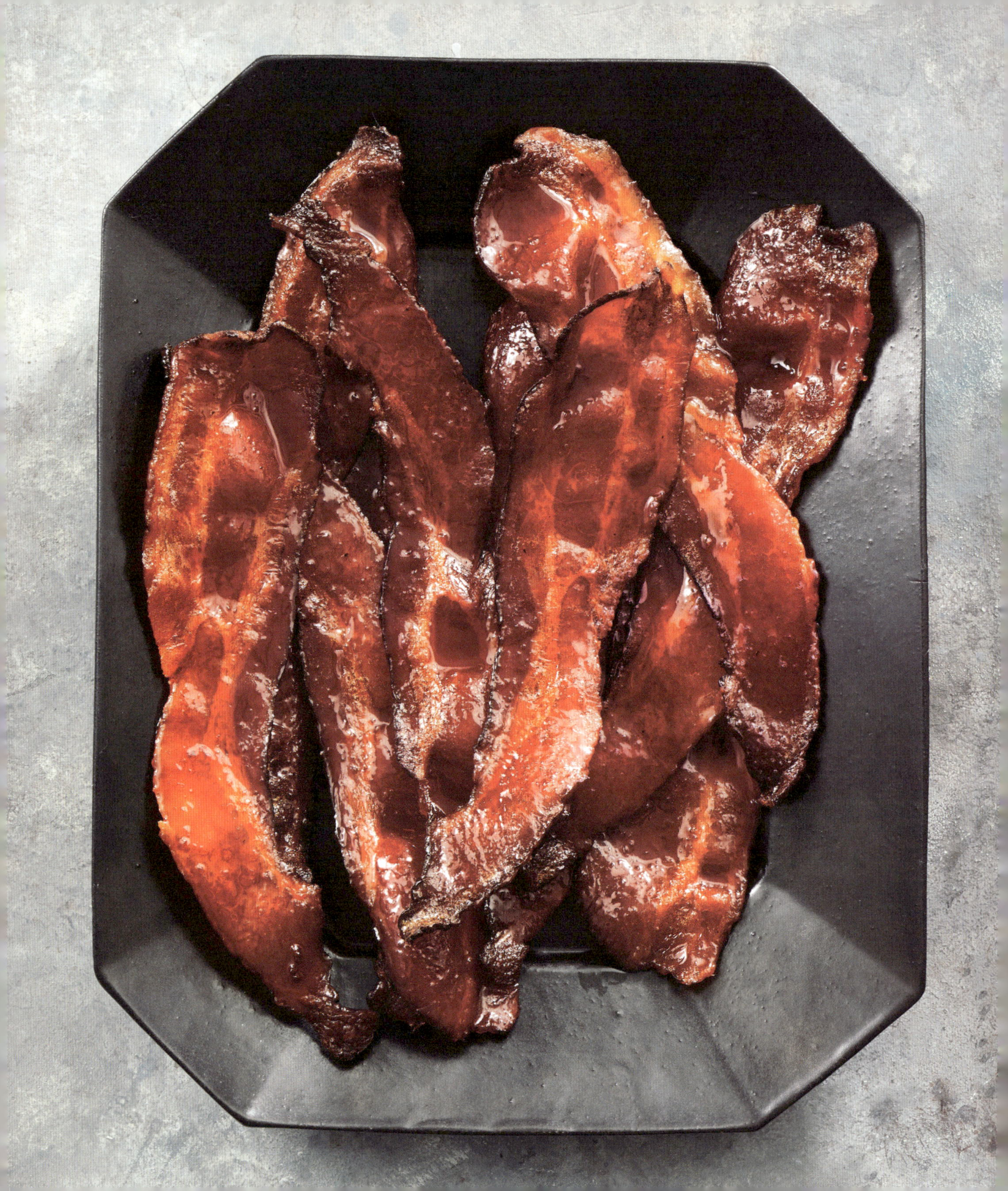

Sriracha-Maple Bacon

- 10 slices bacon (about 12 ounces)
- 1 to 2 tablespoons sriracha
- 2 tablespoons pure maple syrup

Serves 4 to 6 | Active time 5 minutes | Total time 30 minutes

Take crispy bacon to the next level by brushing a spicy-sweet glaze onto each slice. Thanks to a sheet pan (and aluminum foil), cleanup is a breeze.

1. Heat the oven to 400°F. Line a rimmed baking sheet with foil and set a wire rack inside. Arrange the bacon without overlapping on the wire rack and bake 10 minutes. Flip each piece and bake 10 minutes more.

2. In a small bowl, combine the sriracha and the maple syrup. Brush onto the bacon and bake until the bacon is crisp, 8 to 10 minutes.

BACON BONANZA
Keep this sweet and spicy bacon in rotation. Chop it and sprinkle it on deviled eggs, fold it into potato salad or layer it on a sandwich with cucumber, avocado, lettuce and a sunny-side-up egg.

Love Notes

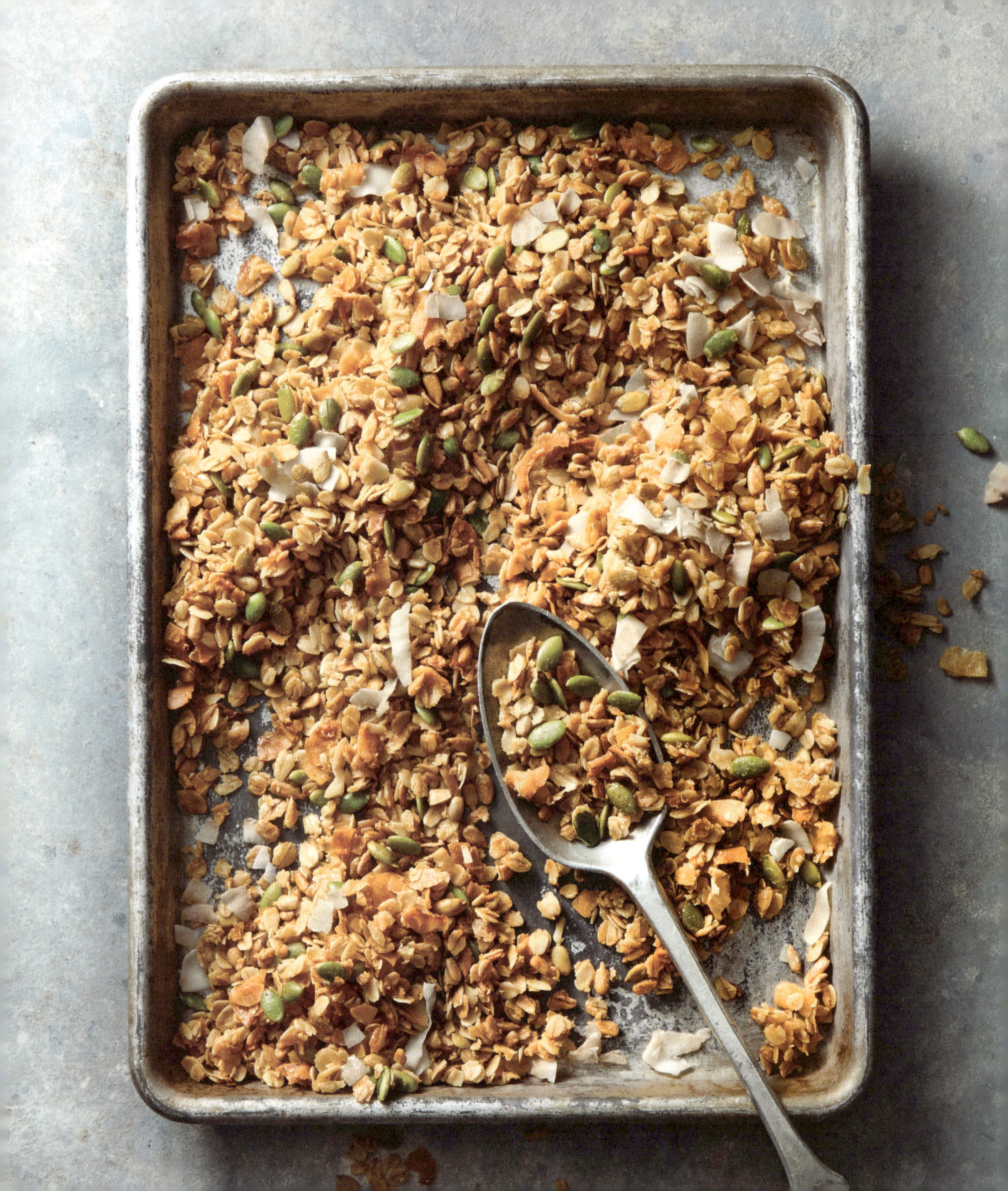

Best Ever Granola

- ½ cup olive oil or extra virgin coconut oil (melted)
- ¾ cup pure maple syrup
- 2 tablespoons turbinado sugar (we used Sugar in the Raw)
- 1 teaspoon kosher salt
- 3 cups old-fashioned rolled oats
- 1 cup unsweetened coconut flakes
- ¾ cup raw sunflower seeds
- ¾ cup raw pumpkin seeds

Makes 7 cups | Active time 15 minutes | Total time 1 hour 15 minutes

Transform a tub of yogurt into an interactive setup with this incredibly easy homemade granola. Bake a batch, then set it out alongside fresh berries and let your guests build their own individual bowls.

1. Heat the oven to 300°F. Line a large rimmed baking sheet with parchment paper. In a large bowl, combine the oil, maple syrup, sugar and salt. Add the oats, coconut and sunflower and pumpkin seeds and stir to evenly coat.

2. Spread the mixture onto a prepared baking sheet and bake, stirring every 15 minutes, until the granola is light golden brown and dry, 45 to 55 minutes. Let cool completely.

Love Notes

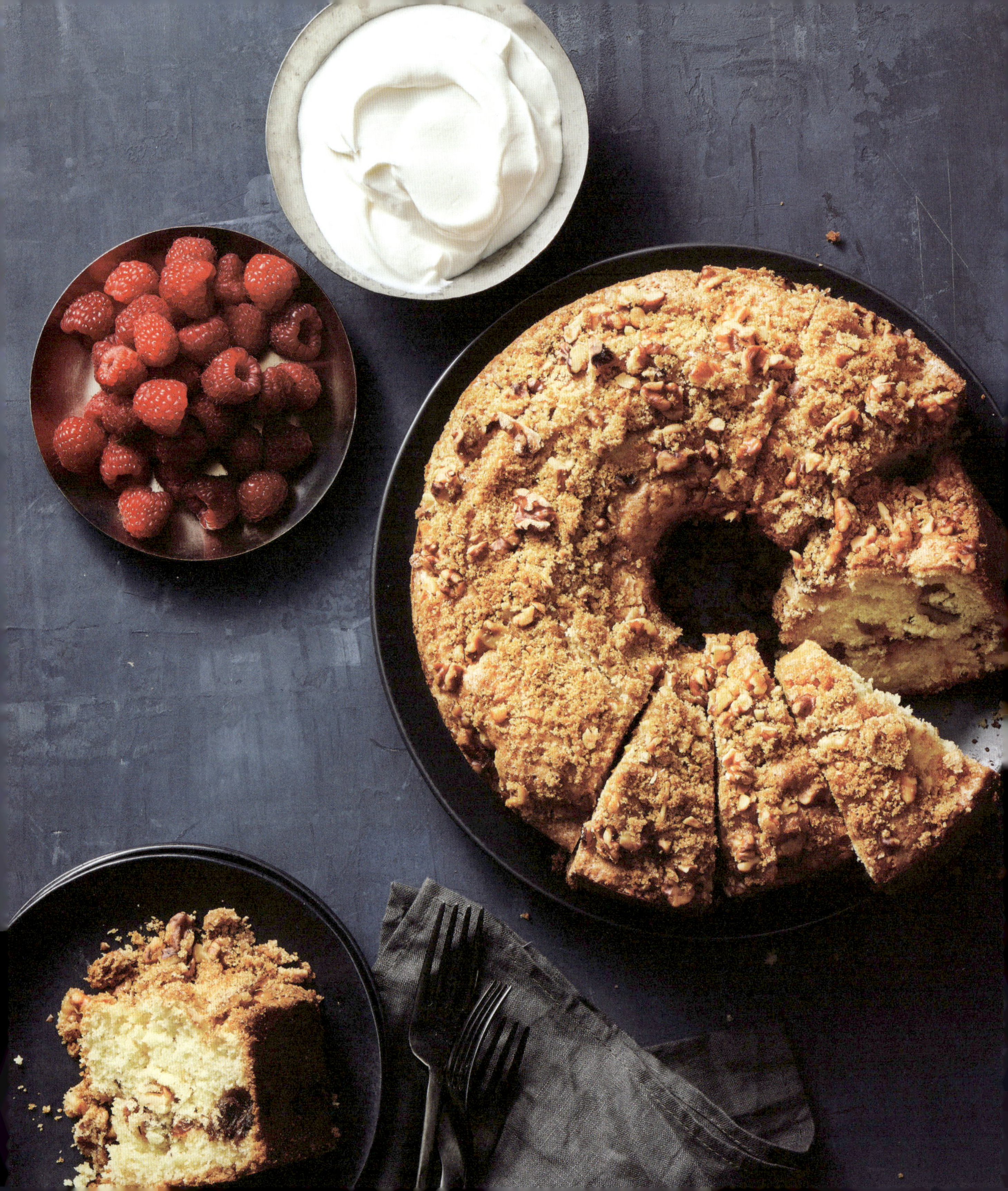

Raisin-Walnut Coffee Cake

Serves 12 | Active time 30 minutes | Total time 1 hour 10 minutes plus cooling

Serving baked goods in the morning doesn't have to mean being up before the sun. Avoid setting an early alarm with this sweet and nutty make-ahead cake you can warm up just before your guests arrive.

- 1 cup (2 sticks) unsalted butter, at room temperature, plus more for the pan
- 2½ cups all-purpose flour
- 2 teaspoons baking powder
- 1 teaspoon baking soda
- ½ teaspoon kosher salt
- 1½ cups walnuts, chopped
- ¾ cup brown sugar
- ½ teaspoon ground cinnamon
- ½ cup raisins
- 1 cup granulated sugar
- 3 large eggs
- 2 teaspoons pure vanilla extract
- 1 cup sour cream

1. Heat oven to 375°F. Butter an angel food cake pan. In a medium bowl, whisk together the flour, baking powder, baking soda and salt.

2. In a small bowl, combine the walnuts, brown sugar and cinnamon; transfer half to a second bowl and mix in the raisins.

3. Using an electric mixer on medium, beat the granulated sugar and butter to combine, 2 minutes. Beat in the eggs, 1 at a time, then the vanilla. Reduce to low and mix in the flour mixture until just combined. Add the sour cream and mix until just combined (batter should be very thick).

4. Spread half of the batter evenly into the prepared pan and sprinkle with the raisin-walnut mixture. Top with the remaining batter and sprinkle with the walnut mixture. Bake 30 minutes. Reduce the oven temperature to 300°F and continue baking until a wooden pick inserted into the cake comes out clean, 20 to 25 minutes more. Cool the cake completely in the pan on a wire rack. Unmold the cake. Slice and serve.

GET AHEAD
You can make this cake, wrap it in plastic and freeze it for up to 3 days. An hour and 15 minutes before serving, let it thaw to room temperature. Then, if desired, warm it in a 375°F oven.

Love Notes

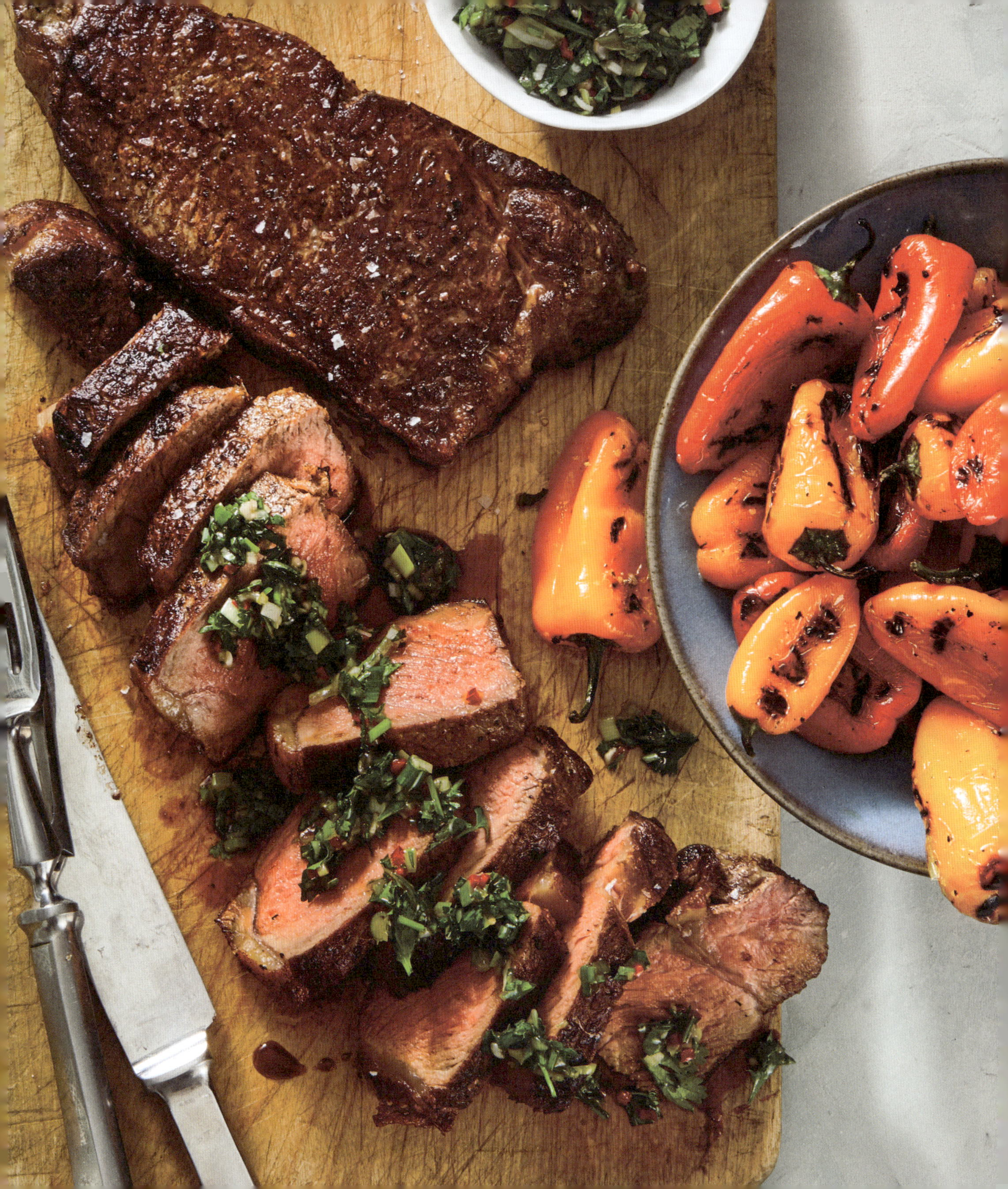

Steak & Grilled Peppers with Chimichurri

Serves 6 | Active time 25 minutes | Total time 25 minutes

- 1 pound mixed baby peppers
- 3 tablespoons olive oil, divided
- Kosher salt and pepper
- 2 12-ounce strip steaks (about 1½ inches thick), trimmed
- 2 tablespoons red wine vinegar
- 2 scallions, finely chopped
- 1 small clove garlic, grated
- ½ large red chile, seeded and finely chopped
- ½ cup flat-leaf parsley, chopped
- ½ cup fresh cilantro, chopped

Sometimes the best way to entertain involves keeping things simple: good steaks, fresh produce and a bright, herby sauce. Tangy Argentinian chimichurri is easy to whisk together ahead of time, so all that's left to do is watch the grill.

1. Heat the grill to medium. In a large bowl, toss the peppers with 1 tablespoon of oil and ¼ teaspoon each of salt and pepper. Season the steaks with ¼ teaspoon each of salt and pepper.

2. Grill the steak and peppers, covered, turning the peppers occasionally, until the peppers are lightly charred and tender, 5 to 7 minutes, and the steak is cooked to the desired doneness, 5 to 8 minutes per side. Transfer the peppers to a platter and the steak to a cutting board and let the steak rest at least 5 minutes before slicing.

3. Meanwhile, in a small bowl, combine the vinegar, scallions, garlic and chile, the remaining 2 tablespoons of oil and a pinch each of salt and pepper. Stir in the parsley and cilantro and serve with the steak and peppers.

TASTY TOPPING
While classic chimichurri features a mix of parsley, oregano, garlic, vinegar and oil, our version includes cilantro and scallions.

Love Notes

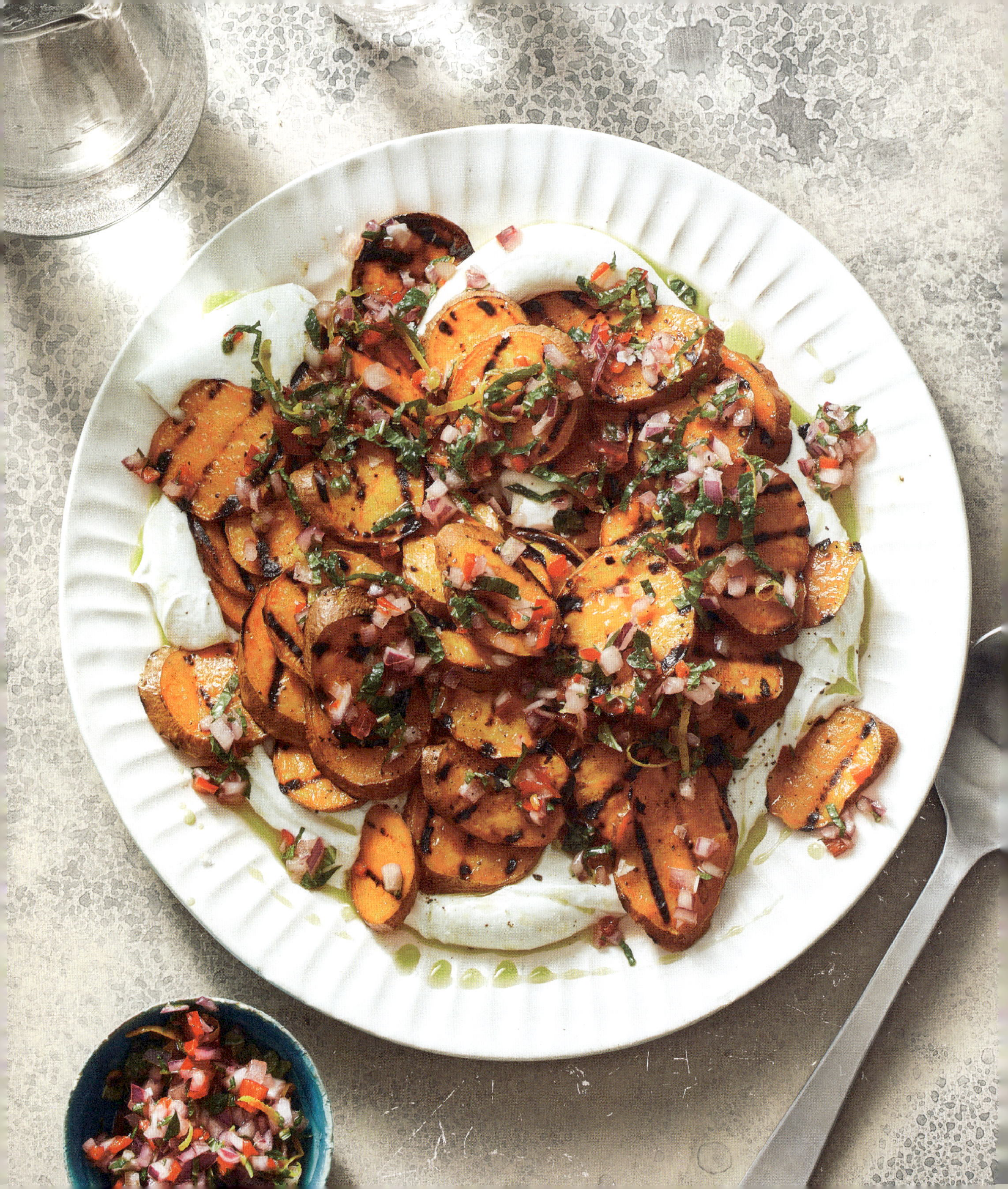

Grilled Sweet Potatoes with Mint-Chile Relish

Serves 6 | **Active time 20 minutes** | **Total time 20 minutes**

- ½ small red onion, finely chopped
- 2 teaspoons grated lemon zest plus ¼ cup juice
- 2 pounds sweet potatoes, well scrubbed and sliced into ¼-inch-thick rounds
- 3 tablespoons olive oil, divided, plus more for serving
- Kosher salt and pepper
- 1 small fresno chile, seeded and finely chopped
- 2 tablespoons hemp seed (optional)
- ¼ cup fresh mint, chopped
- Plain Greek yogurt, for serving

This smoky sweet potato dish makes the perfect addition to your outdoor dinner party. The best part: You don't have to boil or par-bake the spuds before grilling. If you slice them thinly, they'll cook through over the grates.

1. Heat the grill to medium. In a small bowl, combine the onion and the lemon juice. Let sit, tossing occasionally.

2. In a large bowl, toss the sweet potatoes with 2 tablespoons of oil and ¼ teaspoon each of salt and pepper. Grill until slightly charred and tender, 4 to 5 minutes per side.

3. Into the bowl with the onions, stir the lemon zest, chile and hemp (if using) and the remaining tablespoon of oil, then stir in the mint.

4. Spread the Greek yogurt onto a platter and drizzle with oil. Arrange the sweet potatoes over the yogurt and spoon the mint relish on top.

TAME THE FLAME
Hidden underneath the charred potatoes and fiery relish is a swoosh of yogurt that adds a tangy cooling note.

Love Notes

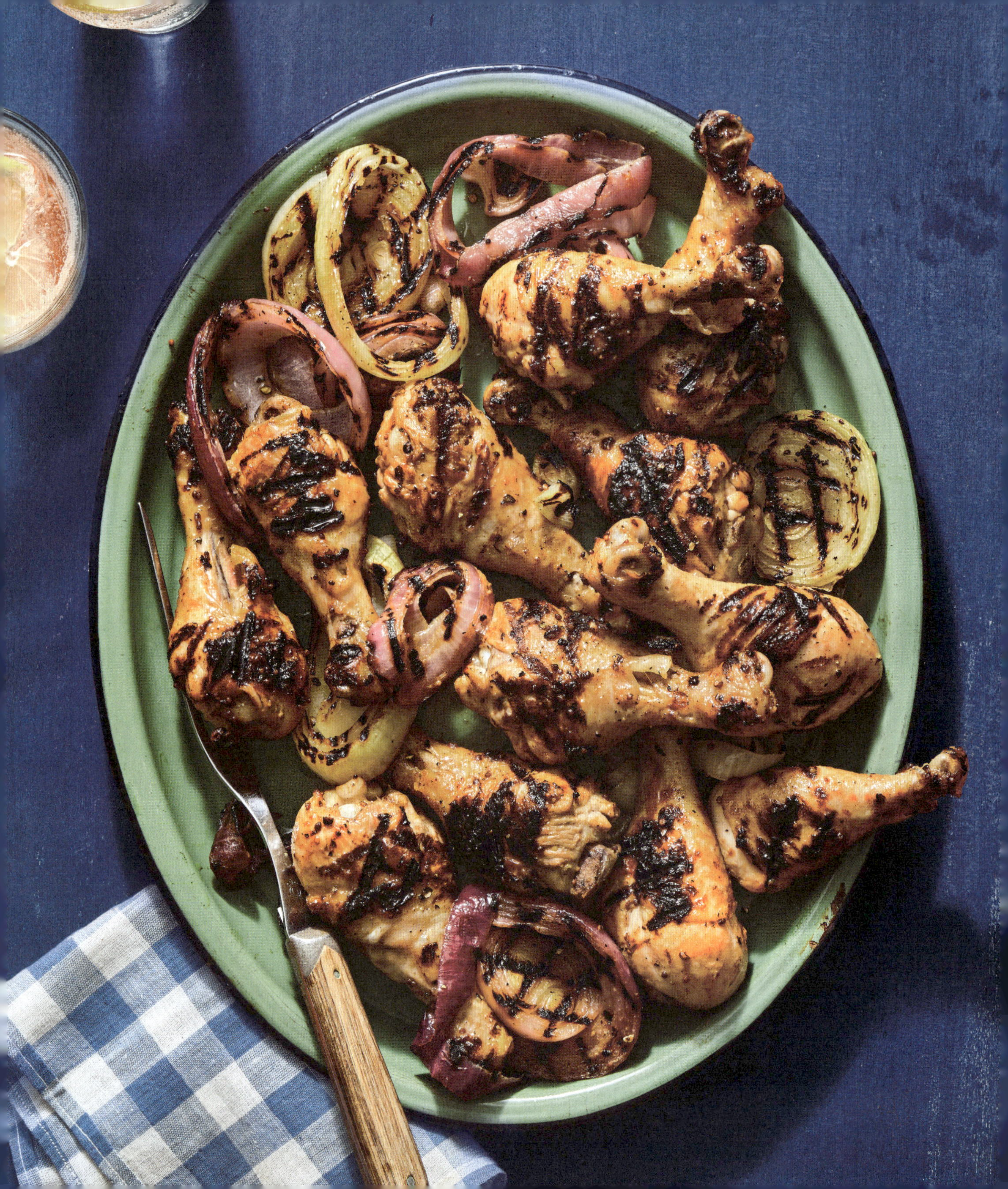

Double Mustard-Marinated Chicken Drumsticks

Serves 6 | Active time 50 minutes | Total time 50 minutes plus marinating

¼ cup whole-grain mustard
¼ cup Dijon mustard
¼ cup apple juice
2 tablespoons white wine vinegar
1 tablespoon olive oil
Pepper
1 medium yellow onion, sliced into ½-inch-thick rounds
1 medium red onion, sliced into ½-inch-thick rounds
12 small drumsticks (about 2½ pounds)

Hosting doesn't have to break the bank. This wow-worthy chicken recipe features an irresistibly tangy marinade of two mustards but is still budget-friendly. Serve it with a crisp white wine and a straightforward salad.

1. In a glass measuring cup, whisk together the mustards, apple juice, vinegar and oil and ½ teaspoon of pepper. Divide the onions, the chicken and the mustard marinade between 2 large resealable bags. Refrigerate at least 3 hours, up to 6 hours.

2. Heat the grill to medium-low. Remove the chicken and onions from the marinade (discard the marinade). Grill the chicken, covered, turning occasionally, until cooked through, 30 to 40 minutes.

3. When the chicken has 20 minutes left to cook, grill the onions, turning occasionally, until tender and slightly charred, 15 to 20 minutes. Transfer the chicken and onions to a platter. Serve warm or at room temperature.

Love Notes

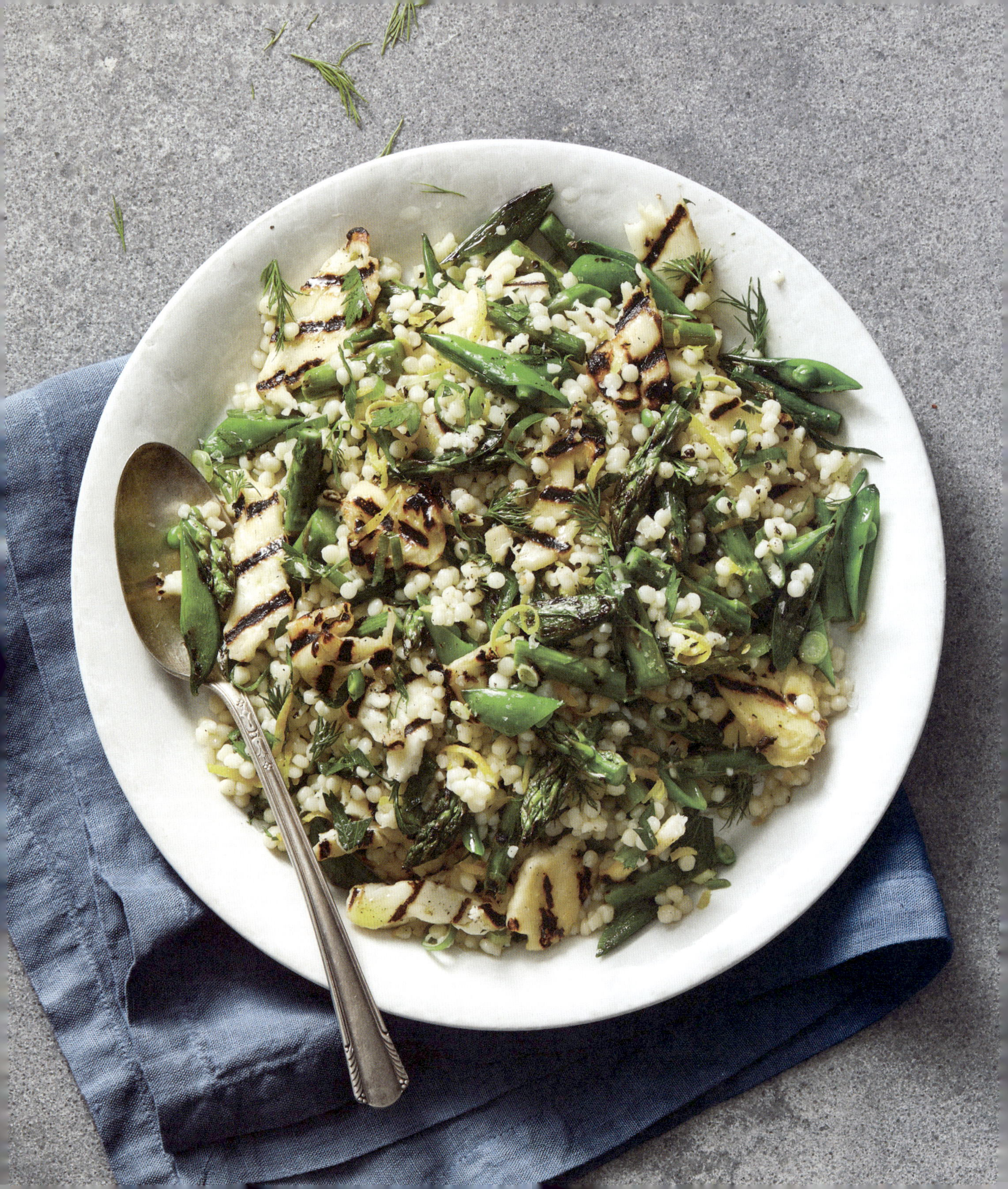

Grilled Halloumi Salad

- 1 cup Israeli (pearl) couscous or quick-cooking farro
- 8 ounces asparagus, trimmed
- 4 ounces snap peas, strings removed
- 3 teaspoons olive oil, divided
- Kosher salt and pepper
- 4 ounces halloumi cheese, thinly sliced (about ⅛-inch thick)
- 1 teaspoon grated lemon zest plus 2 tablespoons lemon juice
- 1 scallion, thinly sliced
- ¼ cup fresh dill, chopped
- ¼ cup flat-leaf parsley, chopped

Serves 4 | Active time 20 minutes | Total time 45 minutes

This squeaky, salty cheese from Cyprus has a unique ability to resist breaking down (read: melting) at high temps, so it's a joy to quickly throw on the grill. Toss it with fluffy couscous and lemony grilled vegetables for a next-level dish.

1. Cook the couscous per the package directions; drain and let cool, then transfer to a large bowl. Heat the grill to medium-high.

2. In a second bowl, toss the asparagus and snap peas with 1 teaspoon of oil and ⅛ teaspoon each of salt and pepper. Grill, turning or rolling once, until lightly charred and tender, 2 to 4 minutes; transfer to a cutting board.

3. Grill the halloumi until lightly charred, about 20 seconds per side; transfer to a plate.

4. Cut the asparagus into 1-inch pieces and the snap peas into halves or thirds and toss with the couscous, the lemon zest and juice, the remaining 2 teaspoons of oil and ¼ teaspoon each of salt and pepper. Fold in the scallion, dill and parsley.

5. Tear the halloumi into bite-size pieces and fold into the couscous.

CROWD PLEASER
If you're planning a big backyard party, aim to serve at least one veg-forward dish that can double as a vegetarian main.

Love Notes

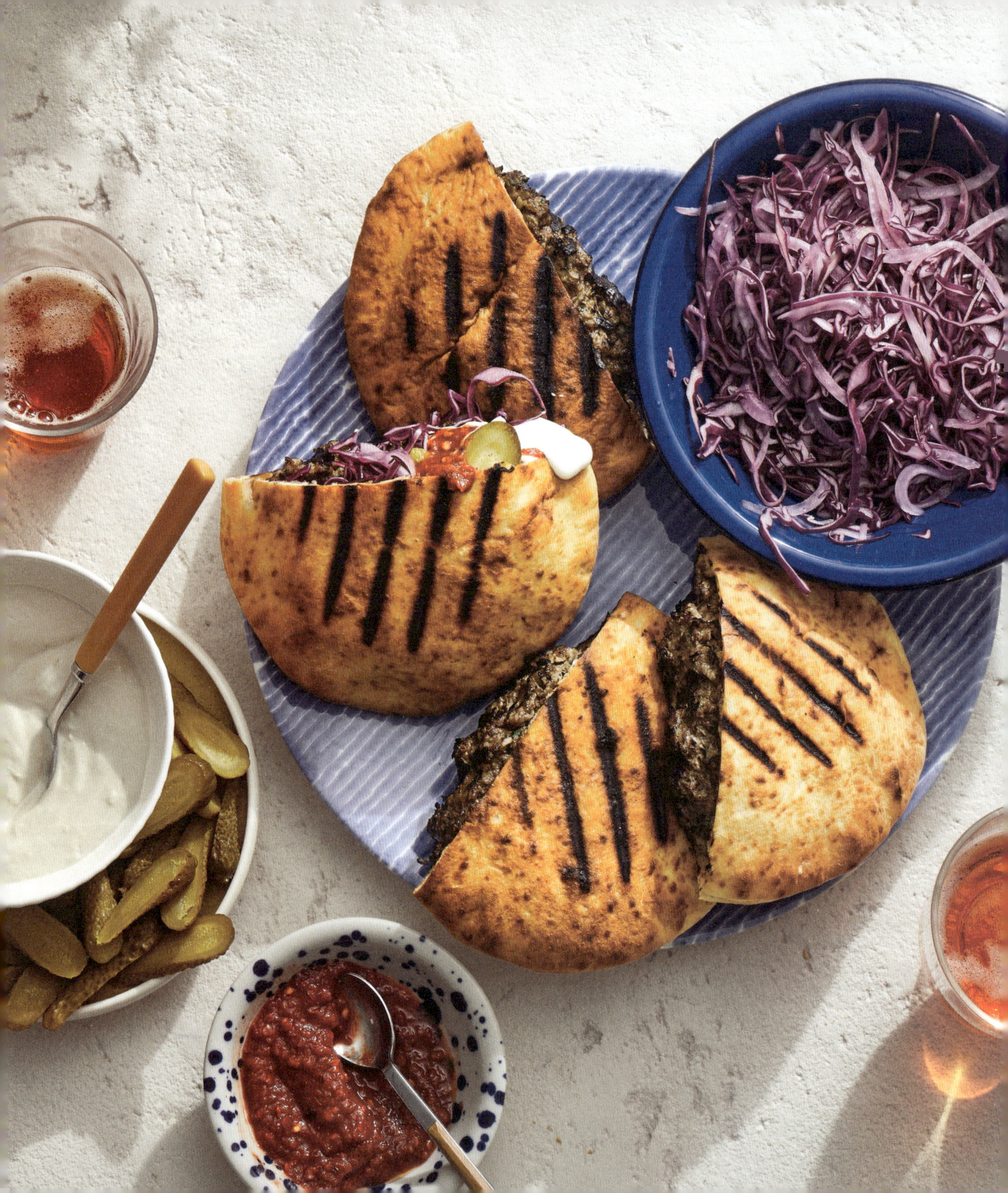

Arayes

Serves 4 | Active time 35 minutes | Total time 35 minutes

- 1½ tablespoons distilled white vinegar
- ¾ teaspoon sugar
- Kosher salt and pepper
- 1 large white onion
- ¼ medium red cabbage (about 10 ounces), cored and very thinly sliced
- ¼ cup flat-leaf parsley leaves, finely chopped
- 1 tablespoon baharat
- 3 cloves garlic, grated, divided
- 1 pound 90% lean ground beef
- 2 pitas, halved
- ½ tablespoon olive oil
- ¼ cup low-fat Greek yogurt
- 2 tablespoons tahini
- 1 tablespoon fresh lemon juice
- Gherkins, sliced, for serving
- Hot sauce, for serving

Add these Lebanese meat-stuffed pitas to your grill rotation and we guarantee that your guests will be impressed. Mix baharat, a versatile smoky-sweet Middle Eastern spice blend, with the beef before grilling.

1. Heat the grill to medium. In a large bowl, whisk together the vinegar, the sugar and ½ teaspoon salt until dissolved. Thinly slice one-fourth of the onion and add to the bowl along with the cabbage. Let sit, tossing occasionally.

2. Meanwhile, coarsely grate the remaining onion into a medium bowl. Add the parsley, the baharat, two-thirds of the garlic and ½ teaspoon each of salt and pepper. Add the beef and mix just to combine. Divide the mixture among the pita pockets (about ¾ cup each).

3. Brush the outsides of the pitas with oil and grill until the beef is cooked medium-well (155°F), 4 to 5 minutes per pita side; then grill the open end of each pita to cook the exposed meat, about 2 minutes.

4. Meanwhile, in a separate small bowl, whisk together the yogurt, tahini and lemon juice; the remaining garlic; 2 tablespoons of water; and ¼ teaspoon of salt, then whisk in more water, ½ teaspoon at a time, until the sauce reaches drizzling consistency.

5. Serve the arayes with the pickled cabbage and the tahini sauce as well as gherkins and hot sauce.

Love Notes

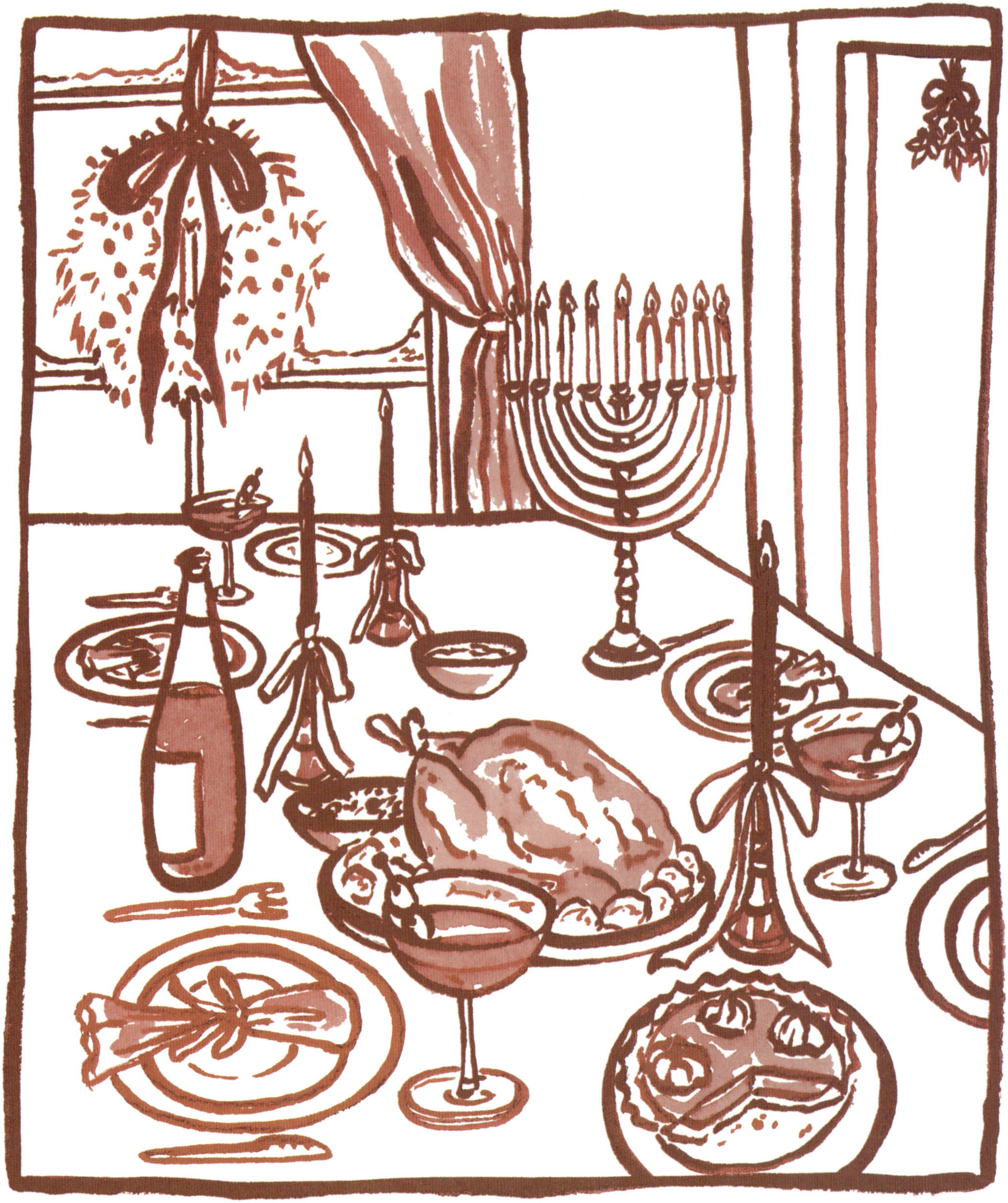

PART 4

Holiday Cooking

Figuring out where to spend the holidays? Wherever you go and whomever you celebrate with, these mix-and-match recipes have you covered. If you're hosting, choose one (or more!) from each category. If attending, offer to bring one of these desserts.

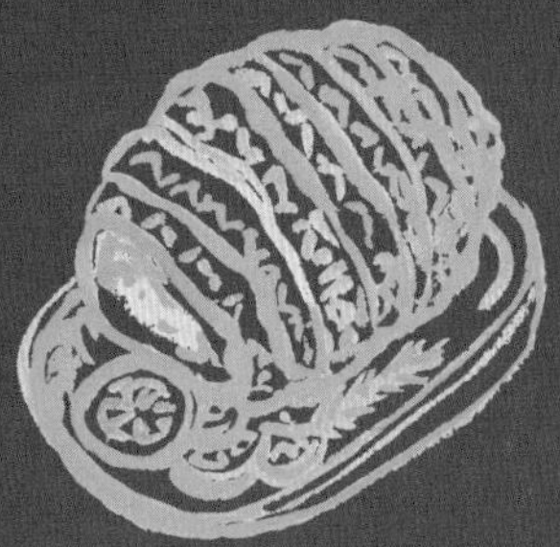

The Main Event

- 209 Roast Turkey Breast
- 211 Everything Bagel Crusted Salmon with Herby Fennel Salad
- 213 Pineapple, Orange & Onion Roasted Ham
- 215 Peppercorn Beef Tenderloin
- 217 Orange-Ginger Roast Chicken with Fennel & Radicchio Salad

Showstopping Sides

- 219 Roasted Root Vegetables
- 221 Fresh Green Bean Casserole
- 223 Sweet & Spicy Brussels Sprouts
- 225 Roasted Carrots & Red Onions
- 227 Dill-Spiked Potato Latkes
- 229 White Bean & Radicchio Salad
- 231 Herby Lentil & Burrata Salad
- 233 Thyme-Scented Mashed Potatoes

Delicious Desserts

- 235 Strawberry Coconut-Crust Cheesecake
- 237 Mixed-Berry Cornmeal Cobblers
- 239 Pecan Pie Brownies
- 241 Peach & Raspberry Galette
- 243 Cookie Cheesecake Bites
- 245 Key Lime Pie
- 247 Dulce de Leche Apple Pie
- 249 Olive Oil–Clementine Cake
- 251 Banana Pudding

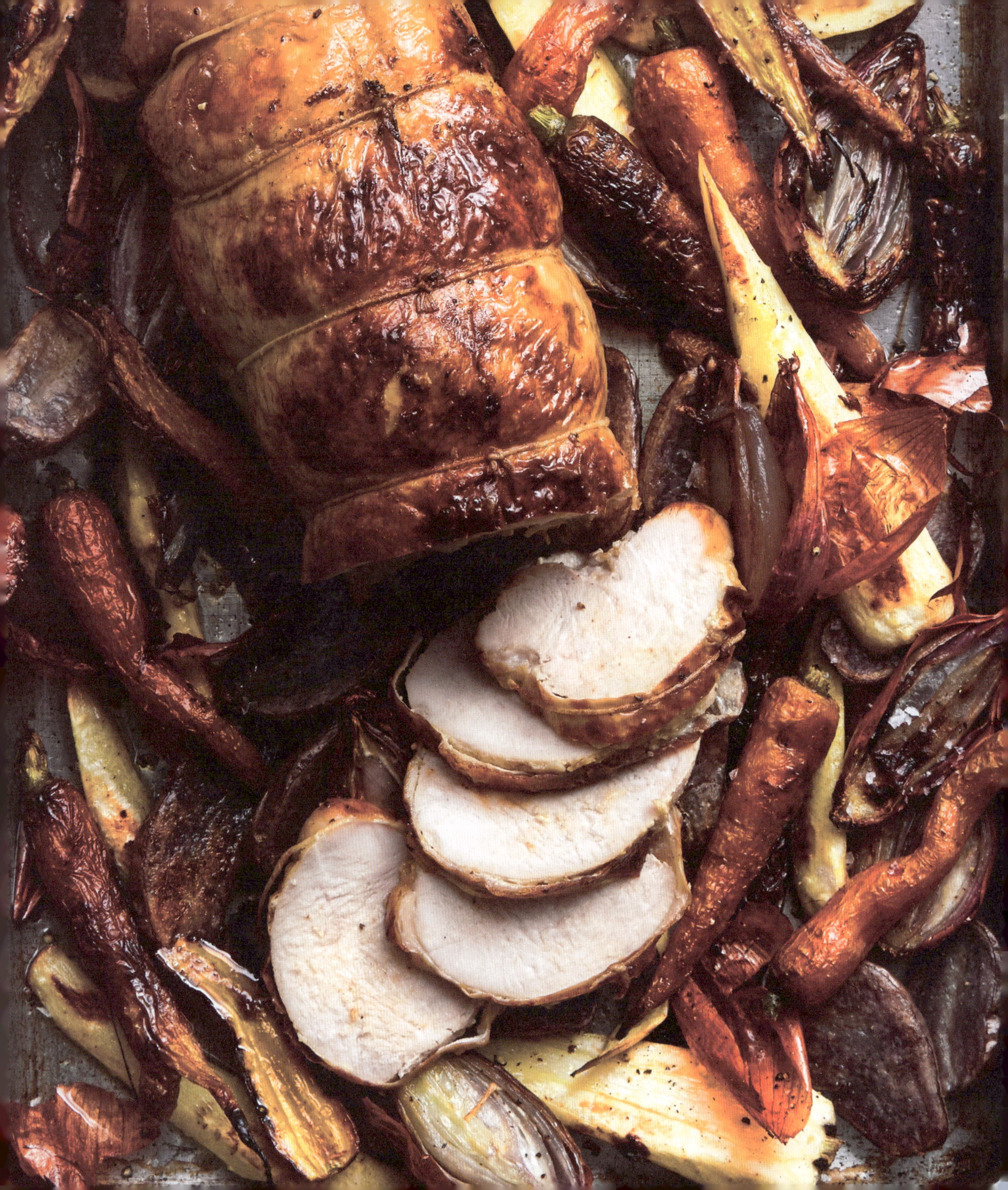

Roast Turkey Breast

Serves 8 | Active time 30 minutes | Total time 2 hours 25 minutes

- 1 lemon
- 6 tablespoons butter, at room temperature
- 4 cloves garlic, crushed with press
- 2 tablespoons Dijon mustard
- Kosher salt and pepper
- 2 (2-pound) turkey-breast halves, deboned
- 1 pound medium shallots, halved lengthwise (left in their skins)
- 1 teaspoon olive oil
- 1 pound small purple potatoes (about 8), scrubbed and halved lengthwise
- 12 ounces small parsnips (about 4), trimmed, scrubbed and halved lengthwise
- 1 pound small thin carrots (about 12), trimmed and scrubbed

This one-dish dinner only looks fancy. Succulent roast turkey breast and savory caramelized root vegetables make for a delicious (and deceptively simple!) sheet pan feast that can feed a crowd.

1. Heat the oven to 425°F. With a vegetable peeler, remove 6 strips of lemon zest, avoiding the white pith; thinly slice crosswise. In a small bowl, combine the butter, garlic, mustard and lemon zest and ½ teaspoon each of salt and pepper; set aside.

2. Remove the skin from turkey-breast halves and set aside. Rub the butter mixture all over the turkey breasts. Place one breast half on top of the other, arranging so 1 thick side and 1 thin side are sandwiched together. Wrap the breasts in skin and tie with butcher's twine to form a log shape.

3. On a large rimmed baking sheet, toss the shallots with oil and ¼ teaspoon each of salt and pepper. Arrange them in the center of the sheet and place the turkey on top. Roast 60 minutes.

4. Remove from the oven and transfer the turkey to a cutting board. Add the potatoes, parsnips and carrots to the baking sheet and toss with the shallots and ½ teaspoon each of salt and pepper; arrange in an even layer. Place the turkey on top of the vegetables and roast until the turkey registers 160°F on an instant-read thermometer and the vegetables are golden brown and tender, 35 to 45 minutes more (remove any vegetables that are done before the turkey).

5. Transfer the turkey to a clean cutting board and let it rest at least 10 minutes before slicing. Serve with the pan juices and vegetables.

Love Notes

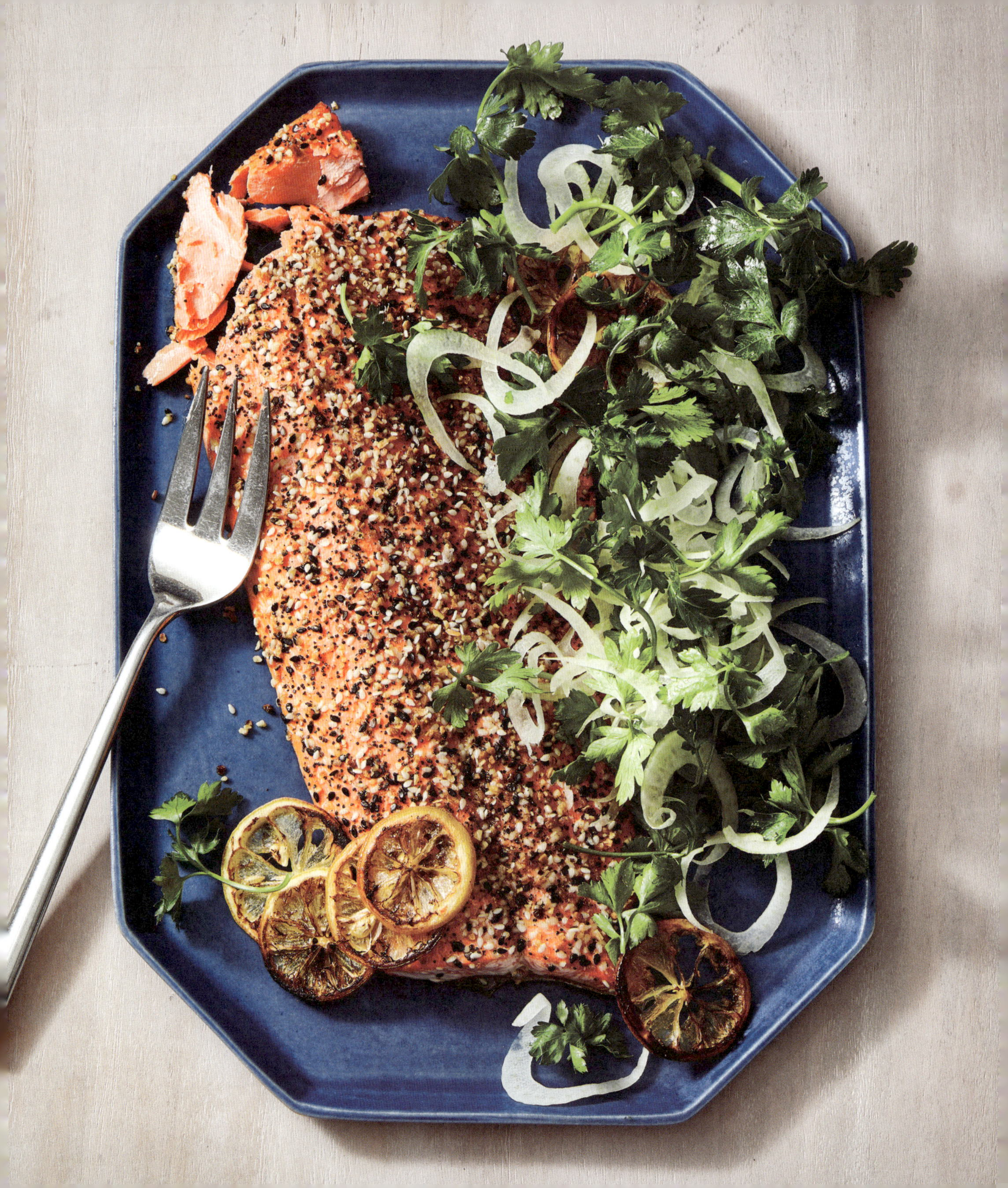

Everything Bagel Crusted Salmon with Herby Fennel Salad

1½ pounds skin-on salmon fillet

2 tablespoons olive oil, divided

Kosher salt and pepper

2 tablespoons everything spice blend

1 lemon

1 small bulb fennel, cored and very thinly sliced, plus ½ cup fennel fronds

3 scallions, thinly sliced

½ cup flat-leaf parsley leaves

½ cup cilantro leaves

Serves 4 | Active time 20 minutes | Total time 25 minutes

Usually made with poppy seeds, toasted sesame seeds, dried garlic, dried onion and salt, this spice blend (plus a squeeze of lemon!) gives incredible flavor to flaky roasted salmon. Round it out with a bright, crunchy fennel salad.

1. Heat the oven to 425°F. Place the salmon, skin side down, on a rimmed baking sheet and rub with 1 tablespoon of oil, then sprinkle ¼ teaspoon of pepper and all of the everything spice on top. Thinly slice half of the lemon and arrange it around the salmon. Bake until the salmon is barely opaque throughout, 18 to 22 minutes.

2. Meanwhile, in a bowl, toss the fennel with juice from the remaining lemon half (about 1½ tablespoons), the remaining tablespoon of oil and ¼ teaspoon each of salt and pepper.

3. Just before serving, toss the fennel with the scallions, parsley, cilantro and fennel fronds. Serve with the salmon and the roasted lemon slices.

SHAKE IT UP
Reach for this seasoning to jazz up avocado toast, potato salad, scrambled eggs and even popcorn.

Love Notes

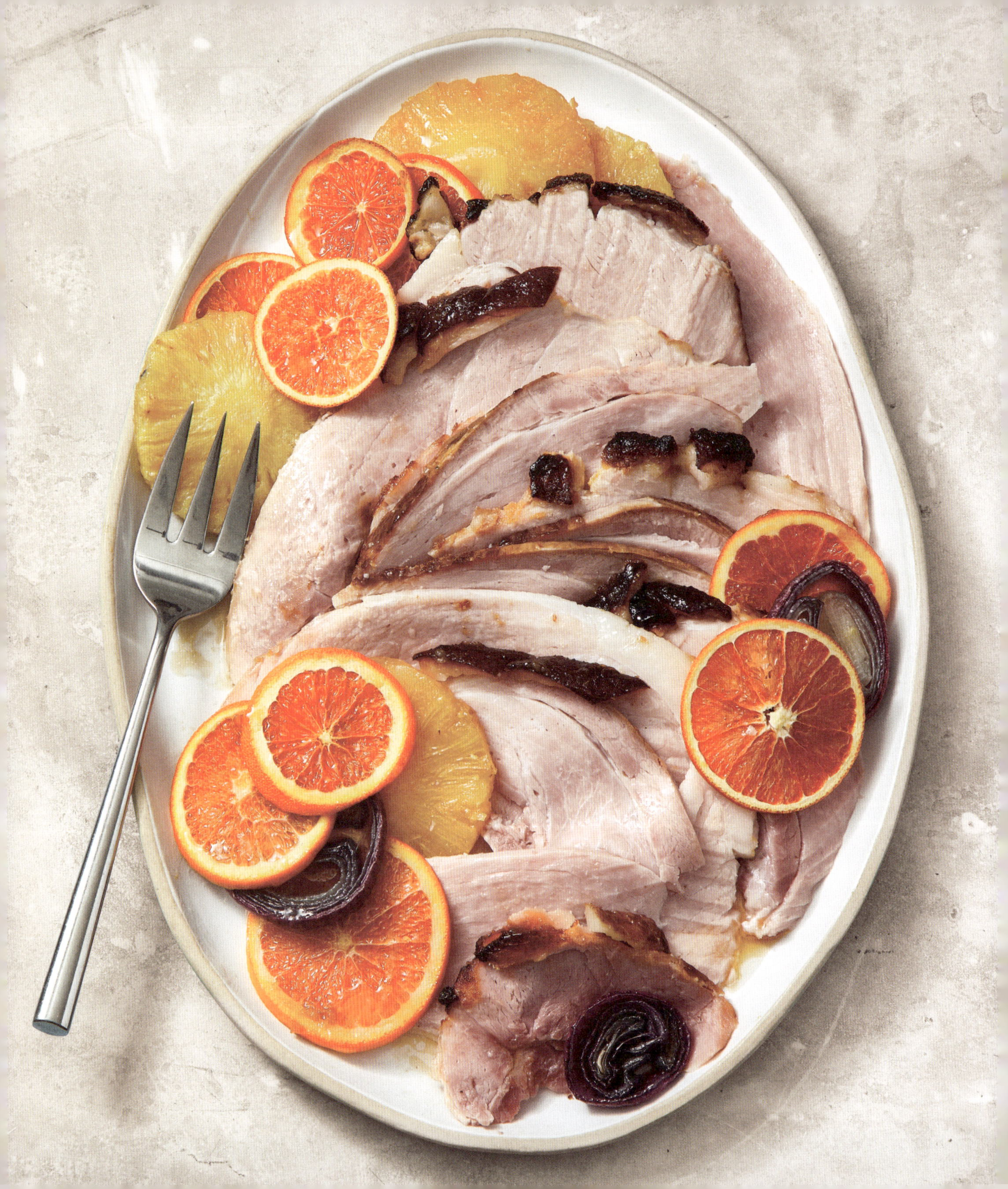

THE MAIN EVENT | **HOLIDAY**

Pineapple, Orange & Onion Roasted Ham

- 1 navel orange, sliced into ¼-inch-thick rounds
- 1 medium red onion, sliced into ½-inch-thick rounds
- 1 pineapple, rind removed, half cut into ½-inch-thick rounds and remaining half roughly chopped
- ½ fully cooked bone-in ham (about 7 pounds total, preferably shank end)
- 1 12-ounce bottle ginger beer, divided
- ½ cup light brown sugar
- 2 teaspoons low-sodium tamari or soy sauce

Serves 10 | Active time 30 minutes | Total time 2 hours 30 minutes

Cutting shallow slits in the top of a ham is called scoring, and it's one of the best ways to boost flavor while making for a prettier presentation. The glaze will sink into all those nooks and crannies to create a glossy, lacquered finish.

1. Heat the oven to 375°F. Arrange the slices of orange, onion and pineapple in a roasting pan. Place a rack on top. Place the ham, cut side down, on top of the rack. Score the ham on all sides in a diamond pattern, cutting only ¼ inch to ½ inch deep. Pour ¼ cup of ginger beer over the ham, cover the entire pan with foil and bake 1½ hours.

2. Meanwhile, in a blender, puree the remaining pineapple and ginger beer until smooth. Transfer to a saucepan, stir in the brown sugar and soy sauce and simmer, stirring occasionally, until syrupy and reduced to 1 cup, 35 to 40 minutes.

3. Brush one-third of the glaze (about ⅓ cup) over the ham and bake, uncovered, 15 minutes. Rotate the ham in the oven, repeat with another one-third of the glaze and bake another 15 minutes. Brush the remaining glaze over the ham and bake until the ham is heated through and the internal temperature registers 140°F, 15 to 20 minutes more.

HOW TO SCORE
With the tip of a small, sharp knife, make ¼-inch- to ½-inch-deep slits in a crosshatched diamond pattern all around the ham.

Love Notes

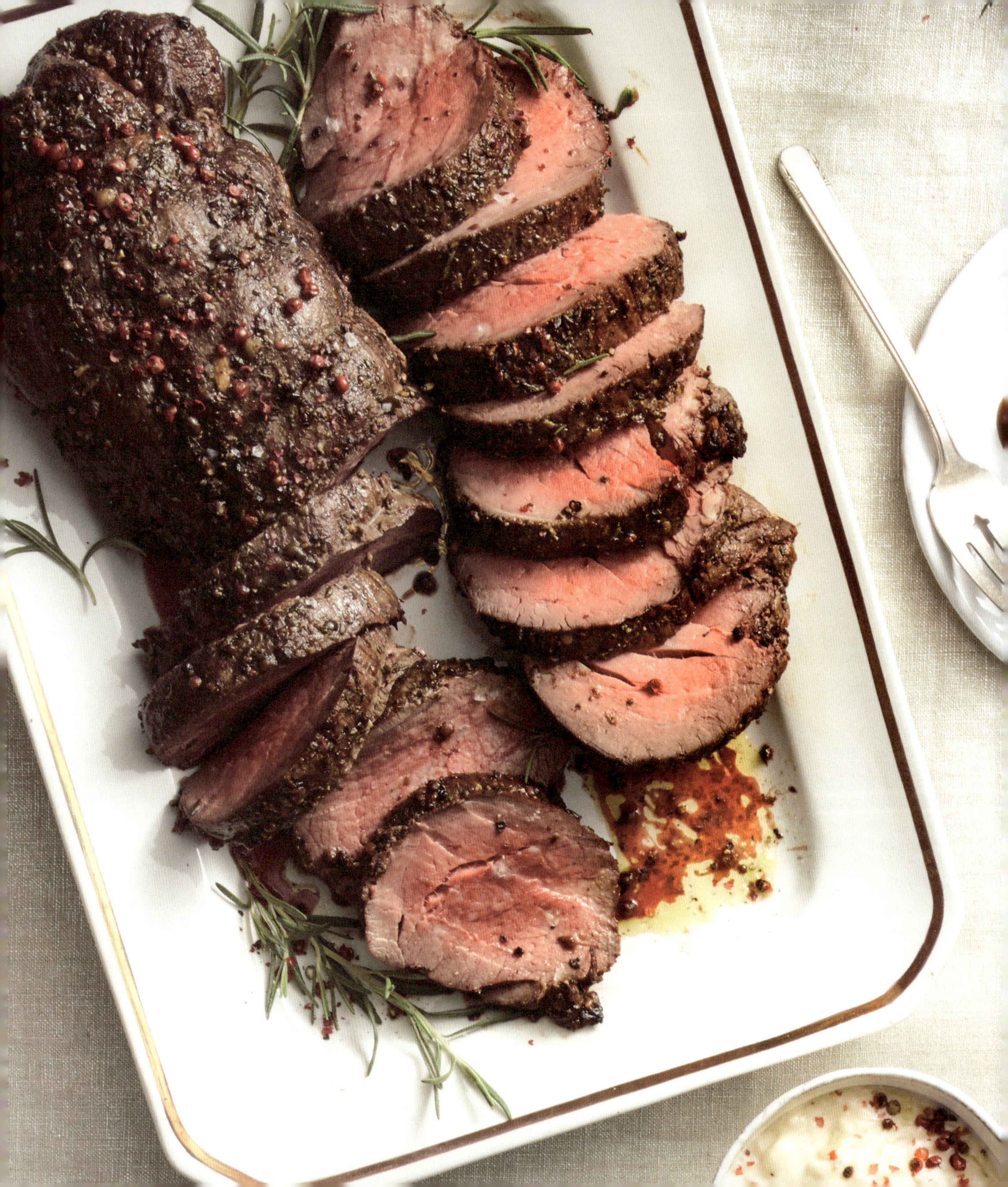

Peppercorn Beef Tenderloin

Serves 12 | Active time 10 minutes | Total time 55 minutes

Forget individual filets: This tenderloin is a worthy centerpiece for any holiday or celebration. It is super tender and packed with flavor thanks to the tricolor peppercorns and horseradish cream sauce. Bonus: it cuts like butter.

1. For the beef: Heat the oven to 425°F. Using a meat mallet or the bottom of a heavy pan, coarsely crush the peppercorns; transfer to a small bowl. Strip the leaves from the rosemary, finely chop it and add it to the bowl with the peppercorns along with the honey and 1 teaspoon of salt, then mix to combine.

2. With paper towels, pat the tenderloin dry. Place on a rimmed baking sheet and rub with the spice mixture. Roast to the desired doneness, 35 to 45 minutes for medium-rare (135°F). Transfer to a cutting board and let rest at least 10 minutes before slicing.

3. While the steak is roasting, prepare the Horseradish Cream Sauce: Melt the butter in a medium saucepan on medium. Add the leek and cook, stirring occasionally, until tender (do not let brown). Add the vermouth and cook until syrupy, about 4 minutes. Stir in the cream and simmer until reduced by half. Remove from the heat and stir in the horseradish, then season with salt to taste. Serve with the beef tenderloin.

FOR THE BEEF

- 2 tablespoons pink peppercorns
- 1 tablespoon green peppercorns
- 1 tablespoon black peppercorns
- 3 sprigs rosemary
- 2 teaspoons honey
- Kosher salt
- 1 4-pound beef tenderloin, trimmed and tied with butcher's twine
- Horseradish Cream Sauce, for serving

FOR THE HORSERADISH CREAM SAUCE

- 1½ tablespoons unsalted butter
- 1 leek, whites only, sliced into half-moons
- ¼ cup dry vermouth
- 1 cup heavy cream
- 1 ounce fresh horseradish, peeled and finely grated (¼ cup)
- Kosher salt

Love Notes

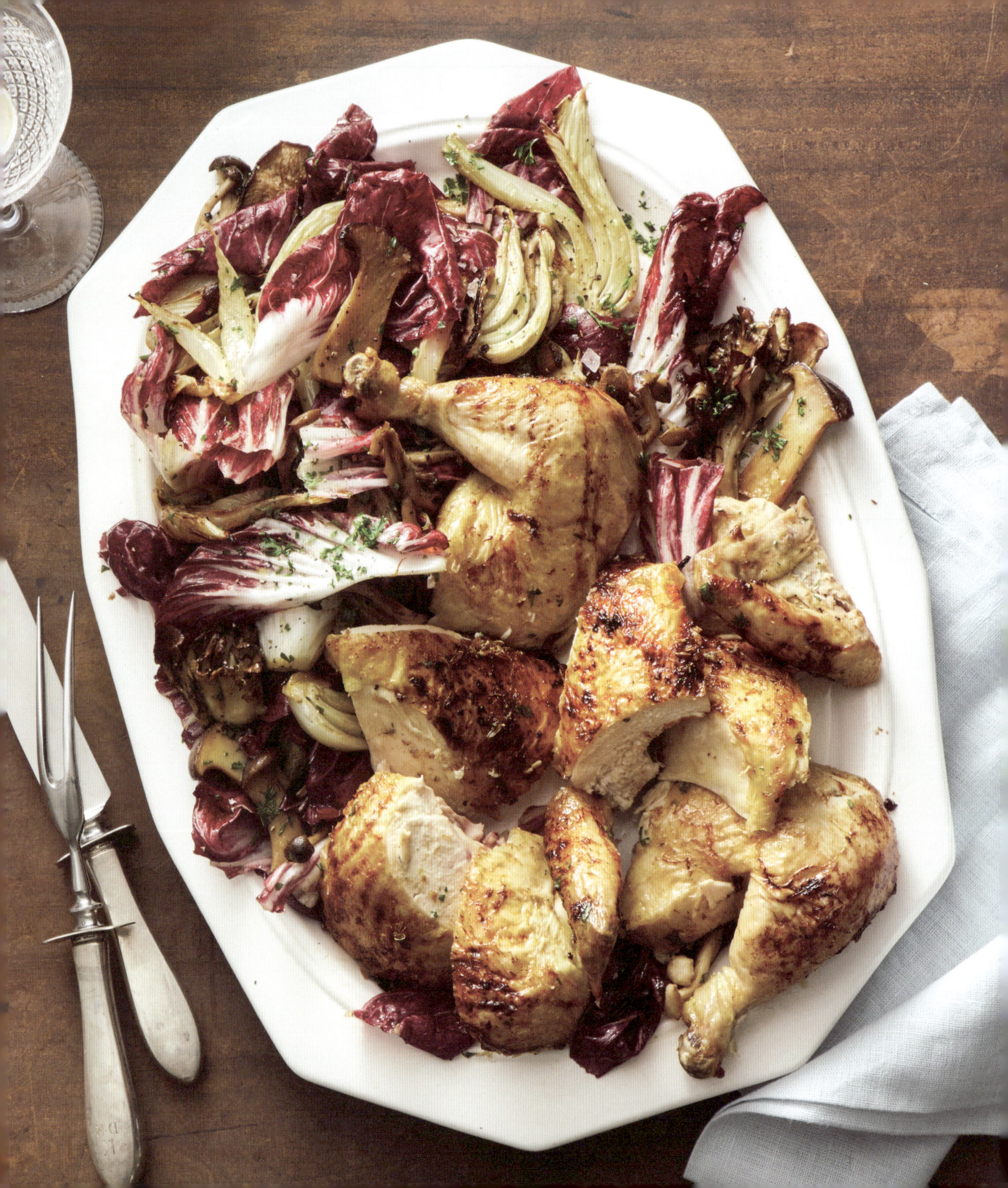

Orange-Ginger Roast Chicken with Fennel & Radicchio Salad

Serves 8 | Active time 10 minutes | Total time 1 hour 30 minutes

A special occasion calls for a meal that turns heads, and a whole roast chicken always delights. Place the bird alongside a bed of fennel, then brush it with a ginger-and-honey-infused orange glaze for an instant upgrade.

- 2 bulbs fennel, cored and sliced into ¼-inch pieces
- 1 tablespoon olive oil
- Kosher salt and pepper
- 1 navel orange
- 2 tablespoons honey
- 2 tablespoons grated fresh ginger
- 2 teaspoons fennel seeds, coarsely crushed
- 1 4- to 5-pound chicken, giblets discarded
- 1 pound mixed mushrooms, cut if large
- 1 tablespoon sherry vinegar
- 1 small head radicchio, torn into large pieces
- Chopped flat-leaf parsley, for serving

1. Heat the oven to 350°F. Line a rimmed baking sheet with parchment paper. On the prepared sheet, toss the fennel with the oil and ½ teaspoon each of salt and pepper. Move to the outer edges of the pan.

2. Grate the zest of the orange into a small bowl, then squeeze in 3 tablespoons of juice (reserve the orange halves). Whisk in the honey to dissolve, then stir in the ginger and the fennel seeds.

3. Pat the chicken dry, place it in the center of the prepared baking sheet and stuff it with the orange halves, then brush it with half of the juice mixture. Roast 40 minutes.

4. Increase the oven temperature to 425°F. Toss the mushrooms with fennel and brush the chicken with the remaining juice mixture. Roast until the temperature reaches 165°F on an instant-read thermometer inserted into the thickest part of the thigh, 25 to 30 minutes. Transfer the chicken to a cutting board and let it rest at least 10 minutes before carving.

5. Toss the mushrooms and fennel with vinegar and season with salt and pepper if necessary, then fold in the radicchio. Serve with the chicken, topped with parsley if desired.

Love Notes

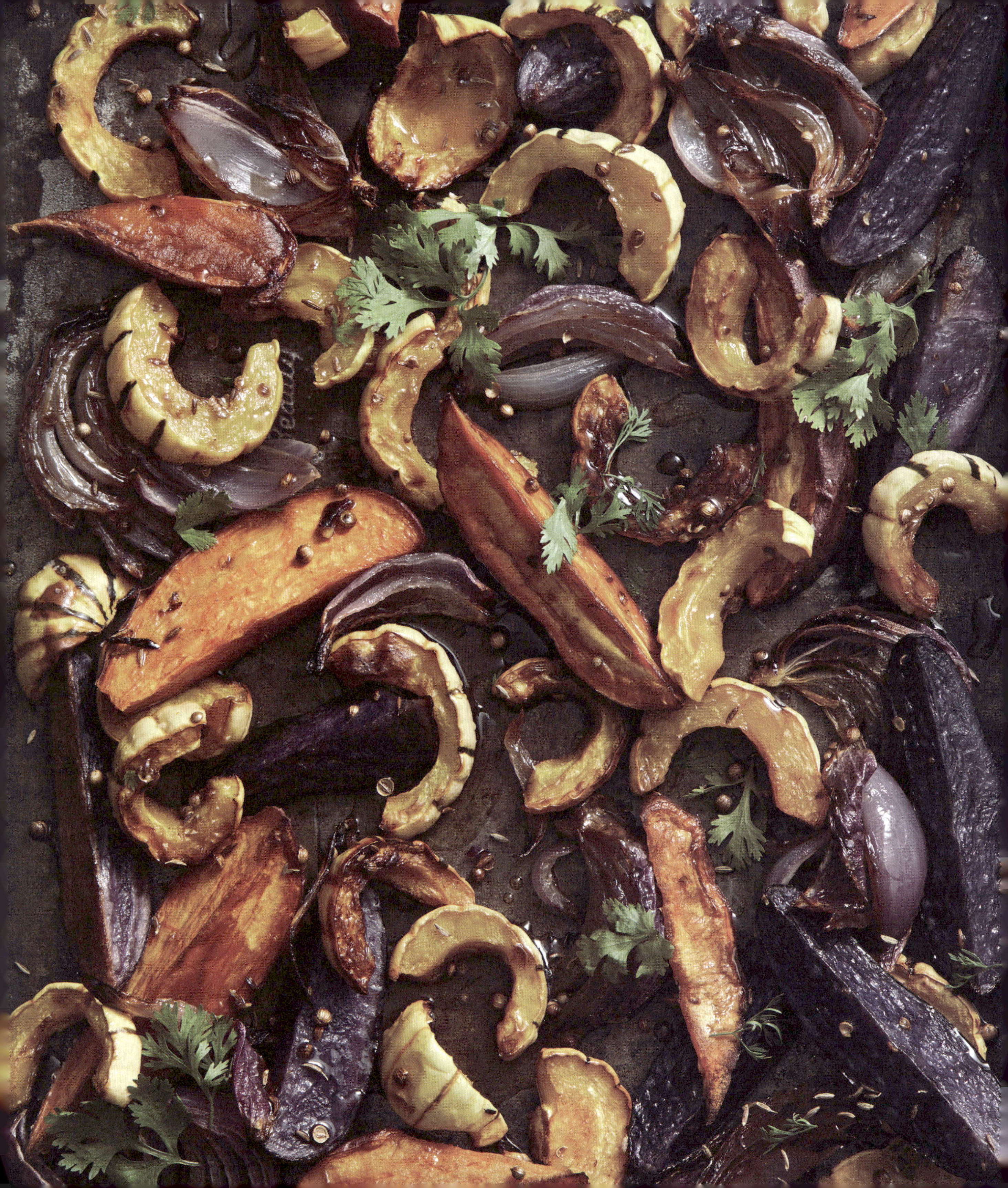

SHOWSTOPPING SIDES | **HOLIDAY**

Roasted Root Vegetables

Serves 8 | Active time 15 minutes | Total time 45 minutes

Getting an aromatic boost from cumin seeds and cracked coriander plus a squeeze of fresh lemon and a drizzle of honey, this colorful vegetable medley pairs well with delicate roast white fish and simple herbed chicken as well as heartier steaks and pork roasts.

- 6 very small purple potatoes (about 1¼ pounds), cut into 1-inch-thick wedges
- 4 very small sweet potatoes (about 1¼ pounds), cut into 1-inch-thick wedges
- 2 small red onions, cut into 1-inch-thick wedges
- 2 small delicata squash (about 1½ pounds), seeded and sliced into ⅓-inch-thick half-moons
- 4 tablespoons olive oil
- 2 tablespoons coriander seeds, roughly cracked or smashed
- 1 teaspoon cumin seeds
- Kosher salt and pepper
- ½ lemon
- 2 tablespoons honey
- Roughly chopped parsley or cilantro, for serving

1. Heat the oven to 425°F. Divide the potatoes, onions and squash between 2 rimmed baking sheets. Drizzle each with 2 tablespoons of oil, then season each with half of the coriander and cumin and ½ teaspoon each of salt and pepper. Arrange the vegetables in an even layer and roast, rotating baking sheets halfway through, until golden brown and tender, 20 to 30 minutes.

2. Immediately remove the baking sheets and squeeze lemon juice over each, then drizzle each tray with 1 tablespoon of honey and gently toss to coat.

3. Transfer the vegetables to a platter and sprinkle with parsley or cilantro if desired.

Love Notes

THE NEWLYWED COOKBOOK **219**

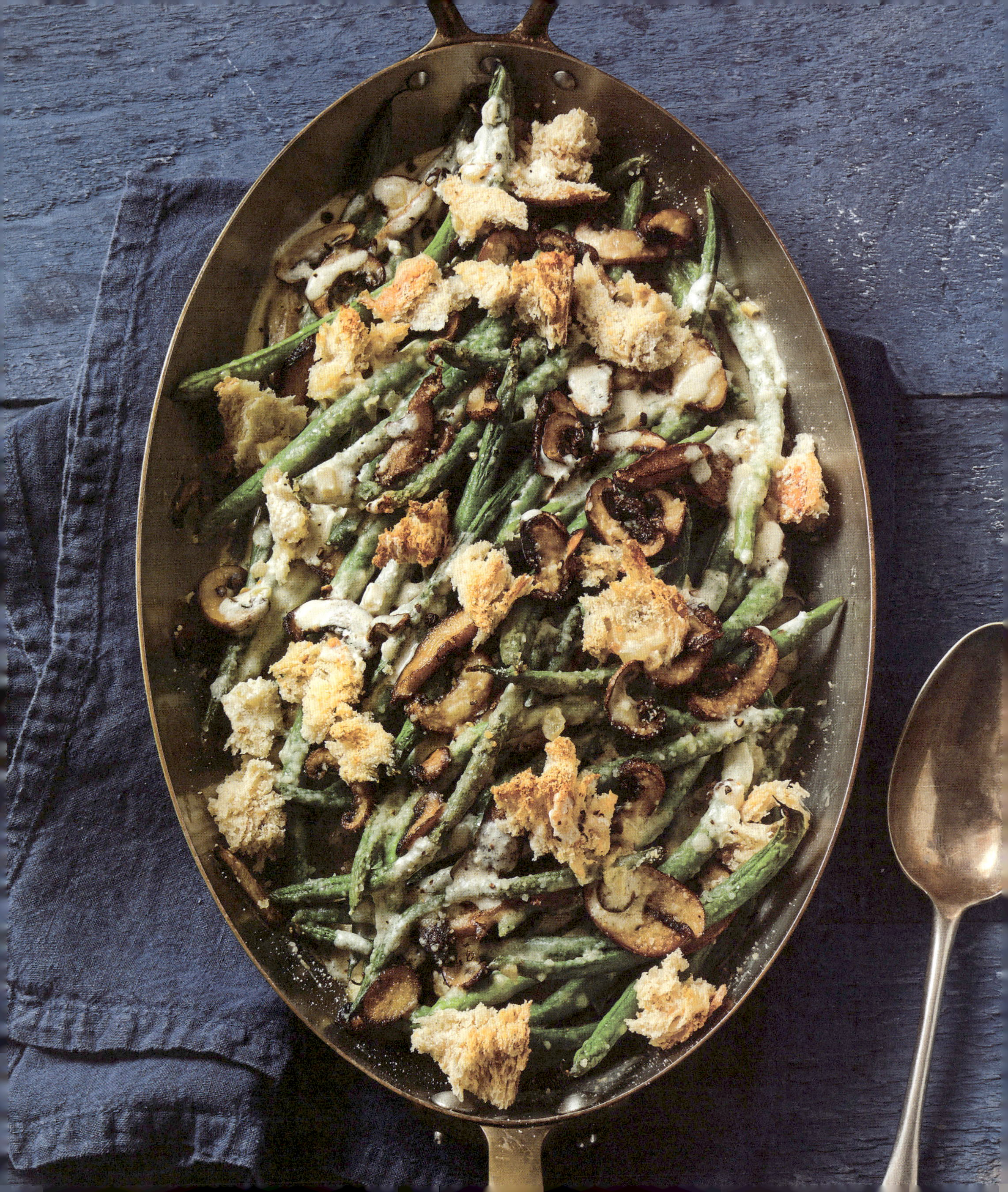

Fresh Green Bean Casserole

Serves 8 | Active time 45 minutes | Total time 55 minutes

This crowd-favorite holiday dish is famous for its shortcut ingredients (here's looking at you, canned green beans and mushroom soup), but you can get the same creamy, crunchy, classic deliciousness with fresh veggies and a fast from-scratch cream sauce.

- 3 tablespoons olive oil, divided, plus more for baking dish
- Kosher salt and pepper
- 2 pounds green beans, trimmed
- 10 ounces mushrooms, trimmed and sliced
- 1 onion, finely chopped
- 1 clove garlic, pressed
- ¾ cup milk
- 4 ounces cream cheese, at room temperature
- 1 tablespoon Dijon mustard
- Pinch of freshly grated nutmeg
- Pinch of cayenne
- ¼ cup plus 2 tablespoons grated Parmesan
- 2 teaspoons grated lemon zest
- 1 cup torn fresh breadcrumbs

1. Heat the oven to 400°F. Oil a 2-quart baking dish. Bring a large pot of salted water to a boil. Add the beans and cook until just tender, 3 to 4 minutes. Drain and run under cold water to cool. Pat dry.

2. Meanwhile, heat 2 tablespoons of oil in a large skillet on medium-high. Add the mushrooms and cook, tossing occasionally, until golden brown and tender, 6 to 7 minutes. Transfer to a bowl.

3. Wipe out the skillet and heat the remaining tablespoon of oil on medium. Add the onion, season with ½ teaspoon of salt and ¼ teaspoon of pepper and cook, covered, stirring occasionally, until very tender, 5 to 7 minutes. Stir in the garlic and cook 1 minute.

4. Whisk in the milk and bring to a simmer. Whisk in the cream cheese, mustard, nutmeg and cayenne and ¼ cup Parmesan and simmer, stirring occasionally, until slightly thickened, 2 to 3 minutes; stir in the lemon zest and toss with the green beans.

5. Fold in the mushrooms and transfer to a prepared baking dish. Sprinkle with the breadcrumbs and the remaining 2 tablespoons of Parmesan and bake until golden brown, 11 to 15 minutes.

Love Notes

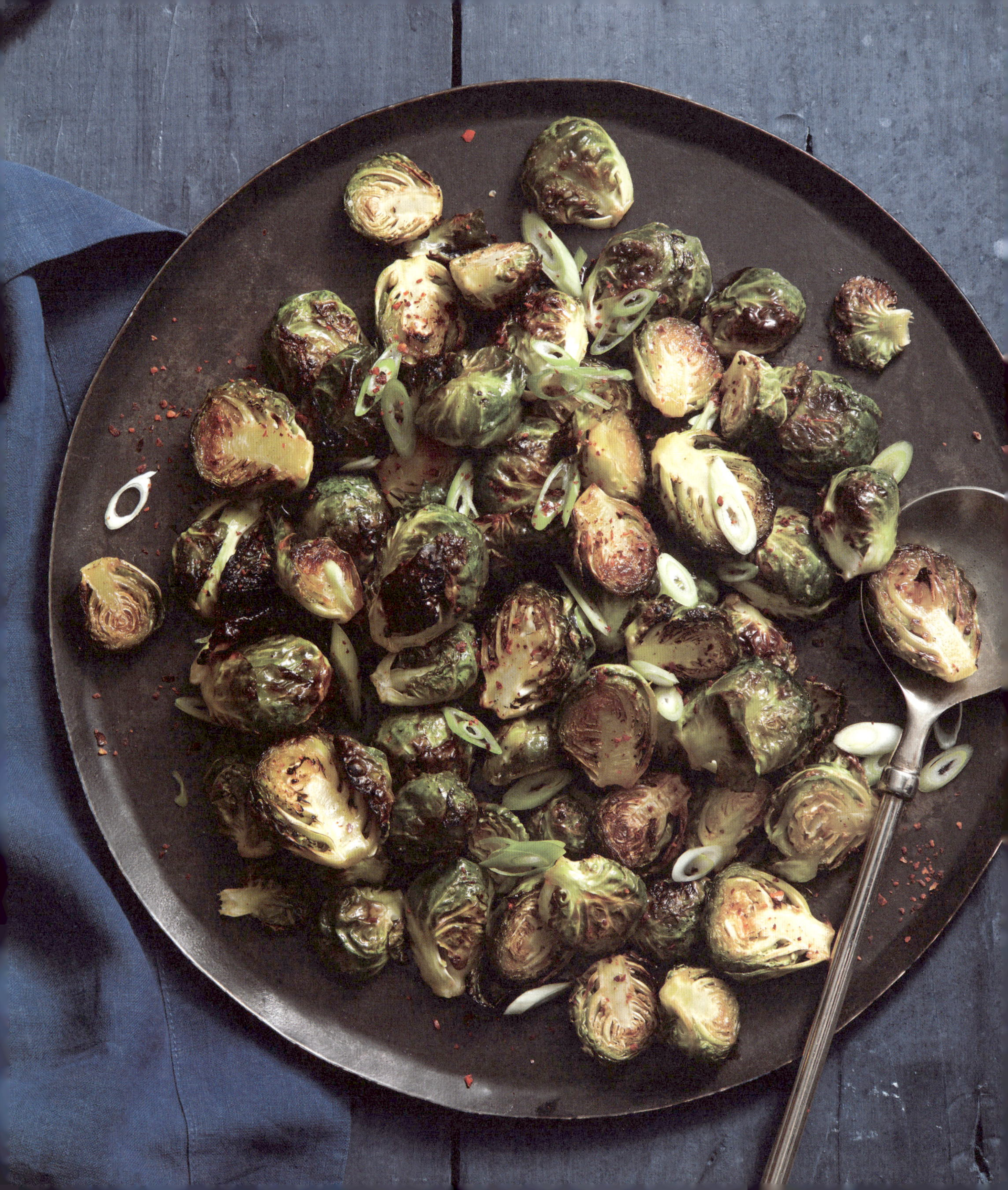

Sweet & Spicy Brussels Sprouts

Serves 8 | Active time 10 minutes | Total time 30 minutes

Take this vegetable to new heights with a maple-sriracha glaze. Seasoning the sprouts before roasting in the air fryer, then tossing them with the sauce after they're charred and crispy is the key to achieving an an intense sweet heat.

- 2 pounds Brussels sprouts, trimmed and halved
- 5 tablespoons olive oil, divided
- ½ teaspoon hot paprika
- Kosher salt
- 6 tablespoons pure maple syrup
- 1½ tablespoons sriracha
- Aleppo pepper and sliced scallions, for serving

1. Heat an air fryer to 375°F. In a large bowl, toss the Brussels sprouts with 4 tablespoons of oil, then the paprika and ½ teaspoon salt. Air-fry the Brussels sprouts in 2 batches until charred, crispy and tender, 9 to 11 minutes.

2. Meanwhile, in a bowl, whisk together the maple syrup, the sriracha and a pinch of salt. Transfer 2½ tablespoons to a small bowl and whisk in the remaining tablespoon of oil; set aside for serving.

3. Transfer 1 batch of the roasted Brussels sprouts to a large bowl and toss with 2 tablespoons of the remaining syrup mixture. Repeat with the remaining Brussels sprouts and 2 tablespoons of the syrup mixture.

4. Transfer to a platter, then drizzle with the reserved maple-oil mixture and sprinkle with Aleppo pepper and scallions if desired.

NO AIR FRYER, NO PROBLEM
Arrange seasoned Brussels sprouts on a rimmed baking sheet, cut sides down, and roast at 425°F until golden brown and tender, 20 to 25 minutes; toss with the maple mixture and serve as directed.

Love Notes

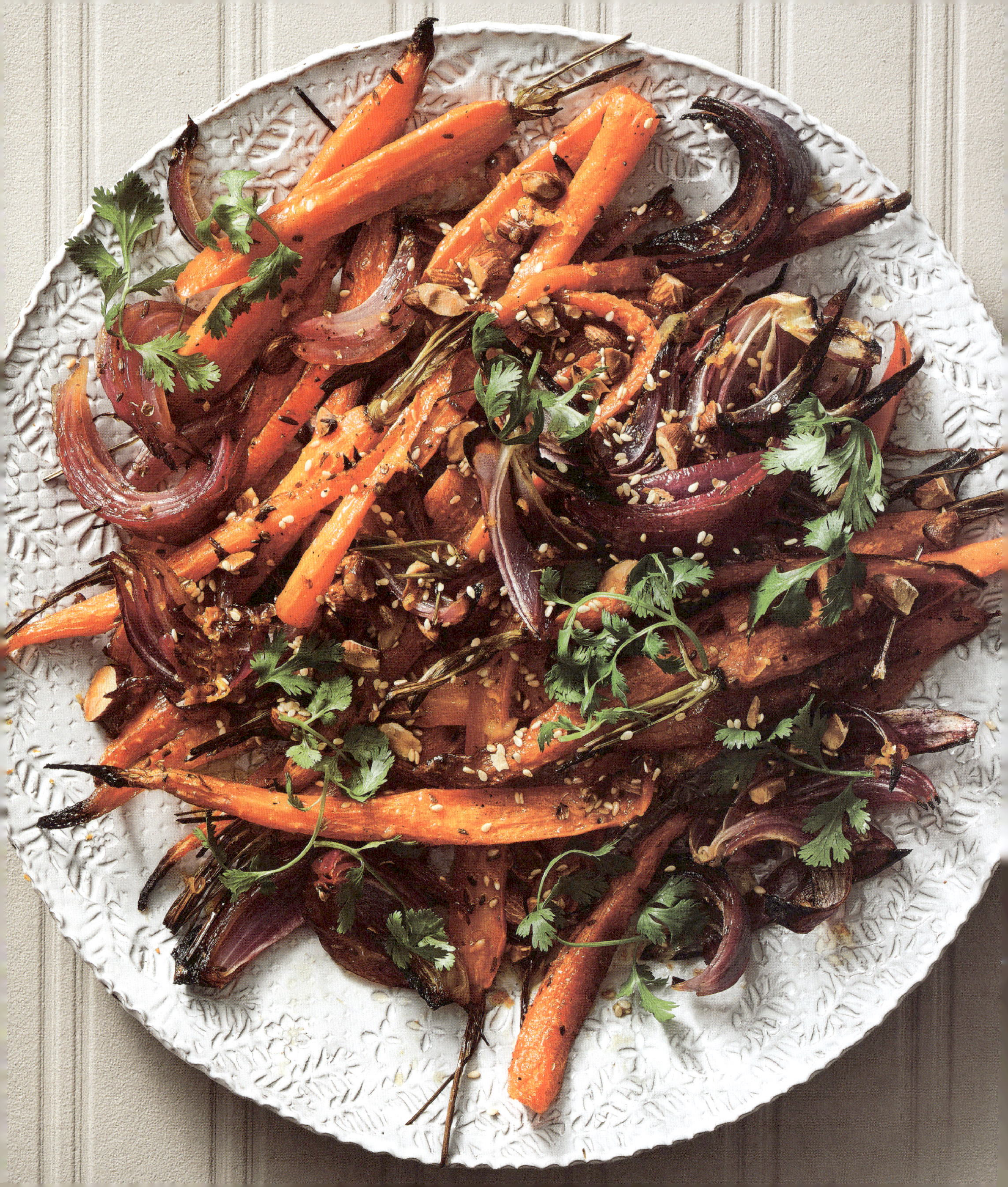

Roasted Carrots & Red Onions

Serves 6 | Active time 25 minutes | Total time 45 minutes

- 1½ pounds carrots, peeled and halved lengthwise (quartered if thick, cut crosswise if long)
- 2 large red onions, cut into ½-inch wedges
- 3 tablespoons olive oil, divided
- 1 teaspoon coriander seeds, crushed, divided
- 1 teaspoon cumin seeds, crushed, divided
- Kosher salt
- ¼ cup almonds, chopped, divided
- 2 tablespoons sesame seeds, divided
- 1 tablespoon sherry vinegar
- 1 teaspoon orange zest plus 1½ tablespoons orange juice
- ¼ cup cilantro leaves

Add some vibrant veggies to your table with this flavor-packed side that pairs well with just about any main. Roasting caramelizes the natural sugars in the carrots and onions, bringing out their sweetness, and toasting the almonds and sesame seeds adds a nutty crunch.

1. Heat the oven to 450°F. Place the carrots on 1 rimmed baking sheet and the onions on a second sheet; toss each with 1 tablespoon of oil, ½ teaspoon each of coriander and cumin seeds and ¼ teaspoon of salt and spread in a single layer. Roast the carrots on a rack in the lower third of the oven and the onions on a rack in the upper third of the oven until nearly tender, 20 minutes.

2. Dividing the vegetables equally between the sheets, sprinkle them with the almonds and sesame seeds, then roast until the nuts and seeds are golden brown and the vegetables are tender, 6 to 8 minutes more.

3. Meanwhile, in a small bowl, whisk together the vinegar, the orange zest and juice, ¼ teaspoon salt and the remaining tablespoon of oil until combined.

4. Arrange the vegetables on a platter, drizzle with the dressing and top with the cilantro.

Love Notes

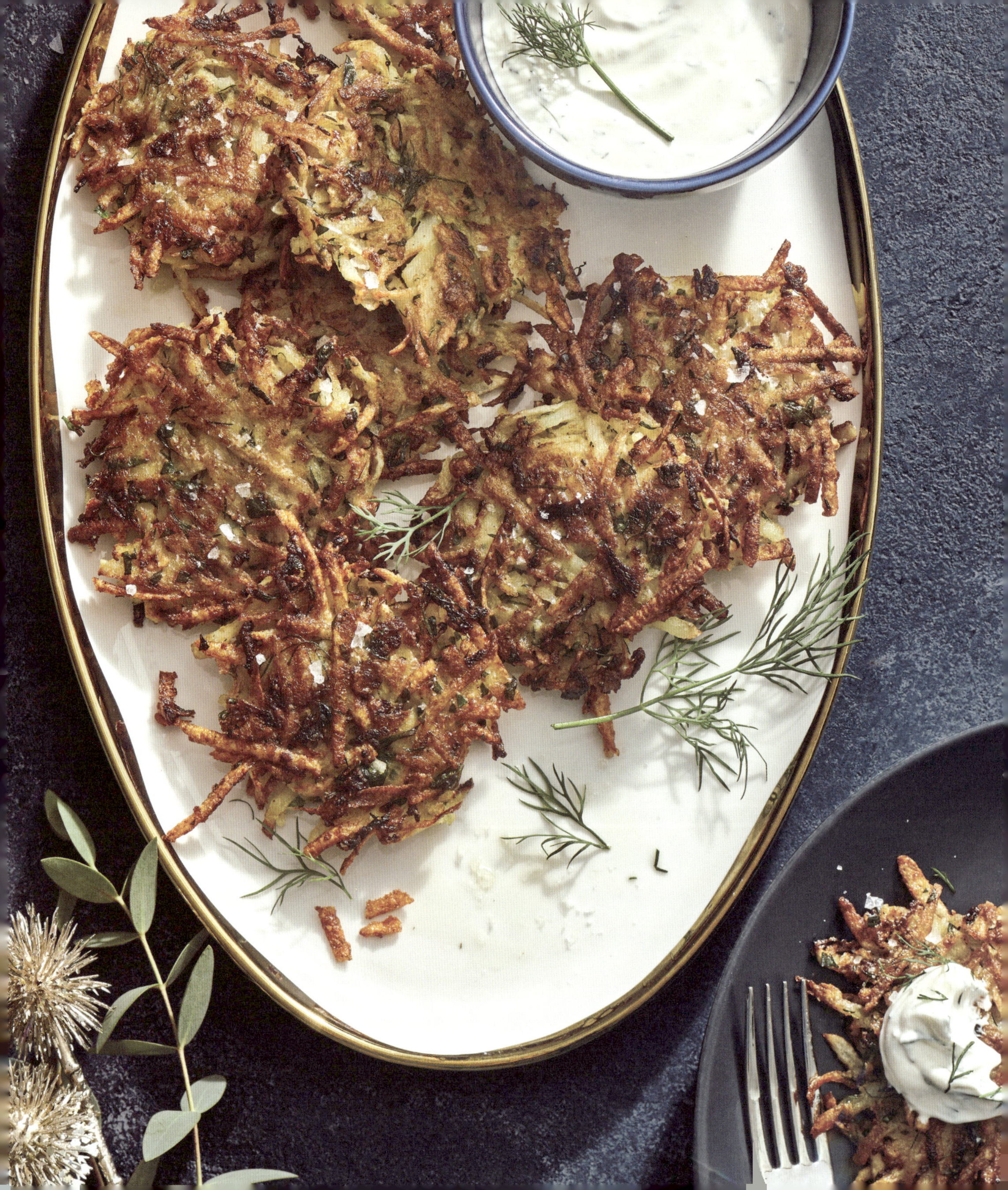

Dill-Spiked Potato Latkes

Makes 20 | Active time 30 minutes | Total time 30 minutes

- 2 large eggs
- Kosher salt and pepper
- 2 pounds russet potatoes, peeled
- 2 medium onions, quartered
- ½ cup matzo meal
- ½ cup flat-leaf parsley leaves, finely chopped
- ½ cup plus 2 tablespoons dill, chopped, divided
- 2 tablespoons olive oil, plus more as needed
- ½ cup sour cream

Classic crispy potato pancakes get a fresh boost from chopped parsley and dill. You can even fry them ahead of time, then warm them in a 350°F oven for 20 minutes. Serve with sour cream or other traditional toppings like applesauce, fresh shredded horseradish and smoked salmon.

1. In a large bowl, whisk together the eggs, 1 teaspoon of salt and ¼ teaspoon of pepper.

2. In a food processor fitted with a large grating disc (or on the large holes of a box grater), grate the potatoes, cutting them as necessary to fit into the feed tube, then grate the onions. Add to the bowl with the eggs and toss to combine. Toss with the matzo meal, then the parsley and all but 2 tablespoons of the dill.

3. Heat 2 tablespoons of oil in a large skillet on medium. Carefully add 5 large spoonfuls of the potato mixture (about ¼ cup each) to the skillet. Flatten into 3-inch pancakes and cook until browned and crisp, 4 to 6 minutes per side; transfer to a wire rack or a paper towel–lined plate.

4. Repeat with the remaining potato mixture, adding more oil to the skillet as needed; when nearing the end of the potato mixture, drain and discard any liquid from the bottom of the bowl.

5. In a small bowl, combine the sour cream with the remaining 2 tablespoons of dill. Serve immediately with the latkes.

Love Notes

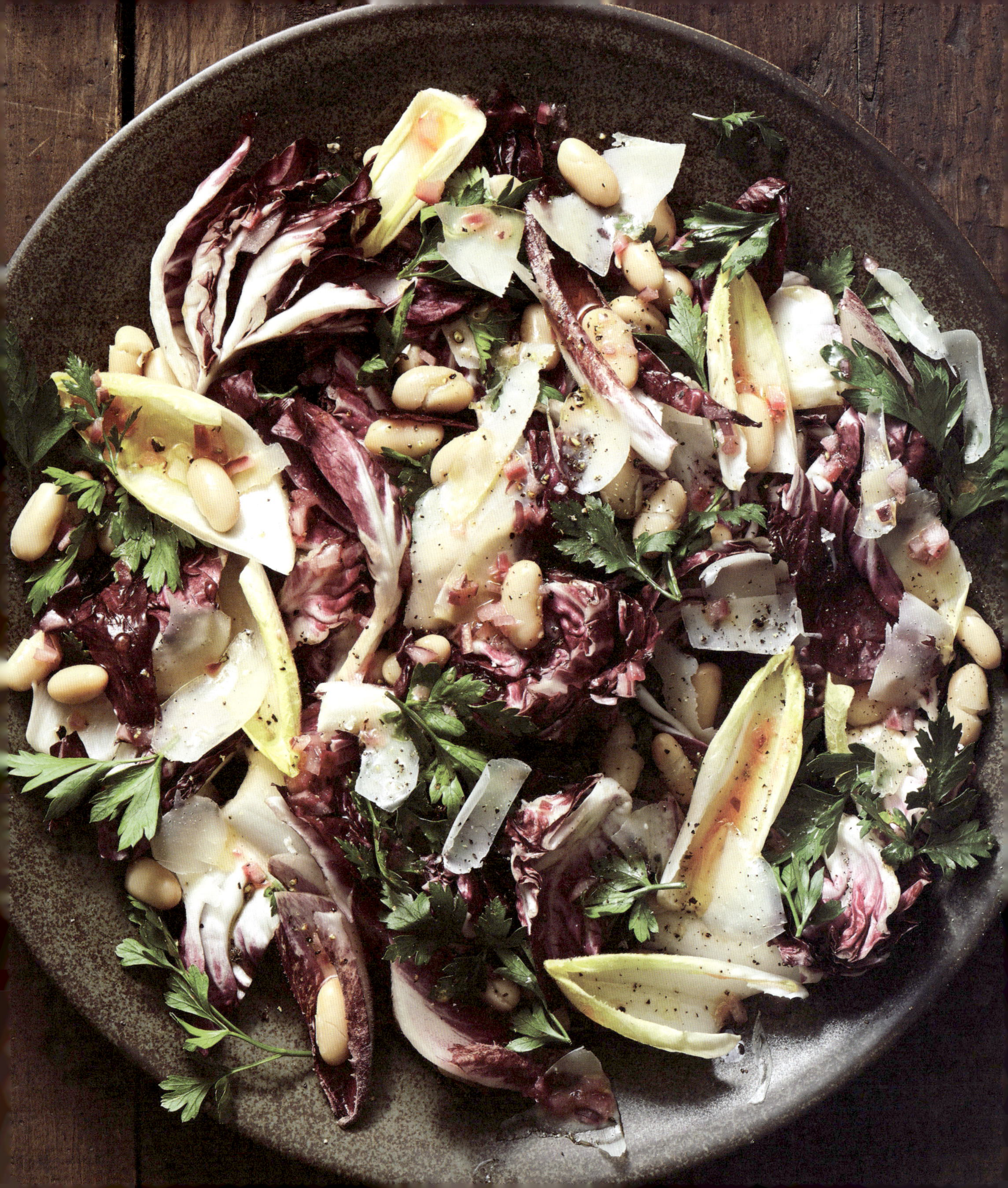

White Bean & Radicchio Salad

Serves 8 | Active time 15 minutes | Total time 20 minutes

- 3 tablespoons lemon juice
- 1 teaspoon honey
- Kosher salt and pepper
- 2 teaspoons Dijon mustard
- ½ medium red onion, finely chopped
- ¼ cup olive oil
- 1 15-ounce can cannellini beans, drained and rinsed
- 2 small heads radicchio, torn
- 2 heads endive, sliced
- 2 cups flat-leaf parsley leaves
- 2 ounces Parmesan cheese, shaved, divided

For a change of pace from the usual bowl of greens, this salad combines crisp and crunchy endive and radicchio with creamy beans and nutty Parmesan. The winter produce brings lots of flavor and texture, but it's the honey-laced Dijon dressing that makes this salad a stunner.

1. In a large bowl, whisk together the lemon juice, the honey and ¾ teaspoon of salt until incorporated. Whisk in the Dijon, then stir in the onion and let sit 5 minutes.

2. Whisk in the oil and ½ teaspoon of pepper and gently toss with the beans.

3. Add the radicchio, endive and parsley and half of the cheese and toss to combine. Serve topped with the remaining cheese.

Love Notes

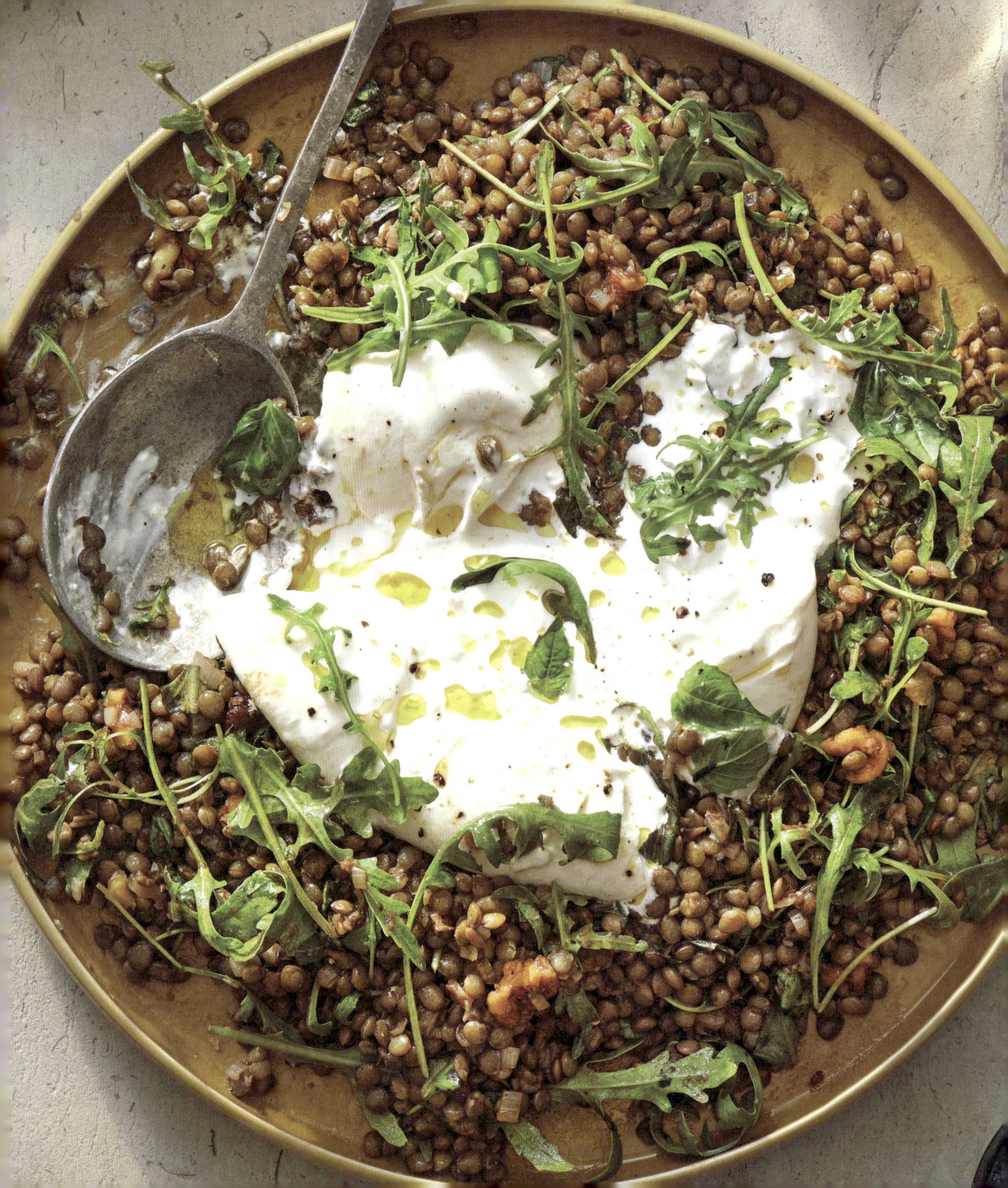

Herby Lentil & Burrata Salad

- 1 cup French green lentils, rinsed and picked over
- ¼ cup olive oil
- ¼ cup raw walnut halves, chopped
- 1 clove garlic, smashed
- 2 sprigs thyme
- 1 medium shallot, finely chopped
- 2½ tablespoons balsamic vinegar
- Kosher salt and pepper
- 2 cups baby arugula
- 1 cup basil leaves, roughly chopped
- 8 ounces burrata, torn

Serves 6 | Active time 20 minutes | Total time 35 minutes

Humble lentils get a serious upgrade with a balsamic vinaigrette and rich, buttery burrata. The ultra-creamy cheese served on top makes this side feel extra-special and wonderfully indulgent.

1. Cook the lentils per the package directions, then drain.

2. Meanwhile, heat the oil in a large skillet on medium. Add the walnuts, garlic and thyme and cook, stirring occasionally, until the nuts are fragrant and golden brown, 4 to 6 minutes.

3. Add the shallot to the walnut mixture and cook, stirring constantly, 1 minute. Remove from the heat and discard the garlic and thyme. Whisk in the vinegar, ½ teaspoon of salt and ¼ teaspoon of pepper.

4. Add the lentils to the skillet, gently folding to coat, then fold in the arugula and basil. Transfer to a platter and top with the burrata.

Love Notes

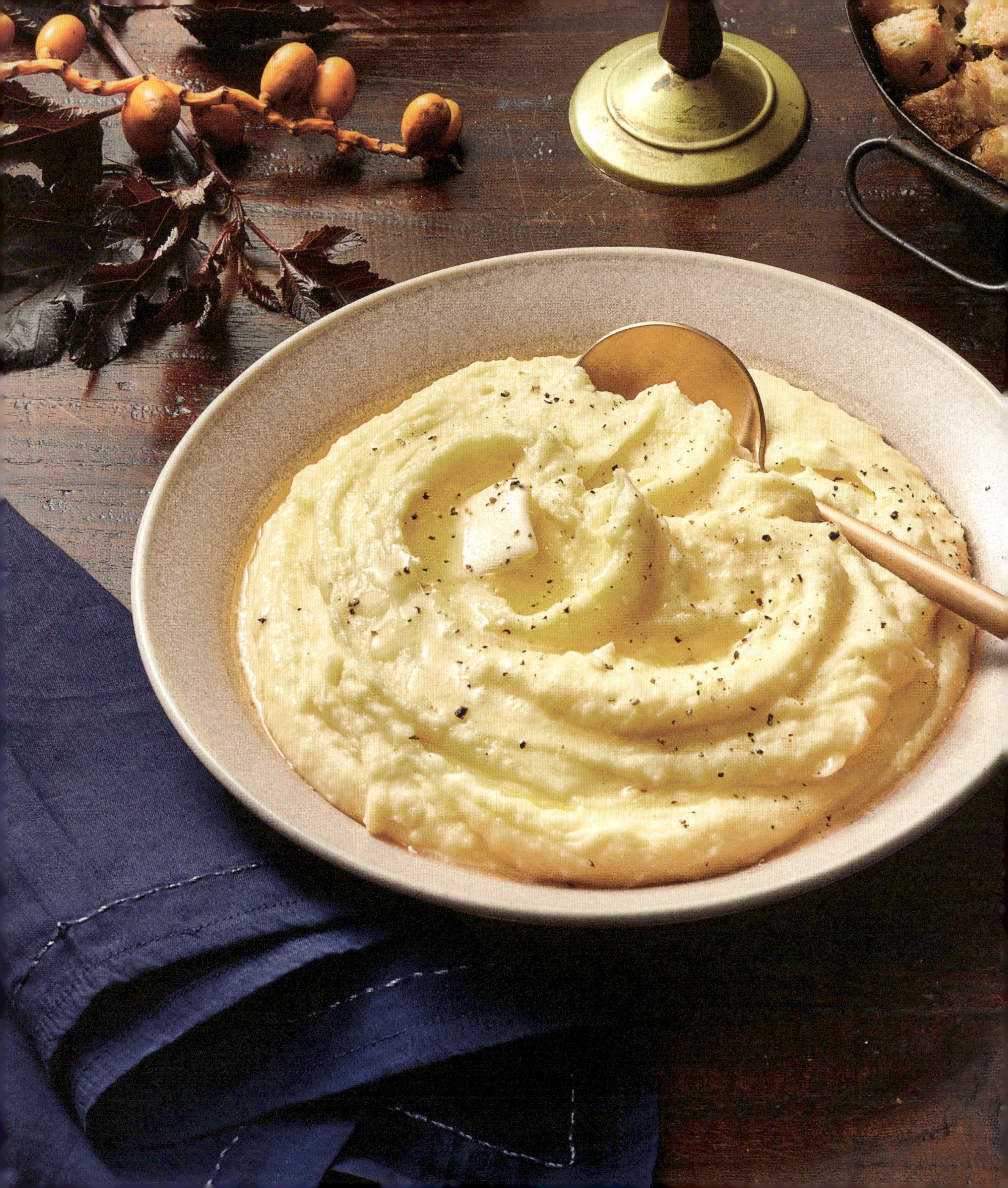

Thyme-Scented Mashed Potatoes

Serves 8 | Active time 15 minutes | Total time 25 minutes

- 4 pounds golden potatoes (about 8), peeled and quartered
- Kosher salt
- 2 cups heavy cream or half-and-half
- 4 tablespoons unsalted butter
- 8 sprigs thyme
- 2 sprigs fresh flat-leaf parsley
- 1 bay leaf
- 6 black peppercorns
- 2 cloves garlic, smashed
- Freshly grated nutmeg, for serving

Take mashed potatoes from "meh" to amazing by infusing heavy cream with aromatics like garlic, thyme and parsley before mixing it into your spuds.

1. Place the potatoes in a large pot, add enough cold water to cover and bring to a boil. Add 2 teaspoons of salt, reduce the heat and simmer until just tender, 15 to 18 minutes. Drain the potatoes and return them to the pot.

2. Meanwhile, place the cream, butter, thyme, parsley, bay leaf, peppercorns and garlic in a small saucepan and bring to a simmer. Simmer 5 minutes, then remove from the heat.

3. Strain the cream mixture into a pot with the potatoes. Add ¾ teaspoon of salt and mash to the desired consistency. Sprinkle with nutmeg before serving if desired.

Love Notes

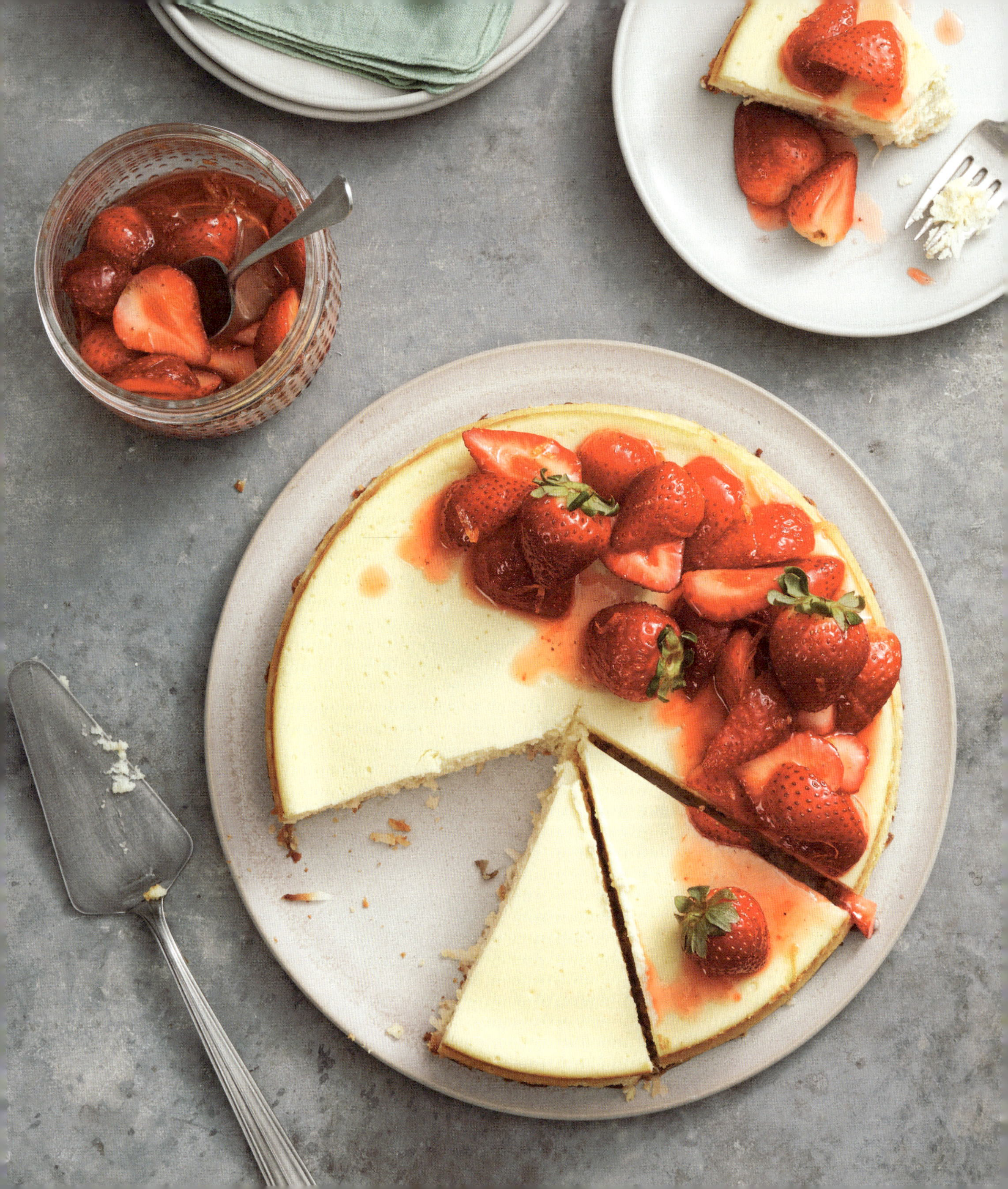

DELICIOUS DESSERTS | **HOLIDAY**

Strawberry Coconut-Crust Cheesecake

- 4 large eggs, divided
- ¾ cup plus 3 tablespoons sugar, divided
- 2 cups sweetened shredded coconut
- 1 lemon
- 3 8-ounce packages cream cheese, at room temperature
- ¾ cup sour cream
- 1 tablespoon potato starch
- 2 teaspoons pure vanilla extract
- 1 tablespoon strawberry jam
- ½ pound small strawberries, hulled and halved or quartered, if large

Serves 12 | Active time 25 minutes | Total time 1 hour 30 minutes plus chilling

Everyone—including those who are gluten-free—will swoon over the rich cream cheese filling, the golden toasted-coconut crust and the zesty, jammy fresh-fruit topping. Like all good cheesecakes, this one needs to chill, so it is the perfect make-ahead treat.

1. Heat the oven to 375°F. Coat a 9-inch springform pan with cooking spray.

2. Separate the whites and yolks from 2 eggs, placing the whites in a medium bowl and the yolks in a small bowl. Add 1 tablespoon of sugar to the whites and whisk until frothy; mix in the coconut. Spread the mixture evenly on the bottom of the pan and bake until the edge is golden brown and the center is dry and set and golden brown in spots, 15 to 25 minutes; let cool 15 minutes. Reduce the oven temperature to 325°F.

3. Meanwhile, zest and juice the lemon (you should get about 2 teaspoons of zest and 3 tablespoons of juice) and set aside. Using an electric mixer, beat the cream cheese, sour cream, potato starch and vanilla; 2 tablespoons of lemon juice; and ¾ cup of sugar in a large bowl until smooth. Beat in the reserved egg yolks and the remaining 2 whole eggs, 1 at a time. Spread the mixture on top of the crust and bake until the edge is set and the center still wobbles slightly, 35 to 40 minutes. Let the cheesecake cool completely in the pan, then refrigerate until chilled, at least 4 hours.

4. While the cheesecake is chilling, in a bowl, whisk together the jam and the remaining tablespoon of lemon juice and 2 tablespoons of sugar. Toss with the berries and let sit at least 15 minutes. Fold in the reserved lemon zest and serve over the cheesecake.

Love Notes

America's Fa

DELICIOUS DESSERTS | **HOLIDAY**

Mixed-Berry Cornmeal Cobblers

Serves 8 | Active time 15 minutes | Total time 50 minutes

- 6 tablespoons (¾ stick) cold unsalted butter, cut into pieces, plus more for pans
- 1 pound mixed berries (raspberries, blueberries and blackberries)
- 8 ounces small strawberries, hulled and halved (quartered if large)
- ½ cup sugar
- 1 tablespoon cornstarch
- 2 teaspoons pure vanilla extract
- ¼ teaspoon kosher salt
- 1 8.5-ounce box Jiffy Corn Muffin Mix
- ½ cup pecans, roughly chopped
- 1 large egg, beaten

This is an easy dessert for summer gatherings: juicy ripe berries nestled under pillowy, golden pecan cornbread. Serving it in mini cast-iron skillets is an adorable touch, but you can assemble it in one large skillet if that's all you have.

1. Heat the oven to 400°F. Line a large rimmed baking sheet with foil. Butter eight 5-inch mini cast-iron skillets and place them on the prepared sheet.

2. In a bowl, toss the berries with the sugar, cornstarch, vanilla and salt. Divide among the prepared pans.

3. Place the corn muffin mix in a bowl with the butter and cut it in or mix it in with your fingers until the mixture is crumbly. Stir in the pecans. Stir in the egg with a fork until the mixture is combined but still crumbly.

4. Sprinkle the mixture over the berries and bake until the fruit is bubbling and the crust is golden brown, 20 to 25 minutes. Let cool at least 10 minutes before serving.

JIFFY CORN MUFFIN MIX

Mabel White Holmes noticed a flat biscuit in her son's friend's lunchbox, and that gave her the idea to create a premade all-purpose baking mix. In April 1930, her experiment became the first prepared baking mix sold to the public, at an affordable price meant to help families dealing with economic hardship.

Love Notes

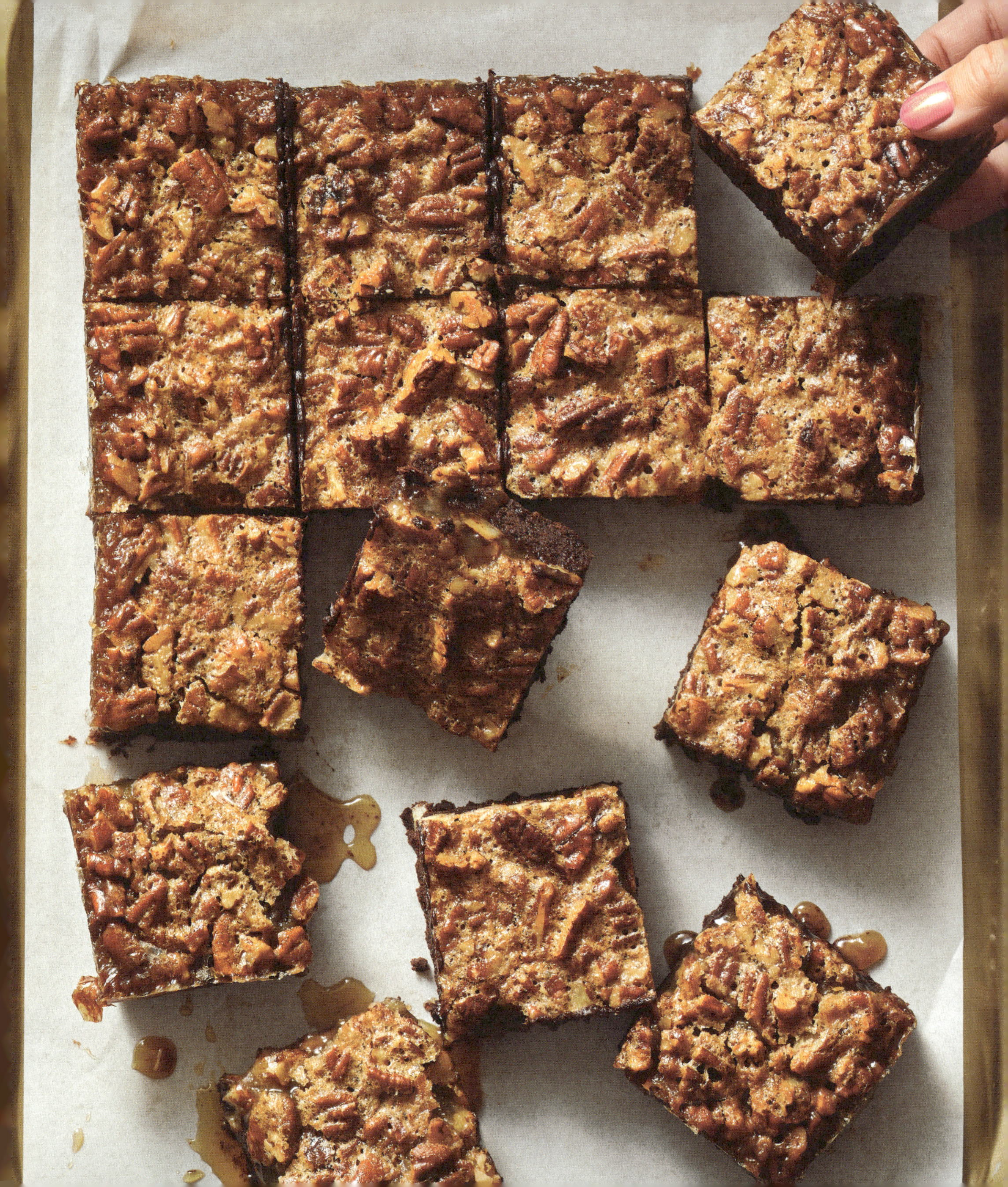

Pecan Pie Brownies

Makes 16 | **Active time 45 minutes** | **Total time 1 hour 15 minutes plus cooling**

Everyone's favorite pie is now in handheld form. These fudgy brownies feature a sticky-sweet topping that will have all the guests begging for the recipe.

FOR BROWNIES
- Nonstick cooking spray
- 1 cup (2 sticks) unsalted butter, cut into pieces
- 1½ cups packed light brown sugar
- ½ cup granulated sugar
- ½ teaspoon kosher salt
- ½ cup bittersweet chocolate chips
- 3 large eggs
- 2 teaspoons pure vanilla extract
- 1½ cups unsweetened cocoa powder (not Dutch process)
- ¾ cup all-purpose flour

FOR PECAN PIE TOPPING
- ¾ cup packed light brown sugar
- ½ cup light corn syrup
- 4 tablespoons unsalted butter, melted and slightly cooled
- 2 large eggs
- 1 teaspoon pure vanilla extract
- ½ teaspoon kosher salt
- 2 cups pecan halves, roughly chopped

1. Make the brownie batter: Heat the oven to 350°F. Lightly coat a 9-inch square baking pan with nonstick cooking spray, then line with 2 pieces of parchment paper, leaving an overhang on all sides. Lightly spray the parchment.

2. In a large bowl, combine the butter, both sugars, the salt and the chocolate chips and microwave in 30-second increments, stirring in between, until the mixture is melted and smooth. Let cool 3 minutes.

3. Whisk in the eggs, 1 at a time, then the vanilla. Stir in the cocoa, then fold in the flour just to combine. Transfer the batter to the prepared pan and smooth the top. Bake until set and a wooden pick inserted in the center comes out clean or with a few moist crumbs attached, 24 to 26 minutes.

4. Meanwhile, make the topping: In a large bowl, whisk together the brown sugar, corn syrup, butter, eggs, vanilla and salt. Stir in the pecans.

5. Remove the brownies from the oven and pour the pecan mixture on top, spreading in an even layer. Return to the oven and continue to bake until the pecan pie topping is set and beginning to turn golden brown, 23 to 25 minutes. Let cool in the pan 30 minutes, then use the parchment overhangs to transfer to a wire rack to cool completely before cutting, at least 3 hours.

Love Notes

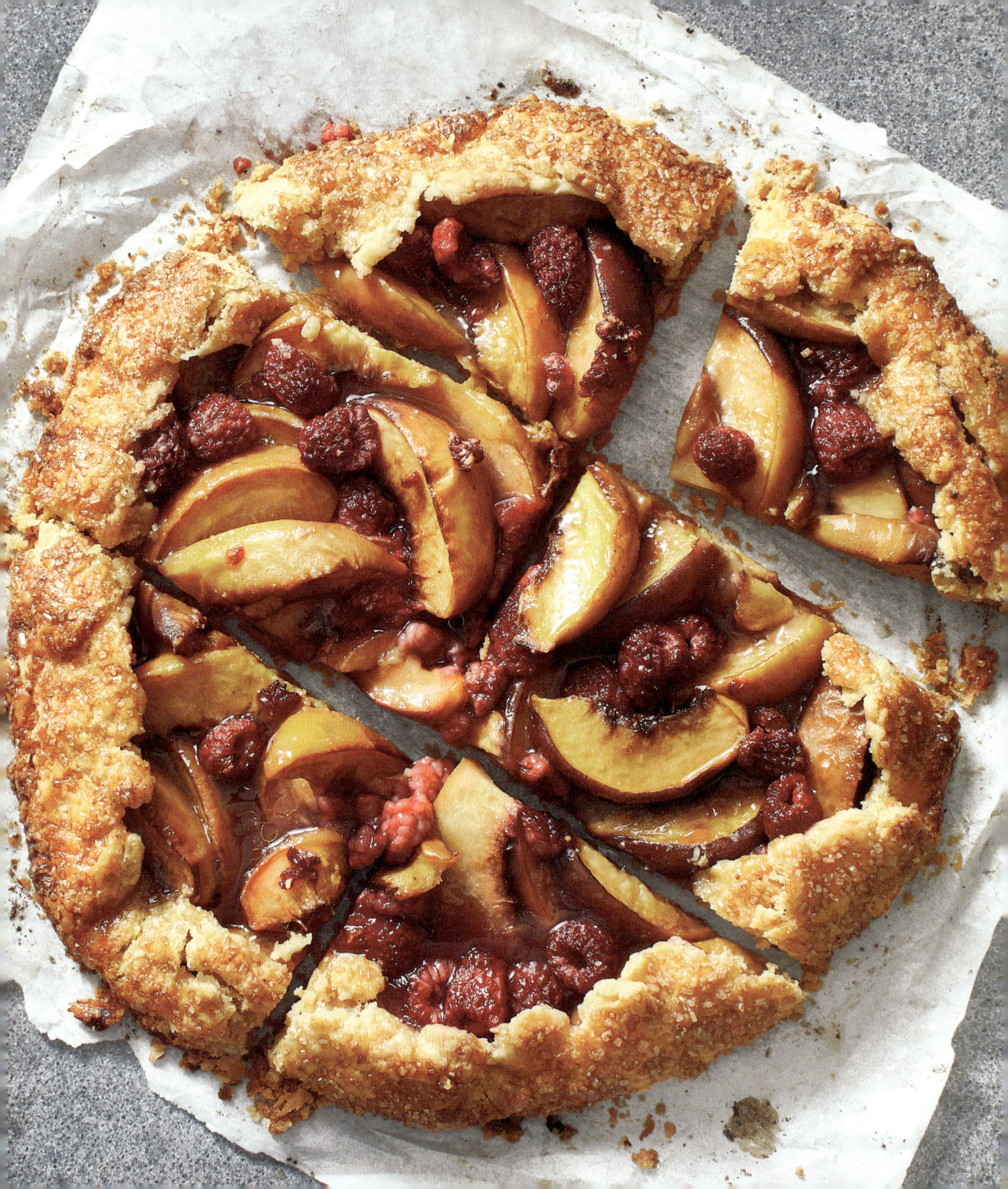

Peach & Raspberry Galette

Serves 6 | Active time 25 minutes | Total time 1 hour 5 minutes

- 1 refrigerated rolled pie crust (or use homemade pie dough)
- Flour, for surface
- 2 medium peaches, cut into ⅛-inch-thick wedges
- ½ teaspoon almond extract
- Pinch kosher salt
- ¼ cup plus 1 tablespoon turbinado sugar, divided
- 1 tablespoon cornstarch
- 1 pint raspberries
- 1 large egg, beaten

Peak summer fruit gets lightly sweetened and artfully arranged on a buttery pie crust in this delightful recipe. There is no blind-baking or fancy latticework needed, and the whole thing comes together on a sheet tray.

1. Heat the oven to 375°F. Unroll the crust onto a lightly floured surface and roll to a 12-inch diameter. Transfer to a parchment-lined baking sheet.

2. In a bowl, toss the peaches with the almond extract, the salt and ¼ cup turbinado sugar. Toss with the cornstarch, then fold in the raspberries. Spoon onto the dough, leaving a 2-inch border around the edge.

3. Fold the dough border over the fruit, crimping the edges as necessary to encase the filling. Brush the border with egg and sprinkle with the remaining tablespoon of turbinado sugar.

4. Bake until the fruit is tender and bubbling and the crust is golden brown, 40 to 45 minutes.

Love Notes

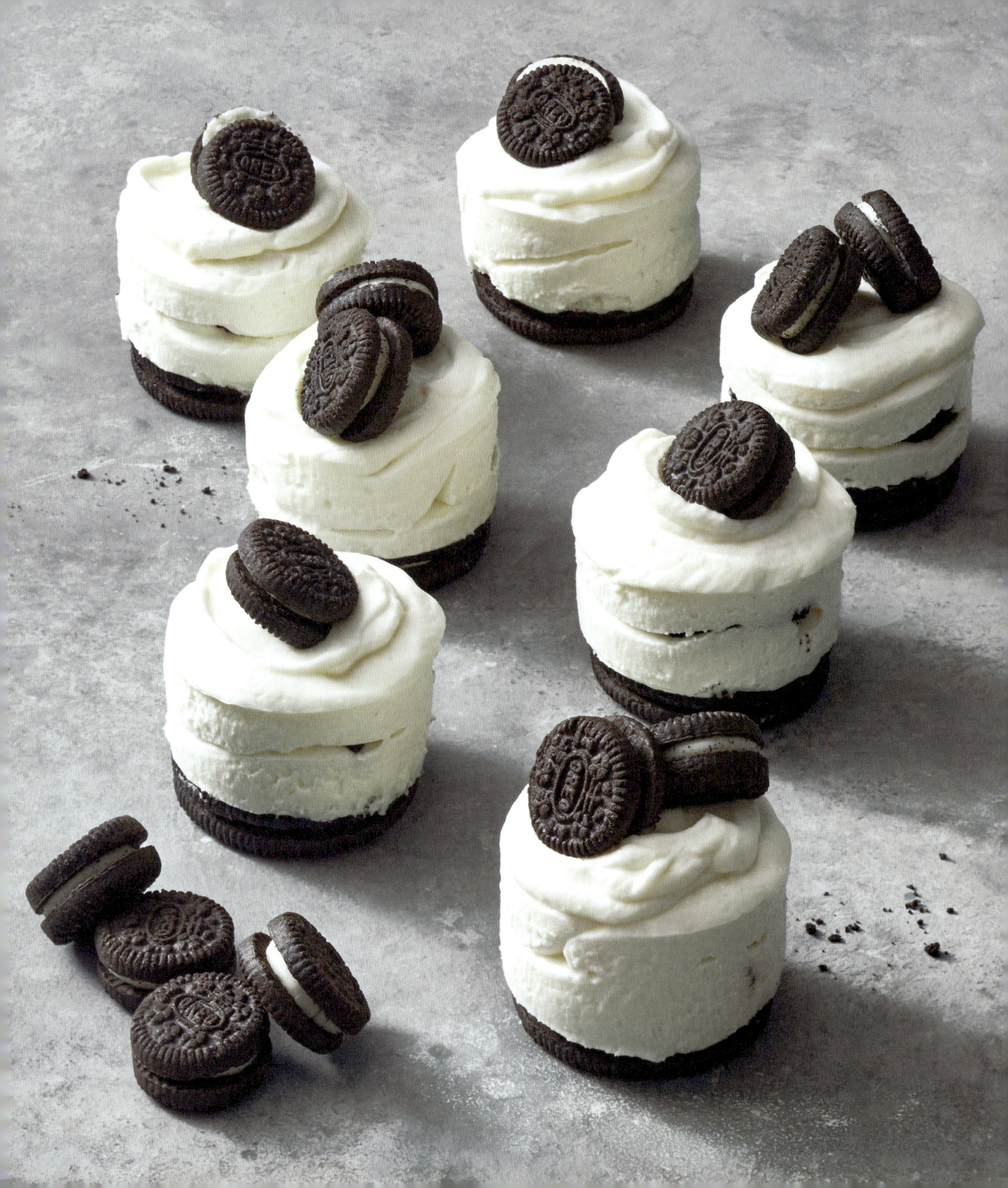

DELICIOUS DESSERTS | **HOLIDAY**

Cookie Cheesecake Bites

- 12 ounces cream cheese (1½ packages), at room temperature
- 3 tablespoons sugar
- 1 cup heavy cream, cold
- 20 chocolate sandwich cookies
- Mini chocolate sandwich cookies, for topping

Serves 12 | Active time 20 minutes | Total time 20 minutes plus chilling

These five-ingredient no-bake mini cheesecakes are creamy, dreamy and poppable, making them a foolproof dessert for any occasion.

1. Using an electric mixer, beat the cream cheese and the sugar until smooth.

2. Reduce the mixer speed to low and gradually add the heavy cream. Increase the speed to high and beat until thick and stiff, about 2 minutes.

3. Roughly break 8 sandwich cookies. Fold into the cream cheese mixture. Place the remaining sandwich cookies in the bottom of a 12-cup nonstick mini cheesecake pan with removable bottoms.

4. Divide the cream mixture among the cups, tapping the pan to set the mixture around the cookies. Top with the mini sandwich cookies and refrigerate until firm, at least 3 hours and up to 1 day.

Love Notes

THE NEWLYWED COOKBOOK **243**

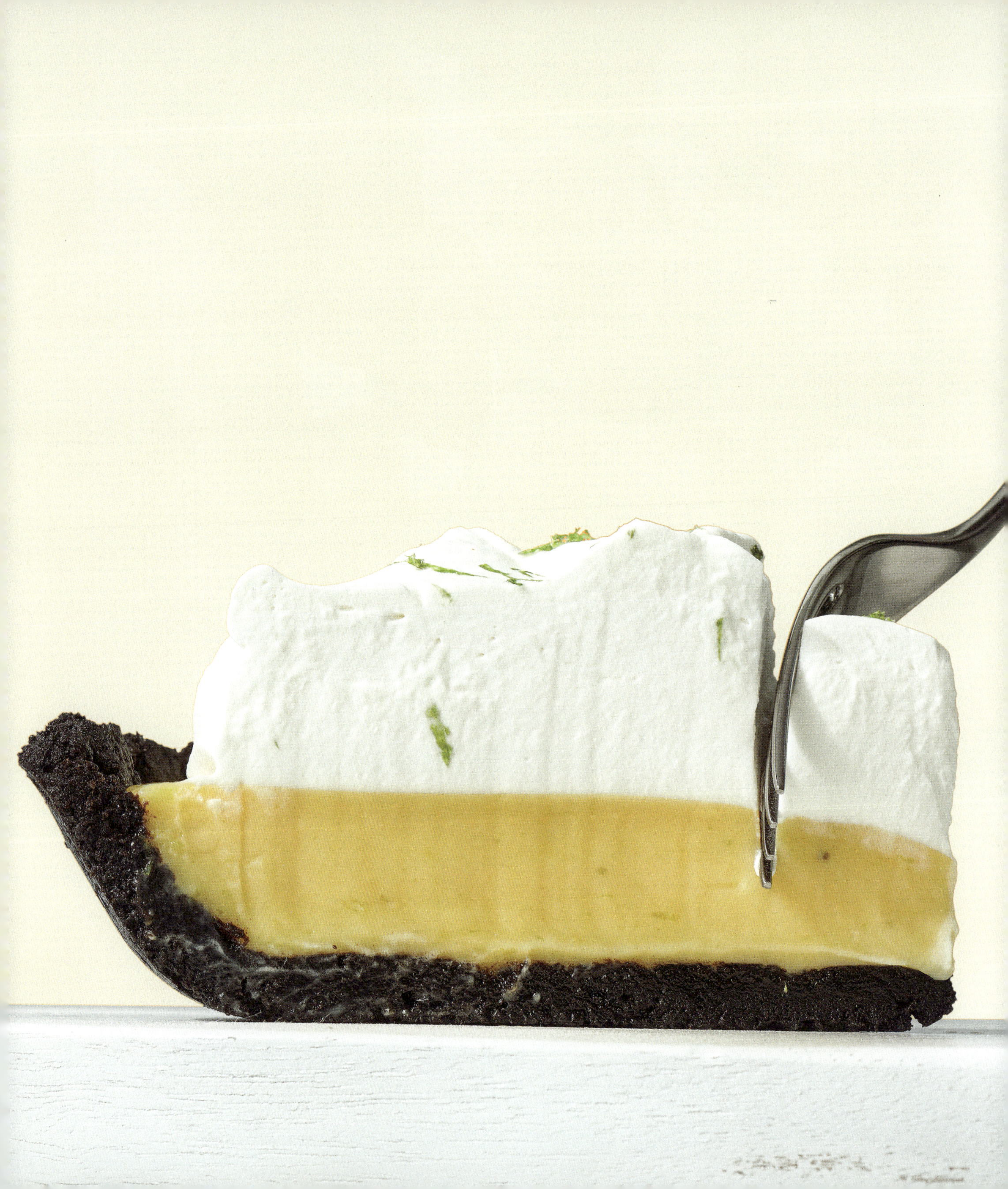

Key Lime Pie

Serves 8 | Active time 30 minutes | Total time 1 hour 15 minutes plus cooling

Give classic key lime flavors a tasty twist by opting for a chocolate wafer crust instead of the typical graham cracker kind.

- 34 chocolate wafer cookies
- Kosher salt
- 6 tablespoons unsalted butter, melted
- 2 14-ounce cans sweetened condensed milk
- 8 large egg yolks
- 1 tablespoon regular or key lime zest (from 5 key limes), plus more for serving
- 1 cup regular or key lime juice (from about 25 key limes)
- 1¼ cups heavy cream
- ¼ cup sour cream
- 2 tablespoons confectioners' sugar
- ½ teaspoon pure vanilla extract

1. Heat the oven to 375°F. In a food processor, pulse the cookies and a pinch of salt to form fine crumbs. Add the butter and pulse to combine. Transfer the mixture to a 9-inch pie plate and press evenly onto the bottom and up the side. Bake until the crust is set and fragrant, 10 to 12 minutes. Transfer to a wire rack to cool.

2. Reduce the oven temperature to 350°F. In a bowl, whisk together the condensed milk, egg yolks, lime zest and lime juice. Pour the mixture into the cooled crust and bake until the center is just set, 12 to 15 minutes. Transfer to a wire rack; let cool completely, about 1 hour, then refrigerate if desired.

3. Using an electric mixer, beat the heavy cream, sour cream, confectioners' sugar and vanilla and a pinch of salt to form medium-stiff peaks. Spoon onto the pie and sprinkle with additional lime zest before serving if desired.

Love Notes

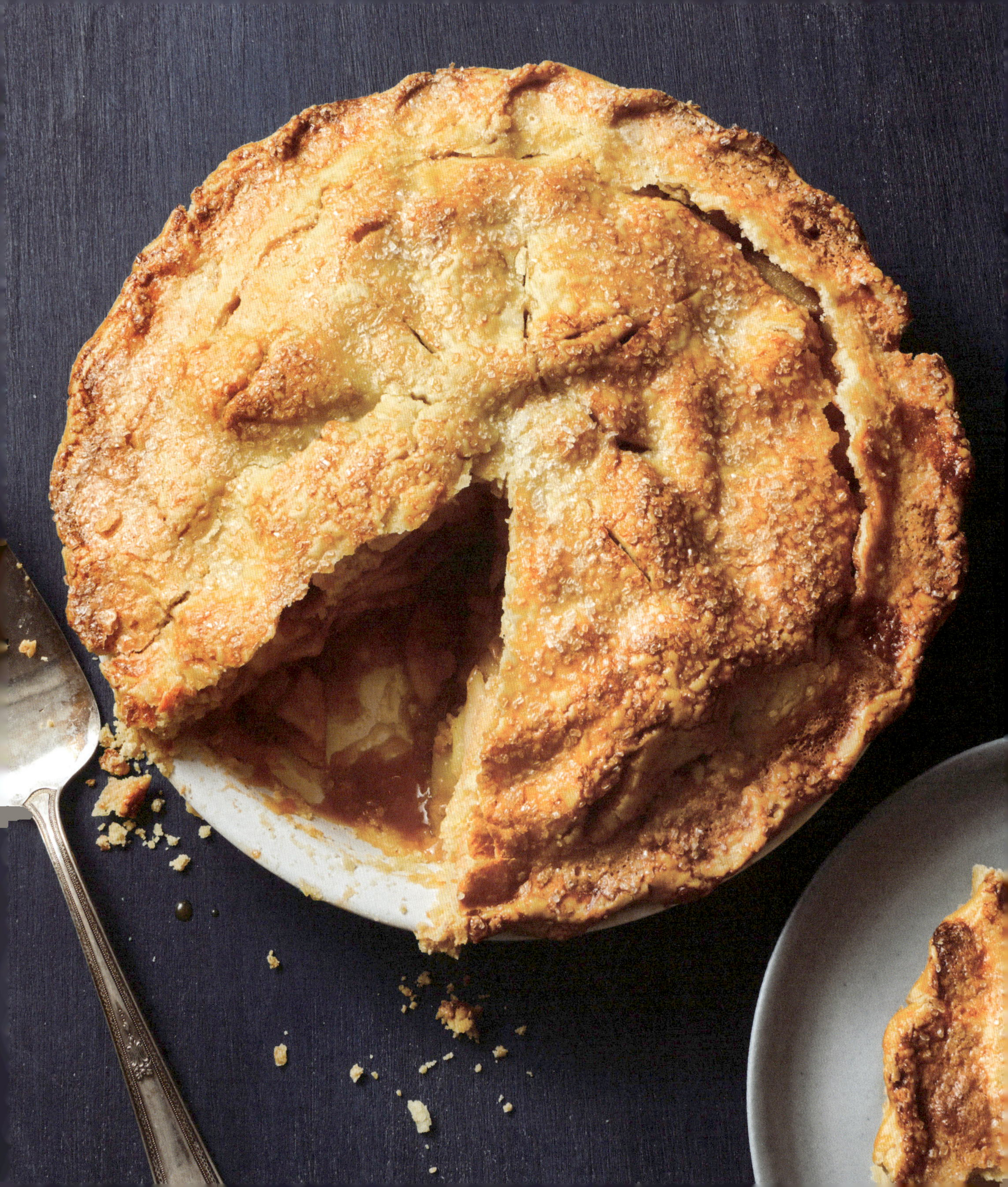

DELICIOUS DESSERTS | **HOLIDAY**

Dulce de Leche Apple Pie

Serves 8 | Active time 1 hour 15 minutes | Total time 2 hours 35 minutes plus cooling

Once you try this indulgent upgrade (read: ooey-gooey caramel), you won't be able to go back to the basic version.

FOR CRUST
- 2½ cups all-purpose flour
- 1 teaspoon plus pinch kosher salt
- 2 tablespoons sugar, divided
- 1 cup (2 sticks) cold unsalted butter, cut into small pieces and frozen 20 minutes
- 6 to 8 tablespoons ice water
- 1 large egg, beaten

FOR APPLES
- 2½ pounds Golden Delicious apples (about 5 large)
- 1½ pounds Granny Smith apples (about 3 large)
- 2 tablespoons fresh lemon juice
- 4 tablespoons sugar, divided
- 3 tablespoons cornstarch
- ¼ teaspoon ground cinnamon
- ⅛ teaspoon freshly grated nutmeg
- 1 cup dulce de leche, divided
- ¼ teaspoon flaked sea salt

1. Make the crust: In a food processor, combine the flour and salt and 1 tablespoon of sugar. Pulse in the butter until it resembles coarse crumbs (a bit smaller than peas). Pulse in 6 tablespoons of ice water until the dough is crumbly but holds together when squeezed, pulsing in more, 1 teaspoon at a time, if necessary; do not overmix. Halve the dough and shape each half on a piece of plastic wrap into a ½-inch-thick disk; wrap and refrigerate until firm, 1 hour.

2. Make the apples: Peel and core the apples and slice them ¼ inch thick. Transfer them to a large bowl and toss with the lemon juice and 2 tablespoons of sugar. Let sit, tossing occasionally, at least 30 minutes and up to 2 hours.

3. On a lightly floured surface, roll 1 disk of dough into a 13-inch circle; fit it into a 9-inch pie plate. Roll the second disk into a 14-inch circle, transferring to parchment halfway through. Slide the parchment (and dough) onto a baking sheet; refrigerate both until ready to use.

4. Heat the oven to 400°F. Combine the cornstarch, cinnamon and nutmeg and the remaining 2 tablespoons of sugar; toss with the apples. Mound the apples in the crust, packing them in along with any juices in the bowl. Drizzle ½ cup of dulce de leche over the top; sprinkle with flaky salt.

5. Let the top crust sit at room temperature until it is pliable without cracking, 5 minutes. Lay it over the filling and trim the edges, leaving a 1-inch overhang. Fold the top crust under the bottom one, creating a thicker crust, and crimp as desired. Refrigerate 10 minutes.

6. Place the pie on a baking sheet, brush with beaten egg and sprinkle with the remaining tablespoon of sugar and a pinch of salt. Cut slits in the top and bake until beginning to brown, 20 to 25 minutes. Reduce the oven temperature to 350°F and bake until the crust is golden brown, 40 to 55 minutes, covering with foil if the crust becomes too dark. Transfer to a wire rack and let cool at least 2½ hours. Serve warm or at room temperature with the remaining caramel.

Love Notes

THE NEWLYWED COOKBOOK 247

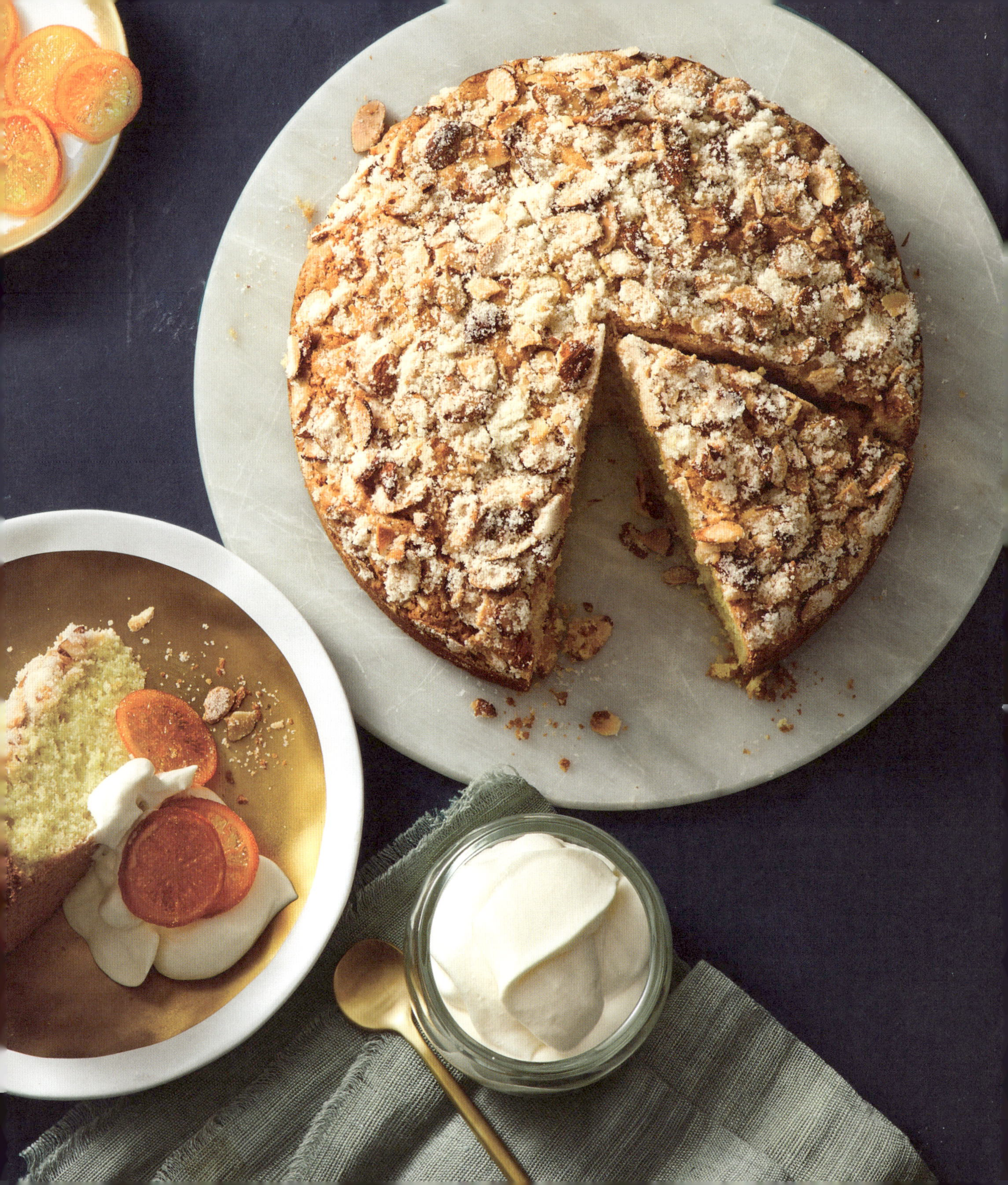

DELICIOUS DESSERTS | HOLIDAY

Olive Oil-Clementine Cake

Serves 8 | Active time 15 minutes | Total time 55 minutes plus cooling

- ¾ cup plus 1 tablespoon extra virgin olive oil, plus more for the pan
- ¾ cup sliced almonds
- ⅓ cup plus ¾ cup granulated sugar
- 1½ cups all-purpose flour
- 2 teaspoons baking powder
- ½ teaspoon kosher salt
- 4 large eggs
- 2 teaspoons finely grated clementine zest plus ¼ cup juice (from about 2 clementines)
- Candied clementines (recipe below) and whipped cream, for serving

This sweet cake is a celebration of winter citrus. Clementine zest and juice are mixed into the batter for a bright boost. Adorn each slice with candied citrus and a dollop of whipped cream before serving.

1. Heat the oven to 350°F. Coat a 9-inch cake pan with oil and line it with parchment paper. In a bowl, toss the almonds with 1 tablespoon of oil and ⅓ cup of sugar.

2. In a medium bowl, whisk together the flour, baking powder and salt. Using an electric mixer, beat the eggs and the remaining ¾ cup sugar until light, fluffy and more than doubled in volume, 4 to 5 minutes. With the mixer on high, gradually add the remaining ¾ cup of oil.

3. Reduce the mixer speed to low and beat in the clementine zest and juice. Gradually add the flour mixture, beating just until incorporated.

4. Spread the batter in the prepared pan. Sprinkle the almond-sugar mixture on top and bake until it is golden brown and a wooden pick inserted in the center comes out clean, 40 to 45 minutes. Let the cake cool 15 minutes, then transfer to a wire rack to cool completely. Top with candied clementines if desired (see recipe at left).

CANDIED CLEMENTINES

In a medium skillet, cook 1½ cups each of granulated sugar and water on low until sugar dissolves. Add 3 small clementines (thinly sliced) and cook for 1 hour. Transfer the clementines to a baking sheet lined with a silicone baking mat and bake at 200°F, turning twice, until dried, about 2 hours. Let cool, then coat the edges in sugar if desired.

Love Notes

THE NEWLYWED COOKBOOK

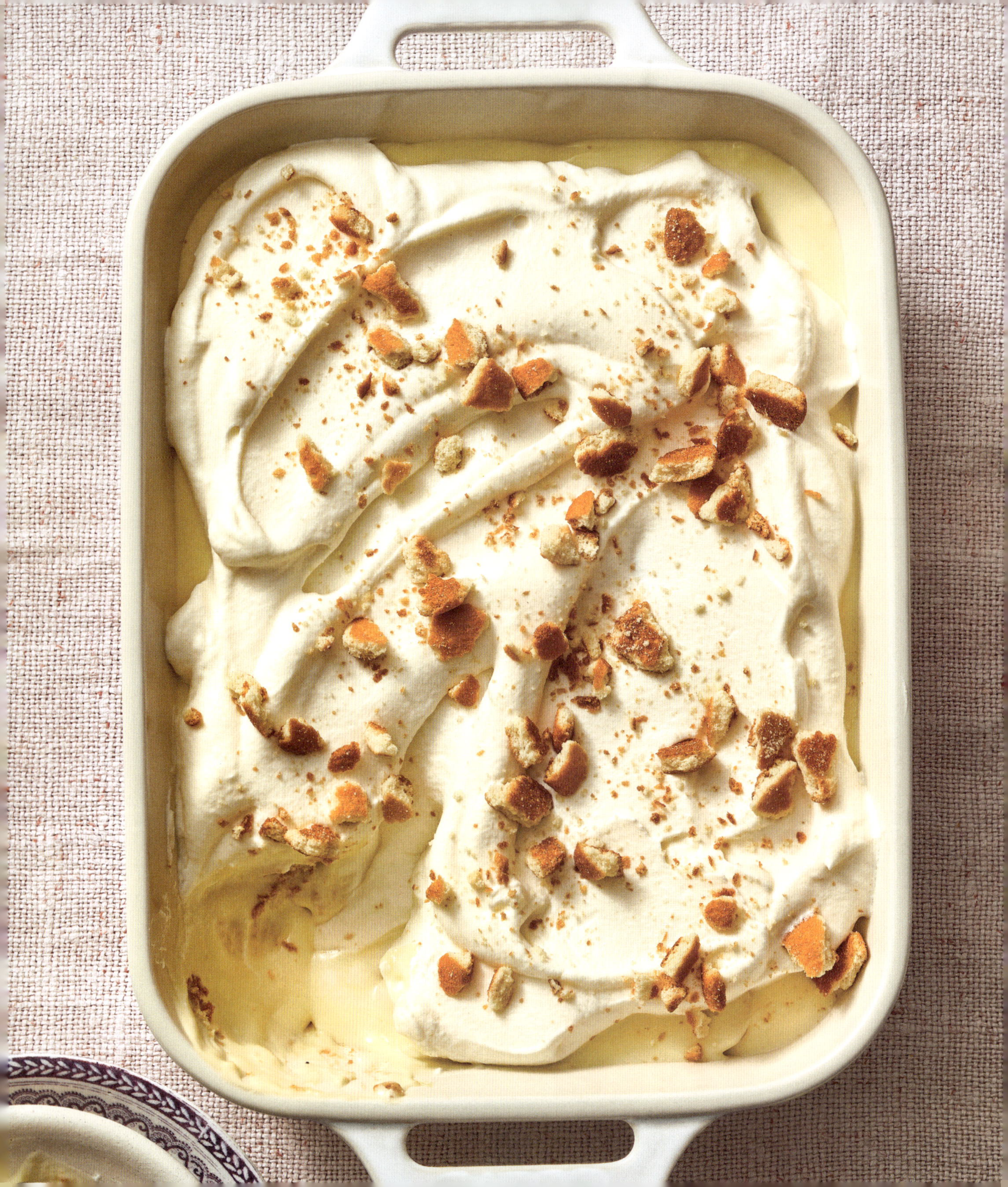

Banana Pudding

Serves 10 | Active time 35 minutes | Total time 35 minutes plus chilling

- 2 cups whole milk
- ½ cup sugar
- ½ teaspoon kosher salt
- 1¾ cups heavy cream, divided
- 4 large egg yolks
- 3 tablespoons cornstarch
- ½ teaspoon pure vanilla extract
- 40 vanilla wafer cookies (we used Nilla Wafers), plus more, crumbled, for topping
- 2 large ripe bananas, sliced ¼ inch thick

Creamy and comforting, this classic dessert is specifically designed to be put together in advance (the cookies need at least six hours in the fridge to soften). Place the plastic wrap directly on the surface of the pudding to keep a skin from forming while it's in the fridge.

1. In a large saucepan, whisk together the milk, sugar and salt and 1 cup heavy cream. In a large heatproof bowl, whisk the egg yolks and cornstarch until combined.

2. Heat the milk mixture on medium-high until just starting to simmer, 3 to 5 minutes. In a slow, steady stream, pour the hot milk mixture over the egg yolk mixture, whisking constantly to prevent the eggs from cooking. Pour the entire mixture back into the saucepan, reduce the heat to medium-low and whisk constantly until the mixture is thickened to the consistency of pancake batter and it bubbles a few times, 5 to 6 minutes. Strain through a fine-mesh sieve into a large bowl, then whisk in the vanilla.

3. Spread a thin layer of pudding onto the bottom of an 8- by 8-inch baking dish. Arrange one-third of the cookies on top, then top with one-third of the bananas. Dollop and spread one-third of the pudding mixture over the bananas. Repeat the layering process twice more, ending with the pudding; smooth the top. Place plastic wrap directly onto the surface of the pudding and refrigerate until it is chilled and the cookies have softened, at least 6 hours.

4. When ready to serve, in a stand mixer fitted with a whisk attachment, beat the remaining ¾ cup of heavy cream on medium-high just until stiff peaks form, 2 to 3 minutes. Spread over the pudding and top with the crumbled cookies.

Love Notes

Index

A

Adobo, canned chipotle in, 22
Adobo-Glazed Portobello Tacos, 119
Air-Fried Falafel Salad, 129
Air-Fried Steak Fajitas, 61
Air fryer, 15
Aleppo Grilled Steak with Farro Salad, 57
Almonds. *See* Nuts and seeds
Apple pie, dulce de leche, 247
Appliances, small, 15–16
Arayes, 203
Asparagus
    Grilled Halloumi Salad, 201
    Sheet Pan Asparagus Frittata, 185

B

Bacon
    about: freezing, 27
    Sriracha-Maple Bacon, 189
Banh mi bowls, pork meatball, 71
Baked Feta Shrimp, 113
Baker, gear list, 17
Bakeware, 13–14
Baking sheets and pans, 13
Banana Pudding, 251
Barista, gear list, 17
Basic Teriyaki Sauce, 29
Beans and other legumes
    about: leftovers, 21; lentils, 23; pantry items, 22, 23
    Air-Fried Falafel Salad, 129
    Black Bean Burgers, 131
    Fish & Chips, 107
    Herby Lentil & Burrata Salad, 231
    Paprika Chicken with Crispy Chickpeas & Tomatoes, 45
    Red Lentil Bolognese, 83
    Saucy Pizza Beans, 59
    Smoky Black Bean & Quinoa Soup, 117
    Steak with Beans & Roasted Broccolini, 69
    White Bean & Radicchio Salad, 229
Beef
    about: leftovers, 21
    Air-Fried Steak Fajitas, 61
    Aleppo Grilled Steak with Farro Salad, 57
    Arayes, 203
    Five-Spice Steak & Broccoli, 73
    Peppercorn Beef Tenderloin, 215
    Sheet Pan BBQ Beef Nachos, 63
    Short Ribs with Creamy Polenta, 179
    Skillet Cheeseburger Hot Dish, 163
    Steak & Grilled Peppers with Chimichurri, 195
    Steak au Poivre with Rosemary Roasted Carrot Salad, 141
    Steak with Beans & Roasted Broccolini, 69
Berries
    Creamy Cannoli Dip, 173
    Crispy Tortilla Bowls with Strawberries & Cream, 157
    Mixed-Berry Cornmeal Cobblers, 237
    Peach & Raspberry Galette, 241
    Strawberry Coconut-Crust Cheesecake, 235
Best Ever Granola, 191
Black Bean Burgers, 131
Blender, 15
Bolognese, red lentil, 83
Bowls
    Crispy Tortilla Bowls with Strawberries & Cream, 157
    Pork Meatball Banh Mi Bowls, 71
    Steak & Rice Noodle Bowls, 91
    Sticky Tofu Bowl, 125
Bread. *See also* Pizza and flatbreads
    about: biscuit mix to stock, 23; freezing, 27; loaf pans, 13; muffin pans, 13–14; panko, 23–24
    Tomato & Scallion Cream Cheese Bagel Bake, 187
Breading meat, alternatives, 47
Bread knife, 12
Broccoli and broccolini
    Five-Spice Steak & Broccoli, 73
    Steak with Beans & Roasted Broccolini, 69
Broth, stocking, 22
Brownies, 239
Brunch, 185–193
    Best Ever Granola, 191
    Raisin-Walnut Coffee Cake, 193
    Sheet Pan Asparagus Frittata, 185
    Sriracha-Maple Bacon, 189
    Tomato & Scallion Cream Cheese Bagel Bake, 187
Brussels sprouts, sweet and saucy, 223
Buffalo Chicken Pizza, 171
Burgers. *See* Sandwiches and wraps
Butternut Squash Curry, 123

C

Cabbage
    Arayes, 203
    Chilled Ramen Salad, 79
Cake pans, 13
California Roll Salad, 111
Canned items, 22
Capers
    about: olives and, 22–23
    Tomato-Poached Cod with Olives & Capers, 147
Caprese, grilled chicken, 49
Carrots
    Carrot-Ginger Sauce, 29
    Roasted Carrots & Red Onions, 225
    Roast Turkey Breast with, 209
    Rosemary Roasted Carrot Salad, 141
Cauliflower
    Creamy Cauliflower Soup with Almond-Thyme Gremolata, 175
    Tandoori-Spiced Cauliflower Chicken Flatbreads, 39
Celery, in Shaved Fennel & Celery Salad, 177
Cereal. *See also* Oats
Cereal, in Spiced Snack Mix, 169
Cheese
    about: leftovers, 21
    Aleppo Grilled Halloumi with Farro Salad (var.), 57
    Baked Feta Shrimp, 113
    Cookie Cheesecake Bites, 243
    Creamy Cannoli Dip, 173
    Creamy Feta Sauce, 30
    Grilled Chicken Caprese, 49
    Grilled Halloumi Salad, 201
    Herby Lentil & Burrata Salad, 231
    Palak Paneer, 133
    pasta with (*See* Pasta and noodles)
    pizza with (*See* Pizza and flatbreads)
    Queso Fundido with Roasted Mushrooms, 167
    sandwiches with (*See* Sandwiches and wraps)
    Sheet Pan BBQ Beef Nachos, 63
    Sheet Pan Chicken Suizas Nachos, 165
    Skillet Balsamic Chicken, 41
    Skillet Cheeseburger Hot Dish, 163
    Strawberry Coconut-Crust Cheesecake, 235
    Tomato & Scallion Cream Cheese Bagel Bake, 187
    Za'atar Chicken with Whipped Feta, 55
Chef's knife, 12
Chicken
    about: breading alternatives, 47; dinners, 37–55
    Buffalo Chicken Pizza, 171
    Chicken à l'Orange, 181
    Chicken Francese Pasta, 89
    Chicken Paprikash, 53
    Crispy Chicken Salad, 47
    Double Mustard–Marinated Chicken Drumsticks, 199
    Grilled Chicken Caprese, 49
    Mojo-Style Sauce, 30
    Moroccan-Spiced Skillet Chicken & Couscous, 43
    Orange-Ginger Roast Chicken with Fennel & Radicchio Salad, 217
    Sheet Pan Chicken Suizas Nachos, 165
    Skillet Balsamic Chicken, 41
    Slow Cooker Chicken Pozole Verde, 51
    Tandoori-Spiced Cauliflower Chicken Flatbreads, 39
    You Married Me Chicken, 153
    Za'atar Chicken with Whipped Feta, 55
Chilled Ramen Salad, 79
Chocolate
    Cookie Cheesecake Bites, 243
    Peanut Butter Molten Chocolate Cakes, 159
    Pecan Pie Brownies, 239
    Tiramisu Dip, 161
Citrus
    about: candied clementines, 249
    Key Lime Pie, 245
    Lemon & Thyme Pear Tart with Apricot Glaze, 183
    Olive Oil–Clementine Cake, 249
    Orange-Ginger Roast Chicken with Fennel & Radicchio Salad, 217
    Pineapple, Orange & Onion Roasted Ham, 213
Classic Pesto, 29
Classic Tuna Melt, 101
Clementines, in Olive Oil–Clementine Cake, 249
Cobblers, mixed berry, 237
Coconut
    about: coconut milk, 24
    Best Ever Granola, 191
    Strawberry Coconut-Crust Cheesecake, 235
Coffee
    about: barista gear list, 17
    Tiramisu Dip, 161
    Coffee cake, raisin-walnut, 193
Colanders, 15
Cookie Cheesecake Bites, 243
Cookware costs, 13
Cooling racks, 13
Corkscrew, 15
Cornmeal. *See* Polenta (cornmeal)
Couscous
    about: 23
    Grilled Halloumi Salad, 201
    Moroccan-Spiced Skillet Chicken & Couscous, 43
Crab Cakes with Creamy Sauce, 103.

See also California Roll Salad
Crabmeat, in California Roll Salad, 111
Creamy Cannoli Dip, 173
Creamy Feta Sauce, 30
Creamy Kale Pasta, 93
Creamy Sauce, 103
Crispy Chicken Salad, 47
Crispy Tortilla Bowls with Strawberries & Cream, 157
Curry
 about: protein alternatives with, 99
 Butternut Squash Curry, 123
 Green Curry Shrimp, 99
Cutting boards, 15

D

Date night in, 141–161
 about: pasta night, 143
 Crispy Tortilla Bowls with Strawberries & Cream, 157
 Ice Cream Float, 155
 Peanut Butter Molten Chocolate Cakes, 159
 Roasted Pork Chops & Pears, 149
 Sautéed Mushrooms & Creamy Polenta, 145
 Shrimp Scampi, 143
 Smoky Mussels Pomodoro, 151
 Steak au Poivre with Rosemary Roasted Carrot Salad, 141
 Tiramisu Dip, 161
 Tomato-Poached Cod with Olives & Capers, 147
 You Married Me Chicken, 153
Desserts. *See also* Raisin-Walnut Coffee Cake
 about: bakeware items (baking sheets/pans; cake pans; loaf/muffin pans; pie plate), 13–14, 17; freezing cookie dough, 27; ice cream/cookie scoop, 15
 Banana Pudding, 251
 Cookie Cheesecake Bites, 243
 Creamy Cannoli Dip, 173
 Dulce de Leche Apple Pie, 247
 Ice Cream Float, 155
 Key Lime Pie, 245
 Lemon & Thyme Pear Tart with Apricot Glaze, 183
 Mixed-Berry Cornmeal Cobblers, 237
 Olive Oil–Clementine Cake, 249
 Peach & Raspberry Galette, 241
 Peanut Butter Molten Chocolate Cakes, 159
 Pecan Pie Brownies, 239
 Strawberry Coconut-Crust Cheesecake, 235
 Tiramisu Dip, 161
Dill-Spiked Potato Latkes, 227
Dinner party, 175–183
 Chicken à l'Orange, 181
 Creamy Cauliflower Soup with Almond-Thyme Gremolata, 175
 Lemon & Thyme Pear Tart with Apricot Glaze, 183
 Shaved Fennel & Celery Salad, 177
 Short Ribs with Creamy Polenta, 179
Dinners (big-batch), freezing, 27
Double Mustard–Marinated Chicken Drumsticks, 199
Dressings. *See* Sauces
Drinks, mixologist gear for, 17
Dulce de Leche Apple Pie, 247
Dumplings
 about: freezing, 27
 Inside-Out Pork Dumplings, 95
Dutch oven, 12

E

Eggplant, in Rigatoni alla Norma, 87
Eggs
 Green Goddess Sandwiches, 121
 Shakshuka, 127
 Sheet Pan Asparagus Frittata, 185
Entertainer, gear list, 17
Entertaining, menus for. *See* Brunch; Date night in; Dinner party; Game day; Grilling
Everything Bagel Crusted Salmon with Herby Fennel Salad, 211

F

Fajitas, steak (air-fried), 61
Falafel salad, air-fried, 129
Farro
 Aleppo Grilled Halloumi with Farro Salad (var.), 57
 Grilled Halloumi Salad, 201
Fennel
 Fennel & Radicchio Salad, 217
 Herby Fennel Salad, 211
 Shaved Fennel & Celery Salad, 177
Fish. *See* Seafood
Five-Spice Steak & Broccoli, 73
Flatbreads. *See* Pizza and flatbreads
Food processor, 15
Freezer, stocking/organizing, 27
Fresh Green Bean Casserole, 221
Fridge. *See* Refrigerator
Fruit, freezing, 27

G

Gadgets and tools, 14–15
Game day, 163–173
 Buffalo Chicken Pizza, 171
 Creamy Cannoli Dip, 173
 Queso Fundido with Roasted Mushrooms, 167
 Sheet Pan Chicken Suizas Nachos, 165
 Skillet Cheeseburger Hot Dish, 163
 Spiced Snack Mix, 169
Gear, kitchen essentials, 12–16
 personal specialties (baker, barista, entertainer, home chef, meal prepper, mixologist, outdoor enthusiast, pasta-maker), 17
Gift registry, 16
Ginger
 about: peeling, 109
 Carrot-Ginger Sauce, 29
Gnocchi with sausage and green beans, 75
Gochujang, sweet and spicy, 30
Granola, 191
Graters, 14
Green beans
 Chicken à l'Orange and, 181
 Fresh Green Bean Casserole, 221
 Seared Salmon with Charred Green Beans, 97
 Sheet Pan Gnocchi with Sausage & Green Beans, 75
Green Curry Shrimp, 99
Green Goddess Sandwiches, 121
Greens, leftovers, 21. *See also* Salads
Gremolata, almond thyme, 175
Grilled Chicken Caprese, 49
Grilled Halloumi Salad, 201
Grilled Sweet Potatoes with Mint-Chile Relish, 197
Grilling, 195–203
 Arayes, 203
 Double Mustard–Marinated Chicken Drumsticks, 199
 Grilled Haloumi Salad, 201
 Grilled Sweet Potatoes with Mint-Chile Relish, 197
 Steak & Grilled Peppers with Chimichurri, 195
Grocery shopping, 19–20

H

Ham, pineapple, orange and onion roasted, 183
Herbs and spices, 25
Herby Lentil & Burrata Salad, 231
Herby Salmon Burgers, 115
Holiday menus, desserts, 235–251
 Banana Pudding, 251
 Cookie Cheesecake Bites, 243
 Dulce de Leche Apple Pie, 247
 Key Lime Pie, 245
 Mixed-Berry Cornmeal Cobblers, 237
 Olive Oil–Clementine Cake, 249
 Peach & Raspberry Galette, 241
 Pecan Pie Brownies, 239
 Strawberry Coconut-Crust Cheesecake, 235
Holiday menus, mains, 209–217
 Everything Bagel Crusted Salmon with Herby Fennel Salad, 211
 Orange-Ginger Roast Chicken with Fennel & Radicchio Salad, 217
 Peppercorn Beef Tenderloin, 215
 Pineapple, Orange & Onion Roasted Ham, 213
 Roasted Root Vegetables, 219
 Roast Turkey Breast, 209
Holiday menus, sides, 219–233
 Dill Spiked Potato Latkes, 227
 Fresh Green Bean Casserole, 221
 Herby Lentil & Burrata Salad, 231
 Roasted Carrots & Red Onions, 225
 Sweet & Spicy Brussels Sprouts, 223
 Thyme-Scented Mashed Potatoes, 233
 White Bean & Radicchio Salad, 229
Home chef, gear list, 17
Homestyle Italian Dressing, 29
Horseradish Cream Sauce, 215

I

Ice cream/cookie scoop, 15
Ice Cream Float, 155
Ingredients. *See also* specific main ingredients
 first in, first out usage, 21
 fridge and freezer items, 26–27
 fridge items, 27
 list to buy, 19
 pantry items, 22–25
 photo of fridge/freezer contents, 19
 planning to buy, 19
 shopping for, 19–20
 storage strategies, 21
Inside-Out Pork Dumplings, 95
Italian dressing, homestyle, 29

J

Juicer/reamer, handheld, 14

K

Kale
 Air-Fried Falafel Salad, 129

THE NEWLYWED COOKBOOK 253

Creamy Kale Pasta, 93
Key Lime Pie, 245
Kitchen
    assessing, organizing, and equipping, 11
    bakeware, 13–14
    cookware costs, 13
    essential gear list, 12–16
    gadgets and tools, 14–15
    knives, types and use, 12
    personal gear lists (baker, barista, entertainer, home chef, meal prepper, mixologist, outdoor enthusiast, pasta maker), 17
    pots and pans, 12–13
Kitchen scissors, 14
Knives, types and use, 12

L

Ladles, 14
Lasagna, three-cheese, 77
Latkes, dill spiked potato, 227
Leftovers, 21
Lemon & Thyme Pear Tart with Apricot Glaze, 183
Lentils. See Beans and other legumes
Liquid condiments, to stock, 24–25

M

Main dishes. See Holiday menus, mains; Plant-powered meals; Weeknight winners; specific main ingredients
Manhattan Clam Chowder, 105
Mayonnaise, about, 24
Meal prep, 21
Meal prepper, gear list, 17
Measuring cups and spoons, 15
Measuring pans, 13
Meatballs, in Pork Meatball Banh Mi Bowls, 71
Menus
    for entertaining (See Brunch; Date night in; Dinner party; Game day; Grilling) for holidays (See Holiday menus entries)
Microplane, 14
Mint-Chile Relish, 197
Mixed-Berry Cornmeal Cobblers, 237
Mixer, electric, 15
Mixing bowls, 15
Mixologist, gear list, 17
Mojo-Style Sauce, 30
Moroccan-Spiced Skillet Chicken & Couscous, 43
Multicooker/slow cooker, 16
Mushrooms
    Adobo-Glazed Portobello Tacos, 119
    Fresh Green Bean Casserole, 221
    Queso Fundido with Roasted Mushrooms, 167
    Red Lentil Bolognese, 83
    Sautéed Mushrooms & Creamy Polenta, 145
    Sticky Tofu Bowl, 125
Mustard
    about: types of, 24
    Double Mustard–Marinated Chicken Drumsticks, 199
    Mustard-Glazed Pork Chops, 65

N

Nachos
    Sheet Pan BBQ Beef Nachos, 63
    Sheet Pan Chicken Suizas Nachos, 165

Noodles. See Pasta and noodles
Nuts and seeds
    about: freezing, 27; nut butters, 22; pantry items, 22, 23
    Almond-Thyme Gremolata, 175
    Best Ever Granola, 191
    Everything Bagel Crusted Salmon with Herby Fennel Salad, 211
    Peanut Butter Molten Chocolate Cakes, 159
    Pecan Pie Brownies, 239
    Raisin-Walnut Coffee Cake, 193
    Sesame Noodles, 85
    Spiced Snack Mix, 169
    Tangy Tahini Sauce, 30

O

Oats
    about: stocking, 23
    Best Ever Granola, 191
Oils, stocking, 24–25
Olive and vegetable oils, 24–25
Olive Oil–Clementine Cake, 249
Olives
    about: stocking capers and, 22–23
    Tomato-Poached Cod with Olives & Capers, 147
Onions
    Onion Flatbread, 135
    Pineapple, Orange & Onion Roasted Ham, 183, 213
    Roasted Carrots & Red Onions, 225
    Roasted Root Vegetables, 219
    Tomato & Scallion Cream Cheese Bagel Bake, 187
Orange-Ginger Roast Chicken with Fennel & Radicchio Salad, 217
Outdoor enthusiast, gear list, 17

P

Palak Paneer, 133
Pans, measuring, 13
Pans, pots and, 12–13
Pantry items, 22–25
    beans and things, 22–23
    freezer items and, 27
    fridge items and, 26
    herbs and spices, 25
    liquid condiments, 24–25
    pasta, grains, etc., 23–24
Paprika Chicken with Crispy Chickpeas & Tomatoes, 45
Paprikash, chicken, 53
Paring knife, 12
Parsnips, Roast Turkey Breast with, 209
Pasta and noodles. See also Couscous
    about: noodle night meals, 77–95; pasta-maker gear list, 17; to stock, 23, 24
    Chicken Francese Pasta, 89
    Chilled Ramen Salad, 79
    Creamy Kale Pasta, 93
    Inside-Out Pork Dumplings, 95
    Red Lentil Bolognese, 83
    Rigatoni alla Norma, 87
    Rigatoni with Sausage-Style Turkey & Arugula, 81
    Sesame Noodles, 85
    Sheet Pan Gnocchi with Sausage & Green Beans, 75
    Shrimp Scampi and, 143
    Steak & Rice Noodle Bowls, 91
    Three-Cheese Summer Skillet Lasagna, 77
Peach & Raspberry Galette, 241

Peanut butter. See Nuts and seeds
Pears
    Lemon & Thyme Pear Tart with Apricot Glaze, 183
    Roasted Pork Chops & Pears, 149
Pecan Pie Brownies, 239
Peppercorn Beef Tenderloin, 215
Pepperoni, in Saucy Pizza Beans, 59
Peppers
    about: canned chipotle in adobo, 22; pantry items to stock, 22, 23; roasted red peppers, 23
    Steak & Grilled Peppers with Chimichurri, 195
Pesto, classic, 29
Pickles, stocking, 23
Pineapple, Orange & Onion Roasted Ham, 213
Pizza and flatbreads
    Buffalo Chicken Pizza, 171
    Onion Flatbread, 135
    Saucy Pizza Beans, 59
    Tandoori-Spiced Cauliflower Chicken Flatbreads, 39
Plant-powered meals, 117–135
    Adobo-Glazed Portobello Tacos, 119
    Air-Fried Falafel Salad, 129
    Aleppo Grilled Halloumi with Farro Salad (var.), 57
    Black Bean Burgers, 131
    Butternut Squash Curry, 123
    Green Goddess Sandwiches, 121
    Grilled Halloumi Salad, 201
    Onion Flatbread, 135
    Palak Paneer, 133
    Sautéed Mushrooms & Creamy Polenta, 145
    Shakshuka, 127
    Smoky Black Bean & Quinoa Soup, 117
    Sticky Tofu Bowl, 125
Polenta (cornmeal)
    about: Jiffy Corn Muffin Mix, 237; polenta, 24
    Mixed-Berry Cornmeal Cobblers, 237
    Sautéed Mushrooms & Creamy Polenta, 145
    Short Ribs with Creamy Polenta, 179
Pork
    about: bone-in vs. boneless pork chops, 149; freezing bacon, 27
    Inside-Out Pork Dumplings, 95
    Mustard-Glazed Pork Chops, 65
    Pineapple, Orange & Onion Roasted Ham, 213
    Pork Meatball Banh Mi Bowls, 71
    Roasted Pork Chops & Pears, 149
    Sriracha-Maple Bacon, 189
Potatoes
    Dill Spiked Potato Latkes, 227
    Fish & Chips, 107
    Mustard-Glazed Pork Chops with, 65
    Roasted Root Vegetables, 219
    Roasted Sausages & Vegetables, 67
    Sheet Pan Gnocchi with Sausage & Green Beans, 75
    Skillet Cheeseburger Hot Dish, 163
    Thyme-Scented Mashed Potatoes, 233
Pots and pans, 12–13
Pretzels, in Spiced Snack Mix, 169

Q

Queso Fundido with Roasted Mushrooms, 167
Quinoa
    about, 24
    Smoky Black Bean & Quinoa Soup, 117

R

Radicchio
    Fennel & Radicchio Salad, 217
    White Bean & Radicchio Salad, 229
Raisin-Walnut Coffee Cake, 193
Raspberries, in Peach & Raspberry Galette, 241
Recipes. *See also specific categories; specific main ingredients*
    dividing portions for storage, 21
    grocery shopping for, 19–20
    meal prep, 21
    planning ingredients lists, 19
    storage/leftover tips, 21
    target search for, 19
Red Lentil Bolognese, 83
Refrigerator
    DIY sauces/spreads/dressings for, 29–30
    stocking and organizing, 26
    storage/leftover tips, 21
Registry, wedding gift, 16
Relishes
    Mint-Chile Relish, 197
    Shallot and Parsley Relish, 69
Rice
    about: cooking ahead, 24; to stock, 24
    Butternut Squash Curry, 123
    Palak Paneer, 133
    Steak & Rice Noodle Bowls, 91
Rigatoni alla Norma, 87
Rigatoni with Sausage-Style Turkey & Arugula, 81
Roasted Carrots & Red Onions, 225
Roasted Pork Chops & Pears, 149
Roasted Root Vegetables, 219
Roasted Sausages & Vegetables, 67
Roast Turkey Breast, 209
Root vegetables, roasted, 219
Rosemary Roasted Carrot Salad, 141
Rubber spatulas, 14
Ruler, 15

S

Salads
    about: breading meat for, 47; spinner for, 15
    Air-Fried Falafel Salad, 129
    Aleppo Grilled Steak with Farro Salad, 57
    California Roll Salad, 111
    Chilled Ramen Salad, 79
    Crispy Chicken Salad, 47
    Fennel & Radicchio Salad, 217
    Grilled Halloumi Salad, 201
    Herby Fennel Salad, 211
    Herby Lentil & Burrata Salad, 231
    Rosemary Roasted Carrot Salad, 141
    Shaved Fennel & Celery Salad, 177
    Smoky Chicken Thighs on Baby Romaine, 37
Salmon. *See* Seafood
Sandwiches and wraps. *See also* Skillet Cheeseburger Hot Dish
    about: mayo magic for golden brown bread slices, 101
    Adobo-Glazed Portobello Tacos, 119
    Arayes, 203
    Black Bean Burgers, 131
    Green Goddess Sandwiches, 121
    Herby Salmon Burgers, 115

Sauce pans, 12
Sauces
    about: DIY for fridge, 29–30; do-it-all dressing, 67; hot sauces, 24; liquid condiments and, 24–25; marinara, 23; salsa, 23; to stock, 22, 23, 24
    Basic Teriyaki Sauce, 29
    Carrot-Ginger Sauce, 29
    Classic Pesto, 29
    Creamy Feta Sauce, 30
    Creamy Sauce, 103
    Homestyle Italian Dressing, 29
    Horseradish Cream Sauce, 215
    Mojo-Style Sauce, 30
    pasta with (*See* Pasta and noodles)
    Sweet and Juicy Gochujang, 30
    Tangy Tahini Sauce, 30
    Saucy Pizza Beans, 59
Sausage
    Rigatoni with Sausage-Style Turkey & Arugula, 81
    Roasted Sausages & Vegetables, 67
    Sheet Pan Gnocchi with Sausage & Green Beans, 75
Sautéed Mushrooms & Creamy Polenta, 145
Scissors, kitchen, 14
Seafood
    about: freezing shrimp, 27; leftovers, 21; pasta night and, 143; prepping mussels, 151; stocking canned fish, 22; suppers, 99–115; surimi (krab/imitation crab), 111
    Baked Feta Shrimp, 113
    California Roll Salad, 111
    Classic Tuna Melt, 101
    Crab Cakes with Creamy Sauce, 103
    Everything Bagel Crusted Salmon with Herby Fennel Salad, 211
    Fish & Chips, 107
    Herby Salmon Burgers, 115
    Manhattan Clam Chowder, 105
    Seared Salmon with Charred Green Beans, 97
    Seared Salmon with Spiced Sweet Potatoes, 109
    Shrimp Scampi, 143
    Smoky Mussels Pomodoro, 151
    Tomato-Poached Cod with Olives & Capers, 147
Seared Salmon with Charred Green Beans, 97
Seared Salmon with Spiced Sweet Potatoes, 109
Sesame Noodles, 85
Shakshuka, 127
Shallot and Parsley Relish, 69
Shaved Fennel & Celery Salad, 177
Sheet Pan Asparagus Frittata, 185
Sheet Pan BBQ Beef Nachos, 63
Sheet Pan Chicken Suizas Nachos, 165
Sheet Pan Gnocchi with Sausage & Green Beans, 75
Shopping for ingredients, 19–20
Short Ribs with Creamy Polenta, 179
Shrimp. *See* Seafood
Side dishes. *See* Holiday menus, sides; Salads; Soups and stews; *specific main ingredients*
Silicone spatulas, 14
Skillet Balsamic Chicken, 41
Skillet Cheeseburger Hot Dish, 163
Skillets, 13
Slow Cooker Chicken Pozole Verde, 51
Slow cooker/multicooker, 16
Smoky Black Bean & Quinoa Soup, 117
Smoky Chicken Thighs on Baby Romaine, 37
Smoky Mussels Pomodoro, 151

Snack mix, spiced, 169
Soups and stews
    about: clam juice for, 105
    Creamy Cauliflower Soup with Almond-Thyme Gremolata, 175
    Manhattan Clam Chowder, 105
    Slow Cooker Chicken Pozole Verde, 51
    Smoky Black Bean & Quinoa Soup, 117
Soy sauce, about, 25
Spatulas, 14
Spiced Snack Mix, 169
Spinach, in Palak Paneer, 133
Squash
    Butternut Squash Curry, 123
    Three-Cheese Summer Skillet Lasagna, 77
Sriracha-Maple Bacon, 189
Steak. *See* Beef
Sticky Tofu Bowl, 125
Storage strategies, 21
Strawberries. *See* Berries
Sweet & Spicy Brussels Sprouts, 223
Sweet and Juicy Gochujang, 30
Sweet potatoes
    Grilled Sweet Potatoes with Mint-Chile Relish, 197
    Roasted Root Vegetables, 219
    Seared Salmon with Spiced Sweet Potatoes, 109

T

Tacos, adobo-glazed portobello, 119
Tahini sauce, tangy, 30
Tandoori-Spiced Cauliflower Chicken Flatbreads, 39
Tangy Tahini Sauce, 30
Teriyaki sauce, basic, 29
Thermometer, 15
Three-Cheese Summer Skillet Lasagna, 77
Thyme-Scented Mashed Potatoes, 233
Tiramisu Dip, 161
Toaster oven, 16
Tofu, Sticky Tofu Bowl, 125
Tomatillos, in Slow Cooker Chicken Pozole Verde, 51
Tomatoes
    about: canned, to stock, 23; stocking ketchup, 24
    Grilled Chicken Caprese, 49
    Paprika Chicken with Crispy Chickpeas & Tomatoes, 45
    sauces with (*See* Sauces)
    Shakshuka, 127
    Smoky Mussels Pomodoro, 151
    Tomato & Scallion Cream Cheese Bagel Bake, 187
    Tomato-Poached Cod with Olives & Capers, 147
Tongs, 14
Tools, gadgets, small appliances, 14–16
Tortilla bowls with strawberries and cream, crispy, 157
Turkey
    Rigatoni with Sausage-Style Turkey & Arugula, 81
    Roast Turkey Breast, 209

V

Vegetable peeler, 14
Vegetables. *See also specific vegetables*
    about: freezing, 27; leftovers, 21
    Roasted Sausages & Vegetables, 67
Vegetarian meals. *See* Plant-powered meals
Vinegars, 25

THE NEWLYWED COOKBOOK 255

W

Weeknight winners. *See also* Plant-powered meals
  about: chicken dinners, 37–55; meaty mains, 57–75; noodle night, 77–95; overview of, 33–35; seafood suppers, 99–115
  Air-Fried Steak Fajitas, 61
  Aleppo Grilled Steak with Farro Salad, 57
  Baked Feta Shrimp, 113
  California Roll Salad, 111
  Chicken Francese Pasta, 89
  Chicken Paprikash, 53
  Chilled Ramen Salad, 79
  Classic Tuna Melt, 101
  Crab Cakes with Creamy Sauce, 103
  Creamy Kale Pasta, 93
  Crispy Chicken Salad, 47
  Fish & Chips, 107
  Five-Spice Steak & Broccoli, 73
  Green Curry Shrimp, 99
  Grilled Chicken Caprese, 49
  Herby Salmon Burgers, 115
  Inside-Out Pork Dumplings, 95
  Manhattan Clam Chowder, 105
  Moroccan-Spiced Skillet Chicken & Couscous, 43
  Mustard-Glazed Pork Chops, 65
  Paprika Chicken with Crispy Chickpeas & Tomatoes, 45
  Pork Meatball Banh Mi Bowls, 71
  Red Lentil Bolognese, 83
  Rigatoni alla Norma, 87
  Rigatoni with Sausage-Style Turkey & Arugula, 81
  Roasted Sausages & Vegetables, 67
  Saucy Pizza Beans, 59
  Seared Salmon with Charred Green Beans, 97
  Seared Salmon with Spiced Sweet Potatoes, 109
  Sesame Noodles, 85
  Sheet Pan BBQ Beef Nachos, 63
  Sheet Pan Gnocchi with Sausage & Green Beans, 75
  Skillet Balsamic Chicken, 41
  Slow Cooker Chicken Pozole Verde, 51
  Smoky Chicken Thighs on Baby Romaine, 37
  Steak & Rice Noodle Bowls, 91
  Steak with Beans & Roasted Broccolini, 69
  Tandoori-Spiced Cauliflower Chicken Flatbreads, 39
  Three-Cheese Summer Skillet Lasagna, 77
  Za'atar Chicken with Whipped Feta, 55
Whisks, 14
White Bean & Radicchio Salad, 229
Worcestershire sauce, 25

Y

You Married Me Chicken, 153

Z

Za'atar Chicken with Whipped Feta, 55

GOOD HOUSEKEEPING

DESIGN LEAD **Laura Formisano**
CHIEF FOOD DIRECTOR **Kate Merker** • DEPUTY FOOD DIRECTOR **Trish Clasen Marsanico**
VISUAL DIRECTOR **Bruce Perez**
GROUP VISUAL STYLING DIRECTOR **Elisabeth Engelhart** • EDITORIAL STYLIST **Alex Mata**
COPY CHIEF **Benay R. Bubar** • COPY EDITOR **Cheryl Della Pietra**

RECIPE PHOTOGRAPHY **Mike Garten, Danielle Occhiogrosso Daly** (pages 171 and 234)
RECIPE DEVELOPERS **Joy Cho, Kristina Kurek, Tina Martinez, Kate Merker**

FOOD STYLISTS **Christine Albano, Simon Andrews, Michelle Gatton, Erika Joyce, Rebecca Jurkevich, Kate Merker**
PROP STYLISTS **Elisabeth Engelhart, Cate Geiger, Raina Kattelson, Christina Lane, Alex Mata**

Leadership & Operations
EDITOR IN CHIEF & EDITORIAL DIRECTOR, HEARST LIFESTYLE GROUP **Jane Francisco**
GROUP EXECUTIVE DIRECTOR, CREATIVE **Melissa Geurts**
DIRECTOR, EDITORIAL OPERATIONS **Dana A. Levy**

Hearst Books
VICE PRESIDENT, PUBLISHER **Jacqueline Deval**
DEPUTY DIRECTOR **Nicole Fisher**
DEPUTY MANAGING EDITOR **Maria Ramroop**

Published by Hearst
PRESIDENT & CHIEF EXECUTIVE OFFICER **Steven R. Swartz**
CHAIRMAN **William R. Hearst III**
EXECUTIVE VICE CHAIRMAN **Frank A. Bennack, Jr.**

Hearst Magazine Media, Inc.
PRESIDENT **Debi Chirichella**
GENERAL MANAGER, HEARST LIFESTYLE BRANDS **Ronak Patel**
GLOBAL CHIEF REVENUE OFFICER **Lisa Ryan Howard**
EDITORIAL DIRECTOR **Lucy Kaylin**
CHIEF FINANCIAL AND STRATEGY OFFICER; TREASURER **Regina Buckley**
CONSUMER GROWTH OFFICER **Lindsey Horrigan**
CHIEF PRODUCT & TECHNOLOGY OFFICER **Daniel Bernard**
PRESIDENT, HEARST MAGAZINES INTERNATIONAL **Jonathan Wright**
SECRETARY **Catherine A. Bostron**

PUBLISHING CONSULTANT **Mark F. Miller**

HEARST HOME

Copyright © 2025 by Hearst Magazine Media, Inc.

All rights reserved.

The book's mention of products made by various companies does not imply that those companies endorse the book. The brand-name products mentioned in the book are trademarks or registered trademarks of their respective companies.

Library of Congress Cataloging-in-Publication Data Available on Request

10 9 8 7 6 5 4 3 2 1

Published by Hearst Home, an imprint of Hearst Books/Hearst Magazine Media, Inc.
300 W 57th Street
New York, NY 10019

Good Housekeeping and the Good Housekeeping logo are registered trademarks of Hearst Magazine Media, Inc. Hearst Home, the Hearst Home logo, and Hearst Books are registered trademarks of Hearst Communications, Inc.

For information about custom editions, special sales, premium and corporate purchases: hearst.com/magazines/hearst-books

Printed in China
978-1-958395-64-6